*Meaningful to Behold*

*Suggested study or reading order for beginners of books by Venerable Geshe Kelsang Gyatso Rinpoche*

How to Transform Your Life
How to Understand the Mind
Joyful Path of Good Fortune
The Mirror of Dharma
The New Heart of Wisdom
Modern Buddhism
Tantric Grounds and Paths
The New Guide to Dakini Land
Essence of Vajrayana
The Oral Instructions of Mahamudra
Great Treasury of Merit
The New Eight Steps to Happiness
Introduction to Buddhism
How to Solve Our Human Problems
Meaningful to Behold
The Bodhisattva Vow
Universal Compassion
The New Meditation Handbook
Living Meaningfully, Dying Joyfully
Ocean of Nectar
Heart Jewel
Clear Light of Bliss
Mahamudra Tantra

---

This book is published under the auspices of the
**NKT-IKBU International Temples Project**
and the profit from its sale is designated for public
benefit through this fund.
[Reg. Charity number 1015054 (England)]
Find out more:
tharpa.com/benefit-all-world-peace

# Venerable Geshe Kelsang Gyatso Rinpoche

# *Meaningful to Behold*

BECOMING A FRIEND OF THE WORLD

THARPA PUBLICATIONS
UK • US • CANADA
AUSTRALIA • ASIA

First published in 1980 by Wisdom Publications.
Second edition 1986; Third edition 1989
Fourth edition 1994 – 3 Impressions
Fifth edition 2007 – 3 Impressions
Sixth edition 2016 - Impression 2 (2019)

The right of Geshe Kelsang Gyatso to be identified as
author of this work has been asserted by him in accordance
with the Copyright, Designs, and Patents Act 1988.

All rights reserved.
No part of this book may be reproduced in any form or
by any means except for the quotation of brief passages
for the purpose of private study, research, or review.

| Tharpa Publications UK | Tharpa Publications US |
|---|---|
| Conishead Priory | 47 Sweeney Road |
| Ulverston, Cumbria | Glen Spey, NY 12737 |
| LA12 9QQ, England | USA |

There are Tharpa Publications offices around the world,
and Tharpa books are published in most major languages.
See pages 577-578 for contact details.

© New Kadampa Tradition – International Kadampa
Buddhist Union 1980, 1986, 1989, 1994, 2007, 2016

Cover design: © NKT-IKBU 2019

Library of Congress Control Number: 2007935978

British Library Cataloguing in Publication Data.
A catalogue record for this book is
available from the British Library.

ISBN 978-1-910368-49-7 – paperback
ISBN 978-1-910368-50-3 – ePub
ISBN 978-1-910368-51-0 – kindle

Set in Palatino by Tharpa Publications.
Printed and bound in the United Kingdom by
Bell and Bain Ltd.

Paper supplied from well-managed forests and other controlled
sources, and certified in accordance with the rules of the
Forest Stewardship Council.

# *Contents*

| | |
|---|---:|
| Illustrations | vi |
| Foreword | vii |
| Acknowledgements | ix |
| Introduction | 1 |
| Chapter 1: The Benefits of Bodhichitta | 11 |
| Chapter 2: Disclosure of Evil | 59 |
| Chapter 3: Full Acceptance of Bodhichitta | 111 |
| Chapter 4: Conscientiousness | 145 |
| Chapter 5: Guarding the Mind with Alertness | 185 |
| Chapter 6: Patience | 233 |
| Chapter 7: Effort | 281 |
| Chapter 8: Concentration | 313 |
| Chapter 9: Wisdom | 397 |
| Chapter 10: Dedication | 505 |
| Conclusion | 519 |
| The Condensed Meaning of the Commentary | 521 |
| Appendix I: *Liberating Prayer* | 543 |
| Glossary | 547 |
| Bibliography | 565 |
| Study Programmes of Kadampa Buddhism | 571 |
| Tharpa Offices Worldwide | 577 |
| Index | 579 |
| Further Reading | 593 |
| Finding Your Nearest Kadampa Meditation Centre | 598 |

# Illustrations

| | |
|---|---|
| Buddha Shakyamuni | x |
| Manjushri | 12 |
| Shantideva | 60 |
| Serlingpa | 110 |
| Atisha | 146 |
| Dromtonpa | 186 |
| Geshe Potowa | 234 |
| Geshe Sharawa | 280 |
| Geshe Chekhawa | 314 |
| Geshe Chilbuwa | 356 |
| Je Tsongkhapa | 396 |
| Je Phabongkhapa | 432 |
| Vajradhara Trijang Rinpoche | 468 |
| Venerable Geshe Kelsang Gyatso Rinpoche *(included at the request of faithful disciples)* | 506 |

# *Foreword*

### *by Vajradhara Trijang Rinpoche*

The excellent expounder, the great Spiritual Master Kelsang Gyatso, studied myriad Buddhist scriptures at the famous Je College of the great monastic university of Sera, Tegchen Ling, practised the meaning of the teachings he received, and became a wise, serious and realized Teacher. From the rain of profound and extensive Dharma that he has bestowed upon his fortunate disciples, he has recently given comprehensive instruction on the great *Bodhisattvacharyavatara* (*Guide to the Bodhisattva's Way of Life*). This commentary has now been made available in English with the title *Meaningful to Behold*, known in Tibetan as 'tong pa don den'.

This text is the heart essence of all the Sugatas of the three times and is the unsurpassed practice of the great Sons of the Conquerors. It explains clearly the mind of bodhichitta developed through equalizing and exchanging self with others – the foundation of the Bodhisattva's way of life. It also explains the benefits of this Mahayana mind, the way we should guard this mind, and how we should practise the great waves of the six perfections once bodhichitta has been cultivated. As a great gathering of the paths of the Mahayana tradition, it is therefore worthy to receive many flowers of praise bestowed with appreciation.

I pray and dedicate that all sentient beings may practise sincerely the meaning of the instructions explained in this text and may thereby accomplish effortlessly the purposes of both themselves and others. May they all swiftly reach the enlightened state of the four bodies [of a Buddha] by accomplishing all the stages of the spiritual grounds and paths.

*Vajradhara Trijang Rinpoche*

# Acknowledgements

The teachings contained in this book were originally delivered as a series of lectures to students at Manjushri Kadampa Meditation Centre in England, by Venerable Geshe Kelsang Gyatso Rinpoche. For more than three months, beginning in late 1977, Venerable Geshe Kelsang gave a verse by verse oral commentary to Shantideva's eighth-century masterpiece, *Guide to the Bodhisattva's Way of Life*, one of the most famous and important texts studied in Mahayana Buddhism.

From the depths of our hearts, we thank the author for his inconceivable kindness in composing this book. Throughout the presentation and revision of these teachings, Venerable Geshe Kelsang has demonstrated by his compassion, wisdom and inexhaustible patience that the Bodhisattva path to enlightenment is still being followed 1,200 years after Shantideva and 2,500 years after the passing away of Buddha Shakyamuni. There can be no greater proof of the immense value of the Bodhisattva's way of life than the living example of such a realized Master.

We also thank all the dedicated, senior Dharma students who assisted the author with the rendering of the English and who prepared the final manuscript for publication.

Please note that numbers in squared brackets throughout the text refer to verse numbers in Shantideva's root text, *Guide to the Bodhisattva's Way of Life*, a full translation of which is available separately. See *Bibliography*.

*Roy Tyson,*
*Administrative Director*
*Manjushri Kadampa Meditation Centre,*
*November 1993.*

*Buddha Shakyamuni*

# *Introduction*

This present text is a commentary to Shantideva's *Guide to the Bodhisattva's Way of Life* (Skt. *Bodhisattvacharyavatara*) and is divided into three parts:

1 The pre-eminent qualities of the author
2 An introduction to the text
3 The explanation of the actual text

### THE PRE-EMINENT QUALITIES OF THE AUTHOR

It is customary at the beginning of commentaries such as this to give a biography of the author, in this case the great Indian Pandit Shantideva (AD 687-763). There now follows a very brief account drawn from traditional sources.

Shantideva was born the crown prince of a royal family in Gujarat, a kingdom in western India. His father was King Kushalavarmana (Armour of Virtue) and his mother was recognized as an emanation of the Tantric Deity Vajrayogini. At his birth the prince received the name Shantivarmana (Armour of Peace).

Even as a very young boy Shantivarmana showed great ability in spiritual matters and by the age of seven was already highly skilled in the inner science of religion. His principal Teacher at that time was a Yogi who had so fully developed penetrating wisdom that it is said he achieved unity with Manjushri, the Buddha embodying the wisdom of all enlightened beings. When Shantivarmana himself engaged in a meditation retreat, he too received a direct vision of Manjushri and many prophetic omens as well.

Shortly afterwards King Kushalavarmana died, leaving Shantivarmana to inherit the throne. The night before his intended coronation, however, Manjushri appeared to him in a dream. He told the prince that he should renounce his kingdom and become a celibate monk. Immediately upon waking, Shantivarmana fled the palace and disappeared into the forest to meditate. Once again he received a vision of Manjushri, who handed him a symbolic wooden sword. Upon taking it Shantivarmana attained eight perfect realizations. He then travelled to the great monastic university of Nalanda where he took ordination from the Abbot Jayadeva (God of Victory) and was given the ordination name of Shantideva (God of Peace).

At Nalanda Shantideva's spiritual development progressed rapidly, especially as the result of his training in the profound and demanding methods of Tantra. However, because he did all his practices secretly at night and rested during the day, it appeared to others that he performed only three activities: eating, sleeping and defecating. For this reason, the other monks sarcastically referred to him as the 'Three Realizations'. Feeling he was a very irresponsible monk and a discredit to their illustrious university, they devised a plan to get rid of him. Incorrectly believing him to be deficient in meditational ability and ignorant of doctrinal theory, they arranged for Shantideva to deliver a discourse before the entire monastery. Their idea was that he would be so humiliated by this exposure of his ignorance that he would be shamed into leaving.

When the day of the scheduled public humiliation arrived, Shantideva mounted the teaching throne and, much to the amazement of those assembled, delivered a discourse which, when written down, became known as *Guide to the Bodhisattva's Way of Life*, still considered the best set of instructions ever written for becoming a Bodhisattva – a being bound for full enlightenment. As he was expounding the ninth chapter dealing with the wisdom apprehending the true nature of reality he uttered the words, 'Everything is like space.' At this point he began to rise into the sky, flying higher and higher until he could no longer be seen although his voice could still be clearly heard. It was in this miraculous manner that the remainder of the ninth chapter and the entirety of the tenth were delivered.

Having no desire to return to Nalanda, Shantideva left for South India. Needless to say, the monks he left behind were profoundly impressed and somewhat bewildered by Shantideva's teachings and his display of miracle powers. Shortly thereafter a dispute arose about these teachings. The Kashmiri Pandits claimed that Shantideva taught only nine chapters, while some of the scholars from Magadha, who possessed great powers of memorization, argued that he had in fact taught ten. It was decided that the only way to resolve this disagreement would be to hear the teachings once again, so several monks left Nalanda in search of the one they had once despised and requested him to repeat his discourse. This he did, and he also gave them the text of his *Compendium of Trainings* (Skt. *Shikshasamuchchaya*), which also explains the practices of a Bodhisattva. From that time onwards the study and practice of Shantideva's works flourished widely throughout India and other Mahayana Buddhist lands.

As Shantideva's fame spread farther and farther, many non-Buddhists became jealous. One of their greatest teachers, Shankadeva, challenged Shantideva to a debate on the condition that the loser forsake his own doctrine for that of the winner. By the use of miracle powers and impeccable logic, Shantideva emerged victorious, thereby bringing Shankadeva and all of his disciples into the Buddhist fold.

On another occasion, when there was great famine in South India, Shantideva announced that he would perform an act of generosity. The next day many people gathered to see what he would do. Shantideva then proceeded to satisfy the hunger of the entire mass of people with a single bowl of rice! Because of this the local people all developed great faith in Shantideva and adopted the Buddhist way of life as their own.

This has been only a brief biography of the great Bodhisattva Shantideva, who throughout his entire life performed countless deeds for the sake of spreading Buddha's teachings, the Dharma, and helping sentient beings. Even today those who are fortunate enough to read, study and meditate on his outstanding texts can find them a source of great insight and benefit.

## AN INTRODUCTION TO THE TEXT

How is Shantideva's *Guide* put together and what does it contain? It is composed of ten chapters and we should try very hard to understand the meaning contained in each one of them. Otherwise we are like the foolish person who was sent to a shop by members of his household to see what was sold there. When he returned home they asked him what was available, and he had to reply, 'I don't know; I have forgotten.' His journey to the shop was a complete waste of time. Similarly, if upon completion of this text we are unable to recall what is contained within each of its chapters, we should be ashamed of ourself. If our study of this text is to be worthwhile and not a complete waste of time, we should not only read the words but also try hard to learn their meaning.

There now follows a brief description of the contents of each of the ten chapters of the root text.

## *Chapter One*

The ultimate goal of Buddhist spiritual practice is the attainment of the fully awakened state of mind. This completely perfected state – variously known as enlightenment, Buddhahood or the highest nirvana – can be achieved by anyone who removes the gross and subtle obstructions clouding his or her mind and develops positive mental qualities to their fullest potential. However, we will not be able to attain this fully awakened state if we do not first develop bodhichitta, the mind of enlightenment. What is bodhichitta? It is the continual and spontaneous state of mind that constantly strives to attain this perfect enlightenment solely for the benefit of all living beings. As will be explained later in this commentary, bodhichitta is developed by training the mind in either of two ways: practising the sevenfold cause and effect meditation (built around the remembrance of motherly love) or exchanging self with others.

In order to generate this precious bodhichitta we must think deeply about its many benefits. A businessman will put a lot of effort into a particular transaction if he understands beforehand that there is much profit to be gained. In the same way, if we see the many benefits of bodhichitta we will strive continuously to develop it. For this reason the first chapter consists of a detailed explanation of these benefits.

## Chapter Two

If we are to develop bodhichitta we must destroy all obstacles hindering its growth as well as accumulate the necessary prerequisites for its cultivation. The main obstacle to developing bodhichitta is evil, defined as that which has the potential power to produce suffering. Because we have a large accumulation of such misery-producing tendencies from the non-virtuous actions we have done in the past, we find it extremely difficult to give birth to the precious and virtuous thought of bodhichitta.

Where poisonous plants grow together in profusion it is virtually impossible for a medicinal seed to sprout. Similarly, the virtuous thought of enlightenment will not arise in a mind choked by the weeds of non-virtue. Therefore, in Chapter Two of his *Guide* Shantideva explains how to prepare the mind for the cultivation of the supremely altruistic attitude by uprooting and weeding out all that is potentially harmful to its growth. This purification of evil is accomplished by exposing our accumulated non-virtue, and then eradicating it by means of the four opponent powers explained in this chapter.

## Chapter Three

However, purifying negativity is not, by itself, sufficient for our purposes. We must also accumulate a great deal of merit, or positive potential energy, and this comes from the practice of virtue. In the same way that it would be unsuitable for a beggar to receive a king in shabby, unkempt surroundings, so too it is impossible for a mind bereft of merit to entertain the precious bodhichitta, the king of all thoughts. Those who wish to invite this honoured guest into their minds must first acquire a great wealth of positive mental energy. After this is done it is then possible to seize and maintain this precious mind of enlightenment. Therefore, in Chapter Three Shantideva explains how to acquire and hold on to bodhichitta.

## *Chapter Four*

Once we have taken hold of the precious bodhichitta, we must prevent it from decreasing. This is done by conscientiously attending to the virtuous actions of our body, speech and mind. This conscientiousness is the subject of Shantideva's fourth chapter.

## *Chapter Five*

Having developed and then stabilized bodhichitta by means of conscientiousness, we must strive to bring this mind to its complete fruition: perfect enlightenment. This is done by taking the Bodhisattva vows and practising the six perfections. Generally the first perfection to be explained is giving. In this text, however, Shantideva discusses giving in his tenth and final chapter together with his dedication. His reason for doing so is that giving, or generosity, is part of the general dedication to all living beings of the good and beautiful things in the universe. Therefore Shantideva begins his discussion with what is generally presented as the second of the perfections – the practice of moral discipline – in a chapter entitled 'Guarding the Mind with Alertness'.

## *Chapters Six to Ten*

Each remaining chapter is devoted to one of the perfections. Chapters six to eight discuss patience, effort and concentration while chapter nine is devoted to an extensive explanation of wisdom. As stated before, the tenth chapter deals with giving and the dedication of merit.

The development of bodhichitta takes place in three stages. The ten chapters of Shantideva's book cover this threefold development, which is outlined concisely in the following often-recited dedication prayer:

> May the precious, supreme bodhichitta
> Grow where it has not yet grown;
> Where it has grown may it not decrease
> But flourish for evermore.

In the first two lines we pray that those sentient beings, including ourself, who have not yet given birth to bodhichitta may do so. Next we pray that those who have already given birth to this altruistic mind may be able to maintain it without letting it decrease. In the final line, we pray that those who have cultivated and stabilized bodhichitta may be able to bring it to its full completion. In the same order, the method of giving birth to bodhichitta is explained in the first three chapters of this text, the way to stabilize it is the subject of the fourth chapter, while chapters five to ten describe the methods whereby the stabilized bodhichitta may be continually increased until full enlightenment is achieved.

If we practise in accordance with the instructions set forth in the ten chapters of *Guide to the Bodhisattva's Way of Life*, it will not be too difficult to attain the exalted state of mind known as enlightenment, or full and complete Buddhahood. In this state all our human potentialities will be fully developed and we will be able to benefit others to the greatest possible extent.

## THE EXPLANATION OF THE ACTUAL TEXT

This has four parts:

1 The meaning of the title
2 The homage of the translators
3 The explanation of the meaning of the text
4 The meaning of the conclusion

## THE MEANING OF THE TITLE

The original Sanskrit title of this text is *Bodhisattvacharyavatara*, the Tibetan translation of which is *Jang chub sem pai cho pa la jug pa*. In English this can be rendered as *Guide to the Bodhisattva's Way of Life*.

It is the custom for all works translated from Sanskrit into Tibetan that the original title be presented first. Why is this necessary? There are two reasons for this practice. First of all, Sanskrit is considered the most sublime of all languages, as well as being the one in which Buddha himself taught. Therefore, having the title in Sanskrit helps plant imprints of this holy language on the mind-streams of those reading the text. Secondly, the title is given in the original language to help us recall the great kindness of those who translated the text from Sanskrit into Tibetan. It is only through the compassion and diligent effort of these translators that the Tibetan people, and subsequently the western world, have had the opportunity to study, meditate on and practise the profound methods contained within this holy scripture.

## THE HOMAGE OF THE TRANSLATORS

Before starting their work on this text, the original Tibetan translators paid homage and made prostration to all the Buddhas and Bodhisattvas in order to remove hindrances and ensure completion of their work.

Such homage is in accordance with the tradition laid down by the great Dharma kings of Tibet. This tradition stipulated that the translator's homage should indicate to which set or 'basket' (Skt. pitaka) of Buddha's teachings the original Sanskrit text belongs. Thus if a particular text belongs to the set of Vinaya – dealing mainly with the training in higher moral discipline – then the homage should be to the Omniscient One. If it belongs to the Sutra Pitaka – dealing mainly with the training in higher concentration – then homage should be paid to the Buddhas and Bodhisattvas. Finally if it is contained within the third set, the Abhidharma Pitaka – dealing mainly with the training in higher wisdom – then homage is paid to youthful Manjughosha, the embodiment of enlightened wisdom. Thus, by reading the homage we can easily tell into which of the three scriptural categories a particular text falls. In this case homage is made to the Buddhas and Bodhisattvas; thus it is clear that *Guide to the Bodhisattva's Way of Life* belongs to the Sutra Pitaka, the set of discourses mainly concerned with meditative concentration.

# *The Benefits of Bodhichitta*

### THE EXPLANATION OF THE MEANING OF THE TEXT

The main body of this commentary is divided into two parts:

1. The preliminary explanation
2. The actual explanation of the stages of the path to enlightenment

### THE PRELIMINARY EXPLANATION

This has three parts:

1. The expression of worship
2. The promise of composition
3. The reason for composition

### THE EXPRESSION OF WORSHIP

[1ab] The actual text begins with Shantideva's homage, or prostration, to the Buddhas (literally, to the Sugatas: those who have gone to bliss), their Noble Sons and Daughters and all other venerable objects of worship. This prostration is in fact Shantideva's way of paying respect to the Three precious and sublime Jewels of Buddhist refuge: Buddha, Dharma and Sangha. A more detailed explanation of these Three Jewels will be given later in this commentary. For now

*Manjushri*

it is sufficient to state that Buddha is a fully awakened being, Dharma is the spiritual teachings such a being gives others to lead them from suffering and dissatisfaction to temporary and ultimate happiness, while the Sangha is the community of those following these enlightening teachings.

Why is it necessary to go for refuge to these three objects? If a sick person is to get well again, he or she must rely upon a skilful physician, effective medicine, and sympathetic and attentive nurses. In the same way, sentient beings caught up in the vicious circle of cyclic existence (Skt. samsara) are all afflicted by the sickness of their delusions, having found nothing in which they can take true refuge. Only by entrusting themselves to Buddha, the perfect physician, the medicine of Dharma and the Sangha nurses will they ever be cured of their ailments. Therefore if there is to be an end to our dissatisfaction and suffering we must discover and entrust ourself to these Three precious and sublime Jewels.

In the first part of verse one Shantideva himself pays homage to the Three Jewels in order to eliminate the obstacles that might arise while composing this text. He prostrates first to the Sugatas, or Buddhas, who are endowed with the Truth Body (Skt. Dharmakaya) of an enlightened being as well as with all Dharma Jewels. He then pays homage to the Sangha by prostrating to the Bodhisattvas, the Buddhas' Noble Sons and Daughters, and lastly he pays homage to the Abbots and Preceptors and all those worthy of veneration. This concludes his expression of worship.

## THE PROMISE OF COMPOSITION

[lcd] Next comes the traditional promise of composition. It was customary for authors to include such a promise at the

beginning of their work to serve as a brief introduction to their intended subject matter. It is Shantideva's intention in this text to present a synthesis of all the paths leading to the attainment of highest enlightenment, Buddhahood. This is the meaning of *Bodhisattvacharyavatara*, for it is only by engaging in the Bodhisattva's way of life – venturing into the activities of the Sons and Daughters of the Sugatas – that we can attain this highest goal.

There are two benefits of studying this precious text. The temporary benefit is that we gain an understanding of the entire path to enlightenment, and are thereby enabled to practise it. The ultimate benefit is that by depending upon this text we will attain the fully enlightened state of Buddhahood.

The ultimate benefit depends upon the temporary benefit, the temporary benefit relies upon the meaning of the text, which in turn relies upon the text itself. This dependent relationship is known as the relationship of the text. Thus Shantideva's promise of composition in verse one indicates that his text has been composed in accordance with Buddha's scriptures and contains the four qualities of meaning, temporary benefit, ultimate benefit and relationship.

## THE REASON FOR COMPOSITION

[2] Next Shantideva explains what his reasons are for composing this text. He admits that it will not contain anything that has not been explained before. Also, since he has no skill in the art of rhetoric or poetry, he has no intention of benefiting others who have already understood the teachings of Buddha. Rather, he wrote this text so that his own virtue would increase, his own understanding of the scriptures

would not decline and his own mind would become better acquainted with the meaning of the scriptures.

[3] He goes on to say that through the power of his faith, composition and wisdom he will explain the meaning of all the scriptures and thus his own realizations will increase for some time. He hopes that if others, equal in good fortune to himself, were to behold this text, it would prove meaningful for them as well.

This concludes the preliminary explanation. With verse four Shantideva begins his presentation of the actual path to be followed by those wishing to enter the Bodhisattva's way of life.

## THE ACTUAL EXPLANATION OF THE STAGES OF THE PATH TO ENLIGHTENMENT

This has two main parts:

1 The exhortation to grasp the significance of this precious human life
2 The method for making this precious human life meaningful

## THE EXHORTATION TO GRASP THE SIGNIFICANCE OF THIS PRECIOUS HUMAN LIFE

[4] Shantideva begins by reminding us that we now have a most rare and precious possession, a fully endowed human life. In contrast to the overwhelming majority of beings in the universe, including most of our fellow humans, we have the opportunity to do something truly meaningful with our lives. We are free of certain restrictions and in possession of certain

abilities and beneficial circumstances that make it possible for us to attain goals far beyond the reach of most beings. But if we do not make use of our present existence in the most worthwhile manner possible, it will be extremely difficult to gain such a beneficially endowed human life again. To appreciate these points more fully we must acquaint ourself with the following detailed analysis.

First of all, why is our present state of existence considered to be so rare and so difficult to attain? The reason is that we were not born human by chance. Every effect has a cause, and our present existence as human beings – and as specially endowed human beings – is the result of a number of specific and hard-to-create causes. In general, birth as a human depends upon having previously practised pure moral discipline and giving. Specifically, each aspect of a fully endowed human life (as described below) has its own appropriate cause. Furthermore, in order to have attained this life we must have generated pure thoughts, or prayers, to receive a bodily vehicle with which we would have the leisure and ability to improve our mind through the continued practice of Dharma, or spiritual teachings. To be effective, such prayers have to be unpolluted by attachment to temporal comforts and happiness. As it is rare that we create even one of these necessary causes, it follows that the fruit resulting from a combination of them all must be extremely rare to find.

Our present situation can be understood in terms of the following analogy. If a person comes across a nugget of gold but does not recognize its rarity and worth, he may easily throw it away. At this moment we have attained a precious human life far more valuable than gold, but if we do not recognize its worth we are apt to squander it in meaningless and purposeless pursuits. Thus it is very important, first of all, to recognize the eight freedoms and ten endowments of this rare and precious opportunity.

The eight freedoms, or leisures, are in reference to being free from eight states of bondage – four encountered even when born as a human being. The four freedoms from the bondage of non-human states of existence are:

(1) Freedom from being born as a hell being
(2) Freedom from being born as a hungry spirit
(3) Freedom from being born as an animal
(4) Freedom from being born as an ordinary god

The four freedoms from obstacles found within human existence are:

(5) Freedom from being born and remaining in a country where there is no religion
(6) Freedom from being born and remaining in a country where there is no Buddhadharma
(7) Freedom from being born and remaining with mental or physical disabilities
(8) Freedom from holding wrong views denying Dharma, such as disbelief in the karmic law of cause and effect, the continuity of consciousness, and so forth

These eight states are called the 'eight freedoms' because they are free from obstacles that oppose or completely prevent our practice of Dharma.

The ten endowments are of two types: the five personal and the five circumstantial endowments. The five personal endowments are:

(1) Being born human
(2) Being born and remaining in a country where Dharma is flourishing – a so-called 'central land'
(3) Being born and remaining with complete powers, free from mental and physical disabilities
(4) Not having committed any of the five actions of immediate retribution. These are killing one's mother, killing one's father, killing an Arhat, shedding the blood of a Buddha with harmful intention, and causing division within a spiritual community
(5) Having faith in the three sets of Buddha's teachings (Skt. tripitaka) and the Buddhist teachings as a whole

The five circumstantial endowments are:

(6) Taking human rebirth in a world where Buddha has appeared
(7) Taking human rebirth in a world where Buddha has taught Dharma
(8) Taking human rebirth in a world where pure Dharma is still being taught
(9) Taking human rebirth in a world where there are people practising pure Dharma
(10) Taking human rebirth in a world where there are benefactors and sponsors for Dharma practitioners

These ten states are called 'endowments' because they complete the conditions conducive to the practice of Dharma.

It is because of our accumulated virtuous actions that we have now attained this precious human life endowed with the eighteen above characteristics. Therefore, now is the time to rejoice at our extraordinary good fortune. What is the purpose of this precious human life and why is it so valuable to us? The purpose and value of such an existence lie in the opportunity it affords us to accomplish one of three outstanding aims. The greatest goal now available to us is the attainment of enlightenment, the complete and perfect awakening of a Buddha. The intermediate goal is the attainment of personal liberation from samsara, the vicious cycle of birth and death fraught with suffering and dissatisfaction; while the smallest goal is to win rebirth as a god or as a human being.

In general we remain completely unaware of the value of our present situation. In particular we are blind to the precious opportunity we now have to attain one of these three goals. Instead we waste our time and squander this precious opportunity by running after the temporary pleasures of this life. If we were to recognize fully the value and potential of this precious human life we would certainly take advantage of it by studying Dharma and seeking one of the three goals. As Shantideva says, 'If no meaning is derived from this precious rebirth now, how can we ever hope to come across it again in the future?'

There is a story that illustrates the importance of taking full advantage of our precious human life. In a remote village in Tibet there lived a man who had no legs. One day as he was making his slow, laboured way across the countryside with the aid of crutches he accidentally fell over the edge of a cliff. As luck would have it he landed on the back of a wild horse grazing below. The horse was so startled that it galloped off with the man holding on for dear life. Quite a long time passed and, to the wonderment of the other villagers, the man showed no signs of tiring of his unusual mount. 'Why don't you get off that horse?' they shouted to him as he raced by. 'Not on your life!' he shouted back to them. 'This is the first time in my life I've ever been on horseback. When can a legless man like me ever hope for such an opportunity again? I'm going to take full advantage of it while I can.' And off he went, clutching on to the back of the wild horse. Just as the man in this story took advantage of his unusual luck, so should we take full advantage of our present fully endowed human life by training our mind in the practice of Dharma.

## THE METHOD FOR MAKING THIS PRECIOUS HUMAN LIFE MEANINGFUL

This has two parts:

1 Contemplating the benefits of bodhichitta
2 How to practise the six perfections once bodhichitta has been developed

### CONTEMPLATING THE BENEFITS OF BODHICHITTA

This section has four parts:

1 An explanation of the benefits of bodhichitta
2 Recognizing bodhichitta
3 The reasons for the benefits of bodhichitta
4 Praise to the one who gives birth to bodhichitta

### AN EXPLANATION OF THE BENEFITS OF BODHICHITTA

As indicated before, the supreme method for making this rare and precious human rebirth meaningful is to use it as a vehicle for attaining the most perfect and complete enlightenment. To work for any lesser goal is to throw away this unique opportunity. Since the attainment of enlightenment depends upon first developing the mind of enlightenment, bodhichitta – the motivation to achieve full enlightenment in order to be most effective in helping others out of their suffering – Shantideva encourages us to develop bodhichitta, and describes its many advantages. These are divided into the following ten outstanding benefits.

## *The conquest of all great evils*

[5] Just as a sudden, powerful flash of lightning on a pitch-dark night briefly illuminates the landscape, so the powerful blessings of Buddha cause worldly people to develop, at least for a short time, the intention to practise virtue.

[6] Usually the virtues of worldly people are weak, while their instincts for non-virtue are strong. Thus we must constantly strive to overcome the great power this evil of non-virtue exerts upon us, replacing it with a strong practice of virtuous actions. Otherwise, if we do nothing to correct our present situation, the sufferings of samsara will be our sole experience. What is the best method for abandoning evil and creating virtue? We must strive to attain the precious bodhichitta. Only it has the power to overcome evil and abundantly increase our virtue. Other than the boundless mind of bodhichitta what else has the ability to subdue such great evil? By reflecting upon this well it becomes clear that we must definitely develop bodhichitta.

## *The attainment of the most sublime happiness*

[7] In general there are many ways in which we can benefit sentient beings, but the Buddhas who have spent aeons examining the best way to help others say that developing bodhichitta is the supreme method. Why is this? Because with the development of bodhichitta we are not only able to attain the supreme happiness of Buddhahood for ourself, but we are also able to lead countless masses of sentient beings to the incomparable bliss of this supreme state. Recognizing the matchless benefits bodhichitta has for ourself and others, we should strive to attain it.

## *Wish-fulfilment*

[8] A further benefit of developing bodhichitta is that all of our wishes will be fulfilled. If we want to be released from the many miseries of samsara and dispel the unhappiness of others, bodhichitta can fulfil these aims. In addition it fulfils the desire of all beings, including ourself, who long to experience limitless and immeasurable joy. Therefore, since this mind of enlightenment grants all wishes, Shantideva advises us to reflect upon its many benefits and never cease striving to attain it.

## *Bodhichitta carries with it a special name and meaning*

[9] Shantideva says that anyone who develops bodhichitta is thereafter referred to as a 'Son of the Buddhas' (literally, a Son of the Sugatas), a Bodhisattva. Such a person becomes an object worthy to be venerated and respected by worldly gods, such as Brahma and Indra, and all of humanity, including

high-born kings and queens. It does not matter if the person developing bodhichitta is a poor, shabbily dressed beggar. Upon his generating the mind of enlightenment he, too, would become an object worthy of the highest veneration.

It is important to remember that we do not need to be a monk or of aristocratic birth or to possess a male body in order to develop bodhichitta. Although Shantideva uses the title 'Son of the Buddhas', he is not using it restrictively. When a woman develops the mind of enlightenment she becomes known as a 'Daughter or Princess of the Buddhas' and likewise becomes an object to be venerated by all gods and humans.

Why does developing bodhichitta entitle us to so much respect? Because all Buddhas – those fully awakened beings from whom supreme happiness derives – are born from Bodhisattvas, who are so-called by virtue of their bodhichitta motivation, their intention to win full awakening for the benefit of all. Thus Buddhas arise from Bodhisattvas who in turn arise from bodhichitta.

To stress the supreme value of bodhichitta, Buddha Shakyamuni says that it is even more important to prostrate, or pay homage, to a Bodhisattva – someone who has developed bodhichitta – than it is to prostrate to a Buddha. He explains this by using the example of the waxing moon. If someone bows down to the new moon it is the same as bowing down to every phase of the moon between new and full. Why? Because by paying respect to a cause we are implicitly paying respect to each of its succeeding effects. Thus, if we prostrate to a Bodhisattva we are implicitly paying homage to all the future states of his or her development, up to and including the attainment of Buddhahood. For such reasons then, bodhichitta is very precious and anyone who develops this mind becomes worthy of veneration.

The great Indian Pandit Atisha had many Teachers and received much instruction from them concerning the development of bodhichitta. But not being satisfied he set out on a dangerous journey to present-day Indonesia in order to receive teachings from the famous Guru Serlingpa (Suvarnadipa). The difficult voyage took thirteen months, but from this Guru Atisha was able to receive flawless and complete instructions on the method for developing the mind of enlightenment.

Although Atisha had over one hundred and fifty Teachers, he referred to Serlingpa as his root Guru. Even many years later when he was in Tibet, if Atisha even heard the name of his root Guru he would immediately descend from his seat and prostrate to him. The Tibetans noticed that he did not do this for any of his other Teachers and asked him why. He replied that from the instructions given him by Guru Serlingpa he realized how to develop the precious bodhichitta. Atisha, the possessor of great learning, held bodhichitta supreme; consequently he venerated Serlingpa above all his other Teachers.

## *Transformation of the inferior into the supreme*

[10] Alchemists assert that there is a special elixir that has the power to transform base metals into gold. If we develop and practise bodhichitta, this impure human body of ours will likewise be transformed into the priceless, peerless jewel of a Buddha's holy body.

The way to meditate on this point is as follows. First we should continually contemplate the impurity of the human body, thinking how undesirable it is to take rebirth constantly in such a gross and impure form. We should abandon whatever desire we might have for this ordinary human body and think instead of the preciousness of the transcendent body of a Buddha. We must develop the strong wish to attain this holy form and consider by what causes we may receive it. Upon continued reflection we will come to recognize that such a form can be achieved solely through the power of bodhichitta. Understanding this, we should then develop a strong determination to attain bodhichitta and mindfully hold this determination.

## *The value of the precious bodhichitta, so difficult to find*

[11] Amongst all jewels the fabled wishfulfilling jewel is the rarest, most priceless, and of foremost importance because it alleviates the poverty of all. Similarly, amongst all kinds of virtue the rarest and most priceless is bodhichitta because it alone can dispel the poverty of those who are poor in virtue. Those who wish to be freed from the sufferings of samsara should firmly maintain this precious bodhichitta.

A skilful oarsman ferries merchants from the mainland to a jewel island. Similarly, Buddha is an oarsman possessing a mind of boundless compassion and skilful methods. This mind is the boat of bodhichitta and in it he ferries all sentient beings across the ocean of suffering to the jewel island of enlightenment. If we make a thorough examination we will clearly see that this boat of bodhichitta is the most sublime and rarest of all methods to achieve happiness.

## *The inexhaustible and increasing fruits of bodhichitta*

[12] Virtues other than bodhichitta are like the banana or plantain tree, the fruits of which are limited and soon

exhausted. For instance, a person becomes rich because of his practice of giving in a previous life, but the fruits of such virtue are gradually used up, and when these riches are finished no more will come.

In contrast, the virtuous fruits from the celestial tree of bodhichitta are inexhaustible. They are like a drop of water that falls into a vast ocean and is therefore never lost until that great ocean itself becomes no more. Even though our virtues in general may be weak, when motivated by bodhichitta their fruits will never be exhausted until we attain complete awakening. Why are the fruits of such actions limitless? There are two reasons for this. First, since the number of sentient beings benefited by a Bodhisattva is countless, the merit arising from actions created for their sake will likewise be limitless. Secondly, since all such merit is dedicated solely for our attainment of enlightenment it will not be exhausted until this enlightenment is reached.

It is said that giving even a little food to a single beggar, if done with the motivation of bodhichitta, produces inexhaustible merit. If we lack such a motivation it does not matter how much gold or silver we give to no matter how many people; the fruits of such virtuous actions are limited and will soon be exhausted. When we realize how abundant are the fruits of all actions proceeding from bodhichitta, we will see that there is nothing more important than striving to attain this precious mind.

## *The power of protection from great fear*

[13] A man travelling in an area where there is great danger from robbers and wild animals will be filled with great fear. However, if he entrusts himself to the protection of a

courageous guide he will immediately be relieved of his anxieties. We human beings, because we have committed very harmful and evil actions in the past, are likewise exposed to the fearful dangers of birth in one of the three lower states of existence – as a hell being, hungry spirit or animal. Even as a human being we fear birth, sickness, loss, violence, old age, death, and the other painful effects of our non-virtuous actions. What has the power to relieve us of this fear? Only the precious bodhichitta. Therefore why do those who are vigilant and wise not devote themselves to the development of this precious mind?

## *The swift and easy destruction of great evil*

[14ab] The world in which we live undergoes great cycles of birth and decay. At the end of the present great aeon our universe will be completely destroyed by fire so that not even the ashes of it will remain. This all-consuming fire will be completely different from the ordinary fires of this world and thousands of times more intense. If we give birth to the precious bodhichitta, the fire of that mind will be similarly intense, sufficient to consume instantly all the immeasurable evil we have accumulated.

## *Scriptural citations of the benefits of bodhichitta*

[14cd] The extensive benefits of bodhichitta were explained to the Bodhisattva Sudhana by Buddha Maitreya in *Stalks in Array Sutra* (Skt. *Gandavyuhasutra*). In the conclusion to this fourteenth verse, Shantideva advises those who wish to learn about these many advantages to consult that famous Mahayana scripture.

If we are to engage in the actual development of bodhichitta we need strong inspiration, and this is only acquired by reflecting on the many benefits of this mind. If we knew of a king who had great wealth, power and knowledge we might easily think, 'How wonderful it would be to become like him!' Such a desire arises only because we have seen the good qualities that king possesses and therefore we wish to emulate him. Similarly, first we must understand the good qualities of bodhichitta and only then will the thought arise, 'How wonderful it would be to give birth to such a precious mind!'

At present, however, if someone were to ask us which we would prefer, to develop bodhichitta or possess a nugget of gold, we would certainly choose the gold. This is because we see the valuable qualities of gold but fail to see the incomparable qualities and benefits of bodhichitta. If we understood these benefits our choice would be different. We would realize that while gold is easily obtained, no amount of money in the world can buy bodhichitta, something not found for sale anywhere. The only way to obtain the precious bodhichitta is to develop it ourself through long meditation.

Until we develop a continuous and spontaneous aspiration to develop bodhichitta we should spend much time contemplating its benefits in general. From Shantideva's list of ten benefits we should select the one that has the strongest positive influence on our mind and meditate reflectively upon it. For such a meditation to be of greatest value it should be continuous and concentrated. Then at the close of the meditation session we should repeat the prayer originally cited in the introduction to this commentary:

> May the precious, supreme bodhichitta
> Grow where it has not yet grown;
> Where it has grown may it not decrease
> But flourish for evermore.

By reciting this prayer we are stating our desire to give birth to bodhichitta as quickly as possible. We can recite this prayer after performing any virtuous action.

We should remember that, without bodhichitta, whatever powers we may have and whatever miracles we may be able to perform are of no real benefit. Being able to fly in the sky is of no importance for even birds are able to do this. We have had such miracle powers and clairvoyance many times in our previous lives, but what have they done for us? Now is the time to control our untamed mind with bodhichitta. With bodhichitta the mind is made peaceful; enlightenment and the fulfilment of all our wishes are not very far away.

It is important to remember that we cannot attain enlightenment if we do not first acquaint ourself with and then master the methods for developing bodhichitta. We must practise these methods as diligently as possible, all the while exhorting ourself to generate this precious attitude. Nowadays, with the world in turmoil, there is a particular need for Westerners to cultivate bodhichitta. If we are to make it through these perilous times, true Bodhisattvas must appear in the West as well as in the East.

To develop bodhichitta we must complete four preparations. It is very important to know these because if we prepare well it is easy to develop bodhichitta. Thus we should (1) acquaint our mind with the benefits of bodhichitta, (2) accumulate a wealth of merit, (3) purify ourself of all non-virtue and (4) understand the method for developing bodhichitta. The last point will be discussed in the next section of this commentary.

## RECOGNIZING BODHICHITTA

This has three parts:

1 The divisions of bodhichitta
2 The benefits of the aspiring mind of bodhichitta
3 The benefits of the engaging mind of bodhichitta

## THE DIVISIONS OF BODHICHITTA

If our meditation on bodhichitta is to be successful we need to understand exactly what the essence of this mind is. As already stated, bodhichitta is a spontaneous and continuous state of mind that seeks enlightenment solely for the benefit of all sentient beings. Shantideva says [15] that this mind is of two types: aspiring bodhichitta and engaging bodhichitta. To understand the significance of and the distinctions between these two types of mind it is helpful to be familiar with the traditional methods of cultivating bodhichitta.

Bodhichitta can be developed by following either of two methods: (1) the sevenfold cause and effect instructions, or (2) equalizing and exchanging self with others. The first method was originally taught by Buddha Shakyamuni and subsequently passed through Maitreya and Asanga in an unbroken lineage to such masters as Serlingpa and Atisha. The second method – equalizing and exchanging self with others – was designed specifically for those of sharp intelligence. It was also taught by Buddha Shakyamuni and passed through Manjushri in an unbroken lineage of Indian Masters to Shantideva himself. Both lineages have survived to the present day and are currently held by accomplished Teachers of all traditions of Mahayana Buddhism.

Equalizing and exchanging self with others will be explained at length in the eighth chapter. What follows is an explanation of developing bodhichitta by means of meditating on the sevenfold cause and effect instructions. This method flourished widely throughout India and Tibet, and by studying it we will see that bodhichitta is not something that can be attained instantly, but rather is the result of a gradual training and development of the mind.

The sevenfold cause and effect is a method involving the successive development of seven realizations, as follows:

(1) Recognizing that all living beings are our mothers
(2) Remembering the kindness of all mother beings
(3) Developing the wish to repay the kindness of all mother beings
(4) Developing affectionate love
(5) Developing great compassion
(6) Developing superior intention
(7) Developing bodhichitta

This method is called the 'sevenfold cause and effect' because these seven realizations are a chain of cause and effect leading to the final realization of bodhichitta. For example, the realization of affectionate love acts as a cause for developing great compassion.

Before we begin our meditation on the sevenfold cause and effect it is helpful first of all to meditate on equanimity. At present our mind is unsettled and biased; instead of looking at all beings equally with the eye of compassion, we feel very close towards some and very distant from, or even hostile towards, others. In such an unbalanced state it is very difficult to recognize all beings as our mothers – the first of the seven cause and effect realizations. Therefore, if our meditation is to be successful we must first try to remove our prejudices by cultivating an attitude of equanimity.

Briefly outlined, the way to develop equanimity is as follows. First we should bring to mind three people we presently regard as our enemy, our friend and a stranger. Then we should ask ourself why we have categorized them in this way. Upon inspection we will find that the person we now call our enemy has received this label because of some harm – great or small, mental or physical, real or imagined – he or she has given us in the past. If we think back, however, we can often remember occasions when this same person treated us with much kindness. And if we could see into our past lives (as will be discussed later) we would undoubtedly discover instances in which this so-called enemy was our selflessly kind mother, feeding us with her own milk and protecting us from harm and fear. Even without considering any lifetime but the present, we can see how temporary and easily subject to change the status of an enemy really is. If tomorrow we were to receive some unexpected assistance, praise or merely a kind word from this person, would we still regard him or her as our foe?

The same considerations can then be applied to the person we now call our dear friend. Although the sight, or even the mere thought, of him or her now elicits a warm feeling in our heart, this was not always the case. There were times, either earlier in this lifetime or in previous lives, when this dear friend or relative was our chief enemy and, as such, inflicted great suffering upon us. And it can easily happen that because of some slight difference of opinion, hasty word, or thoughtless act we suddenly find ourselves estranged from the same person to whom we are now so attached.

In a similar fashion, the stranger has not always been the object of our indifference, nor will he or she always remain so. There have been times when this person – so invisible to us now that we may scarcely be aware of his existence – has been our murderous enemy, and other times when he has been our dearest friend and protector.

By using examples from our own and others' experiences and employing various lines of logical reasoning, we can become convinced that it is extremely short-sighted and ultimately very mistaken to think that anyone is permanently or inherently a friend, enemy or stranger to us. And if this is the case – if these three positions are so temporary and variable – then who is the proper object of our attachment or hatred? If we feel justified in generating hatred towards our present enemy, then we should feel obliged to direct this hatred towards everyone, for sometime in the past we considered each person our enemy. And if it is correct to feel attached and biased towards our present friend because of some benefit we have received from him or her recently, then we should feel similarly towards everyone, because at one time or another everyone has been extremely kind to us, even to the point of being our mother.

If we exert enough energy in meditation, acquainting ourself with the above reasons and examples and try to view people in an altered status, we will come to see how narrow-minded it is to be very close to some beings while remaining hostile or indifferent to others. Instead of assenting, as we do now, to a hard and fast classification of friend, enemy and stranger, and therefore being biased in our outlook, we can develop true equanimity – the basis of the love and compassion necessary if we are to generate the precious bodhichitta and achieve enlightenment. As this is such an extremely worthwhile goal, we should not let our current prejudices go unexamined but expose them in the manner described.

At this point a doubt may arise with respect to the meditation just described. It has been stated that the purpose of developing equanimity is to prepare us to recognize all beings as our mother. We may therefore wonder, 'If it is correct for me to regard all beings as my mother because they have supposedly been my mother in the past, then isn't it likewise correct for me to regard everyone as my enemy for the same reason?' To recognize the fallacy of this conclusion we must understand that whenever we have called anyone our enemy we have done so for basically unsound reasons and as the result of a mistaken view on our part. The habit of blaming our troubles and suffering on others – on the so-called enemy – is a deluded way of thinking, one that fails to realize that it is our own state of mind and not any external circumstance that is ultimately responsible for whatever misery we experience.

At the root of our decision to regard someone as our enemy is a false projection of our mind, a mistaken conception of events. Forgetting such things as the kindness and parental nurturing this person has given us, and unaware of our own culpability for our suffering, we take the harm we receive from another as a valid justification for calling him or her our enemy and treating him with hostility. Although this is something we do all the time, it is in fact completely deluded and ultimately indefensible. On the other hand, as will be explained in the following section, there is nothing false or deluded about regarding all beings as our mother. This is true and verifiable, and not only opens the gateway for continued spiritual growth but provides us with an immediate experience of happiness and well-being.

The goal of equanimity meditation is to remove all biased attitudes of mind and thereby to view all beings without discrimination as our mother. This in turn will motivate us to consider how we can repay their infinite kindness. If, as a result of this meditation, we are able to regard even our most hated enemy as our kind mother, we are ready to gain a realization of the first stage of the seven causes and effects leading to the development of bodhichitta.

## RECOGNIZING THAT ALL LIVING BEINGS ARE OUR MOTHERS

Once we have developed an unbiased outlook towards all beings we are ready to view them all equally as having been our mother. This is the firm foundation upon which the supremely altruistic mind of bodhichitta depends. But how is it possible to recognize all beings as our mother? What are the reasons for believing we have shared the intimate mother-child relationship with everyone?

To answer these questions, consider the following line of reasoning. The woman we presently recognize as our mother is such by virtue of our having been born into the world from her womb. Yet this is not the first and only time we have taken birth. The continuity of our consciousness stretches back over infinite time and the births we have taken have been countless. As we have been born countless times it follows that we have had countless mothers. Thus there is not a single being we meet who, over the incalculable expanse of beginningless time, has failed to be our mother. Despite the altered form and appearance of those we encounter, and the failings of our extremely limited memory, once we become convinced of the logic of the above line of reasoning there will be nothing to prevent us from viewing each being with the same warm recognition we now effortlessly extend to our present mother.

Although the argument presented above is internally consistent, it is obvious that it will be completely lacking in persuasiveness if we do not come to understand and at least tentatively accept the existence of past and future lives. As long as we reject this possibility – as long as we cling to the belief that our birth and death of this lifetime mark the outermost boundaries of our existence – it will be utterly impossible for us to recognize all beings as our mother, except metaphorically. Many other important Dharma topics, such as the workings of cause and effect, also depend for their full understanding on a consideration of past and future lives. Therefore, although this topic may present particular difficulties to some people, especially Westerners, it is very important that we try to keep an open mind and examine the issue with as few preconceptions as possible.

The crux of the matter is our understanding of the nature of the mind, for it is through realizing that our mind is a formless continuum and that this continuum is beginningless that we will be able to understand the existence of previous lives. One way to meditate on this is as follows. We can look at our present stream of thoughts, perceptions and emotions – all the factors we identify as being mental – and trace it backwards to the mind-stream of the previous moment, minute and hour. Then we can trace this mind-stream even further backwards to yesterday, last week and last year. Depending upon the sharpness of our memory, we can trace this mind-stream back year by year until we approach the time of our birth. Even if we can trace it back to our stay in the womb or the moment of conception, we can never point to a time and say, 'At this instant my mind came into being.'

In fact, some people who do this backwards tracing meditation are able to go beyond the moment of conception and remember the mind-stream existing at the end of a previous lifetime. However, as this experience is not shared by very many people (and is the object of many others' doubt) we cannot fairly use it as a proof that mind is a beginningless continuum. Rather, it is much more beneficial for us to gain a closer acquaintance with our own mind and question our own assumptions as to its nature and origin.

To aid in this investigation, here are a few useful questions and observations to keep in mind. When we search for the source of our present body we eventually come to the combined sperm and ovum of our parents. Can this also be the source of our mind-stream? If we answer yes, many difficulties arise. How do we account for the marked differences between our mind and those of our parents and siblings? If our mind is traceable to our parents' germ cells, what is the relation between these cells and our parents' minds? Is the mind something that can eventually be reduced to a physical cause or, being essentially formless, must it not have a non-physical cause of its own quite apart from the source of our physical body?

Some people assert that the mind is a relatively blank slate at birth with but a few pre-natal impressions on it. They say that what we call the mind is merely the learned behaviour we acquire as we grow and develop. Is such a theory satisfactory? Does it take into account differences in temperament between people, differences that have been noted even in newborn infants of the same family? Does it account for the complexity of mental behaviour found in ordinary children, much less the unusual skills and aptitudes of exceptionally gifted youngsters?

If we truly want to understand the nature of the mind and discover whether or not it is a beginningless continuum we must consider these questions carefully. It is a fact that most people, even the educated and those whose professions deal directly with mental phenomena, possess nothing more than a vague idea of what the mind is. If our own views are similarly indefinite – if we do not have a coherent theory to explain the relationship between material form and non-material mind – then it is not wise to reject out of hand a theory based on logic, observation, experience and the testimony of enlightened beings. At the very least we should remain open-minded and look at the issue impartially.

According to Buddhist thought our stream of consciousness was present while we were a foetus. Going even further back to the moment of conception, this mind-stream entered the embryonic cell formed by the union of our father's sperm and mother's ovum. Prior to this entry, this consciousness or mental continuum was the consciousness of a previous lifetime. Furthermore, the consciousness of that life arose from the one before that, and so on back into infinity. Even Buddha Shakyamuni's omniscient mind saw no beginning to this process. Therefore, if the continuity of mind is beginningless, we must have taken countless rebirths and therefore must have had countless mothers. Consequently there is not a single sentient being who has not at one time or another been our mother.

If this is so why do we not intuitively recognize other beings as having been our mother? The reason is that the traumatic experiences of death and rebirth generally rob us of our memories of past lives. In addition, the way beings change form from one life to the next makes it difficult for us to recognize them. For example, if our present mother were to die and be reborn a dog, we would be completely unable to recognize her even if she eventually became our pet. Thus, despite appearances, we are presently surrounded by countless beings, who have each been our mother.

It is important to remember that not all beings lack the ability to recall their previous existence. As a fruit of their meditative practices, in which the gross obscurations of the mind are progressively removed, many Yogis gain the ability to see their past lives. Even some ordinary people, especially young children, have memories of their past lives owing to especially clear imprints on their mind. The fact that most of us, however, do not have such memories is not so surprising. After all, even the obscurations of this lifetime and the general fogginess of our mind are enough to prevent us from remembering events from our early childhood, infancy and stay in the womb.

Considering such lines of reasoning as presented above, and checking carefully to see if they are logical, non-contradictory, reasonable and applicable to our experience, is the process known as 'analytical meditation'. Arising from this process of examination is a conclusion, in this case a strong feeling that all beings have been our mother. The next step is to hold this feeling or conclusion by the power of our mindfulness, and remain upon it single-pointedly. This process is called 'placement meditation'. It is through the continual practice of placement meditation that true realizations dawn in our mind. When we become firm in the recognition that all sentient beings have been our mother, we have attained the realization of the first of the seven stages in the development of bodhichitta.

## REMEMBERING THE KINDNESS OF ALL LIVING BEINGS

If all beings have been our mother, then how are we to recollect their kindness? Our present mother carried us in her womb for nine months. Whether sitting, walking, eating or even sleeping she was ever mindful of our presence. Her only thought was of our welfare and she regarded us as a precious gem. Even though our birth may have caused her intense pain she still thought solely of our welfare and happiness.

As an infant we were little more than a helpless caterpillar, not knowing what was beneficial or harmful. Our mother cared for us and fed us her milk. When we were afraid she warmed us with the heat of her body and cuddled and comforted us in loving arms. She even wore soft clothing so as not to harm our sensitive skin.

Wherever she went she took us with her. She washed and bathed us and cleaned the dirt from our nose. While playing with us she would sing sweet sounds and repeat our name with special tenderness. She protected us continually from the dangers of fire and accident; in fact if it were not for her constant care we would not be alive now. All that we have and enjoy is through the kindness of our mother. She rejoiced in our happiness and shared in our sorrow. Worrying about our slightest discomfort, she would have willingly surrendered even her own life in order that we might live. She taught us how to walk and talk, read and write, and underwent many hardships in order to give us a good education and the very best of whatever she possessed.

Looking upon her child with tenderness, a mother cherishes it from conception until death with great devotion and unconditional love. Bringing to mind the limitless kindness of our present mother makes us realize the infinite loving care we have received from time without beginning from all the countless mothers who have nurtured us. How kind these sentient beings have all been!

## DEVELOPING THE WISH TO REPAY THE KINDNESS OF ALL MOTHER BEINGS

Merely to remember the kindness of all mother sentient beings is not enough. Only the most callous and ungrateful would fail to see that it is our duty and responsibility to repay this kindness. This we can do by bestowing on others material gifts, pleasures or enjoyments and other temporary benefits. However, the supreme repayment for the infinite kindness we have received is to lead all beings to the unsurpassable happiness of full awakening.

## DEVELOPING AFFECTIONATE LOVE

The next stage in the development of bodhichitta is to look upon all beings with affectionate love. This state of mind will arise naturally as a result of meditating for a long time on the three previous stages.

In general, whenever we see our child, husband, wife or parents a heart-warming feeling of affection naturally arises within us and we hold them dear. But such affection does not arise when we see other sentient beings, especially those who disturb us. If we are to develop true bodhichitta this warm feeling must be extended to embrace everyone. If as a result of long and continual meditation our mind becomes accustomed to looking upon each being with affection and warmth, we have realized this fourth stage in the development of the mind of enlightenment.

## DEVELOPING GREAT COMPASSION

Great compassion is the state of mind that wishes each and every being to be free from all suffering. If we have already developed affectionate, heart-warming love and have extended it towards all living beings, then when we meditate deeply on the suffering that others are now experiencing a feeling of great compassion will arise easily. Thus the primary cause of great compassion is our previous development of affectionate love.

The mind of great compassion embraces all sentient beings without exception. At present we are unable to bear our own suffering because we cherish ourself so deeply. In addition we cannot bear to see the suffering of our parents, family and friends because we cherish them as well. However, when we see our enemies in pain we take delight in the knowledge that they are suffering. Why? Because we do not cherish them at all. It is this prejudiced mind that we must tame and transform. We do this by familiarizing ourself with the first four stages until we spontaneously look upon all beings as we do our kind mother. Then, by remembering their suffering and dissatisfaction, we will easily develop great compassion. The measure of this development is that when confronted by a former enemy the spontaneous wish arises that he or she be free from all misery. As has been said, until we have developed affectionate love for all others, we will be unable to develop this great compassion for them.

There are two traditions regarding the development of affectionate love. That of such Indian Masters as Chandragomin and Chandrakirti states that affectionate love is the result of deepening the realization of the first three stages as explained above. According to the tradition of Shantideva, this heart-warming affection is developed mainly through the method of exchanging ourself with others, as will be explained later.

As already mentioned, if we develop affectionate, heart-warming love for all beings and then focus in meditation on their suffering, we can develop the mind of great compassion, wishing them to be released from their misery. If we focus instead on their lack of pure happiness – how they are deprived of true pleasures and joys – then our affectionate love develops into what is known as 'wishing love'. This is the heartfelt wish that no sentient being is ever separated from happiness and its causes.

## DEVELOPING SUPERIOR INTENTION

Upon the full realization of great compassion the thought will arise, 'I myself will undertake the task of liberating all beings from suffering; this is solely my duty and responsibility.' Assuming personal responsibility for the release of all sentient beings in this way is called 'superior intention'. This can be explained further by an example. If a child is drowning in a river, the onlookers will have the heartfelt wish that she be rescued. If the child's father sees this danger, however, he will not be satisfied with merely wishing her to be saved.

Instead there will arise in him the strong intention to act to save his child. He will think, 'I myself will rescue her.' The mind of the onlookers is like great compassion, while the mind of the father is like superior intention.

Someone who has developed this superior intention, although having the strong desire to act for the liberation of all sentient beings, soon realizes that he or she has no power to accomplish this aim. Like a father who is disabled and therefore cannot respond to his child's call for help, such a person is unable to fulfil this altruistic wish. A deep realization of this predicament – the inability to act upon our wishes – leads to the following intended result of this meditation.

## DEVELOPING BODHICHITTA

Through contemplation and examination we will discover that only a completely perfect being who has awakened from the sleep of ignorance, a fully enlightened Buddha, has the complete power to liberate others from their suffering. The truth of this becomes clear when we think about the attributes a true liberator of others must have. Such a being would have to possess the four characteristics of an Awakened One:

(1) Freedom from all obstructions preventing liberation and omniscience
(2) Great skill in liberating living beings from their suffering
(3) Compassion for all living beings without discrimination
(4) Benefiting all living beings whether or not they have helped him

In this world we do not find any ordinary person who has such qualities. Any being who does have these four characteristics is what Buddhists refer to when they use the title 'Buddha'. In the past many people in eastern countries have earned this title by developing supreme qualities through meditation on the Mahayana path. It is my hope that in this present day some Westerners also may develop these precious qualities and likewise achieve Buddhahood.

In conclusion, when the sixth realization, superior intention, has been developed and we subsequently recognize that only a Buddha endowed with the four above-mentioned qualities has the full power to fulfil this pure wish, we achieve the intended result of this meditation. In our mind arises the continuous thought to seek the full enlightenment of Buddhahood in order to benefit all mother sentient beings and remove them from suffering. This is the mind of enlightenment, bodhichitta, and anyone who develops it is called a 'Bodhisattva'.

As Shantideva stated in the previous verse, while there are many types of bodhichitta they are all contained within the following two aspects: the aspiring mind and the engaging, or venturing, mind. [16] These can be likened to the wish to go somewhere and the actual going. First the mind aspiring or wishing to go to the destination arises, and it continues to arise while the journey is being made. In a similar fashion, the aspiring mind of bodhichitta seeks to attain enlightenment for the benefit of all sentient beings, and it continues to arise until this goal is achieved. As for the engaging mind, it begins when the Bodhisattva vows have been received. It is at this point that we actually engage in the practices leading to enlightenment – the six perfections and the other virtues.

The two aspects of bodhichitta are stabilized within our mind by keeping the appropriate precepts and vows. First, in the presence of an actual Preceptor or the visualized assembly of Buddhas, we commit ourself to the aspiring mind. At this time we promise never to abandon this mind but to hold it firmly until enlightenment is reached. Then we take the following eight precepts to prevent this aspiring mind from degenerating in this life and in all future lives. For the sake of this life we vow:

(1) To remember the benefits of bodhichitta six times a day
(2) To generate bodhichitta six times a day
(3) Not to abandon any living being
(4) To accumulate merit and wisdom

As for the four precepts that prevent the aspiring mind from degenerating in future lives, we vow:

(5) Not to cheat or deceive our Preceptors or Spiritual Guides
(6) Not to criticize those who have entered the Mahayana
(7) Not to cause others to regret their virtuous actions
(8) Not to pretend to have good qualities or hide our faults without a special, pure intention

When the aspiring mind has become firm and full of encouragement, the Bodhisattva naturally develops the wish to practise all the perfections, the pure deeds of a Bodhisattva. At this point the vows of the engaging mind are taken, again either in the presence of a Preceptor or before the visualized assembly of Buddhas. At this time we commit ourself to observing all the countless precepts contained within the practice of the six perfections. These six perfections will be explained later in this commentary, and the actual ceremony for taking the Bodhisattva vows will be explained in the third chapter.

When the full set of Bodhisattva vows are taken the aspiring mind of bodhichitta becomes the engaging mind of bodhichitta. If all the precepts are kept purely, the Bodhisattva moves ever closer to the attainment of supreme enlightenment. However, if these precepts are disregarded, violated and abandoned, heavy negative consequences are incurred, removing our mind further from the goal. A full explanation of the eighteen root and forty-six secondary vows of a Bodhisattva can be found in Arya Asanga's *The Bodhisattva's Grounds* (Skt. *Bodhisattvabhumi*) and Je Tsongkhapa's *The Main Path to Enlightenment* (Tib. *Jang chub shung lam*), and in the book *The Bodhisattva Vow*.

## THE BENEFITS OF THE ASPIRING MIND OF BODHICHITTA

It has been said that if we were to offer a universe full of jewels to the fully enlightened beings the merit created would be great indeed. However, Buddha Shakyamuni has said that the merit that arises merely from the mind that seeks enlightenment for the benefit of others is thousands of times greater than this. Such an aspiring mind overcomes the disadvantages and hindrances of samsara, and outshines the qualities of those spiritual practitioners – the so-called Hearers and Solitary Conquerors – who work only for their own liberation. [17] As great as these benefits are, however, an uninterrupted flow of merit does not arise from the aspiring mind in the way that it does from the engaging mind.

## THE BENEFITS OF THE ENGAGING MIND OF BODHICHITTA

[18-19] From the time when the complete Bodhisattva vows are taken with the fearless mind that never turns back from its task of freeing all sentient beings from their suffering and leading them to enlightenment, great and unimaginable merit arises. The merit of such a mind is much greater than that which arises from the aspiring mind, and it comes even when the Bodhisattva is asleep, unconcerned or apparently intoxicated. Moreover, whatever actions of body, speech and mind the person possessing this engaging mind undertakes become the cause for his or her eventual attainment of the highest and most perfect enlightenment.

## THE REASONS FOR THE BENEFITS OF BODHICHITTA

There are two types of reasoning that establish the immense benefits of bodhichitta: reasoning from scripture and from logic. As for the former, [20] in *Sutra Requested by Subahu* (Skt. *Subahupariprcchasutra*) Buddha himself listed the many benefits of developing bodhichitta. Why was this teaching given? In order to persuade those who were inclined to the Hinayana path, which leads only to our own liberation from suffering, to follow the Mahayana path, which leads to full enlightenment for the sake of others.

The reasoning from logic establishing the benefits of bodhichitta follows from the observation that in general there are many types of virtuous or beneficial intentions we might have. For instance, a mother has a beneficial intention towards her child, and we may have a beneficial intention towards the poor and needy. But the beneficial intention of a Bodhisattva, whose great compassion extends to all living beings, is much greater than either of these examples. The difference between an ordinary being's virtuous impulse and that of a Bodhisattva is like the difference between the width of a fingernail and the vast expanse of the sky.

The extensive and unsurpassable benefits of bodhichitta are illustrated by the following story taken from a previous life of Buddha Shakyamuni. It is related that in that particular lifetime he created much negative karma by fighting with his mother and stepping over her head as she lay on the floor trying to block his departure. As a result of such a heavy non-virtuous action he was reborn in a hellish state of existence. In that karmically-created realm he had to endure the continual and excruciating suffering of having his head bored into. Around him were other beings who were all experiencing the same torment. The sight of these suffering beings stirred something within the boy's heart. Implanted on his mind was the karmic imprint of a previous beneficial intention, and when this arose in response to the others' torment he prayed, 'How wonderful it would be if all sentient beings were separated from all pains inflicted on their heads; may all such suffering ripen upon me!' Such was the power of this beneficial intention that all of the negative karma he had collected from harming his mother was completely purified. Immediately he was reborn in a god realm.

[21] Shantideva uses the example of the great merit that arises from a beneficial intention directed merely at relieving the suffering of others' headaches as a standard of comparison. If the merit from such a limited intention is so great, [22] what need is there to speak about the limitless merits of a Bodhisattva's pure intention? For his intention, deriving

from his bodhichitta motivation, is to separate all sentient beings from all their suffering and lead them to the highest state of enlightenment. The Bodhisattva works not only to bring sentient beings temporary happiness but also to lead them to the ultimate happiness of Buddhahood.

[23] Does even our father or mother have the same beneficial intention as the Bodhisattva has towards us? Do the great gods Brahma and Indra or even the wise sages have such a beneficial intention? No. It is true that our kind father and mother wish to dispel our temporary suffering and give us temporary happiness, but it does not occur to them to wish us the sublime joyful state of full awakening, the complete cessation of all our suffering.

In general, ordinary beings like ourself, although we are filled with self-cherishing, strive only for the temporary happiness of this one life. We have no intention to attain the highest state of enlightenment, or even happiness for our future lives. Neither do we have the intention to find release from the sufferings of a hellish rebirth or from the sufferings of samsara as a whole. [24] If the beneficial intention to be released from all suffering and attain enlightenment never arises for our own sake, not even in our dreams, then how will it ever arise for the sake of others? If we have no wish to be free from samsara ourself then how will the wish arise for others to be free from samsara?

If we meditate deeply by considering the constant suffering to which we are subjected we can develop the wish to be liberated from all the unsatisfactory states that make up samsara. This wish to be free is called 'renunciation'. If we reflect on the sufferings of those who are in the same situation as ourself, and realize that all sentient beings are suffering throughout samsara, the wish will arise that they also be freed. This is the development of true compassion, which leads to the generation of the bodhichitta wish.

[25] Bodhichitta is the source of happiness for all sentient beings. It is the universal panacea relieving others of all their suffering. [26] How are we able to measure the infinite, unfathomable merit of this precious jewel-like mind? Is there any wonder comparable to the birth of the precious bodhichitta within our mind?

To benefit another being is certainly a great practice, but for our beneficial intention to be pure it should not be mixed with such defilements as attachment. Only when it lacks such contaminations will great merit follow. [27] And if, as it is said, the pure intention merely to benefit a single sentient being is superior to making vast offerings to infinite Buddhas, what need is there to speak of a Bodhisattva's beneficial intention? With pure bodhichitta he or she wishes to separate every sentient being from suffering and to lead every one to the unchangeable bliss of unsurpassable enlightenment.

To understand the scope of a Bodhisattva's activity and to realize how powerful are the results of his or her motivation, consider the following. If we have a beneficial intention towards one hundred beings then one hundred merits will arise. Similarly if our beneficial intention is directed towards one thousand beings then one thousand merits will arise. If this beneficial intention is directed towards countless beings then the merits that arise will also be countless. Therefore the fruits that arise from the bodhichitta motivation are limitless. Why? Because the object of bodhichitta is the countless sentient beings inhabiting the universe.

[28] Someone might say that a Bodhisattva does not need to dispel the sufferings of sentient beings and lead them to

happiness because they will do this by themselves. But in fact ordinary beings are completely ignorant of the law of actions and their effects. Therefore, although they all wish to be free from misery they nevertheless run straight towards it, which they do by their constant and ignorant creation of non-virtue, the very cause of their suffering. Similarly, although they wish for nothing but happiness they systematically destroy virtue, the cause of happiness, as if it were their worst enemy.

[29] In short, sentient beings do not know the method to attain freedom from suffering. They are deprived of happiness and always afflicted by pain and sorrow. It is the Bodhisattva who, by the power of the precious bodhichitta, dispels their suffering and leads them to happiness. [30] Therefore, where is there a virtue comparable to bodhichitta, the mind of enlightenment that dispels the confusion of all beings, eradicates their suffering and bestows upon them boundless joy? Where is there a friend equal to the precious bodhichitta who accomplishes all benefit and prevents all harm? Where is there merit similar to that of the mind of enlightenment?

## PRAISE TO THE ONE WHO GIVES BIRTH TO BODHICHITTA

[31] In this world we generally respect and praise a person who repays the kindness he or she has received from another. If this is so, how can we even begin to speak of the great kindness shown by the Bodhisattva, that infinitely compassionate being who benefits others whether or not they have benefited him? Bound by great compassion the Bodhisattva unconditionally helps all sentient beings by leading them

in countless ways from suffering to happiness. Is there any need to speak of the praise and veneration due to such a glorious being?

[32] Perhaps there is a person who gives a little food to a few beggars, enough to satisfy them for half a day. Even if he performs this charity with resentment and bad feelings, what is the general reaction to his deeds? The beggars are grateful and the man is praised by others who say, 'He is a great benefactor and has accumulated much virtue.' [33] If this is so then what need is there to speak of the praise and veneration due to the Bodhisattva? This peerless benefactor strives, for as long as samsara exists, to fulfil not only the temporary wishes of countless sentient beings but also the ultimate aim of bestowing upon them the matchless delights of the Awakened Ones. When we understand these reasons well we should always generate the deepest respect for these Bodhisattvas. By merely rejoicing in their beneficial actions we accumulate boundless merit.

Some may wonder what the Bodhisattva does to practise temporary and ultimate generosity towards others. There are a great variety of possible activities because the Bodhisattva always acts according to the different dispositions of individual beings. Sometimes he or she will benefit others by teaching, sometimes by bestowing material aid and sometimes by protecting those in danger or great fear. Very advanced Bodhisattvas are able to manifest in different forms according to the needs of others. Depending upon the situation and the need it is possible for them to manifest as friends, helpers, or even inanimate objects. However, the main way a Bodhisattva benefits others is by teaching them Dharma, for this is the actual method that can lead sentient beings from the sufferings of samsara to the state of highest enlightenment. But, if certain beings lack interest in Dharma the Bodhisattva will be unable to teach them. Therefore, for these beings he manifests according to their temporary needs.

This account of a Bodhisattva's deeds may sound unbelievable, and it may be difficult for us to accept all of this at the present time. But if we become acquainted with and eventually understand the vast Mahayana Dharma, we will realize that a Bodhisattva's deeds are actually like this. Thus first we should listen to Dharma teachings, and afterwards we will begin to understand and appreciate their qualities.

In Tibet there was a Lama named Purchog Jampa Rinpoche who had a disciple called Kachen Yeshe Gyaltsen. This disciple lived beneath the cave of his Teacher and was often without sufficient food and clothing. One day a nobleman came to visit and offered Yeshe Gyaltsen a sack of barley flour, or *tsampa*, and some butter. Afterwards the disciple thought, 'I must be quite a special person for an aristocrat to give me these offerings.'

The next day Jampa Rinpoche gave teachings. In the middle of his discourse he said, 'One of my students is unaware of the fact that a Lama can manifest as tsampa and butter.' Then looking directly at Yeshe Gyaltsen he continued, 'This student thinks that it is solely due to his own merits that these provisions are offered to him.' Suddenly Yeshe Gyaltsen realized that both the nobleman and his gifts were all the manifestation of his Guru, and a feeling of strong devotion and faith arose in his mind.

Stories such as this one, however, are not easily received by new ears. Therefore it may be difficult to accept and believe such things. If we want to know whether a particular food is delicious or not we can only find out by tasting it. In the same way it is only by practising the teachings of Buddha that we will understand the qualities of Dharma. At the moment we have not yet experienced the taste of the Mahayana Dharma, so of course it is difficult to accept. But if we eat this food we will come to know its taste.

As for the Bodhisattva, his or her ultimate work is to lead all sentient beings to the attainment of enlightenment. To do this, preparation is needed. If we were to invite a king or some other high dignitary to our house, we would make elaborate preparation in advance. In the same way, the Bodhisattva wishes to invite all his guests, the countless mother sentient beings, to the banquet of supreme Buddhahood. He prepares for this now by seeking Buddhahood himself. When he attains this lofty state he will be able to relieve all sentient beings of their suffering and place them in the bliss of enlightenment. Thus the Bodhisattva is our kindest benefactor, the one who fulfils all our temporary and ultimate wishes.

At this point a doubt may arise. If, as stated, a Buddha has the ability to relieve all beings of their suffering, why have the countless Buddhas of the past not yet led everyone to enlightenment by now? The answer is as follows. Because Buddhas have overcome all obstructions and limitations they possess all the wisdom, compassion and skilful means necessary for leading others to Buddhahood. However, if sentient beings from their own side do not exert the necessary effort – if they do not bother to follow the path shown to them by the Buddhas –they will remain stuck within samsara. As has often been said, a Buddha cannot remove another's suffering and delusions the way we can pluck a thorn from another's flesh. Without a cooperative effort, nothing can be achieved. Merely relying upon an enlightened being is not enough.

Shantideva continues by advising us how to behave towards a Bodhisattva. [34] He quotes Buddha Shakyamuni as having said that one moment of anger directed towards a Bodhisattva – this peerless benefactor of all sentient beings – contaminates the mind with an enormous non-virtuous residue. As a result we will abide in the intensely suffering realm of the hell beings for as many aeons as there were moments of anger. [35] However, if we generate a virtuous mind, such as faith, towards a Bodhisattva, the fruits of this action will multiply even more abundantly than the results of an angry mind. While anger towards a Bodhisattva is thousands of times more non-virtuous than anger towards an ordinary being, faith in a Bodhisattva is far more meritorious than faith in an ordinary object.

Bodhichitta has so many good qualities and leads to so many beneficial results that the body of one who has developed this supremely precious mind is worthy to be an object of our prostrations. In one of his previous lifetimes as a Bodhisattva, Buddha Shakyamuni appeared as King Maitribala. He was wise, charitable and well-loved by his subjects, and soon his fame spread far and wide. Eventually news of this king reached the abode of five cannibalistic demons. They became very jealous of his good qualities and as a result plotted to murder him. Knowing his reputation for generosity they appeared before him and begged for charity. The king immediately gave them much gold and silver, but instead of accepting this they replied, 'This is an inappropriate offering; we are cannibals so please give us your flesh and blood.' The king assented to this gruesome request and as he gave them some of his blood he prayed, 'As I am now satisfying them with my blood may I one day satisfy them with pure Dharma and thereby be of true benefit to them.'

When this king was later reborn as Buddha Shakyamuni, these five demons were reborn as his first disciples. After listening to Buddha's first discourse, delivered in Sarnath and initiating the first turning of the Wheel of Dharma, these five became Arhats, attaining complete personal liberation from all suffering. [36] Thus even to those who do them harm Bodhisattvas return temporary and ultimate joy and benefit. Since these Bodhisattvas are the foundation for all sentient beings' happiness it is appropriate that we take continuous refuge in them.

Although there are numerous Mahayana practices, of both Sutra and Tantra, there is no practice more important than bodhichitta. By following the path of Tantra it is possible to attain enlightenment in one short lifetime. However, if we have not developed bodhichitta it does not matter how much or for how long we practise; it will be utterly impossible to attain enlightenment. Thus it is a great mistake to think that since Tantra is the quick path to enlightenment we should enter into it immediately and completely forget about developing bodhichitta. Such a misguided way of practising Dharma will be completely empty of results.

It is extremely important to follow the spiritual path correctly and gradually, without omitting any of its stages. To train our mind in this way is to emulate the examples of such great practitioners as Milarepa, who attained enlightenment in one lifetime. Milarepa once said, 'First I feared the eight states of bondage. I meditated on impermanence, death and the shortcomings of samsara. I observed very carefully the law of actions and their effects, and relied solely upon the Three precious and sublime Jewels of refuge. For a long time I trained in the two methods for developing bodhichitta. Later I came to see that whatever appeared to my mind lacked true existence and was like an illusion. Now I have no fear of rebirth in the lower realms.' Such a well-ordered method of practice should be our guide as we follow the Bodhisattva path.

This concludes 'The Benefits of Bodhichitta', the first chapter of the text *Meaningful to Behold*, a commentary to Shantideva's *Guide to the Bodhisattva's Way of Life*.

# Disclosure of Evil

In the first chapter of his *Guide* Shantideva discusses the benefits of developing the mind of bodhichitta. In his second chapter he shows us how we can eliminate obstacles that would normally prevent us from developing this enlightened motive. Thus the outline to the commentary continues as follows:

## HOW TO PRACTISE THE SIX PERFECTIONS ONCE BODHICHITTA HAS BEEN DEVELOPED

This has two parts:

1 Maintaining bodhichitta
2 How to practise the six perfections

### MAINTAINING BODHICHITTA

This section of the outline has two parts, corresponding to the second and third chapters of this commentary:

1 How to destroy obstacles and purify evil
2 How to accept and hold on to the actual bodhichitta

*Shantideva*

## HOW TO DESTROY OBSTACLES AND PURIFY EVIL

As stated before, the main obstacle to developing bodhichitta is our accumulation of negative energy or non-virtue. If we want to develop beneficial states of mind such as bodhichitta we have to purify this non-virtue and replace it with virtuous or meritorious energy. This dual process of accumulating merit and cleansing ourself of non-virtue or evil is accomplished by performing the following preliminary practices and confession:

1 The preliminary limbs of practice
2 The confession of non-virtue

## THE PRELIMINARY LIMBS OF PRACTICE

This has three parts:

1 Offering
2 Prostration
3 Going for refuge

## OFFERING

The first preliminary limb of practice consists of making offerings. Shantideva's discussion of this practice has two parts:

1 The necessity of making offerings, and recognizing the objects of offering
2 The actual offering

# THE NECESSITY OF MAKING OFFERINGS, AND RECOGNIZING THE OBJECTS OF OFFERING

In this second chapter Shantideva is personally taking the part of someone who wishes to purify himself of accumulated non-virtue. He realizes the necessity of following the preliminary practices and declares it openly as follows:

[1] In order to maintain and complete the precious bodhichitta, the source of happiness for all universal beings, I will now make offerings to the objects of devotion: all the Tathagatas (those who have gone to thatness, the Buddhas), the jewel of holy Dharma, and those Sons of Buddha, the Bodhisattvas such as youthful Manjughosha, Avalokiteshvara and others, who possess oceans of excellence.

## THE ACTUAL OFFERING

Shantideva now begins an exhaustive list of the various types of offering that can be presented to these three sublime objects: Buddha, Dharma and Sangha. These types of offering are divided into three parts:

1. Unowned offerings
2. Offering our own body
3. Mentally transformed offerings

## UNOWNED OFFERINGS

[2-7] All of the following I offer up to you. Whatever flowers there are, those that are most beautiful; fruits, medicinal herbs, numerous jewels and pure, refreshing

waters; mountains of jewels, beautiful forest groves, and quiet and joyful places; heavenly trees with the most beautifully blossoming flowers, and trees whose branches bow down with the weight of good fruit.

Exquisite scents from celestial realms, incense, wish-granting trees, jewelled trees, harvests that need no cultivation, and all ornaments worthy of offering. Lakes and pools adorned with magnificent lotuses and resounding with the beautiful sound of wild geese.

From the depths of my heart I offer up all these unowned gifts from the limitless spheres of space, together with all that is worthy of offering, to the supreme beings, the Buddhas and their Sons. O Compassionate Ones, think kindly of me and accept these offerings of mine. I have little merit and no other gifts of beauty or value to offer. By your power, O Protectors, you who are concerned with all others, please accept these offerings for my sake.

Among the rare and beautiful items offered up here Shantideva mentions several – such as mountains of jewels and wish-granting trees – that may seem quite unusual to many of us. Where are such mountains of jewels to be found? What is a wish-granting tree and where is it located? To understand all this we must first know a little about Buddhist cosmology. This system of viewing the universe is quite different from the one presented by current scientific theory, and contains much that would be difficult to accept if interpreted too literally or concretely. However, if we bear in mind the present purpose of this cosmology, namely that it allows us to see the entire universe as an offering to the enlightened ones, the initial strangeness of this system will soon disappear.

Buddha taught that there are countless world systems in the universe; some are like our own while others are vastly different. Our own world system is composed of four 'continents' arranged in the cardinal directions, and we live in the southern continent. At the centre of this world system stands a vast, four-sided mountain. This is Mount Meru. Each side of this central mountain has the nature of a different precious substance. The colour of the sky over each continent is determined by the light reflected from Mount Meru. Because the southern side of Mount Meru is of the nature of lapis lazuli, the sky over the southern continent appears blue. In a similar fashion, the eastern side of Mount Meru is crystal and reflects a white light towards the eastern continent, the western side is the red of ruby and the northern side is the yellow of gold.

The minerals and vegetation on each of these continents are different, and in addition, each continent possesses a special treasure that is its major attribute. These four treasures, which because of their magnificence are offered to the Buddhas, are: a mountain of jewels from the eastern continent, a wish-granting tree from our own southern continent, a wish-granting cow from the western continent, and a harvest of crops that need no cultivation from the northern continent. These gifts, representing all that is most precious and beautiful throughout the universe, together with the sun, the moon and other special items, can be assembled in an imaginative visualization and presented to Buddha, Dharma and Sangha in a form known as a 'mandala offering'. If such a visualized offering is performed seriously, its very vastness and supreme quality can have an extremely positive effect on our mind and thereby lead to the creation of great merit. A detailed explanation of mandala offerings can be found in the book *The New Guide to Dakini Land*.

Making offerings to the Three Jewels – Buddha, Dharma and Sangha – is predominantly an activity of the mind. Actual material gifts are not required and so even the poorest person, provided his or her motivation is pure and visualization expansive, can make the most magnificent offerings. This practice is designed to overcome the narrowness of our miserly attitudes, and its benefits can be vast indeed. The story is told of a small child who wished very much to be able to offer something precious to the Buddha of his day. Since he was poor and could afford nothing, he filled a bowl with dust and held it aloft, visualizing it as resplendent with gold. The strength and purity of his motivation were so powerful that he accumulated vast merit. He was later reborn as the great Buddhist king and benefactor Ashoka. During his reign he did much to establish the Dharma in India and Sri Lanka. In one day alone he caused one million religious monuments to be built, some of which can still be seen today.

If we recognize the enlightened beings as having overcome all obstacles and possessing all good qualities, our practice of making offerings to them will bring us closer to their supreme attainment. Such an attainment depends upon gaining successive realizations along the path and to gain these realizations we need a great wealth of merit, or positive energy. The disciples who lived at the time of Buddha Shakyamuni had great stores of such positive merit, and just by hearing one word of Buddha's teachings some of them quickly attained realizations. At the first turning of the Wheel of Dharma, for instance, when Buddha taught the four noble truths, several disciples gained a direct realization of emptiness, the highest reality, and some even attained the state of nirvana, complete personal liberation from all suffering.

The Dharma taught these days is the same as that taught by Buddha Shakyamuni, and those who teach it are like Buddha himself, so why is it that even though we listen to teachings for months at a time we do not attain realizations? It is simply due to our lack of accumulated merit. Therefore, if we wish to gain realizations we must gather a great wealth of merit, and one of the main methods for doing this is to make offerings to the enlightened ones.

The benefit of making such offerings has been supported by the experience of many meditators in the past. There is the account of a fully ordained nun who received a vision of Avalokiteshvara, the Buddha of compassion, as a direct result of making mandala offerings. The great Spiritual Guide Je Tsongkhapa used the practice of making mandala offerings to gain a direct realization of emptiness. In fact, this practice is recommended by the Teachers of all Mahayana Buddhist traditions.

## OFFERING OUR OWN BODY

[8-9] In all my lifetimes I will offer all my bodies to the Buddhas and their Sons. Please accept me, O Supreme Heroes, as I reverently become your subject and follow your advice. Protected by your power I will remain unafraid of the sufferings of samsara and will benefit others. My previous evils will be purified and in the future I will commit no more.

By offering our own body to the enlightened beings we can accumulate great merit. We will gradually purify the effects of our past non-virtuous actions and refrain from committing further misdeeds in the future. Why is this? The immeasurable non-virtue we have committed since time without beginning has been the fault of our self-cherishing attitude. With a selfish attitude towards our own body we have engaged in innumerable negative actions, trying to get the best for ourself at all costs. Therefore if we are able to offer our body to the enlightened beings, thereby depriving our self-cherishing attitude of its chief object, there will no longer be any reason to commit non-virtuous actions. If we can overcome selfishness and miserliness by mentally offering ourself as a servant to the Buddhas, we will experience many positive results. Moreover, by constantly meditating in this fashion we are preparing ourself to offer our actual body as a servant. The unsurpassed benefits of this action are evident in the life of the great Milarepa who surrendered his body as a servant to his Teacher Marpa and, as a result of his intense Guru devotion, attained full enlightenment within one lifetime.

If we offer not only our present body but also those of our future lives to the Buddhas, we will be free from the fears of samsara. When a person offers himself and his services to a king he receives royal protection, and as a result no one dares to harm him. In a similar fashion, if we offer our body to the Buddhas, it becomes their servant and is beyond the harm caused by human and non-human beings alike.

## MENTALLY TRANSFORMED OFFERINGS

There are two types of mentally transformed offerings:

1 Ordinary offerings
2 Sublime offerings

## ORDINARY OFFERINGS

Shantideva now describes an elaborate visualized ceremony in which twelve mentally transformed offerings are presented to the Buddhas. These are: (1) scented water for bathing the Buddhas, (2) heavenly raiment, (3) ornamental jewels, (4) perfumed oils for anointing the Buddhas, (5) flowers, (6) incense, (7) food, (8) lamps, (9) palaces, (10) jewelled parasols, (11) music and (12) the prayer for a continuous rain of offerings. We should remember when performing the following visualization that the enlightened beings themselves have no impurities of body or mind that need cleansing. From our own side, however, we need to abandon our impure form externally and the evils and obstructions of our mind internally if we are to attain the pure state of a Buddha. Thus, the cleansing and purification that we are about to perform is, in fact, for our own benefit.

[10] First we should visualize the bathing room in which the purification is to take place. The floor sparkles with beautiful crystal and the atmosphere is pervaded by sweet-scented sandalwood. Four jewelled pillars adorned with gems and precious stones stand in the four directions, while from the ceiling are suspended two precious canopies decorated with pearls. In the centre of the bathing room is a pool filled with wonderfully scented waters. From three directions, three steps sparkling with gems lead down into the pool.

[11] Having visualized this beautiful setting we now invite all the Tathagatas and Bodhisattvas to come and bathe in this pool. As we see them arrive we manifest many goddesses from our heart, one for each of the Buddhas and Bodhisattvas. These goddesses take the garments of the

enlightened beings and the Bodhisattvas while others wash them with the pure scented waters held in beautiful jewelled vases, all to the accompaniment of music and song.

[12] Next we visualize the goddesses as drying these guests with towels made from soft and beautifully scented cloth. [13] Then we offer fine robes of suitable colours and many jewelled ornaments to the magnificent Superior beings: Samantabhadra, Manjughosha, Avalokiteshvara and the others. [14] Then, as if polishing pure refined gold, we anoint the radiant bodies of the Buddhas and Bodhisattvas with rare perfume whose fragrance pervades thousands of millions of world systems.

After anointing their bodies in this way we visualize these holy beings in the sky in front of us and send forth beautiful goddesses to them, each one holding a separate offering. [15] To these glorious beings the goddesses present the following: garlands of beautiful and sweet-scented lotuses, mandaravas, upalas and other exquisite flowers; [16] clouds of incense with delicate fragrance; delicious food and drink; [17] lamps arranged on golden lotus buds, whose light dispels the dark ignorance of thousands of millions of world systems; [18] and a most beautiful celestial palace made of pearls and precious gems. Inside this gorgeous palace there are transparent floors carpeted with beautiful flowers, while on the walls hang priceless pearls and gems. Throughout this celestial abode beautiful goddesses sing joyful songs in praise of the Buddhas. [19] Throughout the palace stand many beautifully shaped parasols, vast in diameter, with handles wrought in gold and rims adorned with many kinds of jewels. [20] All these magnificent offerings vibrate with the sound of delightful music, whose beautiful harmonies completely dispel even the traces of all beings' misery.

[21] The final offering of this group is our own prayer that until samsara ends, a continual rain of flowers, incense and precious jewels may fall upon the images and statues of the Buddhas and Bodhisattvas, upon holy Dharma and upon the sacred reliquary monuments.

## SUBLIME OFFERINGS

Sublime offerings are purer than the ordinary visualized offerings just made. They are offerings actually manifested by Superior beings. In emulation of them Shantideva prays:

[22] Just as Manjughosha and Samantabhadra made many beautiful offerings to the Buddhas and Bodhisattvas, similarly may I too make offerings to the Protectors and their Sons.

Supreme beings such as Manjughosha and Samantabhadra have the ability, because of their spiritual realizations, to emanate such offerings as described above. At present we can only visualize such offerings, but Superior Bodhisattvas – those advanced beings who possess both bodhichitta and a direct insight into reality – are able to manifest such things and offer them to the enlightened beings for their use. Such manifestations can also be used by ordinary sentient beings.

Powers of manifestation such as these were not unknown in India and Tibet. In *One Hundred Thousand Songs of Milarepa* (Tib. *Milarepai gurbum*) the story is told of the arrival in Tibet of the great Indian Pandit, Padampa Sangye. Milarepa wanted to test Padampa Sangye's spiritual powers and so he flew miraculously to the mountain near where the Indian was passing. As he awaited the arrival of the Pandit,

Milarepa transformed himself into a flower near the roadside. When Padampa Sangye came by and walked past the flower, apparently unable to see through Milarepa's disguise, the Tibetan Yogi thought that the Indian had no powers of clairvoyance. Shortly after he thought this, however, the Pandit paused, turned around and walked back to the flower. Kicking it sharply he shouted, 'You, Milarepa, stand up!' Milarepa immediately resumed his human form and greeted the Pandit warmly, saying 'Welcome to Tibet. You are indeed a great Master.' To this Padampa Sangye replied, 'You too are very famous in India as a great Yogi.' The story of the competition they then held to demonstrate each other's miracle powers, and the songs of realization Milarepa sang afterwards, can be read in several biographies which have already been translated into English.

If we frequently make ordinary visualized offerings of the twelve types mentioned above, positive imprints will be placed on our minds that will eventually ripen in our ability to make the sublime offerings of Superior Bodhisattvas. However, there is another sublime offering that we can make right at this present moment, and that is to practise the teachings we have received from our Spiritual Guide, or Guru. If our Spiritual Guide gives us instructions on how to abandon non-virtue and practise virtue and we follow these instructions faithfully, then this is a most sublime offering. Milarepa told his Teacher Marpa that he had no material objects to offer to him, but intended instead to repay his Guru's kindness by dedicating his body, speech and mind to the practice of Dharma. Because a Spiritual Guide is solely interested in the welfare of his or her disciples, such an offering of practice is much more pleasing to him than any amount of material wealth.

Another method of making sublime offerings is to transform whatever merit we may have collected from positive actions into gifts suitable for presentation to both enlightened and ordinary beings.

## PROSTRATION

The second preliminary limb of practice is to offer prostration, or homage, to the supreme beings. This is a vast practice and Shantideva summarizes it as follows:

> [23-5] With limitless verses of harmonious praise I will glorify the Buddhas and Bodhisattvas, possessors of oceans of excellence. May clouds of gentle songs of praise extolling their good qualities always ascend to the assembly of Superiors.
> 
> With bodies as numerous as the number of atoms in all the Buddha Lands, I prostrate to the enlightened beings of the three times, to the Dharma and to the supreme Sangha community.
> 
> I also prostrate to the bases for generating bodhichitta, to the stupas containing sacred relics, to all the learned Abbots and Preceptors, and to all the practitioners who have entered the path leading to liberation.

Shantideva specifically mentions two types of prostration here: verbal and physical. Other texts specify a third type, mental prostration, which refers to the attitude of respect and faith we extend towards worthy objects. Praises given to the Buddhas, Bodhisattvas and so forth make up prostrations of speech, while physical prostrations are of many types. In the most beneficial form of practice all three forms of prostration are performed simultaneously.

As for physical prostrations, there are two methods in common use. The first of these is called the 'half-length prostration' and is performed by kneeling down and touching both hands and our forehead to the ground. The complete full-length prostration requires that our whole outstretched body be in contact with the ground. Detailed instructions on the techniques and benefits of these practices were taught by Buddha Shakyamuni, and commented on by later Pandits; and descriptions of the full-length prostration can be found in *Stalks in Array Sutra* (Skt. *Gandhavyuhasutra*). Offering prostration was a major practice of many great Indian Pandits. The famous master Naropa, who was Marpa's principal Guru and the disseminator of profound yogic methods still practised today, used prostrations as his chief external method for accumulating merit.

The practice of prostrations has great power to purify our non-virtue and accumulate positive, meritorious energy. But whether or not this actually happens depends solely on our mind. If we approach this practice with a pure motivation, wishing to overcome our false sense of pride, and keep the qualities of the Three supreme Jewels of Buddha, Dharma and Sangha uppermost in our mind, it is definite that beneficial effects will follow. It is said that as a result of this practice we will be reborn into a high-ranking family, endowed with an attractive and healthy body, and become the object of others' respect. There is even a tradition that says that the merit we gain from paying homage in this way is equal to the number of atoms in the ground covered by our prostrate body.

What is the exact method for performing prostrations? There are various traditions of practice even within Mahayana Buddhism. According to one widely followed tradition, we begin by standing erect and placing the palms of our hands together in an attitude of prayer, the thumbs touching and tucked inside the palms to symbolize a wish-fulfilling jewel. (It should be noted that merely to hold our hands in this or a similar gesture of respect, or even to bow our head slightly, qualifies as a physical prostration; it is not necessary to touch the ground at all.) We then touch our folded hands to four places on our body to plant the seeds to attain various qualities of an enlightened being. First we touch the top of our head in order to attain a Buddha's ushnisha, the crown protuberance that results from paying respect to our Spiritual Guide and which symbolizes a Buddha's inner realizations. We then touch our forehead, throat and heart in order to attain a Buddha's hair curl (a sign of wisdom), power of speech and power of mind respectively. If our motivation and faith are strong, these practices will place powerful potentialities on our mind-stream for our future attainment of a Buddha's transcendent body, speech and mind. After touching these four places we then bend down to do a half-length or full-length prostration and then immediately stand up again. We repeat this process at least three times and then always finish by touching our folded hands to our crown, forehead, throat and heart.

Offering prostrations was a very well-known practice throughout Tibet. Je Tsongkhapa stressed the importance of this practice, and during a retreat with several of his principal disciples performed three and a half million full-length prostrations. Another great Tibetan Teacher, Jampa Rinpoche, who was said to be a manifestation of Maitreya Buddha, claimed to limit his external methods for accumulating merit to just two practices every day: offering one hundred water bowls and making one hundred prostrations.

Even into old age he continued this practice. He was very tall and, because he could cover so much ground with his body, was able to accumulate much merit from his practice. One day he exclaimed, 'How wonderful it would be if I were even taller, then I could accumulate even more merit!'

Prostrations were a popular form of practice even among laypeople in Tibet and many people endured great hardships for the sake of offering them. It was quite common for people to prostrate the entire distance around the capital city of Lhasa. In addition some people were known to have made full-length prostrations all the way from their home district in eastern Tibet to the holy Kailash mountain in the west, a journey that normally took six months by foot.

Although the prostrations that have been described are a physical practice, as with all Dharma practices their true value depends upon our mental attitude. Thus, if during this practice we visualize our body appearing in numberless manifestations, all of which are making prostrations to infinite Buddhas and Bodhisattvas, we will receive benefits as great as our visualization is vast.

In his *Guide*, Shantideva mentions making prostrations to the bases for generating bodhichitta. There are three bases upon which bodhichitta is generated: (1) the Mahayana Dharma, which describes the methods and benefits of generating bodhichitta; (2) the Mahayana Spiritual Guide, who gives us precise instructions; and (3) the actual location where bodhichitta is generated. The generation of bodhichitta is of such great value that even the place where it is developed is worthy of veneration. In India there are many pilgrimage sites marking locations where famous meditators have gained spiritual realizations. Bodh Gaya in particular, where Buddha Shakyamuni demonstrated his attainment of full enlightenment, is considered a very auspicious place to make prostrations. Similarly, his birth place (Lumbini), where he first turned the Wheel of Dharma (Sarnath), and where he passed away (Kushinagar) are all places where pilgrims go particularly to make prostrations.

## GOING FOR REFUGE

The third preliminary practice for purifying negativities and accumulating merit is to turn the mind to the proper and ultimate source of refuge. As Shantideva says:

> [26] From this moment on, until I attain the essence of great enlightenment, I will go for refuge to the Buddhas, the Dharma and the supreme assembly of Superior Bodhisattvas.

The explanation of going for refuge has five parts:

1. The causes of going for refuge
2. The objects of refuge
3. The measurement of going for refuge perfectly
4. The commitments of going for refuge
5. The benefits of going for refuge

If the causes of going for refuge are unknown to us, we will have no motivation to begin this practice; and if we do not know what the proper objects of refuge are, then to whom will we turn? If we do not know the measurement of going for refuge perfectly, we will not know how to complete this practice; and if we remain ignorant of the commitments of going for refuge, we will be unable to fulfil the purpose of this practice. Finally, if we do not know the benefits of going for refuge, we will deprive ourself of the inspiration necessary for undertaking this practice sincerely and repeatedly.

## THE CAUSES OF GOING FOR REFUGE

Going for refuge is a major foundation of the Buddhist path. It signifies our determination to turn away from the endless cycle of confusion and dissatisfaction that has marked our life, and towards a saner, more wholesome way of living. As stated before, our past collection of negative actions of body, speech and mind has been responsible both for our day-to-day confusion and unhappiness and for our difficulty in gaining realizations along the spiritual path. If this uncontrolled pattern of behaviour continues unchecked, it will lead us to even more acute states of suffering and torment in the future. Thus there are two inter-related causes for our taking refuge in Buddha, Dharma and Sangha. First of all we must have a heart-felt dread of the miserable states of samsaric existence towards which our uncontrolled behaviour of body, speech and mind are propelling us. In terms of Buddhist cosmology this dread is interpreted as an intense aversion to the sufferings of the three lower realms of existence or, further, as a feeling of being disgusted with the unsatisfactory nature of all states conditioned by ignorance. In addition to this real dread we must have an unshakeable conviction and faith in the Three Jewels, understanding well how they have the power to protect us from all forms of suffering. Basing our conviction upon reason, proper authority and, most importantly, our own experience, we turn to the Three Jewels of refuge with the thought that only they can show us the path away from fear and dissatisfaction and towards peace of mind.

The Buddhist teachings describe three progressive levels of spiritual practice, and the dual causes for going for refuge described above vary according to which of these three levels we are on. A person at the initial level of motivation sees clearly how his or her mind is polluted by such violent delusions as hatred, jealousy and greed. He fears that without proper training this unruly mind will expose him to the intense suffering of the three lower realms – those states of hellish, ghostly and brutish suffering that result from extremely non-virtuous actions of body, speech and mind. Such a person develops faith and conviction in the power of the Three Jewels to offer protection from this harm.

When a person progresses to the intermediate level of motivation he or she sees how the whole of samsaric existence – the elevated states as well as the lower – is pervaded by dissatisfaction and suffering. Fed up with circling through this unending round of existence, the person turns to the Three Jewels for a method to gain complete liberation from all suffering states of existence.

At the highest level of motivation the spiritual seeker is motivated by great compassion. He or she transcends individual, selfish concerns to see that all other beings are also whirling around in the darkness of their ignorance, creating the causes for more and more suffering for themselves. With an intense wish to help these beings, each of whom he recognizes as having been his mother in previous lives, he turns to the Three Jewels with a conviction that only they can lead him to enlightenment – the fully perfected state in which it is possible to benefit all beings to the greatest extent.

## THE OBJECTS OF REFUGE

It is very important to have a clear idea of what exactly the three objects of refuge are. In Buddhism they are known as the Three Jewels, or the Sublime, Precious Three – Buddha, Dharma and Sangha. A general definition of these three has already been given in the first chapter where Buddha was referred to as an enlightened being (the doctor), Dharma to his teachings (the medicine) and Sangha to the spiritual community of those following these teachings (the nurses). We then go for refuge to these Jewels in the same way that a sick person goes to a physician to be cured, relies upon the prescribed medicine and receives help and support from trained nurses.

As we grow more interested in following the spiritual path, however, it becomes necessary to have a more detailed understanding of these Three Jewels. To gain such an understanding of what are the true objects of refuge, it is useful to be acquainted with the following outline of the Mahayana paths, or states of consciousness leading to and culminating in full enlightenment.

Once we have developed the bodhichitta wish we enter the first of five progressive paths leading to the attainment of Buddhahood. The main work to be done along these paths is the step-by-step removal of all the obstructions that cover our mind and prevent it from exhibiting its basically pure, essential nature. These coverings are classified as delusion-obstructions that prevent liberation and obstructions to knowing that prevent omniscience. We remove these by developing and deeply acquainting our mind with wisdom, specifically the wisdom that has a direct non-conceptual understanding of the true nature of reality.

This understanding removes layer after layer of obscuring ignorance, from the gross to the very subtle, until the clear light nature of our mind is fully revealed.

On the first two of the five paths, the paths of accumulation and preparation, we train in generating an increasingly accurate and profound conceptual understanding of reality by developing powerful concentration and superior seeing (as explained in the eighth and ninth chapters of this commentary). Eventually, as the result of this training and the accumulated strength, or merit, of our mind, our understanding becomes direct, or non-conceptual. At that very moment we enter the third path, the path of seeing, and all our intellectually-formed delusions are removed. We have become a Superior Bodhisattva: a noble Son or Daughter of the Buddhas. The remainder of our training involves the gradual elimination, on the fourth path, the path of meditation, of all the innate delusions and their imprints that still obscure our mind. When this is fully accomplished and there remains not even the subtlest veil covering the clear light nature of our consciousness, we achieve the fifth and final path, the Path of No More Learning, the full enlightenment of Buddhahood. As such an Awakened Being all our actions of body, speech and mind spontaneously and effortlessly work for the benefit of others, as we are impelled by our bodhichitta motivation to lead all beings to the bliss of liberation and enlightenment.

With this brief outline of the Mahayana path in mind we can now return to the objects of refuge and discuss what is meant by Buddha, Dharma and Sangha Jewels. A Buddha Jewel is any being who has progressed through the Mahayana path to its completion and is therefore endowed with the four characteristics of freedom from obstructions, skilful means, universal compassion and impartiality mentioned in the preceding chapter. The Dharma Jewel refers to the second two noble truths, namely true paths (that is, wisdom consciousnesses) that release us forever from any of the obstructions to liberation or omniscience, and true cessations (that is, freedom from any obstruction) achieved through these paths. Lastly, the Sangha Jewel refers to those beings endowed with the Dharma Jewel, namely Superior Bodhisattvas, those noble practitioners who have reached at least the path of seeing and therefore have a direct understanding of the true nature of reality.

## THE MEASUREMENT OF GOING FOR REFUGE PERFECTLY

The true taking of refuge depends upon our clear recognition of the causes mentioned above. Once we have cultivated a dread of various forms of samsaric suffering and an understanding that only the Three Jewels have the power to protect us from such suffering, from the depths of our heart we will place our full reliance firmly upon Buddha, Dharma and Sangha. When we do this sincerely and consistently this is the actual going for refuge. To remind us of this and to deepen our refuge we can recite the following prayer: 'I go for refuge to the Gurus, I go for refuge to the Buddhas, I go for refuge to the Dharma, I go for refuge to the Sangha.'

## THE COMMITMENTS OF GOING FOR REFUGE

Once we have turned to the Three Jewels for refuge there are a number of commitments we should strive to observe purely. These include three actions to be abandoned, three actions to be acknowledged, and six general commitments.

## *The three abandonments*

Once we have taken refuge in the Buddha Jewel, we should abandon going for refuge to teachers who contradict Buddha's view, or to samsaric gods. Having taken refuge in the Dharma Jewel, we should abandon harming others. Having taken refuge in the Sangha Jewel, we should not allow ourself to be influenced by people who reject Buddha's teachings.

## *The three acknowledgements*

Having taken refuge in Buddha, we should regard any image of Buddha, whether it is made of gold, wood or some other material, and regardless of whether it is old or new, as an actual Buddha. Our Dharma refuge requires that we regard any Dharma scripture, even the individual letters, as an actual Dharma Jewel, a Buddha's actual speech. As such, Dharma texts should definitely not be mistreated, placed on the ground or stepped over. Having taken refuge in the Sangha Jewel we should regard anyone who wears the robes of an ordained person as an actual Sangha Jewel.

## *The six general commitments*

The following commitments of going for refuge should also be borne in mind throughout our life. Each of them is designed to enhance beneficial attitudes and maintain the liberating thought of refuge in the forefront of our consciousness. Thus (1) we should go for refuge to the Three Jewels again and again, remembering their good qualities and the differences between them – recognizing their superiority over ordinary worldly forms of refuge. (2)

To offer the first portion of whatever we eat or drink to the Three Jewels, remembering their kindness. (3) With our heart full of compassion – and mindful of living beings' various capacities – always to encourage others to go for refuge. (4) Remembering the benefits of going for refuge, to go for refuge at least three times during the day and three times during the night. (5) To perform every action with complete trust in the Three Jewels – regardless of what situation arises, what frame of mind we are in and whether or not we are healthy. Finally, (6) we should never forsake the Three Jewels even at the cost of our life, or as a joke.

The practice of refuge is extremely vast and profound. There is not a single practice in the lesser or greater vehicles of Buddhism that is not included within the refuge taken by beings of various levels of motivation. When the great Indian Master Atisha first came to Tibet he taught widely on the subject of refuge. As a result the Tibetans jokingly nicknamed him the 'Refuge Lama'. When Atisha learned that the Tibetans were referring to him in this way he was very pleased.

## THE BENEFITS OF GOING FOR REFUGE

There are eight benefits of going for refuge. (1) We become a pure Buddhist, or inner being, and (2) we establish the foundation for taking all other vows – such as lay, ordained, Bodhisattva and Tantric vows. (3) We purify the negative karma that we have accumulated in the past, and (4) we daily accumulate a vast amount of merit. (5) We are held back from falling into the lower realms, and (6) we are protected from harm inflicted by humans and non-humans. (7) We fulfil all our temporary and ultimate wishes, and finally (8) we quickly attain the full enlightenment of Buddhahood.

## THE CONFESSION OF NON-VIRTUE

The three limbs of offering, prostration and refuge are the preliminary practices leading up to the main practice described in this chapter: the confession of non-virtue. This confession, or declaration, of our non-virtuous actions enables us to counteract the harmful effects these actions would otherwise bring upon us. The full and proper completion of this practice depends upon utilizing the four opponent powers listed below. If these four powers are completed properly, with full understanding of their meaning, all our past non-virtue can definitely be purified.

1. The power of regret
2. The power of reliance
3. The power of the opponent force
4. The power of promise

## THE POWER OF REGRET

The first step in purifying the effects of negative actions is to admit to ourself that they were indeed negative and harmful. This sincere admission of the wrongs we have done both to ourself and others allows the process of uprooting these negativities to begin. Thus it is necessary at the outset to develop a strong sense of regret for the harmful actions done while under the sway of deluded states of mind. In the following lengthy paraphrase from the *Guide*, Shantideva takes the part of a spiritual seeker who has become deeply convinced of the extent and gravity of his own non-virtue.

> [27-9] With a deep sense of regret for my past non-virtues, I press my palms together beseeching those

who possess great compassion, all the Buddhas and Superior Bodhisattvas abiding in the ten directions. From beginningless time, in this and in previous lives, having been ignorant of the law of actions and their effects, I have personally committed much non-virtue and have also impelled others to do so. Overwhelmed by deceptive ignorance, I have even rejoiced in the non-virtue others have performed; but now I have recognized all these actions as mistakes, and from the depths of my heart I sincerely declare them all in your presence, O Protectors.

[30-1] Whatever harmful actions of body, speech and mind I have done, my mind being disturbed by delusion, towards the Field of Merit, the Three Jewels, my Spiritual Guide, my parents and others, and all the other wrongs of my defiled mind, today do I openly declare to the deliverers of the world.

[32-3] If I die without cleansing myself of these great evils, I will undoubtedly come to experience unimaginable suffering. I pray to you, please swiftly protect me from all these fears. There are further reasons why I quickly seek your protection. The duration of my life is totally uncertain and to the unpredictable Lord of Death it makes no difference whether I have declared my non-virtues or not. Without waiting for me to complete the work I am engaged in, and unconcerned whether I am sick or healthy, he will suddenly descend upon me. O Protectors, please deliver me from all the fears of dying.

[34-6] During my life I did not understand that my relatives, my body, wealth, possessions and everything would all be left behind, and that I would depart alone from this life for the next. Out of my ignorance I

committed much non-virtue for the sake of my relatives and friends, and did much evil trying to destroy my foes. Now I see the foolishness of such actions and I deeply regret my past deeds. I understand now that my enemies, my relatives and friends, and even myself will all eventually pass away and become as nothing. Similarly my wealth, possessions and everything will become nothing. The pleasures and happiness experienced in a dream become but a faint memory upon awaking. In the same way, the enjoyments of this life will be nothing more than a memory at the time of death. Whatever has passed will not be seen or experienced again.

[37-8] In the brief span of this one life many friends and foes have already passed away and will be seen no more. However, the unbearably evil fruit that has grown from the non-virtuous actions that I have committed on behalf of these friends and foes now stares me full in the face. Not having understood that I would most certainly die, that the time of my death would be utterly uncertain, and that nothing but Dharma could help when I died, I have committed so much evil out of ignorance, attachment and anger. With deep regret I openly declare all of this before you.

[39] Day and night, moment by moment, whether I am sitting, walking, eating or talking, this life ebbs away. This ebbing cannot be halted nor can my life be lengthened. This being so, is there any reason to think that death will not come to me? And what will this death be like?

[40-2] With my non-virtues still undeclared and the practice of Dharma ignored, the Lord of Death

will suddenly swoop down. While lying upon my deathbed, though I am surrounded by a circle of friends and relatives, I alone will experience intense suffering and fear as my life is severed. When I am seized by the frightening messengers of the Lord of Death, of what benefit are these relatives and friends? Had I accumulated merit, taken refuge, practised moral discipline and other virtues, these would have been my protection. But it was these very things that I ignored and now I feel the deepest regret and fear. O Protectors, oblivious of the terrifying suffering of the three lower realms, I have committed a great mine of evil for the sake of this transient life. Deep is my regret.

[43-4] Seized by the authorities and led away to be tortured, the prisoner becomes terrified, his mouth dries and his complexion fades. His eyes bulge and his entire appearance is transfigured. If fears such as these arise owing to the pains inflicted by men, then is it necessary to speak of the great terror that will arise when non-human messengers seize me and I am struck by the fearful panic of death? Completely helpless, my desolation will be extreme.

[45-6] Merely seeing the henchmen of the Lord of Death will bring forth great terror and cries of anguish. With large, gaping eyes I will look in the four directions for someone to give me refuge. But seeing no source of refuge anywhere, I will become enshrouded in gloom and despair. Completely protectorless, exposed to unbearable suffering, what will I do? From this very moment on I must abandon all causes that could lead to such hellish experiences.

Without the strong sense of regret so powerfully illustrated by Shantideva above, we will be unable to purify our non-virtue. Yet, generally, we do not feel even slightly regretful of our past non-virtuous actions. Why? Because we do not fully realize that the fruits of these actions will be nothing but suffering. As long as we remain ignorant of the causal relationship between deluded, non-virtuous actions and the resulting experiences of misery we will neither abandon nor regret our misguided way of life. We will not only be unable to purify the effects of past negativities but will continue to create the causes for even more suffering in the future.

We can cultivate an attitude of regret only when we recognize the connection between the harm we create and the harm we receive. However, it is important not to misunderstand what it means to regret our unskilful actions. We should not view the suffering we experience as an externally applied punishment for our sins; nor is it necessary to feel guilty, thinking we have offended some authority or force that is prepared to take revenge upon us. True regret is not concerned with such extraneous attitudes.

The difference between a proper and an exaggerated attitude in this matter can be illustrated as follows. A boy's parents, recognizing the dangers of fire, have prohibited him from playing with matches. He does so anyway and burns his finger. The proper, most beneficial response would be for the child to regret his carelessness and learn from his painful experience to avoid exposing himself to similar dangers in the future. An exaggerated response would be for the child to think that the match deliberately punished him for disobeying his parents. Such a superstitious reaction only confuses the situation and introduces extraneous considerations, such as guilt, that might in fact reduce rather than increase his ability to deal with future dangerous situations intelligently.

Returning now to the proper application of the opponent powers, we should try to cultivate an attitude of regret towards our unskilful, non-virtuous actions that is based not upon guilt but rather upon a clear understanding that harmful causes bring harmful results. The enlightened beings have called certain actions 'non-virtuous' precisely because of their harmful effects. When we see that we have performed, and are continuing to perform, these potentially misery-inducing actions, sincere regret is a wholly natural and appropriate response.

How is it that harmful results follow from harmful actions? It is through the force of an imprint placed on our mind that the potential to experience future suffering comes about. For example, a person who commits murder plants a very strong negative impression on his or her own mind, and that impression, or seed, carries with it the potential to place that mind in a state of extreme misery. Unless the impression of that non-virtuous action is purified, this latent seed will remain in the mind, its power dormant but unimpaired. When the appropriate circumstances are eventually met, the potential power of this impression will be activated and the seed will ripen as an experience of intense suffering, for instance as rebirth in a karmically created realm of hellish misery.

The situation is analogous to that of an arid piece of ground into which seeds were planted a long time ago. As long as these seeds are not somehow destroyed, they will retain their potential to grow. Should the ground be watered sufficiently, these long-forgotten seeds will suddenly sprout forth. In a similar fashion our karmic actions plant their seeds in the field of our consciousness, and when we encounter the proper conditions these seeds will sprout and bear their karmic fruit.

By performing and neglecting to purify negative, harmful actions we place upon our mind countless seeds of similarly negative potential energy. The fruition of such seeds is not limited to the experience of a lower rebirth. As the result of causing harm to others in a previous life, for example, we may find that this life is filled with much sickness. Also, the mental suffering and unhappiness of the present can be the result of our having disturbed others in the past. In a similar fashion, poverty is the karmic result of miserliness, and having a very disfigured or ugly body is the result of anger. Furthermore, we need not wait until a future life to experience the result of non-virtue committed now; we have all experienced how anger and greed can bring us discomfort and unhappiness almost immediately.

Non-virtuous actions such as theft, divisive speech and malice are committed with other beings serving as their intended objects or victims. There are certain mental actions, however, which are not directed outwardly but instead affect the perpetrator directly. Such mental actions fall into the group known as holding wrong and perverted views, and constitute the heaviest and most damaging of all unskilful actions. For instance, if we hold strongly to the notion that there is no effective refuge from worldly suffering, or if we develop faith in an improper object of refuge, such as our own delusions, or if we stubbornly deny that there is any causal relation between actions and their results, our mind will be misdirected and we will be preventing ourself from gaining a proper view of reality. As a result our ignorance will increase and lead us to create more and more harmful actions of body, speech and mind. If we grasp these truth-denying views strongly enough they can plant very powerful negative seeds upon our mind. One possible effect arising from such seeds is an experience of great difficulty when later trying to study or meditate on the Dharma.

Some people have no aptitude at all for Dharma; they narrow-mindedly reject anything of a spiritual flavour. Such behaviour is also the result of having held wrong views strongly in a previous life. In addition, there are certain countries into which spiritual teachings never penetrate. Such a widespread absence of Dharma is the collective result of past non-virtuous actions committed by the people who have been reborn in that country. Thus, whether it is the experience of individuals or groups of people, misfortune and unhappiness are the results of negative predispositions of mind.

All non-virtuous actions, whether directed inwardly or outwardly, contaminate our mind. Thus if we wish to develop realizations concerning any aspect of Dharma it is necessary to purify our non-virtue as much as possible. Before a dirty pot can be used as a container for a delicious drink it must be thoroughly cleansed, otherwise the beverage will be defiled and unfit for consumption. To use a different image, if we do not rid our mind of its defilements, the sun-like bodhichitta will be unable to dawn within it. On the other hand, if we do manage to purify our non-virtue and accumulate great wealth of merit it is possible to gain deep realizations of even such a difficult topic as the profound view of ultimate reality (the subject of the ninth chapter) without having to receive extensive Dharma teachings.

At this point it might be helpful to talk about the varying degrees of non-virtue. Some people think that the non-virtue of killing a small insect is insignificant when compared with that of killing a large animal. However, the mere size of the victim is not necessarily the most important criterion determining the gravity of our actions. The difference between great and small non-virtue is determined by the inter-relationship of four factors: object, time, action and mind. The heaviest non-virtuous karma will be incurred if the object of our non-virtuous action is venerable and worthy of respect. Such objects include, among others, beings of saintly character, a Buddha, a Bodhisattva, an Arhat, a member of the Sangha, a Spiritual Teacher or our parents. In terms of time, the heaviness of non-virtuous actions increases if they are committed on days set aside for religious and spiritual observance or the taking of vows. The way the non-virtuous action is performed also affects its heaviness. For example, killing another being by slow means, inflicting a great deal of suffering, is a heavier action than swiftly and painlessly taking another's life. Finally, the state of mind we are in when we perform a negative action greatly determines how heavy the results of that action will be. A mind that is strongly motivated by anger and rejoices in actions that harm others is an exceptionally evil mind and the non-virtue accumulated is consequently very great. The more these four types of negative characteristics are present within an action the more harmful will be the accumulated non-virtue.

As stated before, actions are called 'non-virtuous' or 'unskilful' because they lead to future suffering. There are three possible suffering effects of a particular non-virtuous action. The first, the fully-ripened effect of an action, is the future rebirth into which we are thrown by the ripening of the seed planted by that action. For example, if we kill someone and the four conditions of object, time, action and mind are sufficiently heavy, we can be reborn in a state of hellish suffering. The less heavy these conditions, the higher the realm into which we will be reborn. The second result of a non-virtuous action is known as the 'effect similar to the cause'. The specific torments of a life filled with much sickness and a child's possession of a cruel and sadistic temperament are examples of this second type of effect following from the non-virtuous action of murder. Finally, there is the environmental effect of our non-virtuous actions. The place where we must live our life, whether in one of the three lower realms or even when we gain a human rebirth again, will be inhospitable, barren and dangerous as a result of the non-virtuous tendencies killing places upon our mind. The same threefold set of effects applies to all other non-virtuous actions.

As Shantideva pointed out in the passages paraphrased above, all the misery and frustration experienced in the various realms of samsara arise from our non-virtue. If by the power of such non-virtue we take rebirth as a dog, what can be done at that time? Fishermen may now be content to take the lives of fish, but how will they fare when tomorrow they themselves are born as fish? There is nothing permanent about our present human form and no one can say when death will come; it could even be today. Feeling regret for our past non-virtue we must find an antidote to this deadly poison immediately. All our evil deeds must be declared right now.

If we think that we can postpone purifying our negative actions until some time in the future, we should beware! Death is unpredictable and can descend upon us at any time. The Lord of Death does not take into consideration whether his victim has purified non-virtue or not. He cannot be coerced into waiting and accepts no excuses. When death suddenly approaches it will do us no good to say, 'You must come back later, I am supporting a family', or 'I am still very young, come back after a few years', or 'Please let me live a little longer.' All of this is futile. The Lord of Death is uncompromising.

If a sudden breeze arises, a candle large enough to burn for hours can be snuffed out after only a few minutes. While a very ill and elderly man is tenaciously holding on to life for many years, the young people around him may all be dying one by one. We are all going to die, and who can guarantee that death will not come to us tomorrow, or even today?

In Tibet there once lived an astrologer famed for his outstanding ability to predict the future. One day he decided to find out when his own life would come to an end, so he took out his books and charts and began his calculations. Much to his surprise he discovered that he was due to die that very day! 'That's most strange,' he said to himself. 'I wonder if I made a mistake in my figuring. Surely I'm not going to die today, I'm in perfect health.' While musing like this he leaned back, took his grooming kit from his pocket, and began cleaning the wax out of his ear with a needle-like piece of metal he kept for that purpose. 'I wonder where I made my mistake,' he thought as he continued absent-mindedly scraping at his ear. All of a sudden a burst of wind blew open the window he was leaning against. His arm was struck so sharply that the piece of metal was thrust through his eardrum and into his brain, killing him instantly. So who can be certain that death is not about to come?

In light of this uncertainty we must purify our non-virtue immediately. There are many more circumstances that could bring about our death than those that tend to support our life. While all around us people are dying from accidents, war and disease, how can we confidently expect to live out a normal lifespan? By thinking of the everyday examples we find in the news, we should meditate on the uncertainty of the time of death.

Think of our family, friends, relatives and fellow countrymen. Who, among all of them, will still be around after a hundred years have passed? Therefore, why do we commit so much wrong for the sake of beings who will disappear so soon? Yet we have all committed such non-virtue, and if we wish to gain security for the future we must purify this evil immediately. A sense of regret is the foundation of purification. It will arise if we consider impermanence, death and the fruits of our mistaken actions. If three people inadvertently eat poisonous food and one of them dies while the second one becomes sick, what will be the thoughts of the third person? Certainly he will deeply regret having eaten that food. In a similar fashion we should think of the many people who have committed evil, have died and now find themselves in a lower realm experiencing intense suffering, and remember that we have committed the same ill-fated actions.

Out of deep attachment we have lied and stolen for the sake of our friends. With intense anger we have directed much evil towards our enemies. The main cause for all the harm we have done is our ignorance of the law of actions and their effects. Not realizing that suffering will be the sole result of our actions, we ignorantly continue our non-virtuous behaviour.

How difficult it is for us to understand that our life is racing towards the moment of death and there is nothing we can do to prevent it! Second by second our life force slips away. Unlike money, which will remain on deposit as long as we do not spend it, our lifespan is steadily dwindling. Now is the time to admit our non-virtue and practise all that is virtuous.

It is certain that if we do not begin to regret and purify the harm we have done, and thereby establish a new direction for our life, we will be foolishly paving the way towards a future experience of hellish states of existence. Yet some people firmly believe in the non-existence of such realms. They say that because they themselves cannot see such places they must not exist at all. Such logic is ridiculous! We might as well say that because we cannot see what will happen tomorrow and cannot see the earlier civilizations that existed on this planet that the future and the past likewise are totally non-existent. We cannot say that we will not fall sick next month merely because we do not see the cause of this sickness now. Even a learned man who will die in a car accident tomorrow will be unable to foresee that today. Therefore we should not be influenced by a false logic that unjustifiably assumes that what we cannot see does not exist.

Furthermore, although we may question the reality of the hell realms, who can doubt the existence of experiences so horrific that people generally refer to them as 'living hells'? Living for months with the excruciating pain of cancer, being trapped in the depths of paranoia or suicidal depression, having to face death by fire – these are only a few examples of easily recognizable hell-like sufferings experienced within our human realm. If we are to avoid such suffering we must purify the non-virtuous causes in which they are rooted and refrain from all similar negative and harmful actions in the future.

Buddha Shakyamuni and all the learned Pandits who followed him possessed great powers of understanding and clairvoyance. These enlightened beings established the existence of hell realms and the other lower states of existence by means of their own experience and many logical reasons. Although the existence of hell realms is not something we can immediately see for ourself, we should try to keep an open mind about them as much as possible. In this way much benefit will be gained and at the time of death we will have no fear. If we are truly concerned with our future welfare it is best to be aware of the dangers of possible future hell realms and then, in dread of their suffering, practise what is beneficial, purify all evil and enter the path of Dharma.

In many scriptures Buddha went into great detail about the suffering of the hell realms. It was certainly not his intention merely to frighten us. A Buddha has great compassion and love for all sentient beings and wishes to separate them from suffering. It was for this very reason that Buddha Shakyamuni taught about the suffering realms of existence and gave many instructions on how to avoid being reborn there. He taught us to abandon evil and practise virtue not because he wished to frighten us, but because he wished to see us happy.

When a mother explains to her young child the dangers of playing in a crowded street, she does so not because she wishes to scare her child. She teaches out of compassion and concern for the child's safety and out of a realistic understanding of the dangers of the situation. The same is true of the teachings of the enlightened beings. They see the torment that non-virtue will lead us to and they tell us of the danger so that we may avoid it. Otherwise, without such instructions and warnings we would jump straight into the fires of suffering. Thus it is important that we be properly warned. If we did not know that a certain animal was poisonous we might easily walk straight into its path, but who among us would approach a snake that we knew to be deadly?

In terms of our Dharma practice it is important that a dread of lower states of rebirth should be cultivated now and not at the time of death. The fear that makes us cautious about our actions now is helpful, but the fear that arises at the time of death is not helpful at all. What good is it to regret our non-virtue when face to face with the Lord of Death or already experiencing the torments of hell? The only sensible thing to do now is to practise those methods that will keep us from having to experience such suffering in the future. Before the fruits of our non-virtue ripen we should purify our mind-stream. Once these fruits have already ripened, it is too late for even a Buddha to help. Buddhas protect sentient beings by teaching them Dharma and showing them the path away from suffering and towards enlightenment, but they are unable to extract sentient beings from the suffering they have already brought upon themselves. If we do not guard our actions, there is not much even a Buddha can do.

## THE POWER OF RELIANCE

In the next passage Shantideva, full of regret for his misguided actions, turns to the Three Jewels for refuge from suffering:

> [47-53] I go for refuge to all the Buddhas, those who protect all sentient beings from fear. I go for refuge to the Dharma Jewel that is possessed by these Buddhas. I go for refuge to the assembly of Superior Bodhisattvas. I go for refuge to you, the Three Jewels, and pray for protection from non-virtue, the cause of rebirth in hell.

I offer my body to you, Arya Samantabhadra, and I pray that you protect me from the fears of hell. I offer my body as your servant, Arya Manjushri, and I pray that you also protect me from these fears. I cry mournfully to you, Lord Avalokiteshvara: please protect me for I have been an evil-doer. From my heart I pray to you, O Compassionate Ones, Arya Akashagarbha, Arya Ksitigarbha, Arya Sarvanivaranaviskambini and Arya Maitreya: please protect me! And I go for refuge to you, Arya Vajrapani, upon sight of whom the messengers of the Lord of Death flee with terror to the four directions.

O Buddhas, previously I have transgressed your advice and have committed great evil, but now I see the results of this, the great torments of hell, and I go to you for refuge. By relying upon you, may all those evils and fears be swiftly purified.

Here Shantideva states that his regrettable non-virtuous actions were all performed because he failed to heed the teachings of the enlightened beings. As purification of all evil depends upon following these teachings sincerely, Shantideva invokes the power of reliance by going for refuge to Buddha, Dharma and Sangha from the depths of his heart.

In the Mahayana tradition the power of reliance refers to going for refuge and generating bodhichitta. To understand why these actions are called the 'power of reliance' consider the following analogy. If we slip and fall down on the ground, the way we raise ourself up again is by relying upon that very ground, that is, by using it as a support to lift ourself up. Similarly, if we wish to raise ourself up after committing an unskilful action, we do so by relying upon the objects against whom we committed that action. In terms of the object, all non-virtue can be included within two categories: non-virtuous actions directed against the Three Jewels, and those directed against sentient beings. Purifying actions committed against the former, therefore, entails relying upon the refuge we take in Buddha, Dharma and Sangha. If our actions are committed against sentient beings, the power of reliance entails regenerating the precious thought of bodhichitta, thereby reminding ourself that we are seeking enlightenment solely for the sake of those beings we have regrettably harmed.

## THE POWER OF THE OPPONENT FORCE

It is this third power, when combined with a deep sense of regret, that will actually purify the effects of our negative actions. In general there are six types of activity used as opponent forces to evil, but there is nothing magical about them. They are only effective when based on a strong foundation of regret and combined with a sincere desire to purify our negativities. These six traditional methods are: (1) reciting the names of Buddhas, (2) reciting mantras, (3) reciting Buddhist Dharma scriptures, (4) meditating on the profound view of reality (emptiness), (5) making offerings and (6) constructing, painting or repairing images of a Buddha's body, speech and mind.

If we wish to purify non-virtue, any positive virtuous action can be used as the opponent power. Even sweeping a shrine room, if done with sincere regret and a strong intention to purify non-virtue, can be a very powerful opponent force. To illustrate this there is the famous story of the monk called Lam Chung, who lived at the time of Buddha Shakyamuni. Before he became a monk he had already gained the unenviable reputation of being dull and unteachable. He was sent to school but soon expelled because his teachers said he was unable to remember any of his lessons. Later his parents sent him to a Brahmin so that he might learn the Vedic scriptures. Again he was unable to remember or understand anything he was taught and was once again expelled.

Thinking that a monastic situation might be more to his liking, his parents sent Lam Chung to his elder brother, Arya Lam Chen, who ordained him as a monk. Lam Chen took responsibility for his younger brother's education and began by teaching him one verse of Dharma. Lam Chung studied this verse for three months but never mastered it! If he memorized it in the morning he would forget it by the evening, and if he memorized it at night he would forget it by the following morning. He tried studying out of doors, hoping this would be helpful for his mind, but with no success. He recited the verse so often while up in the hills that even the shepherds minding their flocks came to memorize and understand it, but poor Lam Chung still could not master it. The shepherds themselves tried teaching him, but still Lam Chung was unable to learn it. As a result of his repeated failure, even his older brother Lam Chen was compelled to dismiss him.

Lam Chung was completely desolate. He felt utterly depressed and cried as he walked slowly along the road. He thought to himself, 'Now I am neither a monk nor a layperson. How miserable I am!' Through the power of his clairvoyance, Buddha saw all that had taken place with Lam Chung and went to meet him. He asked him why he was crying and Lam Chung replied, 'I am so stupid I cannot memorize even one verse of scripture. Now even my own brother has given up on me.'

Buddha told him not to worry. As a method to purify his mind of past negativities, Buddha taught Lam Chung just two words of Dharma and appointed him as the sweeper at the temple. Lam Chung was very happy with his new position. He swept the temple with great dedication, reciting as he did so the few words that Buddha had taught him.

He swept and swept for a long time, but through the power of Buddha, whenever Lam Chung swept the right side of the temple more dust would appear on the left side, and whenever he went and swept the left side of the temple dust would appear again on the right side. Undaunted, he continued to sweep and purify, just as Buddha had instructed. The situation remained like this for a long time until, all of a sudden, Lam Chung was struck by the realization that the dust he was constantly sweeping lacked true, independent existence. This was a profound realization and through it he gained a direct understanding of emptiness, the ultimate nature of reality. By meditating on this emptiness continuously he was soon able to attain complete liberation from suffering. He had become a glorious Arhat.

Buddha Shakyamuni saw that the purification techniques he had given Lam Chung had been profoundly successful and decided to proclaim Lam Chung's new qualities publicly. He directed his disciple Ananda to inform a certain community of nuns that from then on their new Spiritual Guide was to be Lam Chung. The nuns were very upset and felt, 'How can we accept as our Abbot a monk who is so stupid that he could not even remember one verse of the teachings over months and months?' They decided that if they exposed Lam Chung's inadequacies in public they would not have to accept him as their leader. So they spread the word in a nearby town that a monk who was as wise as

Buddha himself would be coming soon to give teachings, and that all those who attended would certainly attain great realizations. To increase his expected humiliation the nuns even erected a large, ostentatious throne and purposely failed to provide it with any steps leading up to its elevated seat.

When the day of the scheduled teachings arrived, Lam Chung made his way to the nuns' community where over a hundred thousand people had gathered, some to listen and others to see him humiliated. When he saw the large throne without steps he realized that it had been constructed in this way to make him look foolish. Without hesitation he stretched out his hand so that it seemed like an enormous elephant's trunk and with it he reduced the throne until it was but a small speck. Then he returned the throne to its former size and, to the increasing amazement of the gathering, flew up to the top of it! After a brief period of meditation he flew into the sky and circled the gathering before returning to the throne. Seated once more he said: 'Listen carefully. I will now give a week-long discourse on the meaning of one verse of Dharma. This is the same verse that in the past I could not remember or understand even after three months of trying.'

When the seven days of teaching were complete, many thousands in the audience had attained a direct understanding of reality while others attained the elevated states of a Stream Enterer, a Once Returner, a Never Returner and full Arhatship. Others who were present were able to develop the precious bodhichitta, and those who came to test him increased their faith in the Three Jewels. Afterwards Buddha himself prophesied that among all his disciples Lam Chung would possess the greatest skill in taming the minds of others. Even today we can see pictures of Lam Chung, who is one of the sixteen Arhats often depicted in Buddhist art.

This story illustrates how even an unconventional practice, if done sincerely and with the proper motivation, can serve as an opponent to our non-virtue. However, no remedy, no matter how powerful, can ever be effective if we do not apply it; and we will only be motivated to do so once we have become aware of the need for a cure.

A seriously ill person who thinks that he might not have long to live will take the advice of a doctor because of his fear of death. [54] If we need to comply with a doctor's advice when frightened by a common illness, then is there any need to mention the necessity of listening to and following the spiritual advice of the most skilled physician, the compassionate Buddha? His powerful medicine of Dharma can cure the diseases that have plagued us since beginningless time – the poisonous delusions of attachment, anger and ignorance.

It does not take many causes for us to be reborn in a hell realm. If we were to indulge in but a moment of anger towards a Bodhisattva and this were not purified, we would soon find ourself in hell. The power of the disease of anger is that strong! [55] Neither it nor the other pernicious world-consuming mental diseases – attachment, jealousy, pride and the like – can be cured by an ordinary doctor or his medicine. Only the great physician Buddha and his medicine of Dharma can overcome these diseases. [56] If we do not take the remedy offered to us, where else can we possibly find relief? It is extremely foolish and ignorant to wish to be rid of samsaric suffering but to neglect the pursuit of spiritual practices, which are the only effective way of gaining the desired release.

[57] If we need to be cautious when walking near the edge of a cliff, what need is there to mention the caution required near the edge of a precipice that drops down to the depths of hell? This is like a pit thousands of miles deep and we are plunged into it for an extremely long time because of our creation of non-virtue.

Therefore we must quickly purify all our non-virtue. [58] It is unwise to think that we can enjoy ourself today in the conviction that we will not die. No one has the power to say with confidence, 'Death will not come to me today.' Inevitably there will be a time when we become nothing. When this time comes others will speak of us as we now refer to those who have already departed.

Shantideva concludes this section on the power of the opponent force by asking:

[59] Who can possibly say to me, 'You have committed evil but I will protect you'? No one. When I think that death is definite and the time of death so uncertain, how can I become free of this intense fear? If it is inevitable that the time will arrive when I will become nothing, how can I relax and continue to enjoy myself this way?

The last line of the above passage does not mean that we should never relax and enjoy ourself. However, we should realize that at the present moment we have found a precious human life. To waste all of our time engaged solely in the concerns of this lifetime, committing non-virtuous actions because of our heedlessness, is to lead a life no different from that of a dull-witted animal. If we want to make this precious human life truly meaningful we should guard our future lifetimes by practising Dharma now, according to our capacity, and thereby take advantage of this rare opportunity. Purifying the effects of non-virtue by applying the proper opponent force is one of the most important ways of proceeding.

## THE POWER OF PROMISE

The last of the four powers included in the confession of non-virtue is our firm promise never to repeat particular non-virtuous actions again. If these four powers are employed properly, it is certain that all our evil can be purified completely.

In past lifetimes we have been born in high positions, have possessed beautiful and handsome forms, have been endowed with great riches and wealth, and have experienced all the pleasures and joys of samsara over and over again. However, as Shantideva says:

> [60-1] What remains of those experiences now? From all of these we have gained no benefit; they were empty of meaning. Even the richest man must leave all his wealth behind at the time of his death, for he departs alone. At the time of our death the only things we will carry with us will be the fruits of our own actions. Now we engage in worldly pleasures, thinking them to be important, but they are illusory and meaningless. Yet we remain attached to these mundane pleasures and for their sake transgress the advice of our Spiritual Guides. Since this body, and my family, friends and riches must all be left behind when I die and go elsewhere alone, what is the sense of endangering myself for the sake of such transient concerns?

Shantideva emphasizes the senselessness of our unceasing efforts to gain the transitory pleasures of this world. He points out that not only have we experienced these pleasures countless times in the past but in our efforts to satisfy our insatiable desires we engage in actions that only bring us future suffering.

We have many other wrong views concerning our pleasures and comforts. For instance, we generally think that all our possessions and wealth have come about as the result of our own efforts in this lifetime. We also assume that the happiness we experience is caused by ourself while all our suffering is caused by others. These attitudes, however, are incorrect.

We should realize that there are two kinds of cause for all our experiences of pleasure and pain. The substantial cause of each of our experiences was created in a previous life, or earlier in this life; while the circumstantial causes are the necessary conditions occurring in this life that bring the substantial cause to fruition. It is true that a rich man may well have worked very hard in this lifetime to become wealthy, but the work he did is still only a circumstantial cause of his wealth. The main, substantial cause of his becoming rich was his practice of giving during a previous lifetime. Buddha taught that the principal cause of happiness in this lifetime is our practice of virtue in the past; and similarly the suffering we experience now is the result of non-virtue we committed in former lives.

The importance of the proper substantial cause can be illustrated as follows. There are two brothers who decide to go into the same business independently of each other, and so they set up separate shops. Although they have been brought up by the same parents, have received the same type of education, have begun their separate businesses with the same capital investment and so forth, one brother meets with great success and becomes rich while the other encounters much difficulty and goes bankrupt. This is only one simple illustration, but we are all acquainted with similar situations from our own experience. What is the reason for such different results? In our example, both brothers have created the proper circumstantial causes for becoming rich, so why did they end up so differently? The reason is that the principal cause for success, in this case the practice of giving that leads to the attainment of wealth in the future, was created by only one of the brothers. If the other brother lacks this cause as an unripened seed upon his consciousness, he will never become rich no matter how hard he tries.

The experience of suffering also has substantial and circumstantial causes. For instance, a person with a digestive problem falls ill and experiences physical suffering. Again, his or her suffering has arisen because of two causes. The circumstantial cause was that the food he ate was not digested correctly, but the substantial cause was some non-virtuous action he committed previously. It was this action that planted in his mind the seed to experience suffering upon encountering the proper circumstantial cause. If he had not committed that non-virtuous action, and therefore had not created the proper substantial cause, then even if he ate food that gave others indigestion he would never experience this suffering himself. He would be like a peacock who is able to eat poisonous plants and, instead of becoming ill, grows stronger. These examples, although insignificant in themselves, serve to illustrate the point that all our happiness and suffering arise from a combination of circumstantial causes in this lifetime and previous substantial causes.

Shantideva summarizes the power of the promise and the entire practice of confessing non-virtue in the following concluding passage:

> [62-5] All suffering arises from non-virtue; all happiness arises from virtue. Thus throughout the day and the night I must consider how I can be free from non-virtue, the source of all misery.
>
> Through my ignorance I have committed countless non-virtuous actions, breaking vows or engaging in deeds that were by nature wrong. All this non-virtue I humbly declare in the presence of you Buddhas and Bodhisattvas. With my palms pressed together, prostrating again and again, I beseech you to free me from these great evils. That which was non-virtuous I will not do again.

This concludes 'Disclosure of Evil', the second chapter of the text *Meaningful to Behold*, a commentary to Shantideva's *Guide to the Bodhisattva's Way of Life*.

Serlingpa

# Full Acceptance of Bodhichitta

Before our mind is ready to accept and hold the precious thought of bodhichitta, it must be cleansed of its defilements and endowed with great merit. This process is similar to that by which a farmer prepares his field for a crop. First he must remove the rocks and weeds, and then he must make sure that the ground is provided with sufficient water and proper nourishment. Only then can he feel confident that the seeds he sows will sprout, grow and ripen as he desires.

While preparing our mind for the precious bodhichitta there are traditional methods of purifying non-virtue and accumulating merit that should be followed. These are all contained within what is known as the 'practice of the seven limbs'. The first three limbs have already been introduced in chapter two: (1) prostration, (2) offering and (3) the confession of non-virtue. Shantideva introduces the remaining four in this chapter: (4) rejoicing in virtue, (5) requesting the Buddhas to turn the Wheel of Dharma, (6) beseeching the Buddhas not to pass away and (7) dedicating merit.

Each of the seven limbs serves as a direct opponent to a particular delusion, although the effect of the seven-limb practice is more far-reaching than this. Specifically, prostration destroys the delusion of pride, while the practice of making offerings helps overcome our miserliness. The confession of non-virtue through the application of the four opponent powers fights all three poisonous delusions of ignorance, attachment and anger, but is principally directed against our ignorance. Rejoicing in the virtues of others overcomes jealousy, while requesting the Buddhas to turn the Wheel of Dharma helps to purify our wrong views and any previously committed irreligious acts. By beseeching the Buddhas not to pass away we remove dangers and obstacles to our own life and plant seeds that eventually ripen in our attainment of the indestructible body of a Buddha. Finally, by dedicating our merit to the benefit of all sentient beings we overcome the demon of self-cherishing.

In this chapter Shantideva explains how the seven limbs of practice – specifically the last four – prepare us for full acceptance of bodhichitta through our formal taking of the Bodhisattva vows. Thus this chapter can be outlined as follows:

## HOW TO ACCEPT AND HOLD ON TO THE ACTUAL BODHICHITTA

This section has three parts:

1 The preparatory practices for accumulating merit
2 Fully accepting bodhichitta
3 Concluding activities

## THE PREPARATORY PRACTICES FOR ACCUMULATING MERIT

As indicated before, this section consists of the last four of the seven limbs, with an additional explanation on training the mind in the practice of giving. Thus this section is divided into five parts as follows:

1. Rejoicing in virtue
2. Requesting the Buddhas to turn the Wheel of Dharma
3. Beseeching the Buddhas not to pass away
4. Dedicating merit
5. Training the mind in giving

## REJOICING IN VIRTUE

Rejoicing is a joyful mind, free of jealousy and pride, which takes delight in witnessing the virtuous actions of others or even ourself. Rejoicing in the virtue of others brings us great merit, while rejoicing in our own virtue increases our merit abundantly. It is said that rejoicing is a principal practice of a Bodhisattva. Even though we may be unable to rejoice as fully as such a high-minded being we can still practise in a similar way. It is a vast practice extremely effective for taming the wild elephant of our mind; it is entirely appropriate to spend an entire lifetime in the practice of rejoicing.

Jealousy is the opponent of the mind of rejoicing. It generally arises towards someone more learned or fortunate than ourself. While rejoicing in others' good fortune brings us happiness and benefit, jealousy does nothing but harm our mind. If we can practise rejoicing sincerely, two beneficial results will follow. Firstly, we will plant seeds for gaining good qualities similar to the ones in which we are rejoicing. Secondly, by cultivating this mind of joy we can overcome the poison of jealousy. This is extremely worthwhile. Jealousy not only destroys our virtue and pulls us down, but also makes it impossible for us to develop the precious bodhichitta.

When we rejoice in the happiness and comfort of others we create the cause for enjoying such experiences ourself.

However, if the comfort of others provokes jealousy in our mind, we will experience unhappiness in both the present and the future. How wonderful it would be if this poisonous mind could be eliminated forever! It has not a single positive aspect but instead is responsible for many of the disputes and conflicts plaguing the world today. From fights between neighbours to wars between nations, a frequent source of conflict is the deluded mind of jealousy.

How can jealousy be uprooted? As with all delusions, the ultimate solution is to understand that the root of jealousy is our self-grasping ignorance. Only the direct realization of emptiness – the direct realization that all things lack inherent existence – can cut through the root of this ignorance. However, before we are in a position to apply this ultimate solution we can and should use the temporary antidotes presented in Dharma teachings. Thus in the same way that our anger is lessened by our practice of love and patience, and our attachment can be lessened by meditating upon a desirable object's unpleasant or repulsive characteristics, so too can we counteract the jealous mind by rejoicing in the virtues of others. By weakening and then utterly uprooting our delusions in this way we can eventually gain complete liberation from all suffering.

One who has gained such freedom for him or herself is called an 'Arhat', or 'Foe Destroyer'. Yet after eradicating all the delusions, the imprints of the delusions still remain. These imprints are called 'obstructions to knowing' or 'obstructions to omniscience' because they prevent the mind from gaining an uninterrupted perception of the true nature of all phenomena. Through developing bodhichitta and practising Mahayana teachings, even these subtle obstructions to omniscience can be removed. One who has not only eradicated all his or her delusions but removed the shroud of their imprints as well has become a fully enlightened being, a Buddha. Abandoning delusions is like removing musk from a box, and purifying the imprints preventing enlightenment is like removing the odour that remains behind.

The path leading to the attainment of enlightenment is a steady development of our positive qualities of mind. Each step of spiritual training brings us closer to the goal. Of all the practices on the path, the simplest and most effective is to rejoice in virtue. As the great Tibetan meditator Gungtang Jampelyang said, 'If you wish to accumulate a great deal of merit even while lying down then rejoice in the virtue of others.' When King Prasenajit asked Buddha Shakyamuni for a spiritual practice he could follow without having to abandon his family or his kingdom, Buddha advised him to practise rejoicing, cultivate bodhichitta and dedicate his merits. Even someone who is very busy with the affairs of the world has time to engage in these three practices, and a great deal of positive energy can be generated by each of them.

The ability to rejoice wholeheartedly in the virtuous actions of ourself and others is based on our appreciation of the positive effects of these actions. The more we understand that happiness will be the result of a particular practice the more we will be able to rejoice in it. In his *Guide*, Shantideva mentions three areas of activity worthy of rejoicing: activities involved in achieving (1) a higher state of birth either as a god or human, (2) complete liberation from suffering and (3) the fully enlightened state of a Buddha. The first result of virtuous activity, achieving happiness in future states of existence, is often called the 'temporary result' of spiritual practice. The ultimate result of spiritual practice is known as 'definite goodness' and comprises the attainment of personal liberation for the practitioner mainly concerned with his or her own welfare, and full enlightenment for the practitioner mainly concerned with the welfare of others. These three states of attainment are characterized by increasing levels of happiness and peace of mind, and are therefore worthy of our rejoicing.

[1] Shantideva begins this section by rejoicing in the virtuous causes and effects of fortunate states of existence. The causes for being born in one of these states as either a human or god include the practices of moral discipline, giving and stainless prayer. By engaging in selfless giving, keeping our moral discipline pure, practising patience, making the appropriate prayers and so forth, we can avoid the three lower realms and gain a higher rebirth. In addition, if we rejoice in others who are also following these pure practices, this will be the cause of even more benefit and merit for ourself.

The story is told of the king mentioned before, Prasenajit, who invited Buddha and his entire retinue to his palace for a grand feast. Standing at the door was a beggar who rejoiced in the king's generosity but was saddened to think that he did not have the opportunity to perform such virtuous actions himself because he was poor. At the end of the banquet Buddha who understood the minds of all who were present, dedicated the merits of the beggar, and not those of the patron of the meal as was customary! The king, with great surprise, asked Buddha why he had done this. Buddha replied, 'On this occasion the beggar has practised purer virtue than you. The virtue of your offerings has been stained with worldly thoughts of reputation, pride and the like, whereas the virtue of the beggar's rejoicing was unmixed with such impurities. Thus I have dedicated his merits.'

[2] Next, Shantideva rejoices in the teachings that lead all sentient beings from their pain and suffering in samsara to the rest and peace of liberation. There are many paths that lead to the attainment of liberation but they are all included in the three higher trainings of moral discipline, concentration and wisdom. Ordinary moral discipline, abandonment of the ten non-virtuous actions, can lead to rebirth as a human or god, but is not adequate by itself for the attainment of liberation. For this, the moral discipline of renunciation for the whole of samsara is required. When moral discipline is conjoined with the thought of renunciation it earns the title 'higher moral discipline'. In a similar fashion, with renunciation as their base the practices of single-pointed concentration and insight into the true nature of reality become the trainings in higher concentration and higher wisdom. When these three higher trainings are completed the practitioner will definitely attain liberation.

Having rejoiced in those causes leading to the attainment of higher rebirth and liberation, Shantideva now turns to those actions that lead to the full enlightenment of Buddhahood:

> [3-4] I rejoice in the great enlightenment of the Buddhas and in its cause – the ten spiritual grounds or levels on the virtuous path of the Bodhisattvas. With gladness I rejoice in the virtue gained by developing bodhichitta: the mind of a Bodhisattva who wishes happiness for all beings and benefits them according to their capacities and dispositions.

If we rejoice in the virtues of others and pray strongly to be able to practise those virtues ourself, great benefits will follow. By recognizing the incomparable help that

Bodhisattvas bestow upon sentient beings, by rejoicing in their merit, and by praying strongly to become like them, eventually we ourself will undoubtedly become Bodhisattvas. This will follow naturally from the power of our rejoicing and prayer, and the law of actions and their effects.

What are the virtuous causes and effects of great enlightenment? The primary cause is, as we have said, the precious mind of bodhichitta. Someone who has developed this mind automatically gains the title of Bodhisattva and enters the first of the five Bodhisattva paths, the path of accumulation. Through the force of single-pointed concentration, the Bodhisattva then meditates on the profound view of emptiness, and when he or she develops superior seeing, he attains the second Bodhisattva path, the path of preparation. He continues this meditation on emptiness until he gains a direct realization. Through the force of this glorious achievement he becomes a Superior Bodhisattva, attains the path of seeing, and enters the first of the ten spiritual grounds of a Superior Bodhisattva.

On attaining the third path, the path of seeing, he abandons all intellectually-formed aspects of self-grasping. However, the Superior Bodhisattva still has to abandon innate self-grasping, of which there are nine levels ranging from the biggest of the big to the smallest of the small. By continuing to familiarize his mind with emptiness meditation, the Superior Bodhisattva abandons these innate forms of self-grasping, from the gross to the subtle, and progresses through the various levels of the fourth path, the path of meditation. By the time he has reached the eighth spiritual ground on the fourth path, the Superior Bodhisattva has abandoned all forms of delusion. However, the imprints of these delusions, the obstructions to omniscience, still remain, and these are removed by continual meditation on emptiness through the eighth, ninth and tenth spiritual grounds. Finally, even the last traces of the imprints of delusion are removed, and the Superior Bodhisattva attains the fifth path, the Path of No More Learning, the state of perfect and complete enlightenment. The Bodhisattva has finally achieved his or her goal and become a Buddha.

It is useful to be acquainted with even this brief outline of a Bodhisattva's path because we can better understand and rejoice in the causes and effects of his practice. The more clearly we understand the path of higher beings, the more we are able to rejoice in each of its levels. This plants the seeds for our being able to travel through these levels ourself and thereby attain the full enlightenment of Buddhahood.

## REQUESTING THE BUDDHAS TO TURN
## THE WHEEL OF DHARMA

Shantideva next prays as follows:

> [5] With my palms pressed together in devotion, I beseech all the Buddhas residing in every direction: please listen to me. For the sake of all sentient beings who continuously suffer in the dark gloom of ignorance, please kindle your lamp of Dharma.

Requesting the Buddhas to turn the Wheel of Dharma or, as Shantideva says, to light the lamp of Dharma, is a very important practice. If practised throughout our lifetime and at the time of death, it will plant strong seeds upon our consciousness to meet an enlightened being in the future and receive teachings from him or her. Even if we do not meet an actual Buddha we will certainly be able to meet a Mahayana Teacher who can show us the way to enlightenment.

Even though we may no longer be holding wrong views, the imprints of such views held in the past are so strong that they continually interfere with our practice. We may accept the teachings on a certain level but inwardly still have grave doubts about the existence of past and future lives, lower realms of existence or even the reality of Buddhahood. When we try to meditate on such topics as the four noble truths, the twelve dependent-related links or the profound view of reality, our mind becomes foggy and enshrouded in gloom. Who can dispel this darkness? Only the Spiritual Guide who lights the lamp of Dharma can remove this darkness from our mind. Therefore we should entreat the Buddhas and all the Spiritual Guides to kindle this lamp for the sake of all beings who, like ourself, still wander in the darkness of ignorance.

## BESEECHING THE BUDDHAS NOT TO PASS AWAY

[6] With my palms pressed together in devotion I beseech the Buddhas who wish to pass away and enter parinirvana to remain instead for countless aeons for the sake of all bewildered sentient beings who wander like blind men without a guide.

A Buddha's actual body does not die for it has been delivered from the round of birth and death. Therefore why is it necessary for us to beseech the enlightened beings not to pass away? To understand this we must know something of the four bodies of a Buddha.

When all delusions and imprints have been eradicated from the mind and all positive qualities have been fully developed, the fully purified state of Buddhahood is attained. At this time we attain the four so-called 'bodies' of a Buddha: the Wisdom Truth Body, the Nature Body, the Enjoyment Body and the Emanation Body. The Wisdom Truth and Nature Bodies are, respectively, the omniscient mind and the emptiness of the omniscient mind of a Buddha and are known collectively as the Truth Body (Skt. Dharmakaya). The Dharmakaya and the completely purified form body, the Enjoyment Body (Skt. Sambhogakaya), are indestructible. Thus, they are known collectively as the 'vajra body'.

The Truth Body can be perceived only by other Buddhas, and the Enjoyment Body only by Buddhas and Superior Bodhisattvas. Therefore, in order to benefit ordinary sentient beings, Buddhas manifest various Emanation Bodies (Skt. Nirmanakaya). Because such bodies exist solely to benefit others they may assume a wide variety of forms. For example, in order to benefit men and women a Buddha may manifest in a human form, while appearing as a god, an animal or even an inanimate object if it is beneficial to do so. A Buddha may appear in any form whatsoever if it proves helpful for specific sentient beings' minds. It is such an Emanation Body, seen to be no different from our own, that appears to die when a Buddha passes away. Since this is the only form to which we can relate at present, it is an important practice to request the Buddhas not to pass away but to remain with us for countless aeons until we have all reached enlightenment.

## DEDICATING MERIT

Dedication is a prayer made at the conclusion of a specific practice so that the positive energy of that practice will be directed towards a specific result. This accumulated positive energy, or merit, is like a horse that will carry us in whichever direction we determine by means of our dedication. If the merit of a virtuous action is dedicated to the attainment of birth as a human or god, that action will become the cause for rebirth in those realms. Similarly, if we dedicate for the attainment of liberation, enlightenment, the development of bodhichitta or the realization of emptiness, the merit will ripen as directed. In this chapter the merit generated from the first six limbs of practice is dedicated for the sake of all sentient beings.

When we practise within the Mahayana tradition, we should always remember to dedicate our accumulated merit for the generation of the precious mind of bodhichitta. This is the purpose of the prayer, mentioned twice earlier, in which we give voice to our hope that bodhichitta will grow, never decrease and flourish abundantly.

There are important things to remember at the beginning and the end of any virtuous action. If we want that action to be pure and effective we should make sure that our initial motivation is uncontaminated and correct. Then, when the action is completed, we should dedicate the merit generated towards the desired goal. At the least our motivation before engaging in meditation or entering a retreat should be that of renunciation. This ensures that our practices are not being used for a worldly purpose. Finally, at the close of the session, whatever virtue has been gained should be dedicated to the attainment of enlightenment for the sake of all beings. Without a pure motivation our meditation will not be a pure Dharma practice, and without proper dedication the aim of our meditation will not be fulfilled.

If we develop the heartfelt wish to attain bodhichitta, and direct our motivation and dedication accordingly, then even a simple action such as offering flowers or incense to a visualized image of a Buddha will bring about great results and lead to our swift development of the precious mind of bodhichitta. Through the power of our prayers and the Buddhas' blessings we will certainly be able to develop bodhichitta, attain single-pointed concentration and gain a realization of the profound view of emptiness.

If the merit of our virtuous actions is not dedicated, many hindrances can arise. Virtue left undedicated is like a door left unlocked and anger is the thief capable of stealing whatever merit we may have created. However, if the merit of a virtuous action has been properly dedicated towards our attainment of bodhichitta, no amount of future anger will be able to destroy it. Thus it is very important that we conclude all our actions, especially our spiritual practices, with a complete and heartfelt dedication.

In Shantideva's *Guide* the following four types of dedication are mentioned:

1 General dedication
2 Dedication for the sick
3 Dedication to relieve hunger and thirst
4 Dedication to fulfil the wishes of sentient beings

## GENERAL DEDICATION

[7] Through the merit collected from prostration, offering, confession and other virtues, may the suffering of all sentient beings be dispelled.

## DEDICATION FOR THE SICK

[8] May I become the doctor, medicine and nurse for all sentient beings throughout the universe for as long as they remain in sickness.

We should pray to be able to answer the various needs of all those suffering from disease. Through the power of such prayers and their heightened concentration it is possible for advanced Bodhisattvas to manifest actual medicine to be taken by those who are ill. Even though these powers are beyond us now we should dedicate our merit to be able to benefit others as much as possible in the future. To make our prayers deep and effective we should first think of the pains and misery that the sick experience. We can meditate on those who are confined to a hospital, those sick and dying alone without a friend to care for them, and those whose tears we have seen and whose cries we have heard. Then we generate compassion towards these suffering beings and pray to become a doctor, medicine and nurse for all those who are sick.

## DEDICATION TO RELIEVE HUNGER AND THIRST

[9] May a rain of food and drink dispel the sufferings of hunger and thirst. During the aeon of severe famine may I myself become food and drink for all.

By dedicating our merit in this way we create the cause to become a benefactor of all living beings in the future. At the present time the hunger and thirst experienced in this world are small compared to that which will be experienced during a future age. At that time a severe famine will affect sentient beings throughout the universe. That unfortunate aeon will be followed by an age of weapons, a time of continual fighting and killing. When that aeon of slaughter draws to a close our entire world system will be consumed by fire until it is completely empty. To be reborn a human during the aeon of famine will be like being reborn in the lower realm of the hungry spirits; and those humans born during the following age of destruction will feel as if they were in a hell realm. Thus in order to help not only the beings who suffer at present but also those who will suffer even more severely in the future we should pray as Shantideva does.

## DEDICATION TO FULFIL THE WISHES OF SENTIENT BEINGS

A mother, full of love and compassion for her children, prays continually for their welfare, success and prosperity. With great love and compassion for all sentient beings we should pray to become whatever it might be that others require:

> [10] May I become an inexhaustible treasury for those who are poor and destitute. In accordance with sentient beings' needs may I become whatever they desire and always be at their disposal.

This concludes the first four of the five preparatory practices for accumulating merit. What remains is to train our minds in the expansive practice of selfless giving.

## TRAINING THE MIND IN GIVING

Shantideva declares:

> [11] From this moment on, without any sense of loss,
> I shall give away my body and likewise my wealth,
> and my virtues amassed throughout the three times –
> past, present and future – to help all living beings, my mothers.

It is beyond our ability at present to make such a bold declaration as this, but by training our mind in the proper way we will certainly be able to engage in such selfless giving in the future. If we can destroy our attachment to our body and our possessions by meditating on their shortcomings and lack of essence, and if we think deeply about the many benefits that will arise from giving what we have to others, we will eventually be able to emulate the deeds of the Bodhisattvas. When we can do this, it will be as Shantideva says:

> [12ab] All sorrow will be transcended and I will attain the body and excellences of a Buddha.

It is important to train our mind well now in the thought of giving up our body and possessions because, [12cd] as Shantideva next points out, we will have to give up everything we own at the time of death anyway. If, as we pass from this life, we cling possessively to our body and wealth, we will experience great inner torment and plant the seeds for a lower rebirth. Therefore, before the time comes when everything will be taken from us involuntarily, it is wise to acquaint ourself with the thought of giving what we own to others. To be able to give our body and possessions to others voluntarily is the best way to extract meaning from them.

What does it mean to give our body to others? Certain higher beings who have trained their mind to overcome attachment and self-cherishing, and in addition have meditated upon great compassion and the profound view of emptiness, are able, if the need arises, to surrender their body without difficulty and give it to others. They experience no sense of loss from this practice and are able to view their body as if it were an insignificant object. Whether we can practise in the same way, however, is doubtful. As long as we are governed by self-cherishing it would be more harmful than helpful to sacrifice something as precious as our body. Furthermore, it is a mistake to give up this precious human vehicle unless there is a great need and purpose for so doing. Yet it is still an important practice to rejoice in the actions of those Bodhisattvas who can actually give away their body and possessions, and to pray that some day we will be able to do the same.

In the final chapters of the *Perfection of Wisdom Sutra* (Skt. *Prajnaparamitasutra*) Buddha Shakyamuni tells the following story of Bodhisattva Sadaprarudita who perfected the practice of selfless giving as part of his spiritual path. Sadaprarudita was a sincere practitioner who, like a thirsty man in search of water, looked everywhere for a Teacher who could explain to him the profound view of emptiness. One day he heard a voice from the sky tell him to go to the East where a great Teacher, the Bodhisattva Dharmodgata, lived, for he was the Guru who could teach him. Sadaprarudita became very happy at the thought that now he would receive teachings. As a sign of his sincerity and devotion he wanted to bring the Bodhisattva Dharmodgata an offering of gold and silver but was too poor to afford even the smallest gift.

At that time the thought came to his mind, 'The only thing of value that I possess is my body. I will sell this, and with the money I receive I will be able to buy offerings for my Teacher.' He immediately went to a nearby town, and stood in the street and cried out, 'Who will buy my body? I will sell it to whoever wants it.' Yet despite his loud and desperate cries no one came forward to take up his offer. Depressed that now there was no way for him to raise the money for his Teacher's gift, Sadaprarudita sat down and began to cry.

From his abode in the celestial realms, the great Lord Indra, chief of the gods, saw all that had happened and decided to test the young Bodhisattva. Transforming himself into a high caste Brahmin, Indra appeared before Sadaprarudita and asked why he was crying. When the Bodhisattva explained his plight and why he needed the money, the Brahmin said, 'Normally I have no need for human flesh and blood. It so happens, however, that today I must perform a special sacrifice and need unusual ingredients. Therefore, I would gladly pay for some of your flesh.' Sadaprarudita was ecstatic that he had finally found someone to whom he could sell his body. He started to cut some flesh from his right thigh and, picking up a large rock, was about to break the bones of his leg.

The daughter of a local merchant lived in a house nearby, and witnessed the unusual scene taking place out in the street. Greatly alarmed she ran outside and asked the Bodhisattva why he was mutilating himself so horribly. Sadaprarudita calmly explained that he was selling his flesh so that he could make offerings to the Teacher Dharmodgata in order to receive the wisdom teachings from him. 'What is the great benefit of these teachings for you to harm yourself this way?' she asked. The Bodhisattva replied that by meditating upon the teachings on emptiness one could attain the full enlightenment of Buddhahood. The merchant's daughter then asked about Buddhahood and the young Bodhisattva explained to her all the excellent qualities of a fully enlightened being. Hearing of these surpassing qualities, the young woman developed great faith in the Three Jewels, Buddha, Dharma and Sangha. She implored Sadaprarudita not to harm himself any further and declared, 'My father is very wealthy and I will provide all the riches you require to make an offering worthy of the great Teacher Dharmodgata.'

Seeing the Bodhisattva's willingness to sacrifice himself and listening to his conversation with the merchant's daughter, the great god Indra realized the extent and the depth of Sadaprarudita's great compassion. He immediately transformed himself back into his original shape and proclaimed, 'All the Buddhas of the past attained their enlightenment with the great mind and the effort that you now possess. It is truly wonderful that for the sake of Dharma you are prepared to sacrifice your body. Please tell me if there is anything in the entire universe that I can give you now?' Sadaprarudita replied, 'The only thing that I require is the path that leads to enlightenment.' Hearing this, Indra was forced to admit, 'I can give you anything in the universe, but only an enlightened being has the ability to fulfil your request.' Then the Bodhisattva made the following prayer, 'If without deception I gave my body for the sake of Dharma, then through the power of that pure offering may I be restored to full health.' Instantly upon the conclusion of this prayer his body was made whole again.

The merchant's daughter escorted the Bodhisattva into her house and asked her father to give Sadaprarudita gold and silver as an offering to his Teacher. When the merchant heard his daughter's story he too was filled with strong devotion and bestowed upon the Bodhisattva five hundred carts laden with gold and silver and delectable food. Then the Bodhisattva Sadaprarudita and the merchant's daughter, accompanied by five hundred maidservants, embarked upon their journey to see the Teacher Dharmodgata. When they arrived they presented their offerings and Dharmodgata taught them all the perfection of wisdom. Hearing these teachings Sadaprarudita gained a direct understanding of the profound view of emptiness.

Afterwards Dharmodgata entered into a meditation of single-pointed concentration and remained in that state for seven years while Sadaprarudita waited to receive more teachings. During all of this time Sadaprarudita did not think about food and drink but waited patiently, intent only upon receiving more teachings. When Dharmodgata finally emerged from his meditation, Sadaprarudita requested further instructions on emptiness and began to prepare a large area with suitable offerings. However, he encountered many hindrances while trying to arrange the area properly; there was dust everywhere and no water with which to settle it. Undeterred, the brave Bodhisattva cut his own body and with his blood settled the dust on the ground, the merchant's daughter and the five hundred maidservants doing likewise. Their blood instantly transformed into sandalwood-scented water and Indra himself appeared, offering many celestial flowers, which the Bodhisattva scattered upon the ground. Sadaprarudita then constructed a large throne and a beautiful canopy, and decorated the area with many jewels, religious objects and precious ornaments.

On the following day Dharmodgata taught the perfection of wisdom to many thousands of people. The earth trembled, flowers rained from the sky and many other miracles occurred. The merchant's daughter and the five hundred maidservants all meditated deeply upon emptiness and as a result attained high stages on the Bodhisattva path. Sadaprarudita himself attained the eighth of the ten Bodhisattva grounds, and suddenly flew up into the sky to see his Teacher. When he asked him why all these miracles had occurred, Dharmodgata replied that this was an auspicious indication of the great benefit received that day. Owing to Sadaprarudita's request and to Dharmodgata's own teaching, many thousands of beings had realized the correct view of emptiness and developed the precious mind of bodhichitta. This story illustrates the power of a high-level Bodhisattva to give his or her body to others without any difficulty. As Shantideva says:

[13-14] Having given up my body completely, it does not matter to me what sentient beings choose to do with it. For their pleasure I have given up my body to others; let them play with it, ridicule, beat or even kill it if it so pleases them. Because I have given it to others, what is the point of holding my body dear any longer?

Buddha Shakyamuni said that with a realization of emptiness – that all things lack true or independent existence – it is not difficult to give up our body and even easier to give up our possessions. Therefore Shantideva continues:

[15-16] I give this body to sentient beings without causing problems or harm to anyone, solely in order to practise virtue. When others encounter me, may it always prove meaningful and beneficial for them. Whether a person has anger or faith towards me, may his wishes be fulfilled.

It is difficult for us to look upon a friend and an enemy in the same way. If someone harms us anger arises; if someone praises us we are filled with pleasure. But a Bodhisattva is not moved by praise or abuse. If such a high-minded being were to sit between two people, one of whom cut him with a knife while the other anointed his body with perfume, the Bodhisattva would look upon them both with equal love and compassion.

Shantideva continues his prayers to be able to benefit others as follows:

> [17-22] No matter if others harm me physically or insult me verbally, may whatever they do become the cause of their enlightenment.
>
> During all my lives may I become a protector for those who are protectorless. May I become a guide for those who travel, and a boat, a ship and a bridge for those who wish to cross the water. May I become an island for those in trouble, and a lamp for those who travel in darkness. May I become an abode and place of rest for those desiring one, and a servant for those who want a servant.
>
> May I become a wish-fulfilling jewel for those with special wishes, a treasury of wealth, powerful mantras and effective medicine. In all my lives may I become a wishfulfilling tree and an inexhaustible wish-granting cow that satisfies all beings.
>
> Just as the great elements of earth, water and so forth support the life of sentient beings, so may I too become the foundation of sustenance for all. May I become whatever is beneficial for all sentient beings in the realms reaching to the ends of space until they attain complete and unsurpassable enlightenment.

Why is it necessary to make prayers like this? If we wish to develop the precious bodhichitta we must cultivate a beneficial intention towards all sentient beings. We can train ourself in this way by paying close attention to the situation of others. Whenever we see sentient beings suffering we should think, 'What can I do to dispel their misery and bring them happiness?' We should train our mind constantly with this beneficial thought.

At present we are not able to give boundless help to all living beings, but by dedicating our virtues for the benefit of others as suggested above we will plant the seeds to accomplish this altruistic goal in the future. If we dedicate our merit, praying to be a Spiritual Guide for those who lack such a guide or praying to become a benefactor for the poor, in the future these wishes will definitely be fulfilled.

At this time we have been born human and therefore have the precious opportunity to think, consider and train our mind. If we do nothing but engage in our usual self-cherishing thoughts, then we are not much different from animals. Even birds and insects go from here to there trying to search for happiness and relieve their suffering. If we are to make our humanity useful, we should try to elevate our view beyond such selfish concerns. Shantideva's teachings on mind training are a powerful method to gain such an elevated view.

## FULLY ACCEPTING BODHICHITTA

In the first chapter the method of developing bodhichitta by means of the sevenfold cause and effect instruction was explained, and also the eight precepts of the aspiring mind. When we have prepared and developed our mind sufficiently to be able to practise the six perfections leading to enlightenment, we are ready to take the actual Bodhisattva vows. The purpose of taking these vows is to accomplish the aim of a Bodhisattva. What is this aim? To attain enlightenment for the benefit of all mother sentient beings. It is not sufficient just to wish to attain Buddhahood for the benefit of others, we must take the proper vows and engage in all the necessary practices.

When we understand the commitments involved in taking the Bodhisattva vows and feel that we are able to keep them, the time has come to engage in the actual Bodhisattva's way of life. This is what it means to accept fully the bodhichitta mind.

The ceremony for taking the actual Bodhisattva vows can be outlined as follows. If these vows are to be received from our Spiritual Guide, we should first set up extensive and beautiful offerings and prepare the place where the vows will be given. When the Spiritual Guide arrives, we should make an offering of the prayer of seven limbs, outlining the seven preliminary practices given above, and then offer a mandala, presenting all the rare and precious things of the universe for our development of bodhichitta. After all these preparations have been made, we should request the Spiritual Guide to grant us the Bodhisattva vows.

We should begin with the following request: 'O Preceptor, please listen to me.' (If the ceremony is held in the presence of the visualized Buddhas and Bodhisattvas, we should begin as follows: 'O Gurus, Buddhas and Bodhisattvas please listen to what I now say.') Then recite the following verses from Shantideva's *Guide*:

> [23-24] Just as all the previous Sugatas, the Buddhas, generated the mind of enlightenment, bodhichitta,

and accomplished all the stages of the Bodhisattva's training, so will I too, for the sake of all beings, generate the mind of enlightenment and accomplish all the stages of the Bodhisattva's training.

We recite these verses three times, and at the end of the third recitation we receive the Bodhisattva vows.

What do these verses mean? All the previous Buddhas achieved their exalted state by following the practices of a Bodhisattva. Motivated by their desire to help all sentient beings they gave birth to the precious bodhichitta, received the Bodhisattva vows and followed a progressive path of practice that included the six perfections and other beneficial deeds. Because we too wish to become fully enlightened for the sake of others, we vow to follow these stages of practice in exactly the same way.

These promises are made to our Spiritual Guide or to the visualized assembly of Buddhas and Bodhisattvas. The Spiritual Guide from whom we receive these vows must be fully qualified. He or she should have received the Bodhisattva vows and be skilled in explaining each one of them individually. He must be able to bestow the vows upon others and give a skilful explanation of all the practices involved in the six perfections.

From our side, if we had previously developed aspiring bodhichitta, upon receiving the Bodhisattva vows we will develop engaging bodhichitta. It then becomes necessary to refrain specifically from the eighteen root and forty-six secondary downfalls. (In practice, however, there is no limit to the moral and ethical precepts a Bodhisattva joyfully adopts in his or her selfless dedication to the welfare of others.) Once these sixty-four vows have been made in the presence of our Teacher, we can frequently retake them on our own in the presence of visualized Buddhas and Bodhisattvas. If we break any of our vows it is possible to take them again in a similar ceremony. By engaging in these ceremonies and dedicating our mind to the practices of a Bodhisattva, we will be fully accepting the precious mind of bodhichitta.

## CONCLUDING ACTIVITIES

So far Shantideva has described the various preparatory practices useful for accumulating merit, and the ceremony involved in fully accepting bodhichitta. The activities that seal and conclude our full acceptance of the mind of enlightenment can be explained in three sections as follows:

1 Meditating on the happiness of fulfilling our own wishes
2 Meditating on the happiness of benefiting others and fulfilling their wishes
3 Exhorting others to meditate on happiness

### MEDITATING ON THE HAPPINESS OF FULFILLING OUR OWN WISHES

Once we have developed the precious bodhichitta we will realize the great extent of our good fortune and rejoice accordingly. [25] In order to enhance all the qualities associated with bodhichitta we should be full of praise and encouragement, uplifting ourself with joy:

[26ab] Now my life has borne great fruit, my human life has attained great meaning.

We should think how privileged we are to have taken the Bodhisattva vows and how this action has given great meaning to our human rebirth, making it truly fruitful. Thinking in this way we will be filled with profound happiness.

Having studied Mahayana Dharma, and meditated on and developed bodhichitta, we have discovered qualities of life that are not ordinarily possessed. This very precious mind of bodhichitta is not easily found in this world. Though scholars may study hard and obtain doctorates and other advanced degrees, these qualifications cannot begin to compare with the precious mind of bodhichitta. Therefore, the person who has developed this precious mind has great reason to rejoice and be happy. We should think:

> [26cd-27] Today I am born into the lineage of Buddha and have become a Bodhisattva. All my actions from now on shall accord with this noble lineage; and upon this lineage, pure and faultless, I shall never bring disgrace.

[28] It is very rare to find a precious jewel in a heap of rubbish, and rarer still for a blind man to discover such a jewel. If a blind man were to be so fortunate how happy he would become! In a similar fashion, it is very rare to find a person who is even interested in trying to develop bodhichitta and rarer still to find one who has actually developed it. If we were to develop such a precious mind, how happy and joyful we would be! There is no quality in life greater than having developed the engaging mind of bodhichitta.

A Kadampa Geshe, a great Teacher of the past, was once asked, 'Which is better, developing miracle powers and clairvoyance, receiving visions of our personal Deity or developing bodhichitta?' He answered that bodhichitta is a thousand times greater than any other accomplishment or power. Why? In many previous lives we have developed miracle powers and have even been able to fly in the sky. During the first aeon of this world age all beings possessed clairvoyance and had bodies of the nature of light, but where is the essence of these powers now? What benefit have they brought any of us? Everything is changing and we are still caught up in the round of samsara, experiencing suffering and dissatisfaction continuously. However, if we had previously developed the thought of bodhichitta and engaged in its practices, by now we might have gained the enlightenment of Buddhahood and be free from the problems of samsara.

Developing bodhichitta is even more important than receiving visions of our personal Deity and engaging in related Tantric practices. By meditating on our channels, winds and drops we can develop inner heat, and even be able to levitate into space. However, without bodhichitta all this is meaningless. If we have developed bodhichitta and gained an understanding of emptiness, such Tantric practices can be very useful in increasing our realizations, but if we lack this foundation we will be completely unable to practise the Tantric path. Many people nowadays are attracted to Tantra because they believe it will provide a shortcut to enlightenment, or at least endow them with magical powers, but these people have no understanding of how important the foundation of renunciation, bodhichitta and emptiness is for this higher path. Practising Tantra solely for the sake of benefiting this life, hoping to gain renown or special powers, does nothing but plant the seeds for hellish suffering in the future. Anyone who practises like this is like a misguided person who uses precious sandalwood to kindle a fire. Or, to cite other examples, such an ill-motivated practitioner is like a person who uses bank notes to light a cigarette, or a Rolls Royce to cart manure. If we wish to make the practice of Tantra meaningful, bodhichitta is indispensable.

## MEDITATING ON THE HAPPINESS OF BENEFITING OTHERS AND FULFILLING THEIR WISHES

This section involves meditating on the happiness of being able to accomplish the three following activities:

1 Relieving others of their suffering
2 Eliminating the two obstructions
3 Bestowing great benefit and happiness upon others

### RELIEVING OTHERS OF THEIR SUFFERING

When we develop bodhichitta we will gain the ability to help other beings in numerous ways. In this section Shantideva discusses five of these beneficial ways by comparing the precious bodhichitta with nectar, an inexhaustible treasury, supreme medicine, a celestial shady tree and a universal bridge.

[29ab] First of all bodhichitta is like supreme nectar that is able to overcome the great power of death. It destroys the suffering of death by leading all sentient beings to the eternal unsurpassable state of complete Buddhahood. [29cd] Bodhichitta is also like an inexhaustible treasury that eliminates the poverty of all sentient beings by satisfying all their wishes. How do Buddhas and Bodhisattvas – those supreme beings who possess bodhichitta – eliminate poverty? By providing us with inexhaustible Dharma teachings and

material gifts they can temporarily fulfil our spiritual and physical needs. Furthermore, by leading us to the everlasting state of happiness and complete enlightenment they can ultimately free us from all poverty. It is in this respect that bodhichitta is like an inexhaustible treasury.

If bodhichitta has such power, why is it that so many beings in this and other realms are still experiencing poverty and so forth? The reason is that the power of enlightened beings is like an iron hook, and for us to be pulled up from our suffering we must make a connection with this hook by our own ring of faith. If we do not turn our mind to the Three Jewels there is no way for them to help us; the causes for our release are not yet complete. If we remain passive, waiting for our salvation to come from the outside without doing anything from our own side to develop our mind, we will continue to experience suffering as we have always done.

Returning to Shantideva's analogy, [30ab] bodhichitta is like supreme medicine that can relieve the mental and physical sickness of all sentient beings. Once we have taken the medicine of bodhichitta, we will gradually be cured of all diseases of mind and body. With his or her mind continuously filled with the medicine of bodhichitta, a Bodhisattva is immune to suffering.

[30cd] Just as a shady tree provides refreshment for a tired traveller, bodhichitta provides shade and rest for the exhausted sentient beings wandering along the paths of samsara. [31ab] Finally, bodhichitta is like a universal bridge that leads beings from the suffering of the lower realms to the happiness of the higher realms and ultimately to Buddhahood.

## ELIMINATING THE TWO OBSTRUCTIONS

As mentioned earlier, there are two sets of obstructions affecting the mind: obstructions to liberation and obstructions to omniscience. Bodhichitta has the power to eliminate both of these. [31cd] It is like the moon dispelling the unbearable suffering of sentient beings caused by their delusions, and in this way it eliminates the obstructions to liberation. Furthermore, [32ab] it is like the sun dispelling the darkness of the imprints of ignorance, thereby removing the obstructions to omniscience.

If we develop the precious bodhichitta and cultivate the two wings of method and wisdom we will be able to fly over all obstacles and reach the supreme citadel of enlightenment. Bodhichitta is like the hand holding the axe of wisdom, and by wielding the realization of emptiness we can cut through the root of self-grasping's imprints and attain complete omniscience.

[32cd] In summary, when the milk of Dharma is churned by wisdom, the quintessential butter we receive is the precious bodhichitta.

## BESTOWING GREAT BENEFIT AND HAPPINESS UPON OTHERS

[33] Bodhichitta is like a host who invites sentient beings as his or her guests to a banquet of higher rebirth, liberation and the unsurpassable delight of enlightenment. Through the power of his bodhichitta a Bodhisattva brings others to the states of happiness and complete fulfilment. All living beings are wandering, lost in the desert of samsara and thirsting for happiness. Who is able to lead them from this

wilderness? The one who possesses the precious mind of bodhichitta.

## EXHORTING OTHERS TO MEDITATE ON HAPPINESS

Shantideva summarizes the third concluding activity that seals our full acceptance of bodhichitta as follows:

> [34] Today, in the presence of the Protectors, I invite all sentient beings to a banquet of unsurpassable delight. Let all those who appreciate Dharma – you gods, demi-gods, nagas and humans – rejoice and be happy!

So far Shantideva has given extensive explanations of various Dharma methods, but how do we actually put them into practice? We do this by means of analytical and placement meditation on the teachings we have received. First we must take a critical look at each subject, trying to understand its meaning and relevance for our lives. Judging, testing and trying to understand the teachings in this way is called 'analytical meditation'. Once we have done this and have come to some conclusion concerning the object of meditation we should place our mind upon it single-pointedly. This is known as 'placement', or 'formal', meditation. If we think that meditation is sitting with an empty mind we will receive no benefit no matter how long we meditate.

The object of meditation can be a particular aspect of the teaching, such as the benefits of bodhichitta, or the form of a personal Deity or even our breath. Whatever object we choose, we should examine it fully to gain a clear idea of it. For example, in order to develop single-pointed concentration we can meditate on the visualized figure of a Buddha, choosing such a figure because it represents all the wisdom and methods of the path. We begin by selecting a painting or a statue that represents such a figure clearly. We should examine this image minutely, scrutinizing it from the crown of its head to its feet and back to the crown again. By doing this well we will gain a rough mental image of a Buddha's body. This then becomes our object to visualize in meditation. When we sit quietly and try to see this image in our mind's eye, holding the object with mindfulness and checking with alertness, we will be engaged in placement meditation.

This entire process can be likened to setting out on a journey. If we wish to go to London we must first gain an accurate understanding of which road to take, otherwise we might arrive in Manchester! In a similar fashion, if we want to engage in placement meditation and dwell upon an object single-pointedly, we must first gain a thorough understanding of that object by means of analytical meditation. Otherwise our efforts will be wasted and many faults will arise. This point cannot be overstated: it is a big mistake to try to meditate on nothing. If we have a proper object of meditation there is the possibility that we can progress along the nine levels of concentration and achieve the single-pointed concentration of tranquil abiding (Skt. shamatha). Without a proper object of meditation there will be little to show from even a thousand years of sitting.

Everything that has been explained so far in this commentary, and everything that is to follow are objects for meditation. There is not a single teaching in Shantideva's text that is not to be meditated on. Thus it is very important to learn the art of meditation correctly, and to be able to apply it in our everyday life.

This concludes 'Full Acceptance of Bodhichitta', the third chapter of the text *Meaningful to Behold*, a commentary to Shantideva's *Guide to the Bodhisattva's Way of Life*.

# *Conscientiousness*

### HOW TO PRACTISE THE SIX PERFECTIONS

Having discussed the benefits of the mind of enlightenment, how to purify the non-virtue preventing the development of this mind and how to accept this mind fully, Shantideva is now ready to explain how we can keep our bodhichitta from degenerating and how we can increase it through the practice of the six perfections. Thus the remainder of the text is divided into the following four parts:

1. Meditating on conscientiousness so that the bodhichitta practice and precepts do not degenerate
2. How to train in moral discipline by practising mindfulness and alertness
3. Explanation of the four remaining perfections: patience, effort, concentration and wisdom
4. Dedication and the practice of giving for the benefit of all beings

### MEDITATING ON CONSCIENTIOUSNESS SO THAT THE BODHICHITTA PRACTICE AND PRECEPTS DO NOT DEGENERATE

It has previously been explained how the practitioner generates the mind of bodhichitta and takes the Bodhisattva

*Atisha*

vows, dedicating him or herself to the attainment of full enlightenment for the sake of others. However, if a Bodhisattva is careless with his three doors of body, speech and mind, he will be unable to follow the practices correctly or keep his vows purely. Therefore, in order to prevent the precious bodhichitta from degenerating, Shantideva teaches the method of conscientiousness. Conscientiousness is a mental factor that is vigilant in preventing us from wandering towards delusions and being distracted by meaningless activities of body, speech and mind. Its opposite is a careless attitude of recklessness or unconcern leading to deluded activity, the creation of negative karma and the degeneration of our practice and precepts.

Recklessness can manifest through any of our three doors. To be careless with our body is to engage in actions that are in conflict with Dharma. These include such things as killing, stealing, engaging in sexual misconduct, letting ourself become intoxicated, becoming addicted to gambling, and other similarly deluded misdeeds. In terms of our speech, recklessness manifests as lying, divisive speech, hurtful speech and idle chatter. Finally, recklessness of mind includes all deluded thoughts such as covetousness, malice and wrong views.

If we are conscientious about our behaviour, our understanding and realizations will automatically increase while the defilements of our three doors will decrease. Conscientiousness is essential for our practice of pure moral discipline. Generally, when a conscientious person speaks he is polite, saying things that will benefit others as well as himself and communicating about Dharma matters. The reckless person, on the other hand, speaks under the influence of delusion. His behaviour is impolite and what he says invariably upsets others and himself as well.

Being conscientious about our three doors is the way to ensure that our positive, virtuous qualities – including whatever bodhichitta we have developed – are stabilized and abundantly increased. If we wish to practise Dharma well, we must develop conscientiousness. All Dharma communities have codes of discipline and ask the people living there to refrain from certain actions such as smoking, drinking, gambling and fighting. What is the reason for this discipline? It is not to punish the practitioners, though it might appear this way to some. Rather, these rules are laid down in order to help people practise conscientiously. Spiritual Guides continually remind us to abandon non-virtue and keep our mind from the influence of delusion. They do this so that our actions of body, speech and mind will be pure and we will be able to gain the fruits of spiritual practice.

All vows and precepts serve the same purpose: to help the practitioner develop along the path to liberation and enlightenment. Buddha Shakyamuni specified two hundred and fifty-three vows for his fully-ordained monks to keep. This was not a punishment for them; it was to aid their practice. The Bodhisattva also has vows to keep and these too are to help him or her attain the fruits of the path.

The story is told of a monk who lived for a long time in a cave engaging in meditation and observing pure moral discipline. He was supported by a family who served as his benefactors, and every day the daughter of the family would bring him food and drink. Her secret aim, however, was to seduce him into making love to her but she was never successful in arousing his interest. Finally one day she openly declared her desire for him. Calmly he answered her, 'I cannot make love to you for it is against my vow of celibacy.' Disappointed, the young woman went away.

Shortly afterwards she went to see him again, this time bringing with her a jug of alcohol and a goat. Entering his cave she declared, 'Today I have three requests to make of you. If you don't grant me at least one of them I will kill myself. My first and most heartfelt request is that you make love to me and not reject me as before.' But again the monk had to decline, explaining that it was against the rules laid down by Buddha for monks to engage in any sexual conduct whatsoever.

'All right,' the woman said, 'if you won't grant my first request then listen to my second one. Kill the goat I've brought with me so that we can share a meal of its flesh.' The monk was astonished and replied, 'We Buddhists try hard never to harm any living being. It is impossible for me to do as you ask.'

'If you won't grant either of my first two requests then you must grant the third or I will certainly kill myself,' cried the woman. 'You must join me in drinking the alcohol I brought.' For a few minutes the monk remained in a quandary. 'What a perplexing situation!' he thought. 'This young woman is obviously quite desperate and will certainly kill herself if I don't grant one of her outrageous requests. But which one should I choose? I definitely can't have sex with her; that would destroy my vows. As for killing the goat, that would be contrary to all that I believe. As for drinking alcohol, that too would be a violation of my vows. And yet of all three the last choice seems the least harmful.'

And so, out of fear that she would kill herself if he refused, the monk chose to drink the alcohol with the daughter. As a result, however, he got completely drunk. Then, in a state of total intoxication and heedlessness, he proceeded to make love to the woman and afterwards slaughtered and ate the goat! In the end, therefore, not one of the non-virtuous actions he feared was left undone. Such is the power of a breach of mindfulness!

Because the person who wishes to develop and maintain the mind of bodhichitta must be ever mindful of the actions of his or her three doors, Shantideva devotes the fourth chapter of his *Guide* to a full explanation of conscientiousness. If we understand how to practise conscientiousness and teach it to others, great benefits arise. If students heed this advice, they will be led into the practice of virtue and be able to reach their goals. In this text the explanation of conscientiousness has three parts:

1 An introduction to conscientiousness
2 An extensive explanation of conscientiousness
3 Summary

## AN INTRODUCTION TO CONSCIENTIOUSNESS

Shantideva introduces this subject by stating:

[1] Having firmly accepted the aspiring and engaging minds of bodhichitta as outlined previously, the Bodhisattva practises the six perfections and, with conscientiousness, continuously guards the practices and precepts of the two bodhichittas.

## AN EXTENSIVE EXPLANATION OF CONSCIENTIOUSNESS

This section, which constitutes the main body of the present chapter, has two principal parts:

1 Meditating on conscientiousness with respect to bodhichitta
2 Meditating on conscientiousness with respect to the precepts

## MEDITATING ON CONSCIENTIOUSNESS WITH RESPECT TO BODHICHITTA

The first major subdivision of this chapter has two parts:

1 The reasons why it is unwise to abandon bodhichitta
2 The faults of abandoning bodhichitta

## THE REASONS WHY IT IS UNWISE TO ABANDON BODHICHITTA

If we do not firmly hold the bodhichitta we have developed it can easily degenerate; therefore it is important that we guard it vigilantly. Once we have developed bodhichitta it is very unwise to abandon it. Why is this? [2] In our ordinary affairs we sometimes promise to take responsibility for particular tasks without having done much examination beforehand to see if we can keep our promise or not. As a result it is sometimes appropriate to abandon the task before it is completed. [3] This should not be the case with our bodhichitta wish and promise. Bodhichitta is only developed after we have deeply contemplated its benefits and made a thorough examination of all the reasons for cultivating this precious attitude. Having become convinced of the importance of developing bodhichitta, we make the solemn promise to benefit all sentient beings by attaining the full enlightenment of Buddhahood. To go back on such a deeply considered promise by being careless about our bodhichitta is therefore extremely unskilful.

## THE FAULTS OF ABANDONING BODHICHITTA

This has three parts:

1 We are led to the three lower realms
2 The benefit to others will decrease
3 We are far removed from the Bodhisattva grounds

## WE ARE LED TO THE THREE LOWER REALMS

As Shantideva says:

[4-7] If, having promised to attain enlightenment for the sake of all sentient beings, I reject this promise by failing to practise, I will be deceiving everyone. What greater evil is there than this? Where else will I be reborn but in unfortunate states of existence?

Buddha has said that the person who intends to give even the smallest, most ordinary thing to another but later changes his mind because of miserliness will later be reborn as a wandering, hungry spirit. As for me, I have promised to invite all sentient beings to a banquet of unsurpassable excellence. If I break this promise, how will I ever be reborn in the higher realms? Only an omniscient Buddha can understand how someone who abandons bodhichitta can ever be free from suffering.

The last sentence refers to a story told of Shariputra who was one of Buddha Shakyamuni's main disciples and is often depicted in paintings at the right side of Buddha's throne. At one point he developed bodhichitta and became a Bodhisattva. In order to test the depth of his commitment, an evil demon approached him one day and asked him for his right hand. Shariputra immediately cut it off and offered it to him with his left hand. The demon acted insulted and cried out, 'How dare you extend your left hand towards me! Have you no sense of politeness?' He continued to abuse the new Bodhisattva in this way for some time and then left. Shariputra was deeply saddened by this unreasonable behaviour and thought, 'If sentient beings are as unreasonable as this, how can I ever benefit them?' With that thought he abandoned his bodhichitta and returned to his former path of seeking liberation for himself alone. He eventually reached that goal and attained Arhatship in that very life.

If, as has been stated above, a person who rejects bodhichitta will be reborn in the three lower realms, why was Shariputra not reborn in hell? How was he able to attain Arhatship? Shantideva's answer is that only an omniscient one who sees the whole range of actions and their effects can understand how he escaped from the suffering of the three lower realms. It is beyond the power of limited minds to comprehend this fully. However, it is clear that while Shariputra did forsake his bodhichitta motivation he did not abandon his renunciation for samsara or his wisdom of emptiness. By meditating upon these two continuously he was able to reach nirvana and gain complete personal liberation from all suffering.

## THE BENEFIT TO OTHERS WILL DECREASE

If we take the Bodhisattva vows as described in the third chapter we commit ourself to certain behaviour of body, speech and mind. [8] The most important commitment is never to give up our bodhichitta motivation. If, by a lack of conscientiousness, we should do so, this is the heaviest of all violations of our vows and greatly weakens our ability to benefit others. Our whole basis of working for the welfare of others is lost. [9] Similarly, whoever interrupts a Bodhisattva's practice of virtue creates extremely negative karma. Why is this? Whatever a Bodhisattva does or accumulates in the way of virtue is solely for the welfare of others. Therefore, if he or she is hindered even for one moment in this practice, all sentient beings will be harmed indirectly.

Because we cannot tell who is and who is not a Bodhisattva, we should never interrupt someone who is practising virtue. We accumulate great non-virtue even if the person we interfere with is merely aspiring to practise Mahayana teachings. Any harm we give him or her affects the joy and happiness of all. [10] And, if negative results follow from destroying the happiness of one sentient being, is there any need to speak of the evil created by destroying the happiness of all sentient beings as vast as space? Is it possible to measure the suffering results of such a non-virtuous action?

If we can develop bodhichitta and practise Mahayana Dharma it is certainly excellent, but if we cannot practise we should have no objection to others who wish to do so. Mahayana Dharma can be followed by anyone who wishes to develop the precious bodhichitta; it is not a practice restricted solely to monks and nuns.

There are further misconceptions concerning the practice of Mahayana Dharma. Some people think that a person who merely aspires to practise Mahayana Dharma is not actually practising. They think this way because the person is apparently not benefiting anyone, but this is wrong. Although a Mahayana practitioner may be unable to benefit others now, he is training his mind to be able to do so later. This is a very realistic approach. Until we have tamed our own mind we cannot really help others. Though our main aim is to benefit all sentient beings as much as possible, we must first control and purify our own mind because it is polluted by the three delusions of attachment, hatred and ignorance. This is our primary task.

When we sow seeds in a field, the crops and fruit do not suddenly appear. To expect startling results in a short time is completely mistaken. In a similar manner, while it is immensely worthwhile to train our mind we must realize that it will take time before the expected benefits to ourself and others will arise. To demand immediate results from our meditation practice is foolish. To obtain the fruit of the path we should meditate continuously, year after year. The fully enlightened Indian Master Guru Padmasambhava said, 'By amassing many meditations throughout years of practice, realizations will be received.' If we have the sincere wish to attain enlightenment for the sake of others, we should take these words of advice to heart and develop a firm and steady practice over a long period of time.

## WE ARE FAR REMOVED FROM THE BODHISATTVA GROUNDS

[11] As explained earlier, if we take the Bodhisattva vows and break them we can retake them at another ceremony. However, if we keep taking the vows only to break them again and again, we will be seriously harming our practice. As Shantideva says, we will be preventing ourself from

reaching the higher stages of the Bodhisattva path: the ten grounds along which the Superior Bodhisattva proceeds on his or her way to enlightenment.

This advice does not apply merely to the development of bodhichitta. It is very difficult to gain any realizations at all if our meditation practices are constantly interrupted. If we want to attain tranquil abiding in which we can develop true single-pointedness of mind, we will be unable to do so if we meditate for a month, abandon our practice and then resume it a few months later. No practice done in such a fitful manner will ever bear fruit. We cannot bring water to a boil if we are forever turning the heat on and off. Just as the stove should be kept at a constant temperature, so our meditation practices should be steady and continuous.

How did great Yogis such as Milarepa gain their realizations while we are still suffering in samsara? Our body is no different from theirs, and the Mahayana Dharma available to us is the same as the teachings they followed. What, then, accounts for the great differences between us? The only reason there can be is that we have not collected all the causes to make our practice fruitful. Perhaps our motivation is impure or we do not understand the methods we have been given. The most important reason, however, is that we fail to practise steadily day by day. This must be corrected if we are ever to reach our desired goal.

This completes the first major section of this chapter, conscientiousness with respect to maintaining bodhichitta. In the next section Shantideva discusses how conscientiousness should be extended to all the practices of a Bodhisattva.

## MEDITATING ON CONSCIENTIOUSNESS WITH RESPECT TO THE PRECEPTS

The precepts arising from the Bodhisattva vows are vast but they are all included within the practice of the six perfections and the four ways of gathering disciples. In this section Shantideva divides the precepts into the following three areas of practice:

1 Conscientiousness in abandoning non-virtue
2 Conscientiousness in meditating on virtue
3 Conscientiousness in abandoning delusions

### CONSCIENTIOUSNESS IN ABANDONING NON-VIRTUE

During the Bodhisattva vow ceremony in the presence of our Spiritual Guide or the visualized Buddhas and Bodhisattvas we promised to attain enlightenment for the sake of all sentient beings. [12] Shantideva reminds us to act with diligence in accordance with this promise and warns us that if no effort is made to keep our vows we will descend to the lower states of existence. Some people may argue that it is not necessary for us to keep the precepts we have taken because the compassionate Buddhas will certainly protect us. This is a mistaken belief. If from our side we have committed heavy non-virtuous actions, and we have done nothing to purify these actions or to accumulate merit, then even a fully enlightened Buddha is unable to rescue us from drowning in the ocean of samsara.

[13] In the past countless Buddhas have appeared, but owing to our faults and imperfections we have not been the direct object of their care and thus have not been rescued

by them. What is the reason for this? Although Buddha Shakyamuni attained enlightenment under the Bodhi Tree in Bodh Gaya, turned the Wheel of Dharma and led countless sentient beings to liberation and enlightenment, we are still floundering in samsara. Why? Buddha's disciples also led many beings to liberation from suffering but we are still caught in the swamp of samsara. Why are we still suffering?

When Buddha Shakyamuni appeared in India 2,500 years ago did he not know that we were wandering in samsara? Of course he did. Did he not have great compassion for us, and the power to show us the path? Certainly. From our side, however, we had not completed all the secondary causes necessary to become a member of his retinue and receive teachings from him at that time. Because of our previous non-virtuous actions perhaps we had taken rebirth in the three lower realms. If we were fortunate enough to be born human, perhaps we lived in a place where there was no Dharma or even no practice of moral discipline. And if we were born as humans in close proximity to Buddha Shakyamuni, perhaps we held wrong views and disliked the teachings he gave. As Shantideva says, it is solely because of our own faults and misdeeds that the Buddhas are unable to rescue us from the ocean of samsaric suffering.

For as long as we lack faith in enlightened beings, disbelieve the law of actions and their effects, refuse to consider the continuity of consciousness and the existence of past and future lives, and reject the practice of Dharma, then even a Buddha is powerless to help us. He cannot free us from the bonds of suffering with which we have tied ourself. If we continue to cherish our mistaken views there will be no way for us to practise Dharma purely and benefit from the teachings the enlightened beings have given us.

Then Shantideva says:

[14] If I continue to come under the influence of wrong views, after my death I will be reborn in the three lower realms again and again and undergo the suffering of sickness, death, bondage, laceration and the shedding of blood.

Buddha has stated that for as long as sentient beings are under the influence of ignorance they must experience the four characteristics of samsara: (1) birth inevitably leads to death, (2) that which is collected together must eventually disperse, (3) those holding high positions must eventually fall to lower states, and (4) all meetings eventually result in parting. We should examine these four characteristics very carefully. Whoever possesses a high rank, a good reputation or wealth must eventually see it decrease, fall and ultimately vanish. Is there any real pleasure to be had from these attainments, and can any of them help us at the time of death? Can our husband or wife, our friends or family, our possessions or our government help us when it is time to die? To think that we will live in this world permanently is a gross self-deception. This world has no permanent residents. Of all the billions of people alive now, who will still be here in one hundred years? We are merely travellers passing through this world, and as travellers we must think to provide ourself well for our journey. Yet what do we need to take with us? None of the temporal pleasures mentioned above are of any value at the time of death; only Dharma practice – the training, controlling and purifying of our mind – can protect us from suffering.

Some people pray to be able to practise Dharma in their next life because they feel they have no opportunity to practise now. This is foolish. At this moment we have found a perfect human rebirth, have met the Mahayana teachings and have the rare chance to practise Dharma. [15] If we do not take advantage of this opportunity now, how will we ever find such a perfect human rebirth again in the future? It is rare for a Buddha to appear in this world, rare to find a fully endowed precious human rebirth and difficult to develop faith in an enlightened being. Therefore, as we have already attained these precious circumstances, we should practise Dharma now.

We should not waste this precious human life, which we have attained with great difficulty, only for the sake of this present life's comforts. Instead we must use this rare opportunity to develop the precious mind of bodhichitta. At the moment we have clear sight, good hearing, a fresh mind and good health. If we do not practise Dharma now it will be too late to do so even if we live to be eighty or ninety. Although we may have the intention at that time to practise Dharma, our senses will be declining, our mind unsteady and our body unhealthy. A Tibetan proverb says, 'If you don't practise Dharma when you are young, when you've grown old you will regret it.'

Gungtang Rinpoche, a great meditator of the past, summarized the decrepit state of old age graphically by saying:

> Your hair is now as white as a conch shell, not because you have rid yourself of the blackness of non-virtue but because the Lord of Death has spit on you and his spittle has fallen upon your head in the form of white frost. The wrinkles on your forehead are not the folds in the skin of a plump baby but rather the lines marked by the Messenger of Time numbering your many bygone years.

Some people think that they will practise Dharma once they have finished with their worldly business. This is a mistaken attitude because our work in the world never finishes. Work is like a ripple of water continually moving on the surface of the ocean. It is very difficult to break free from our occupations in order to practise Dharma. The busy work with which we fill our lives is only completed at the time of our death.

[16] Even though we are now young and healthy, nourished by good food, adorned by fine clothing and free from unfavourable circumstances, life can suddenly deceive us. Our body is an object loaned to us for only a short time. If we want to generate the precious bodhichitta, we must do so in this lifetime. Day by day, hour by hour, minute by minute and moment by moment, our life is passing by. Even while we are asleep our life span is draining from us. We cannot be confident that death will not suddenly descend upon us. Despite all this everyone thinks, 'I will not die today . . . or even tomorrow.' Even when we are lying sick in bed we continue to think like this. And even on the day our death actually comes, instead of thinking about our imminent death we will probably be making vain plans for a future we will not live to see. But we are all going to die; this is why life is so deceptive.

If our body belonged to us permanently we could take it with us when we died, but at the time of death we will have to leave it behind like all our other borrowed possessions. Why should we cling to this body, which was born from the union of our mother's ovum and our father's sperm, as if it were ours, truly ours? Instead we should think of this life as a momentary deception, realizing that second by second the tide of life ebbs away. Reflect deeply upon the certainty and suddenness of our death's approach and remember that our body is merely an object on loan. If we can gain a deep understanding of these points our mind will definitely change. We will no longer waste our time and a new meaning and purpose will be given to our life. Otherwise we will merely be marking time until death comes.

[17] If we do not practise virtue we will be wasting this precious human life. Moreover, if we practise non-virtue we will make it impossible for ourself to find another perfect human rebirth in the future. If we fail to find such a human form again and are reborn instead in the three lower realms, our life will be darkened by confusion. There will be absolutely no opportunity to practise Dharma and we will not even hear of virtue, much less be able to follow it. [18] At the moment, while we are still human, we have the opportunity to practise Dharma and to realize that benefits arise from practising virtue while many faults arise from following non-virtue. If we are reborn in the three lower realms, our confusion will be so great that we will not be able to discriminate between the effects of virtue and non-virtue any longer.

As Shantideva says:

[19] Committing nothing but non-virtue and being unable to practise even a single virtuous deed, we will remain in hell for a hundred million aeons where even the words 'a happy life' will not be heard.

[20] Buddha Shakyamuni gave an example to show how difficult it is, once we have descended into the three lower realms, for us ever to find a higher rebirth again. Imagine that on the surface of a vast ocean a golden yoke is floating, blown here and there by the currents and winds. Once every hundred years a blind turtle, living at the bottom of the ocean,

swims up to the surface only to return to the depths once again. The chances of that blind turtle surfacing at the precise point to insert his head through the golden yoke can be likened to the chance we will have of finding another human rebirth once we have fallen into the lower realms. If we do not practise now, when can we ever hope to practise again?

## CONSCIENTIOUSNESS IN MEDITATING ON VIRTUE

This section has six parts:

1. Striving to abandon the infinite evils collected in previous lives
2. Merely experiencing the sufferings of lower realms will not lead to release
3. Not applying effort to the practice of virtue now that we have attained a precious human life is self-deception
4. If we do not practise virtue now we will experience suffering in this life
5. If we do not practise virtue now we will experience the sufferings of lower realms in future lives
6. Following from the above, it is appropriate to strive to abandon non-virtue and practise virtue

## STRIVING TO ABANDON THE INFINITE EVILS COLLECTED IN PREVIOUS LIVES

Shantideva says:

[21] Buddha taught that a moment of evil leads to rebirth in the lowest hell for many aeons. If we neglect to use the four opponent powers and purify those evils

that we have committed since beginningless time, is there any need for us to speak of our failing to be reborn in the happy realms of existence?

## MERELY EXPERIENCING THE SUFFERINGS OF LOWER REALMS WILL NOT LEAD TO RELEASE

[22] When the seeds of our non-virtuous karma ripen we are thrown into one of the three lower realms of rebirth. There we will remain until the fruit of that karma has been exhausted. When that karma is completed are we freed from suffering? No, we are not. Although we have exhausted the fruit of certain seeds of non-virtue, while in the lower realms we committed even more non-virtue through the power of our ignorance. When a being is born in one of the lower realms he or she is unable to practise virtue; his life is spent in the accumulation of non-virtuous actions. All these actions plant seeds in his mind that will ripen in the experience of future suffering.

For as long as we are still in samsara and living a life conditioned by ignorance, we cannot say that we have ever finished with suffering. Those fortunate beings who have achieved liberation from suffering did so not by letting their negative karma exhaust itself or by waiting for their experiences of misery to cease, but by following a path of meditation and uprooting the very cause of suffering. When their sentences are up prisoners are released from their bondage, but no one is sentenced to a time after which he or she will automatically be released from samsara. The only way to escape is to recognize that ignorance is the root of our suffering and then to meditate on the path of wisdom that cuts through this root.

There is no real happiness in samsara. We may think that kings and presidents are in some way happier than the rest of us, but they too must experience much suffering during their lives. From the poorest beggar to the most exalted world leader, everyone must experience many sufferings, either mentally, by not obtaining what is desired and by meeting that which is not desired, or physically, by having to endure the pains of birth, sickness, old age and death. There is no doubt that from the cries of a newborn baby to the lamentations of one who is on his deathbed, there is always the experience of dissatisfaction and pain. When a baby cries at birth, he is not crying because he is happy.

If we want to exhaust our suffering we need to study both the cause and the remedy of samsara. It is only in Dharma that these matters are analyzed fully. What is meant by Dharma? It means 'to hold'. What is held depends upon the scope of our practice. At the initial level, Dharma practice holds us back from falling into the three lower realms. At the intermediate level, we are held back from being reborn anywhere in samsara. Finally, at the highest level, that of the Mahayana practitioner, we are held back from all the faults and disadvantages of self-cherishing and shown the way to full enlightenment. There is no Dharma practice that is not included within one of these three scopes. Therefore if we wish an end to our suffering, we must practise Dharma conscientiously.

## NOT APPLYING EFFORT TO THE PRACTICE OF VIRTUE NOW THAT WE HAVE ATTAINED A PRECIOUS HUMAN LIFE IS SELF-DECEPTION

[23] Now that we have found a precious human life possessing the eight freedoms and the ten endowments

mentioned earlier, if we do not strive to practise Dharma there can be no greater self-deception or folly. Buddha illustrated this point with the following example. There once was a merchant who went to sea in search of precious jewels. After many difficulties he finally arrived at an island and, to his delight and amazement, discovered it was filled with gems of every description. But soon he became involved in the sensual pleasures of the island, took to drinking and gambling and completely wasted his time in meaningless activities. When he finally returned to his native country he had nothing to show for his troubles but the debts he had incurred. Was he not extremely foolish? Yet such a man is not nearly so foolish as those who let themselves be distracted by the temporal pleasures of the world, neglecting to use their precious human life to achieve the goals of spiritual practice.

If we were to lose or squander a hundred pounds we would become upset even though, with a little effort, it is possible to replace this money later. Yet we think nothing of wasting this human life that, once lost, can never be bought again no matter how much gold or silver we might have. When the Lord of Death comes we cannot hire armed guards to keep our body from him, nor can we escape, fight back or beg to be excused. When this pitiless Lord announces 'It is time for you to come with me', we have no choice but to leave our loved ones and possessions behind and depart alone and empty-handed. If we have neglected to practise one of the three scopes of Dharma and are forced to proceed to the lower realms with nothing to show for having been born human, there can be no greater self-deception than this.

## IF WE DO NOT PRACTISE VIRTUE NOW WE WILL EXPERIENCE SUFFERING IN THIS LIFE

Shantideva continues by saying:

> [24] This precious human rebirth is extremely rare and difficult to find. If, confused about the law of actions and their effects, I neglect the practices of virtue, then at the time of death I must depart alone, choked by regret, fear and intense panic.

In Tibet there once lived a man named Mondrol Chodak. He was very knowledgeable and possessed other good qualities, so his neighbours would regularly ask him for advice. He was a natural leader and much respected by everyone. He was very busy until one day he was struck down by a fever. Lying down in the sunshine he reflected deeply on the course of his life and thought, 'I've done every conceivable worldly action but I've never practised Dharma.' Intense regret overwhelmed him as he realized that the only thing that could help him at the time of his death was Dharma, but this he had neglected to follow. For a long time he continued to lie there, full of regret and fear.

His grandmother saw him and called out loudly, 'Don't lie in the sun like that!' But he was so filled with remorse that he did not hear her. After a while she called out to him again, this time with scorn in her voice. 'What is the matter with you today?' she asked. 'You don't normally act like this.'

Mondrol Chodak looked at her sadly and said, 'Today I have realized how all of my relatives and friends have been deceiving me. You have always told me how clever, wise and helpful I am. But now I can see that all of my actions, without an exception, have been involved in the petty concerns of this world. Distracted by these worldly activities and the praise I received for them, I did everything but practise Dharma. The one thing that could have protected me is the one thing I avoided. Is there anyone in the world more foolish than I?' With tears falling from his eyes he sobbed, 'How wonderful if I weren't Mondrol Chodak! If only I were someone else.' Immediately after saying this he died.

Dying with regrets like this is not at all unusual. If we waste our life in meaningless activities we will end up exactly as Mondrol Chodak did. First we will be struck down with a sickness or injury; then, as we are lying in bed, the Lord of Death will make his approach. The doctor comes to visit us but can do nothing except tell our relatives that our disease is incurable. Prayers now cannot avert our death. Our close family surrounds our deathbed, their eyes full of tears as they give up all hope for us. With our final breath we make our last requests: 'When I die please take care of so and so . . .' After a while our mouth dries up, our nose sinks, our eyes stare vaguely upwards and our breathing becomes irregular. As we think of the family and friends we will never see again, our heart is filled with pain. All the non-virtuous actions of the life now finishing flash before our mind's eye and we are overcome by grief and regret. Our limbs begin to shake and we find it difficult to let go and just die. Urine and excrement flow uncontrollably from our body and, because of the evil we have left unpurified and the force of illusory appearances, horrifying visions manifest before us. Finally, we breathe out one last time and are unable to bring the breath in again. At last the unavoidable moment of death has come.

It is very important for us to contemplate the way death approaches and to think deeply about the probable experiences of our own death. We should not do this contemplation once or twice, but over and over again until we are filled with the firm determination not to waste even a moment of this precious and fragile human life. Only through a realization of our mortality can we extract the true essence of our existence. Remembering death is our greatest incentive for practising Dharma conscientiously.

## IF WE DO NOT PRACTISE VIRTUE NOW WE WILL EXPERIENCE THE SUFFERINGS OF LOWER REALMS IN FUTURE LIVES

Shantideva now declares:

> [25] Now that I have obtained this precious human life, if I do not practise virtue but instead solely commit non-virtue, I will be reborn in the depths of hell. My body will blaze for an immeasurable length of time amidst unbearable flames. At such a time is it not inevitable that my mind will also be consumed by overwhelming regret?

## FOLLOWING FROM THE ABOVE, IT IS APPROPRIATE TO STRIVE TO ABANDON NON-VIRTUE AND PRACTISE VIRTUE

Shantideva concludes this section as follows:

> [26-27] By some extremely good fortune I have found a precious human rebirth endowed with the leisure that is extremely difficult to find. If, while being able to discriminate between the faults of non-virtue and the benefit of virtue, I allow myself to be led to a hellish

rebirth, it is as if I did not possess a human mind at all. It is as though my mind were bewildered by a powerful spell, unable to function or to understand why it is confused. What kind of ignorance dwells within me?

To be able to see the difference between positive and negative actions and to understand the relationship between actions and their effects, yet still to lead a life full of non-virtue is a definite sign that our mind is steeped in the darkest ignorance.

This concludes the discussion of conscientiousness in relation to meditating on the importance of practising virtue.

## CONSCIENTIOUSNESS IN ABANDONING DELUSIONS

This has three parts:

1 Contemplating the faults of delusions
2 The inappropriateness of grieving over the hardships to be endured while abandoning delusions
3 Contemplating the joy of being able to abandon delusions

## CONTEMPLATING THE FAULTS OF DELUSIONS

Shantideva's discussion of the faults of delusions is divided into six parts:

1 Delusions give us no choice
2 Delusions bring infinite sufferings
3 Delusions harm us for a long time
4 Following delusions as if they were friends is unwise

5  Being patient with delusions is unwise
6  Developing encouragement to dispel delusions

## DELUSIONS GIVE US NO CHOICE

Shantideva characterizes the hold our delusions have over us as follows:

> [28] Although my enemies of hatred, attachment and so forth have neither weapons, legs nor arms, still they harm and torture me and treat me like a slave.

According to Dharma our worst enemy is delusion. This refers to any mental factor that disturbs and harms our peaceful mind. If we wish to be free of all suffering we must be able to identify the various delusions and understand how they harm us. Generally we all try to be aware of our external enemies, but we pay scant heed to the inner enemies infecting our own mind. If we do not recognize the delusions and see how they harm us, how can we ever overcome our suffering? Buddha identified the six root delusions that poison our mind as follows: (1) attachment, (2) anger, (3) pride, (4) ignorance, (5) deluded doubt and (6) deluded view. These will now be explained as follows.

### *Attachment*

Attachment is a mental factor that perceives an object, considers it to be beautiful or pleasing, and wishes to obtain, touch, possess and not be separated from it. Attachment works in two related ways: wishing to obtain a beautiful object not yet possessed, and wishing never to be separated from that object once it is possessed. The ordinary relationship between two members of a couple illustrates both types of attachment. In the beginning they wish to be with each other; this is the first type of attachment. Afterwards the desire arises never to be apart from each other; this is the second type of attachment. Attachment can also arise in relation to material objects. Under the influence of this delusion our mind is absorbed into the desired object in the same way as oil is absorbed into cloth. Just as it is very difficult to separate oil from the cloth it has stained, so it is difficult to separate the mind from the object of attachment with which it has become absorbed.

It is because of our attachment that we continue to wander in samsara and experience infinite suffering. The prerequisite for achieving liberation or full enlightenment, or even for ordination as a monk or nun, is the mind of renunciation. Attachment to the transitory pleasures of this world prevents the mind of renunciation from arising.

From beginningless time we have been unable to free ourself from the prison of samsara. Attachment is what keeps us bound in this prison. If we have the sincere wish to practise Dharma we must renounce the whole of samsara, and we can do this only by reducing our deluded attachment.

Once we have recognized our attachment there are two ways of abandoning it. We can overcome this delusion temporarily by meditating on the repulsiveness and the impurity of the desired object and then considering the many faults of the delusion itself. If we practise continuously in this way we can definitely reduce our attachment. In the eighth chapter of this text Shantideva explains this practice in more detail.

The method described above is only a temporary antidote for our attachment. If we want to remove it completely we must uproot the underlying cause not only of attachment but of all the delusions: self-grasping. Only by meditating on emptiness (Skt. shunyata) are we able to uproot self-grasping completely. To attain complete liberation from suffering we need to develop not only a realization of emptiness but also of renunciation, tranquil abiding and superior seeing. Shantideva discusses the meditations on tranquil abiding and superior seeing in chapters eight and nine respectively.

## *Anger*

The second root delusion is anger. This is a mental factor that exaggerates the unpleasant characteristics of an object and wishes to harm it. As with attachment, anger can be directed towards what is animate or inanimate. How are we harmed by our anger or hatred? Buddha has said that hatred decreases or destroys all our collections of virtue and can lead us into the lowest of the hell realms. A moment's anger directed towards a Bodhisattva, for instance, can destroy all the merit we may have accumulated previously to take rebirth in a higher realm.

Anger is the fire that burns the wood of our virtue. It lurks behind all disputes whether they are domestic quarrels between a husband and wife or a war between two nations. It causes our face to become red, and disturbs not only our own mind but the peace of others as well. An extensive explanation of the many faults of anger, as well as methods for preventing it arising, will be presented in the sixth chapter of this text.

## *Pride*

Pride is a mental factor causing us to feel higher or superior to others. Even our study of Dharma can be the occasion for the delusion of pride to arise if we think that our understanding is superior to that of anyone else. Pride is harmful because it prevents us from accepting fresh knowledge from a qualified teacher. Just as a pool of water cannot collect on top of a mountain, so a reservoir of understanding cannot be established in a mind falsely elevated by pride.

## *Ignorance*

The fourth root delusion is ignorance. This refers to not knowing and being confused, and manifests primarily as self-grasping. If our meditation on emptiness is done incorrectly and our mind is led into darkness, this is also a form of ignorance. The faults of such an ignorant, confused mind are many. Even in worldly affairs we must have a clear understanding of what we are doing if we wish to perform our actions well. In a similar manner, if we do not know the methods involved in travelling the path leading to liberation and full enlightenment it will be impossible for us to attain any of these states. All our wrong views, such as denying the continuity of our consciousness and the workings of actions and their effects, or karma, are caused by the mental factor of ignorance.

## *Deluded Doubt*

Deluded doubt is a mental factor that obstructs our belief by fluctuating between the extremes of truth and untruth. For example, we may lack belief in the workings of karma because our mind is plagued by doubt and thinks, 'Maybe it's true; maybe it's not true.'

Doubt keeps our mind from becoming stabilized and prevents us from travelling the path to liberation. Buddha

Shakyamuni synthesized the entire path to liberation into the four noble truths, but if our mind is filled with deluded doubt we will never be able to attain this liberation. Such doubt makes it impossible for us to practise seriously and prevents us from receiving any fruit from our meditations.

There are two ways of dispelling our doubt about a particular subject. The first is to examine it logically by employing a valid line of reasoning. Buddha Shakyamuni always emphasized that his teachings should be examined in this way before they are ever accepted. Sometimes, however, we are unable to come to a definite conclusion by means of our reasoning. Perhaps we do not know enough yet about the subject matter to draw a logical conclusion. In this case we should dispel our doubt by relying on the instructions of a fully qualified Spiritual Guide in whom we can confidently place our trust. If we do not try to remove our doubts in either of these two ways, our Dharma practice will never develop properly.

## *Deluded View*

Deluded view is the sixth and the last of the root delusions. There are many types of deluded view but the principal one is grasping the I or self to be inherently existent. This view, as well as its remedy, is explained more fully in the ninth chapter. For now it is enough to say that this view conceives the I as something having no relationship with either the mind or the body. For example, when we are walking near the edge of a dangerous cliff we do not think 'My body might fall' or 'My mind might fall', but rather 'I might fall!' The I that we hold at such a time is unrelated to and independent of our body, our mind or the combination of them both. This mistaken way of looking at ourself is the chain that binds us to samsara. It is the root of all our delusions; if this view is abandoned all our delusions will be cut.

This deluded view of believing things to be independent and inherently existent is the source from which all other delusions, such as attachment, anger and pride, arise. These delusions in turn impel us to create karma, and by the power of this karma we are born again and again in samsara. There we experience the sufferings of birth, hunger, thirst, sickness, old age and eventually death. All of these sufferings have their source in our deluded view that conceives things as inherently existent. If we wish to overcome our sufferings we should meditate daily on the faults of holding such a deluded view.

Now we can see why Shantideva says that our delusions are our worst enemies, keeping us enslaved within the prison of samsara. What impels us to sell our time, energy, sweat and indeed our very life force for the sake of a little money, a few possessions and the bubble of reputation? We are urged on in this way by our delusions, primarily our attachment. Anger enslaves us as well. What else urges us on to fight despite the dangers, fears and threats of death? Nothing but delusion has the power to harm us in so many ways.

## DELUSIONS BRING INFINITE SUFFERING

[29ab] We are sometimes harmed externally by ordinary enemies but, since time without beginning, the enemy of delusions has dwelt within our mind and unceasingly harmed us at its pleasure. This enemy is so mixed with our mind that it is very difficult to identify it. Only by studying this enemy can we recognize it for what it is. There is no other method.

We say that a particular physician is skilful if he or she is able to identify and diagnose diseases of the body. In fact, however, such a diagnosis is not very difficult to perform and can be carried out largely by means of the physician's eyesight. It requires much more skill to be able to distinguish a virtuous mind from a non-virtuous one for this cannot be done by the power of our eyes. How can we make such a subtle diagnosis? First we must hear many teachings about the nature of the mind, and then check what we have heard and what we observe about our mind by means of analytical meditation. This is how we can train ourself in Dharma.

There are various states of mind. Some are virtuous, some are non-virtuous and others are neither of the two. To be able to recognize those minds that are non-virtuous and then apply the correct remedy to remove them is to be truly skilful. Once we understand which of our states of mind are deluded and can see how they cause us continual harm, we can surely exert a great deal of effort trying to overcome them. If there is a group of people and one amongst them is subversive, when the other members realize who he is and what he is up to they will waste no time in expelling him. Similarly, if we recognize the root delusion of self-grasping for what it is – our most dangerous enemy – we will make every possible effort to eradicate it from our mind. It is not right to be complacent with such an enemy in our midst.

Shantideva summarizes the dangers to which our delusions expose us as follows:

[29cd-31] For me to remain patiently under the influence of self-grasping is a source of great shame. This is no time to be patient! If all the gods, demi-gods and sentient beings throughout the universe were to rise

up against me as one enemy they would only be able to harm me during my present lifetime. They do not have the power to lead me to the roaring fires of the deepest hell and throw me in. However, the power of the delusions is such that it can instantly cast me into the flames of hell, flames so strong that they can reduce Mount Meru to a heap of ashes.

## DELUSIONS HARM US FOR A LONG TIME

[32] All our external enemies, no matter who they are, are unable to remain our enemies forever. However, the inner enemy of delusion has harmed us since beginningless time and, if we do not defeat it during this present lifetime, it will continue to harm us for infinite lifetimes to come.

## FOLLOWING DELUSIONS AS IF THEY WERE FRIENDS IS UNWISE

[33] We can turn an ordinary, external enemy into our friend merely by agreeing with him and entrusting ourself to him. If we do this he will return joy and benefit to us and will cease to harm us. However, if we make friends with and entrust ourself to the inner enemy of delusions it will only cause us more suffering and pain in the future. Therefore we must never regard a delusion as our friend.

## BEING PATIENT WITH DELUSIONS IS UNWISE

Shantideva continues as follows:

> [34-35] Delusions are my worst enemy and have the longest duration; they are the principal cause increasing

my suffering, fear and misery. As long as this enemy dwells within my heart, how can I remain without fear and be joyful while still in samsara? Delusions are the guards of this prison of samsara. They cast me into hell and butcher and torture me incessantly. As long as the net of delusions is permanently spread in my mind, how will I ever experience happiness?

## DEVELOPING ENCOURAGEMENT TO DISPEL DELUSIONS

Now that Shantideva has outlined the various faults of delusions he encourages us to make the strong determination to fight against this enemy incessantly:

> [36] In this world those who are filled with self-importance are unable to sleep until the enemy who has given them slight and short-lived harm has been vanquished. They display tireless effort to dispel this petty foe. Taking this as an example I will not abandon my efforts until that inner enemy of mine is slain before my very eyes!

This concludes the discussion of the faults of delusions. In the following section Shantideva continues with the imagery of warfare.

## THE INAPPROPRIATENESS OF GRIEVING OVER THE HARDSHIPS TO BE ENDURED WHILE ABANDONING DELUSIONS

There is really no reason to kill our ordinary enemies; death will come to them naturally in the future anyway. [37]

Despite this fact there are some soldiers who engage in fearsome battles, willing to fight even though their enemies have superior weapons. They ignore the pains of battle and continue to fight until they are victorious. If there are people who are willing to expend such great effort in order to kill an ordinary enemy, [38] why do we not strive unceasingly to destroy the worst enemy of all: the delusions that are the cause of all of our suffering? To overcome such a powerful foe we must certainly expect to experience great hardships, but is there any need to mention the absolute necessity of attacking this enemy diligently?

[39] Soldiers who receive battle scars later show them off proudly as if they were ornaments. For petty reasons they have endured much suffering and hardship and now enjoy wearing the scars inflicted upon them. However, how infinitely more worthwhile it is to endure the problems and hardships encountered while accomplishing the greatest purpose of all! Therefore, we should be prepared to endure all the difficulties we meet along the spiritual path.

[40] Fishermen, hunters and farmers endure the sufferings of heat and cold merely for the sake of making a temporary livelihood. If they endure these sufferings while working for their own sake, we should think, 'Why am I not patient and forbearing in the face of suffering and hardship while working for the benefit of others?' There can be no doubt that the hardships encountered while working for our own and others' welfare – the twin goals of the Mahayana path – should be gladly endured.

We may wonder why it is necessary for us to abandon our own delusions in order to dispel the suffering of others. Shantideva answers as follows:

[41-42] If I am not free from delusions and am unsure about my future lives within samsara, then my promise to liberate all sentient beings in all ten directions from their delusions and suffering was surely the words of a madman! Therefore I should strive along the path of Dharma without ever ceasing to abandon my own delusions.

If we first abandon our own delusions we will gain the power to release all sentient beings from their suffering. Our ultimate aim as followers of the Mahayana path is to benefit others, but to be able to do this we must first gain control over our own mind. Only by doing this can we truly be of help to others. Shantideva next emphasizes the necessity of overcoming our own delusions by returning to the warfare imagery used earlier:

[43-44] Hold a strong grudge against delusion and let the battle commence! Under no circumstances will I surrender to delusion, whose sole task is to cause me harm. There is no fault in holding such a grudge because its object is what obstructs our Dharma practice. Such a grudge is anger only in appearance but not in reality. It would be better for someone to set my body on fire or cut off my head than for me ever to bow down under delusion or fall under its influence.

In Tibet there was a very famous practitioner by the name of Geshe Ben Gungyel. A disciple noticed that at night he neither slept nor recited any prayers, and asked what his practice was. Ben Gungyel replied, 'I have two practices: to be aware when delusions arise and to control them. I have no other practice than this. If I see that delusions are not arising

I am happy. But if delusions do arise I try to be mindful of them and apply the appropriate opponents. My Dharma practice is not from my mouth. My practice is to eradicate delusion.' Ben Gungyel's method of practice was greatly praised by the famous Teachers of his day. It would be very wise for us to try to emulate him.

## CONTEMPLATING THE JOY OF BEING ABLE TO ABANDON DELUSIONS

This section, the third aspect of practising conscientiousness in the abandonment of delusions, has three parts:

1 Unlike ordinary enemies, delusions cannot return once they have been eradicated
2 As the cause of delusions is wrong views, with diligence they can be abandoned
3 For these reasons it is suitable to abandon delusions

## UNLIKE ORDINARY ENEMIES, DELUSIONS CANNOT RETURN ONCE THEY HAVE BEEN ERADICATED

Shantideva declares:

[45] When an ordinary enemy is banished from one country he may regain his strength abroad and then return to seek revenge. The inner enemy of delusions, however, is not able to do this. When delusions are completely abandoned they can never return again.

## AS THE CAUSE OF DELUSIONS IS WRONG VIEWS, WITH DILIGENCE THEY CAN BE ABANDONED

Someone might wonder, 'I understand how delusion harms me but is it really possible to uproot delusion completely?' Yes. If the one root of all delusions is cut, then all delusions are abandoned forever. Self-grasping is this root, and all the other delusions are like branches. If the root of an ordinary tree is cut, all of its branches, fruit and so forth will wither and die. In the same way, if we uproot our self-grasping, all of our delusions will cease. If we know how to go about this properly we will have no problems in our practice. The weapon we need to cut through the root of self-grasping is the sword of wisdom, the realization of emptiness. [46] If we have the eye of wisdom we can pierce through delusions and eradicate them completely.

## FOR THESE REASONS IT IS SUITABLE TO ABANDON DELUSIONS

Some people may think that delusions are self-existent and therefore cannot be abandoned. But this is a mistake; nothing is self-existent, not even our delusions. Once a delusion has been dispelled from our mind it becomes completely non-existent. How can it possibly abide anywhere else and arise again to harm us? Even though we may be weak-minded, if we strive diligently why should we not be able to destroy our delusions?

If we think that a delusion is self-existent, we should search for it. [47ab] But a delusion cannot be found to abide either in the object, in the sense powers or between the two, and nor can it be found anywhere else. Therefore how does a delusion arise to harm sentient beings? From where does it come? Our inability to discover the exact location of a delusion indicates that while it does function to disturb our mind it is not self-existent. Attachment and all the other delusions are merely like an illusion. Recognizing this fact, Shantideva cries out:

> [47cd] If there has been no good reason, why have I suffered so long in hell? Seeing this, I will put away all my fear and strive resolutely to abandon all delusions completely.

## SUMMARY

Shantideva concludes the entire discussion of conscientiousness as follows:

> [48] Thinking about conscientiousness I will strive to integrate all these precepts into my Dharma practice as they have been explained above. I will try to keep these precepts as purely as I am able. A patient who ignores his doctor's instructions will never be cured. In the same way, if I do not listen to and practise Buddha's teachings, how can I ever be cured of the disease of delusion?

This concludes 'Conscientiousness', the fourth chapter of the text *Meaningful to Behold*, a commentary to Shantideva's *Guide to the Bodhisattva's Way of Life*.

# Guarding the Mind with Alertness

Once we have taken the Bodhisattva vows and have understood the importance of practising conscientiously, we are ready to begin the actual method for attaining enlightenment. This entails the practice of the six perfections. As explained in the introduction, although giving is generally presented first, in Shantideva's text the first perfection to be discussed is that of moral discipline. Because discipline requires mindfulness and alertness, this chapter is explained largely in terms of these two mental factors.

## HOW TO TRAIN IN MORAL DISCIPLINE BY PRACTISING MINDFULNESS AND ALERTNESS

This section has five parts:

1 The method of guarding the practice is to guard the mind
2 The method of guarding the mind is to practise mindfulness and alertness
3 How to practise moral discipline by means of mindfulness and alertness
4 How to prevent our practice from degenerating
5 In conclusion, the necessity of following the meaning and not merely the words of the practice

*Dromtonpa*

## THE METHOD OF GUARDING THE PRACTICE IS TO GUARD THE MIND

[1] If we wish to avoid falling under the influence of delusion we must guard our mind and prevent it from wandering. We cannot practise moral discipline purely if we have an unguarded mind. If we can learn how to protect our mind from delusion and yoke it to the practice of virtue, our moral discipline will grow in strength and eventually be perfected. If we neglect to guard our mind, however, many faults will arise.

[2] If we let a wild elephant loose in a populated area it will cause massive destruction, but the uncontrolled wild mind can cause much more harm than such a crazed beast. If the deluded, wild elephant of our mind is not subdued it will create much suffering for us in this life and will cause us to experience the sufferings of the deepest hell in the future. In fact, if we investigate we can see that the creator of all the sufferings of this and future lives is nothing but our unsubdued mind. To subdue this wild beast is much more important than bringing a jungle elephant under our control.

[3] Many benefits follow from taming our mind. If we take the rope of mindfulness and tie our elephant mind securely to the post of virtue, all our fears will swiftly come to an end. All positive and virtuous attainments will fall into the palm of our hand. If we wish to elevate our mind we must merge it with the practice of virtue by steadily applying the power of mindfulness. This is the very heart of meditation.

If we do not develop mindfulness our meditations will be hollow and empty. There will be nothing to keep our wild elephant mind from running back and forth in its customary, uncontrolled manner between objects of attachment, anger, jealousy and so forth. While we are sitting on our meditation cushion our mind may be miles away, wandering through distant cities or visiting our family and friends. Just as a potter needs two hands to shape his wares, so do we need mindfulness and alertness if we are to meditate properly and gain realizations along the spiritual path.

[4] If we learn how to control our mind properly, we will overcome all our fears. Neither tigers, elephants, lions, bears, snakes, all other enemies, the guardians of hell, evil spirits nor even cannibals can frighten us. Why is this so? [5] Because all fear comes from the mind that is untamed. Thus a Bodhisattva who has trained his mind has no reason to fear any of the creatures just mentioned because he is always happy to surrender his body and possessions to others. For us, however, it is quite different. Because we have not controlled our self-cherishing mind, fear arises immediately whenever we encounter anything even slightly threatening. The only way to overcome such fear is to tame the mind.

A story about one of Buddha Shakyamuni's previous lives illustrates the protection afforded by a subdued mind. At that time he was born as an Indian king named Chandra. One day from another land came a young man who had turned cannibal. Whenever people saw this bloodthirsty person draw near they fled in all directions; everyone except King Chandra. He remained where he was and even walked calmly towards the youth and introduced himself. The youth immediately lunged at him but King Chandra neither felt nor displayed even a trace of fear. To someone who had become accustomed by now to having people run away from him, the king's behaviour was surprising indeed! 'Aren't you afraid of death?' the young man cried in amazement. The king replied that he was prepared to sacrifice his body then and there if need be.

The youth was stunned that someone as young, handsome and powerful as this king was unafraid to die. 'Surely he must have a strong mind,' the young man thought and asked the reason for his lack of fear. King Chandra replied, 'Because I have trained myself in the practice of virtue I no longer have anything to be frightened of.' As soon as he heard these words the young man developed strong faith in the practice of virtue. He listened attentively as the king told of the suffering results that would certainly follow from his harmful and vicious actions. After receiving many teachings on the workings of actions and their effects, the youth felt deep regret for his past evils and promised from the depths of his heart never to commit any more. The subduing of the young man and the overcoming of danger were all accomplished because King Chandra had eradicated all fear by controlling his own mind. In the same way, if we secure the wild elephant of our mind to the proper object of virtue, our fears will likewise be overcome.

[6] As the fully perfect Buddha Shakyamuni stated in *Cloud of Jewels Sutra* (Skt. *Ratnameghasutra*), all the infinite miseries and fears of this and future lives arise from our mind. Not only by scriptural authority but also by logical reasoning can we understand that all our faults and problems depend upon our mind. Yet most of us do not stop to consider whether this is true or not; we automatically assume that both our suffering and our happiness arise only because of external causes and conditions. We believe that outer circumstances are the sole factors determining our state of mind. Some Indian schools of philosophy, for example, believe that everything is the creation of the gods Ishvara or Brahma. They believe all our experiences depend entirely upon them.

Buddhist philosophy offers a different explanation. According to its teachings, suffering and happiness arise principally from the mind. In fact, the entire universe and all the beings in it originate from the power of mind. Everything that exists is shaped by the power of mind and all that we encounter and experience is determined by our mind.

This is a complex subject and we will return to it later in the ninth chapter. But let us investigate it here a little further. When we see our relatives and friends in a dream we believe at that time that they are really there, existing as something external to us. This, however, is not the case; what we have seen were dream images that merely arose from our own mind. Furthermore, when we watch the images on a motion picture screen we receive the impression that these pictures originate from somewhere in front of us when in fact they are being projected from behind us. Just as dream and motion picture images seem to have a certain 'external' existence in the ways described, when in fact they do not exist in their apparent manner at all, so the appearance of people and things in the universe seems to exist externally to us when in fact this appearance actually originates from our own mind. People without any Dharma understanding – those who have never done any in-depth analysis of the relation between appearance and reality – may perhaps laugh at such a view, but if we are ever to obtain an ultimate realization of the true nature of reality, the emptiness or lack of inherent existence of all phenomena, we must investigate this view thoroughly. This issue is too important to be dismissed lightly.

If all the places in the universe and the living creatures dwelling therein did not originate from the mind, then, as Shantideva asks in one of the most famous verses of this text:

[7] Who purposely creates all the weapons of hell? Who creates the burning iron ground? And where do the enticing women come from?

[8] Because every environment and all living beings have come into existence as a result of sentient beings' accumulation of collective and individual karma, and because karma is created by the mind, within the entire scope of the universe there is nothing to fear but our own uncontrolled and evil mind.

Every Dharma practice also depends upon the mind. Shantideva next explains how the six perfections of giving, moral discipline, patience, effort, concentration and wisdom are all primarily activities of the mind and depend upon it for their substance and effectiveness.

[9] We may ask why, if Buddha Shakyamuni and the other enlightened beings have perfected giving, are there so many beggars and still so much poverty remaining in the world? The reason is that giving is not perfected by eradicating all poverty, but by familiarizing ourself completely with the thought that is prepared to give up everything we have – our body, possessions, and the fruits of virtue – to other beings. The practice of giving does not merely entail bestowing gifts upon others, although this is definitely part of it. [10] Rather, giving is a mental training and involves acquainting ourself with the thought of giving without desiring anything in return. This perfection is not aimed at eradicating external poverty, though it undoubtedly helps alleviate want, but at eradicating our own internal miserliness. Therefore we can see that the true practice of giving depends entirely upon our mind.

In a similar manner, [11] the perfection of moral discipline does not merely entail such actions as saving the lives of others, for instance, by removing fish, deer and other animals from situations of danger and placing them in safety. Instead, moral discipline refers to a mind that abandons all non-virtuous actions. It is the maintenance and guarding of this mind that constitutes the true practice of moral discipline. Once the mind has become completely accustomed to abandoning every trace of non-virtue and transgression of vows, it has achieved the perfection of moral discipline. Thus this perfection, too, depends entirely upon the mind.

The next perfection is that of patience. It concerns the way we react to the beings and objects that harm us. [12] We must realize that there is no way for us to overcome all our external foes. If we defeat one enemy, another always arises to take his or her place. If we kill someone who has harmed us, his relatives and friends will attack us in revenge. How is it possible, Shantideva asks, to be free from all enemies who are as infinite as the expanse of space? Only by defeating our own anger can we overcome those who would harm us.

[13] If we want to be protected while walking over rough and rocky ground it is not realistic to think of covering the earth with leather. This would be impossible. Yet if we had enough leather merely to cover the soles of our own feet we would be able to walk anywhere. [14] In a similar manner, it is far better simply to control our own anger than to try to defeat our external foes. Abandoning anger depends upon training the mind. Perfecting patience does not merely entail refraining from retaliating when we are harmed. It depends on familiarizing our mind with the willingness to endure the pains and discomfort of suffering. As with the others, this practice is predominantly a mental one.

[15] There are many spiritual practices that can lead us into states of unimaginable happiness and good fortune. For example, by collecting the type of karma that is created when we develop a concentrated mind of equipoise we can take rebirth in one of the god realms of Brahma and so forth. Achieving such states of intense pleasure is not possible through practices involving our body or speech; it is only by training the mind that such results can be experienced. However, in order to generate a sufficiently powerful and concentrated state of consciousness to achieve such an extraordinary rebirth we need to train our mind with great perseverance and diligence. Thus, the perfection of effort also depends upon how well we train our mind.

[16] Reciting mantras, prostrating, fasting and so forth are all practices that can generate a great deal of positive energy. But if our mind wanders during these practices they will be without benefit or meaning. The perfection of concentration concerns training the mind so that it remains focused upon an object of our choice. When this concentration becomes effortless and completely unwavering the state of tranquil abiding can be attained. This is a very significant achievement and, as is obvious, does not depend primarily upon our body or speech but upon the state of our mind.

[17] We all wish to be free from suffering and to obtain happiness but this will not be possible if we fail to uncover the sublime secret of the mind, the most significant of all Dharma realizations: the emptiness of true existence. To gain this subtle understanding and develop the wisdom realizing emptiness depends mainly upon our mental effort; physical and verbal activities by themselves are not sufficient. Therefore wisdom and all the other perfections, as well as all the delusions and imperfections they overcome,

are mental factors and depend upon the mind for their very existence.

[18] There is no point in engaging in the many different practices of Dharma if we do not guard our mind well, but what exactly is to be guarded? It is the five sense consciousnesses – eye, ear, nose, tongue and body consciousness – and mental consciousness. How, for example, do we guard our eye consciousness? We do this by preventing our attention from wandering to those visual objects that cause attachment, anger or other delusions to arise. Similarly our ear consciousness should be guarded from distracting sounds that foster delusions. The same is true for all the other consciousnesses; they should be kept in check and prevented from wandering towards what is non-virtuous. This is what is meant by guarding the mind.

Of these six the most important is the mental consciousness, which we normally refer to as the mind itself. This is primarily what must be guarded if we wish to train ourself according to Dharma and overcome all negativities. For example, our eye consciousness might perceive an object of attachment, but if our mental consciousness is well guarded the delusion of attachment will not arise. We need not shut ourself off from all visual stimuli in order to overcome our delusions; if we gain control over our mind there are no external objects that can possibly harm us. Gaining this control is especially important during our meditation practices, most specifically when we are trying to develop deep concentration. If we do not learn how to guard our mind properly we will not receive results from even the most advanced Dharma practices.

Shantideva emphasizes the importance of guarding our mind by drawing the following analogy:

[19-20] If a part of our body were wounded and we had to walk through a jostling crowd, we would be especially careful to guard and cover that wound. In a similar manner, when we are dwelling among harmful people or objects that cause our delusions to arise, we should guard the wound of our mind carefully.

If we are anxious to protect an ordinary wound that can at most give us but a little temporary pain, then surely we should be highly motivated to guard the wound of our mind. If our mind remains unprotected and uncontrolled it can lead us into hellish experiences of deep suffering and torment until we feel we are being crushed between two mighty mountains.

It is true that being in the centre of a crowd can be a very beneficial experience. We can consider everything we see as a dream. As Milarepa said, 'I don't need to read books; wherever I go and whatever I see serves to develop my mind.' However, there are certain circumstances during which it is especially important to exercise control over our mind and guard it from delusion. [21] If, for example, we must associate with people who are so uncontrolled and irreligious that their only practice is non-virtue, we must guard ourself well or we will be tainted by their many faults. If we spend a lot of time in the company of those who deny the existence of actions and their effects, the continuity of consciousness, the possibility of liberation and so forth, we run the risk of falling under their influence. If our mind is well guarded, however, we will remain unaffected. Furthermore, those who have taken certain ordination vows must be careful when entering situations that could lead to a transgression of these vows. Monks and nuns, for example, should be particularly careful when associating with the opposite sex; at such times they should post a strong guard at the door of their mind. Lay people as well should exercise caution whenever they find themselves in circumstances of great temptation or non-virtue. The best way to keep our good qualities and our vows from degenerating is to be diligent in guarding our mind. As Shantideva says:

[22] It is far better to let our body, honour, livelihood, wealth and other virtues decline than to let our practice of guarding the mind decline.

Therefore, from this moment on we should try our best to gain control over our life and keep whatever good qualities we have developed from degenerating.

## THE METHOD OF GUARDING THE MIND IS
## TO PRACTISE MINDFULNESS AND ALERTNESS

In this section Shantideva introduces the mental factors of mindfulness and alertness, the two forces we employ when guarding our mind. The importance of employing these two mental factors is explained under the following six headings:

1. A brief presentation of the two factors
2. Without mindfulness and alertness our virtue will have little power
3. Without mindfulness and alertness we will not develop pure wisdom
4. Without mindfulness and alertness we cannot practise pure moral discipline
5. Without mindfulness and alertness previously accumulated virtue will degenerate

6 Without mindfulness and alertness new virtue cannot be accumulated

## A BRIEF PRESENTATION OF THE TWO FACTORS

Shantideva begins this section with the following request:

> [23] With my palms pressed together, I beseech those who wish to guard their minds from delusion: be diligent and hold on to mindfulness and alertness at all times!

What exactly is mindfulness? This mental factor can be explained according to three characteristics: its object, nature and function. First of all, mindfulness focuses on an object with which the mind has previously become acquainted. Second, it is the nature of mindfulness not to forget this object but to hold it. Finally, the function of this mental factor is not to wander away from the object it is holding. Thus it is obvious that without mindfulness we can make no progress in our studies. At the beginning, middle and end of our practice, mindfulness and alertness are of the utmost importance in attaining virtuous qualities.

The mental factor alertness is a type of wisdom. For example, if we have placed our mind on an object with mindfulness, alertness is the factor that checks to see if our mind has fallen under the control of mental sinking or mental excitement. It looks to see whether our meditation is proceeding well or badly. Thus it is a type of wisdom that examines our mind and understands how it is functioning. Alertness is the fruit of mindfulness and has a very close connection with it. While mindfulness holds on to its object, alertness observes whether or not the mind has wandered from that object.

We can illustrate how these two mental factors operate together as follows. Let us say we are trying to visualize the figure of Buddha Shakyamuni. First we look at a painting or a statue and then we try to generate a mental image of what we have seen. This mental picture becomes the object of our visualization, and having found this object our mindfulness holds it and does not wander away. When the mind is placed upon the object single-pointedly, this is what is known as 'concentration'. As we practise concentration we should occasionally check to see if our meditation is progressing well or if interruptions and obstacles have arisen. This spy-like function of the mind is alertness. If alertness discovers that the mind has fallen under the influence of sinking or excitement we can grasp the object once again with mindfulness and continue our meditation.

## WITHOUT MINDFULNESS AND ALERTNESS OUR VIRTUE WILL HAVE LITTLE POWER

[24] A man who is afflicted by sickness is powerless to act as he wishes. In the same way, if our mind wanders towards delusion because our mental factor of mindfulness has declined, we will be powerless to accomplish any virtuous deed.

## WITHOUT MINDFULNESS AND ALERTNESS WE WILL NOT DEVELOP PURE WISDOM

[25] If a vase has a leak in it, it cannot be used to hold water. A mind that lacks mindfulness and alertness is similar to such a broken vase. It cannot retain whatever is placed in it through the three wisdoms of listening, contemplation and

meditation. Such excellent qualities as the wisdom that realizes emptiness cannot grow in such a weak mind.

## WITHOUT MINDFULNESS AND ALERTNESS WE CANNOT PRACTISE PURE MORAL DISCIPLINE

[26] We may have deep faith in Dharma and have heard and studied many teachings, but without mindfulness and alertness it is certain that many faults will arise in our behaviour. We run the risk of breaking our vows and thereby polluting our mind. If we wish to keep pure moral discipline therefore, we must grasp these two mental factors firmly.

## WITHOUT MINDFULNESS AND ALERTNESS PREVIOUSLY ACCUMULATED VIRTUE WILL DEGENERATE

[27] If our wealth and possessions are not safely secured within our homes, thieves can easily break in, steal what we own and leave us empty-handed. In the same way, the virtue we have accumulated in the past can be stolen by the thief of anger if it has not been secured by the mental factors of mindfulness and alertness. Furthermore, through a lack of mindfulness we will be led to commit non-virtuous actions in the future and will therefore fall into the three lower realms.

## WITHOUT MINDFULNESS AND ALERTNESS NEW VIRTUE CANNOT BE ACCUMULATED

[28] If we become separated from these two mental factors, not only will our previous virtues degenerate but we will be powerless to create new ones. Furthermore, whatever potential we have created to be reborn in the fortunate realms of

existence will be destroyed. In addition, the possibility of our attaining liberation or enlightenment is completely eradicated.

Of the two mental factors we have been talking about, it is more important for us to develop mindfulness because alertness arises naturally from it. [29] Thus we should never let mindfulness stray from the doorway of our mind. If we feel that our mindfulness is about to decline, we should immediately reflect upon the sufferings of the lower realms and renew the hold of our mind upon its object.

If we wish to develop mindfulness there are both outer and inner circumstances that can help us. [30] The outer circumstances refer to following the instructions of our Spiritual Guide, which will remind us of the suffering of the lower realms and of the need to honour the vows we have taken before our Abbot or Preceptor. Such recollection will re-establish our mindfulness and, if we follow our Spiritual Guide continuously, we will not only remember the good qualities of Dharma that we once knew but will become aware of many other positive qualities as well.

[31] As for arranging the inner circumstances, this refers to cultivating the thought: 'I am always dwelling in the presence of all the Buddhas and Bodhisattvas.' This is a very beneficial practice because we will be unlikely to commit a non-virtuous action if we remember that the enlightened beings can see all things without obstructions.

A Buddha's omniscient mind encompasses all objects of knowledge, and wherever his omniscience pervades his body also manifests. There is no place where a Buddha does not exist. Therefore, whenever we remember the enlightened beings they are in fact present at that very place. We cannot say that because we fail to see a Buddha there is no enlightened being present. At our stage of development we do not possess the eye that can see a Buddha's actual form. Thus, even though they are not visible to us at the moment, we should always remember that we are dwelling in their presence.

[32] If we can train our mind to think in this way, we will grow circumspect about our behaviour. This will be based upon our respect for the Three Jewels and our dread of the ripening effects of non-virtuous karma. Our body, speech and mind will be kept free from defilements and we will be able to practise Dharma purely. On the other hand, if we fail to recognize that we are always dwelling in the presence of the Buddhas and Bodhisattvas, we will remain engrossed in the worldly concerns of gain and loss while associating with others, and we will harbour non-virtuous thoughts when remaining by ourself. If we develop strong faith in the Buddhas and Bodhisattvas and follow their advice faithfully we will be able to maintain a firm state of mindfulness. [33] With the door of our mind thus guarded from delusion we will naturally develop alertness. When we have cultivated these two mental factors well, we will be able to engage in the various types of moral discipline described next.

## HOW TO PRACTISE MORAL DISCIPLINE BY MEANS OF MINDFULNESS AND ALERTNESS

The practice of moral discipline is the main topic of the fifth chapter and is presented in terms of its three aspects:

1. Practising the moral discipline of restraint
2. Practising the moral discipline of gathering virtue
3. Practising the moral discipline of benefiting sentient beings

Moral discipline is defined as the intention to abandon all faults, downfalls and non-virtue. Every practice of moral discipline is contained within the three headings listed above.

## PRACTISING THE MORAL DISCIPLINE OF RESTRAINT

The moral discipline of restraint is an extensive subject but its primary concern is simply to prevent improper conduct of our body, speech and mind. Because we have taken Bodhisattva vows we should take Shantideva's words on this subject as advice and try to practise in strict accordance with it. [34] The basic practice is as follows: at the very beginning of any action, whether it is thought, word or physical deed, we should examine our motivation to see whether it is virtuous or non-virtuous. If we discover that the motive behind the action we are contemplating is defiled by one of the delusions such as jealousy, greed or ill will, we should bring to mind the faults of that delusion and immediately abandon it.

This superior method of guarding the mind through the application of mindfulness and alertness will not always prove effective. If we are not familiar with this method of checking the mind, or if our delusions arise too strongly to be banished immediately, then we have to resort to other methods of guarding our behaviour. One effective way to deal with strong delusions is to remain for a short while as if we were a piece of wood – unmoving, non-reactive and without thought. If we can avoid giving expression to our delusions in this way, the object that aroused the defiled mind will soon be forgotten and the delusion itself will subside. Examples of how to employ this particular method will be given later.

Shantideva now gives specific advice on how we should conduct ourself so that we can avoid non-virtuous actions. As practitioners emulating the Bodhisattva ideal, we should train our body according to the Bodhisattva precepts. [35] When walking we should not let our gaze wander about in a distracted manner, looking here and there for no purpose. We should cast our eyes downwards and look at the ground on which we are about to tread. Of course [36] if there is a need or if we wish to relax, we may look around us. During our walk we may encounter others, and we should greet them warmly. [37] As we continue walking we should occasionally look in the four directions to be certain there are no dangers or obstacles. [38] When we have examined the situation well, we should proceed.

Although it is important to be mindful of our actions, we should not fall to the extreme of thinking, 'I am a Bodhisattva guarding my behaviour; it is beneath my practice to socialize with worldly people.' Our conduct should not only be pure but also well-mannered. As long as there is a good reason for adapting our behaviour to comply with local custom and others' expectations, we should do so without thinking that it contradicts our precepts.

[39] In terms of our bodily conduct, we should check again and again to see whether or not it is virtuous. [40] And just as our bodily conduct must be stainless, so too must our mental conduct be impeccable. Binding the wild elephant of our mind to the pillar of Dharma virtue [41] we should remain undistracted by delusion. With the power of alertness we should examine all of our actions with great vigilance.

[42] As was said earlier, there is no moral precept that a Bodhisattva fails to practise and observe. However, circumstances may arise in which it is better to commit certain

normally non-virtuous actions than it is to bind ourself to a specific moral code. Of course it takes wisdom to determine when it is appropriate to relax our moral discipline and when it is better to be strict. If we keep our bodhichitta motivation in mind, however, we will find it much easier to make the correct discriminations. Our basic consideration should be: 'What is more beneficial for others? What is the best way of dealing with the situation so that they receive the most good?'

Our practice should always be realistic. We have to take into account not only our own limitations but also the changing circumstances around us. There are situations, for example, in which our own life or that of someone else may be in great danger; at such times it may not be possible or even preferable for us to refrain from lying. We have to deal with the total situation and do whatever is most appropriate and beneficial. Although Bodhisattvas take vows not to engage in idle singing, dancing or the playing of music, there are certain times when it serves a greater purpose to engage in these actions. We should do whatever is most important at the particular moment; we must use our intelligence as much as we can.

It may help to give specific examples of situations in which a Bodhisattva is permitted to break the vow not to lie. Imagine that a man is pursuing a dog in order to kill it. If a Bodhisattva saw where the dog was hiding, then even if he is asked by its pursuer if he has seen the dog, he is permitted to reply, 'No, I don't know where it is.' The Bodhisattva's primary duty and responsibility is to save the dog from being killed.

If he fails to do so, thinking that it is more important to avoid lying, then he is breaking the more important

Bodhisattva vow of working for the benefit of all sentient beings. In this situation the Bodhisattva should see that the practice of protecting others from fear – one aspect of the perfection of giving – served a more important purpose than refraining from the non-virtue of lying. The Bodhisattva should realize that to tell an untruth to a would-be killer is not actually lying because his motivation is undefiled by delusions or the thought of self-cherishing. Only a being whose mind is pervaded by great compassion, however, can make such discriminations between what is proper and what is improper in many of these situations.

The previous illustration is an example of when it is appropriate to lie in order to protect the lives of others. There are even circumstances in which it is appropriate to lie to save our own life. For certain beings in certain situations it is better for them to give up their own lives than to engage in any non-virtuous action whatsoever. Generally, however, our life is of such great value that it would be wrong to give it away for an unimportant reason. This precious human body is the vehicle in which we can travel along the Mahayana path to full enlightenment. To give it up for no great purpose would prevent us from proceeding along this path and being of benefit to others. Our death would indirectly harm all those whom we could have helped had we remained alive. Therefore it is generally much more important to preserve our own life, provided we are motivated by a compassionate impulse, than it is to comply too rigidly with a lesser moral injunction and allow ourself to be killed.

There is another traditional example used to explain how a Bodhisattva can even commit murder if this is beneficial to others. In a previous life Buddha Shakyamuni was a ship's captain and one day he was ferrying five hundred merchants across the sea. With his powers of clairvoyance he realized that one of the merchants was planning to kill all the others. He thought to himself, 'If he carries out his plan he will not only cause four hundred and ninety-nine people to lose their lives but will also create the cause for being reborn in the lower realms.' The captain realized that if he killed the would-be assassin he could prevent all five hundred people from being harmed. Therefore, with the motivation of great compassion he killed that merchant. As a result of this selfless action the captain purified much negative karma accumulated throughout many aeons and also collected limitless merit. This story illustrates the range of a Bodhisattva's actions, but most of us are not able to practise like this at the moment. We should be aware of our level of attainment and understand our limitations for, as the saying goes, if a jackal tries to jump where a tiger leaps he will only break his neck!

[43] After we have checked our motivation and have decided upon a virtuous course of action we should try to perform that action with a high degree of mindfulness. We should do one thing at a time and do it well. It is unwise to start one thing, switch to something else, return to the original task and so on. If we behave in such an inconsistent manner we will never receive the fruits of any of our actions. [44] On the other hand, if we check our motivation well, decide upon a particular practice or activity and then complete what we have started, we will be able to maintain a superior level of alertness. By means of this alertness we will automatically prevent any of the root or secondary delusions from polluting our mind. In this way we can transform all of our daily experiences into the practice of Dharma.

Shantideva now gives specific advice on how to deal with a wide range of potentially disturbing situations. He says that [45] when we are associating with people engaged in senseless chatter or when we are watching a spectacle or a drama, we should keep our mind free from all attachment. With mindfulness and alertness we should keep a watch on our mind and avoid falling under the influence of desire and distraction. We should also control the mindless activities of our body. [46] Unless there is some purpose for our doing so, we should not dig the earth, cut the grass, draw patterns on the ground or engage in any other meaningless activity. We should recall the advice of the enlightened beings, bring to mind the heavy consequences of mindlessness and refrain from all senseless actions.

[47] If we are engaged in some activity and the intention arises to move about and say something we should immediately examine our mind. Should we decide that our motivation is defiled and our intended behaviour is unworthy of a Bodhisattva, we should seize the mind and make it firm. We should not let our habits dominate our behaviour or act as if we were sleepwalking. It is important to be as alert and mindful as possible at all times. [48] If attachment arises or we notice the tendency for anger to overwhelm us, we should think deeply about the many faults of these two delusions and reject them completely. If this is not possible at the moment, then for a short period of time we should remain like a mindless piece of wood, neither doing nor saying anything.

As was mentioned earlier, we do not always possess the strength of mind to abandon our delusions the moment they arise or to transform them into something beneficial. Because our mind is not yet well trained, it will often happen that our deluded impulses are too powerful to be wrestled with in this manner. When this is the case, instead of attempting the impossible we should merely be as unresponsive as possible to the thoughts flooding our mind. By depriving them of energy in this way, we will prevent our delusions from motivating our behaviour and they will soon fade away of their own accord. This is an extremely skilful and realistic way of dealing with our mind and is an excellent method for increasing our moral strength.

[49] Shantideva then mentions specific instances when it is advisable to remain like a mindless piece of wood. We can do this when our mind is very distracted or when the thought arises to belittle, slander, or abuse others. [50] If pride, haughtiness or the intention to find fault with others arises, we can also remain impassive until our deluded motivation fades. Feeling pretentious, thinking to deceive others and wishing to praise our own qualities, wealth, or possessions are all occasions when it is wise to pretend that we are made out of wood. Whenever we have the desire to blame others, speak harshly or cause disruption we should practise this technique of non-reaction.

[51] Furthermore, we should not give in to the desire to seek worldly gain, reputation, honour, veneration, fame and so forth. Whenever the wish arises to gather a circle of admirers or to be served by others we should also remain like wood. [52] And if, because the mind is distracted, the thought arises to work only for our own benefit and neglect the welfare of others, or to say something from this selfish motivation, we should again be unresponsive. [53] Should our practice of Dharma be interrupted by impatience, laziness, fear, shamelessness or the desire to speak without meaning, it is wise not to give energy to any of these thoughts. Finally, if strong attachment arises to our relatives or friends we should remain as impassive as wood.

[54] Thus the Bodhisattva should always be guarding his or her mind against the arising of disturbing thoughts and the desire to engage in non-virtuous and meaningless activities. Whenever he sees a danger arise, he should apply the appropriate counter-measure and hold firmly on to his mind. [55] Practising virtue resolutely and generating such positive qualities as faith, steadfastness, respect, politeness, sense of shame and consideration for others, the Bodhisattva maintains a peaceful mind and a dread of committing non-virtuous actions, and strives diligently to bring happiness to all.

It may often happen that a Bodhisattva's selfless actions provoke jealousy and so forth in others. [56] If we are trying to emulate a Bodhisattva's deeds and this happens to us, we should not become disheartened. We should realize that such reactions are merely the whims of the immature. Even if we receive harm from the person we are trying to befriend we should remember that he is only acting in this way through the force of his delusions. Knowing what a burden it is to be forced to live with such defiled thoughts, we should develop even more love and compassion for this unfortunate being and wish that he may soon be removed from his suffering.

[57] While working for the benefit of others we should try to keep our mind free from defilements and avoid transgressing our vows. We should try to overcome pride in our actions and keep our mind well-balanced. Having accustomed our mind to the correct view of reality, we should regard everything and everyone we encounter as if they were a magician's illusion. [58] It is also extremely important to reflect on the great significance and the rarity of having attained this precious human life. By holding on to our mind with mindfulness and alertness we should try to make it as firm as Mount Meru, the unshakeable king of all

mountains, and thereby extract the greatest value from this unique opportunity to give meaning to our existence.

The essence of Dharma practice is to abandon non-virtue, practise whatever is virtuous and gain control over our mind. If we are unable to do this then our claim to have done a lot of meditation and many retreats is empty of meaning. If we meditated for a full year and then, upon examination, discovered that our delusions had not subsided at all and that our mind was as wild as before, then that year of meditation was purposeless and produced little fruit. As Buddha Shakyamuni himself said:

> Not to commit any evil action,
> To accumulate a wealth of excellent virtue
> And to tame our mind –
> This is the teaching of the enlightened ones.

The nature of our mind is like the pure, blue sky. However, at present our mind is obscured by the myriad clouds of delusions and our wild disturbing thoughts. Only the practice of Dharma dispels these clouds of obscuration and allows the pure nature of the mind to shine forth freely. Anyone who has removed all traces of delusion from his or her mind and has attained the state of complete purity is called a 'Buddha'. Therefore, no matter what practice we may be doing, we should check to see that it is actually decreasing our delusions and bringing our mind under control. We should keep this criterion in mind at all times and judge our practices accordingly. There is no value in reciting the mere words of a practice if our mind is not receiving any benefit.

The three types of moral discipline discussed in this chapter are mainly practised by those who have taken the Bodhisattva vows. We may therefore think, 'Since I am not a

Bodhisattva, what need is there for me to study and practise in this way?' This is a mistaken way of thinking. Even before vows are formally taken we must train in developing bodhichitta and try to observe the appropriate moral behaviour. It is only by training in this way that we can prepare ourself for the actual practices of a Bodhisattva. As beginners we may not be able to do everything a Bodhisattva does, but if we practise the three types of moral discipline according to our own capacity we will be creating the cause to achieve the actual state of a Bodhisattva in the future.

For someone who has taken the Bodhisattva vows, the moral discipline of restraint means to refrain from all defilements and faults. A layperson who has not yet taken the Bodhisattva vows practises the moral discipline of restraint by refraining mainly from the ten non-virtuous actions. These include the three non-virtuous actions of body (killing, stealing and engaging in sexual misconduct), the four of speech (lying, divisive speech, hurtful speech and idle chatter) and the three of mind (covetousness, malice, or ill will, and holding wrong views). If we practise restraint with respect to our body, speech and mind we will be able to ensure that these non-virtuous actions are not committed and will therefore be free of their harmful effects.

It may be beneficial to give a brief outline of the ten non-virtuous actions in terms of the four factors needed to bring each action to full fruition. These four are (1) the object of the action, (2) our intention while performing the action, (3) the type of action and (4) the completion of the action. If we understand these four factors well we will be in a position to decrease the strength of, and eventually eliminate, all our non-virtues. The four factors for each of the ten non-virtuous actions are as follows:

## *Killing*

(1) The object of killing is any other living being.
(2) Our intention is to kill that being.
(3) The action involves making an effort to kill by means of poison, weapons and so forth.
(4) The action is complete when the being dies before we do.

## *Stealing*

(1) The object is anything that does not belong to us or has not been freely given to us.
(2) Our intention is the desire to possess that object.
(3) The action involves removing the object by any means including fraud and deception.
(4) The action is complete when we regard the stolen object as our own.

## *Sexual Misconduct*

(1) The object is someone other than our partner, someone else's partner, or someone who is not a legitimate or willing object of our sexual attentions. Even our own partner can be the object of sexual misconduct if the action takes place in any of the following circumstances: before images of the Buddhas and Bodhisattvas or on days when special vows have been taken.
(2) Our intention is the desire to have sexual intercourse.
(3) Our action involves making an effort to accomplish this intention.

(4) The action is complete when we accept with delight the feelings resulting from our action.

## *Lying*

(1) The object can be any other person.
(2) Our intention is to distort the truth by claiming, for example, that something is true while it is actually untrue.
(3) The action involves uttering falsehoods or misleading others in any way, even by means of bodily actions.
(4) The full completion of this action occurs when the lie is accepted by the other person as being true.

## *Divisive speech*

(1) The object must be two or more people.
(2) Our intention is to cause disunity between these people.
(3) The action is making an effort in spreading rumours, sowing doubt and so forth.
(4) The action is complete when our divisive speech is heard by others, and as a result disharmony between them either arises or increases.

## *Hurtful speech*

(1) The object can be any other person.
(2) Our intention is the wish to speak out of anger in a hurtful manner.
(3) The action is to speak hurtfully to another.
(4) The action is complete when another person hears and understands our words.

## *Idle chatter*

(1) The object can be any other person.
(2) Our intention is to utter nonsense or even sing without any purpose.
(3) The action is to communicate this nonsense or purposeless speech to others.
(4) The action is complete whenever these words are spoken.

## *Covetousness*

(1) The object of this action is anything that belongs to others.
(2) Our intention is to get the object.
(3) The action involves repeatedly planning how to get the object.
(4) The action is complete when we abandon any sense of shame or fear of blame from thinking in such a covetous manner.

## *Malice*

(1) The object is any other person.
(2) Our intention is to kill or otherwise harm that person.
(3) The action is to make plans for accomplishing this aim.
(4) The full completion of this action is to fail to see how it is non-virtuous.

## *Holding wrong views*

(1) The object includes virtuous and non-virtuous phenomena.

(2) Our intention is to hold on to views concerning these objects that are contrary to the teachings of Dharma.
(3) The action involves believing firmly in our mistaken views. These include maintaining that karma and its fruit are non-existent, that the four noble truths are deceptive, that there is no such thing as the continuity of consciousness, and that phenomena cannot be classified as virtuous or non-virtuous.
(4) The action is complete when we have become totally convinced of the correctness of our mistaken views and have no understanding with which to oppose them.

This concludes the discussion of practising the moral discipline of restraint. A Bodhisattva should recognize any fault of body, speech and mind as soon as it arises and abandon it immediately. However, in situations of great danger or when the greater good of others is involved – in short, whenever there is a greater purpose – the skilful Bodhisattva is permitted to break any of the restraints of body or speech. At no time, however, is he or she to commit any of the non-virtuous actions of mind for this would be to abandon his intention to work for the benefit of all sentient beings.

## PRACTISING THE MORAL DISCIPLINE OF GATHERING VIRTUE

This has two parts:

1 Abandoning attachment to the body
2 Practising virtue with skilful means

## ABANDONING ATTACHMENT TO THE BODY

If we do not reduce attachment to our own body it will be impossible for us to keep pure moral discipline. For the sake of protecting our body we harm others and engage in a host of other non-virtuous actions. Therefore we should ask ourself, [59] 'Why do I cherish this body so strongly? Why do I guard it and think that it is mine?' When death separates us from our physical form we will depart alone without friends. Who will guard our body then? If we cannot protect it at that time, why are we so anxious to guard it now?

Who will inherit our body once we have died? In some countries the discarded body becomes a banquet for vultures and jackals. In others it is cremated and becomes little different from firewood. In still others it is buried and becomes like the mud and dirt. Finally, a corpse might be thrown into the sea where it is slowly devoured by fish. If we can recognize that the body we care so much for now is potentially a banquet, firewood or dirt, we will not cling to it with such strong attachment and feel it is truly ours. If after such considerations we still desire to guard our body, then we must guard it well because the uncompromising Lord of Death will soon descend.

[60] We are not the same as our body and soon we will be separated from it. Therefore, is there any meaning or purpose in protecting and being attached to it? We might argue, 'Because this body has been mine for a long time I should continue to guard it.' Yet such an answer betrays the confusion of an ignorant mind. To begin with, there is no independent, self-existent I that possesses anything. And why should we hold on to our aggregates, pus, blood, limbs, excrement, urine and so forth as if these were truly 'I'

or 'mine'? [61] If we want to guard something it would be much more sensible to guard a clean wooden form than to be possessive of this putrid machine filled with impurities.

The type of guarding or protecting that Shantideva is talking about here is that which is based upon the delusion of attachment. In order to overcome this delusion we should analyze our body minutely to see if we can discover anything that is clean and pure and worthy of such exaggerated possessiveness. [62] Mentally dissect the body. Peel the skin away from the flesh and check to see if the skin is pure or not. Cut the flesh from the bones and ask ourself if this is clean? [63] What about the marrow inside the bones? With the scalpel of wisdom we should make a thorough investigation and see what we find. [64] If after such close analysis there is no essence at all to be found, why are we still attached to our physical form? Where is that pure essence that we instinctively hold to be our I? As Shantideva so graphically states:

> [65-66ab] Our body is so dirty inside, of what use could it possibly be? It is unfit to eat, our blood is unfit to drink and our intestines are unfit to suck. Perhaps the only reason we are guarding our body is to be able to feed it to the vultures and jackals later on.

[66cd] The only reason for us to be protective of our body is if we are going to use it for the practice of virtue. [67] Otherwise we are doing nothing more than preparing food for jackals. [68] If our body is not going to be useful to us, then nourishing it with food and kindness is like paying wages to a servant who does no work. If we regarded our body as our servant instead of our master as we normally do, we would develop a more realistic attitude towards its care and feeding. [69] We would be glad to pay it its proper

wages if it helped us to engage in the practice of Dharma for our own and others' benefit, but critical and strict whenever we discovered that it was not benefiting anyone.

[70] Another way to look at our body is as if it were a boat. Our consciousness could then be viewed as a traveller seeking the jewelled island of enlightenment. In order to sail across the ocean of samsara and reach our goal it is very important to maintain our boat – the precious human body – until we achieve our destination and acquire the wishful-filling jewel that is the fully purified body of a Buddha.

In summary, we need to strike a balance by reducing our clinging, possessive attitude to the body while still maintaining it as a vehicle for our spiritual practices. The best way of achieving this balance is by decreasing or preventing our attachment and this can be accomplished in two ways. The first is to contemplate the body's impurity by analyzing each of its five parts: skin, flesh, bone, marrow and inner organs. The second is to meditate on the body's lack of inherent existence by seeing that nowhere among its parts is there an essential entity to be found. This second analysis, which will be explained more fully in the ninth chapter, will dissolve our concrete conception of what the body is and who we are, and thereby destroy the very foundations upon which attachment arises. By meditating on impurity and emptiness we can also reduce and eventually eliminate the attachment that arises towards someone else's body. A basic question we should always ask ourself is: 'Exactly what is it that I am attached to?'

## PRACTISING VIRTUE WITH SKILFUL MEANS

The second aspect of practising the moral discipline of gathering virtue is divided into three sections:

1 Following pure conduct of the body
2 Following skilful conduct when associating with others
3 Following skilful conduct of body, speech and mind

## FOLLOWING PURE CONDUCT OF THE BODY

[71] When we meet others we should display a smiling face towards them, abandon all frowns and, as a friend of the world, generate love and compassion. A Bodhisattva communicates with others honestly and, motivated by a kind heart, speaks gently and endearingly to them.

[72] We should try as much as possible to be considerate of others, especially when they are meditating. We should not handle things noisily or move furniture around needlessly. We should open doors quietly and gently, without making any noise. A Bodhisattva takes delight in acting discreetly with total humility. [73] Just as a stork, a thief and a cat move silently and accomplish their tasks, so does a Bodhisattva act. However, these practices are not restricted to Bodhisattvas; all those who aspire to what is virtuous should try to follow such exemplary behaviour.

## FOLLOWING SKILFUL CONDUCT WHEN ASSOCIATING WITH OTHERS

[74] When we are with our friends or acquaintances we should urge them skilfully and subtly to practise Dharma. We should also regard ourself as the pupil of others and accept any unasked for advice we may receive with gladness and respect. If another person should lecture us on Dharma

we should put away all pride and receive such teachings gratefully.

We should never be arrogant and think, 'I am a Bodhisattva and therefore superior to others.' Even Bodhisattvas on the higher stages of the path should associate with others according to the patterns of conventional conduct.

[75] Whenever we see others engaged in virtuous activity we should rejoice and give them praise or talk about their good qualities to others. [76] And if we hear someone else being praised we should join in and extol that person's virtue and good qualities even further. What should we do if we ourself are praised for having certain qualities? We should not become inflated with pride but merely recognize if we actually do possess these qualities or not.

In brief, we should let all our actions of body, speech and mind be directed towards the happiness of others. [77] Such beneficial conduct is rarely found in the world. Whether we are travelling, working, eating, drinking or engaging in any other activity whatsoever, let it be for the benefit of all beings. And especially when we speak we should consider only the welfare of others.

[78] What is the benefit of acting in this way? In this world it is an observable fact that if we are helpful and please others our kind deeds will be repaid; without question we will receive kindness from others. We will be liked and dearly appreciated and will find great happiness not only in this life but in future lives as well. On the other hand, if we are jealous of other peoples' good qualities, ungrateful and overly critical, our own mind will become unhappy and disturbed and we will be planting the seeds to experience much suffering in the future.

Instead of looking for faults in others' behaviour and extolling our own good qualities we should do just the opposite. It is the discipline of Dharma to examine our own behaviour regularly, face up to our own shortcomings and recognize good qualities in others. While the practices of Dharma are so vast that it is difficult to understand and follow them all, it is sufficient merely to train ourself in two disciplines: abandoning our faults and rejoicing in the good qualities of others. As the great Indian Teacher Atisha said:

> Do not look for faults in others, but look for faults in yourself, and purge them like bad blood.

> Do not contemplate your own good qualities, but contemplate the good qualities of others, and respect everyone as a servant would.

## FOLLOWING SKILFUL CONDUCT OF BODY, SPEECH AND MIND

[79] When communicating with others we should speak confidently, coherently and endearingly. We should not utter words out of attachment or anger but rather speak gently and with moderation. [80] Whenever we see another person we should think, 'Because of this very sentient being I can attain the enlightenment of Buddhahood', and look upon every living being the way a mother looks upon her only child.

[81] Whenever we think to engage in a particular practice we should first contemplate its benefits and thereby develop a strong aspiration for what we are about to do. For instance, if we are going to practise giving we can encourage ourself by bringing to mind the good qualities of generous giving

and also by thinking about the faults of miserliness, its opponent. If we do this type of contemplation beforehand our practices will be greatly strengthened.

Shantideva now mentions three groups of objects to which our virtuous activities can be directed. These he refers to as the 'field of excellence', the 'field of benefit' and the 'field of suffering'. These three can be explained by taking as our example the practice of giving. The field of excellence is the Three Jewels of refuge, and any offerings we make to them will lead to our accumulation of great benefit and merit. Because the objects of our practice possess the highest quality of realizations, the positive effects of our giving will be greatly increased. Next is the field of benefit, which refers to our own mother and father, and all others from whom we have received great kindness. Any giving we direct towards these kind benefactors will accumulate much merit. Finally, the field of suffering refers to all sentient beings who are tormented by disease, poverty and the like. To give aid, protection and so forth to these unfortunate beings will certainly be fruitful.

In general, giving is a highly meritorious activity no matter to whom it is directed. However, greater results follow if we are generous towards these three fields rather than towards ordinary beings not included in these categories. This is because the objects in these fields possess special qualities – excellence, great kindness and intense need, respectively – that increase the value of our virtuous actions and the merit created by these actions. By the same token, causing harm to these three fields creates heavier non-virtue than causing harm to ordinary beings or strangers.

[82] For our Dharma practices to be solid and well-based we need to have a clear understanding of them and

deep faith in their value. If these two conditions are met the results of our efforts will fall naturally into the palm of our hand. Attempting to practise Dharma, however, without first understanding the methods to be used is like trying to climb a steep mountain without using our hands. Furthermore, trying to meditate without faith and confidence in our practice is like trying to walk along a pathway with our eyes closed. There are people nowadays who say, 'Although I have meditated for a long time, I have not attained any realizations. Why is this?' Perhaps it is because they have not completely understood the method of practice and therefore lack faith and confidence in it. Shantideva points out that in order to practise Dharma correctly we must first study the teachings so that we can understand the methods. If we do this we will be able to engage in the actual practice without having to depend on anyone else.

[83] This section is concluded with a reminder that we should not abandon greater, more important virtuous actions for the sake of practising small virtues. We should try to cultivate a realistic attitude towards our practice and be balanced in what we do. Taking all things into consideration, we should try to determine which course of action is the most beneficial. For instance, although there are times when giving our body to others is a very advanced form of giving, we should not waste our precious human form merely to satisfy another's hunger. [84ab] We should always try to determine what will ultimately be more beneficial for others and then proceed with confidence and understanding.

## PRACTISING THE MORAL DISCIPLINE OF BENEFITING SENTIENT BEINGS

The two types of moral discipline so far discussed, those of restraint and gathering virtue, are primarily intended to tame our own mind. The person who is well-trained in these two types of moral discipline makes continuous efforts to practise the third: working for the welfare and benefit of all living beings. However, because the desires of living beings are limitless we may wonder if our moral discipline will become defiled by trying to fulfil these desires. The answer is that if our mind has been well-tamed there will be no danger of our morality declining.

[84cd] The compassionate Buddha who sees into the future and knows the course of all actions, prohibited those of lower motivation and those with self-cherishing from committing the seven non-virtuous actions of body and speech. However, in *Sutra on Skilful Means* (Skt. *Mahaguhyaupayakaushalyasutra*) he gave permission for Bodhisattvas, who have trained their minds to work for the benefit of all beings, to break any of these restraints when necessary. For those exalted beings whose minds have been tamed and whose motivation has been completely purified, there is no danger of experiencing harm from performing actions that would be dangerous for those of lesser mental development.

Therefore, those who wish to train themselves in the Bodhisattva's way of life should understand well that the first thing that must be done is to tame their own mind completely. After we have accomplished this we will be able to be of actual benefit to countless sentient beings. As Atisha said, 'Now is not the time to subdue the mind of others; now is the time to subdue your own mind.' The prerequisite for benefiting others is to train ourself beforehand.

If we want to be of true benefit to others there are certain specific qualities that we must first develop. We need the Dharma eye of wisdom, clairvoyance, skill in teaching Dharma, and patience in enduring the harm received from others. In addition, we must be free from self-cherishing attitudes and be completely familiar with the state of mind that holds others more dear than ourself. Of course, we can give temporary benefit to a few other sentient beings without having developed all the qualities just mentioned, but such benefit is limited. To quote Atisha once again: 'Just as a bird without wings cannot fly, someone who has not attained clairvoyance is not able to benefit all sentient beings.'

The following story illustrates how clairvoyance, which can be attained once the mind has been properly tamed, is necessary to ensure that our good intentions do not lead to disaster. A long time ago there was a kind-hearted man who discovered a large fish that had been dropped by a passing fisherman. Seeing it struggling on the dry land, the man felt very sad for the fish and, wanting to save its life, took it home with him and dropped it into a small pond. Unfortunately, the kind man was unaware of the type of fish he had saved; when it recovered it followed its natural instincts and ate all the other smaller fish in the pond. When the men who owned the pond came by they were very upset. When they saw the large intruder and understood what had happened, they killed it immediately. In the end, therefore, the fish that had been saved from dying was killed anyway, but not until it had killed many other fish as well.

What this story demonstrates is that although the kind-hearted man had acted benevolently, because he did not have a clear view of the situation he did not realize how dangerous his well-intentioned action really was. Even though he did bring some small benefit to one fish, he indirectly caused much harm to many others. The point is that if we wish to benefit others to the greatest possible extent we should first tame our mind, attain realizations and develop the wisdom that understands the consequences of our actions. This does not mean, however, that we should wait until we are well advanced before giving help to others. On the contrary, we should do as much as we can to help others, whether it is nursing the sick or saving an insect from drowning. We should merely realize that what we can do now is insignificant compared to the benefit we could bestow if we had a fully controlled mind. With this realization in mind, we should pray to be able to emulate the deeds of the exalted Bodhisattvas, and strive to attain such an advanced state ourself.

How then can we practise the moral discipline of benefiting others? Shantideva now gives a number of specific examples. [85] In relation to food, for instance, he advises us not to think solely about our own benefit but to divide whatever food we receive among the poor, the protectorless, the helpless, animals and especially Dharma practitioners. Whatever we do eat we should eat in moderation.

It is important to discriminate between what we should and should not give to others. In general, we can give whatever we possess, but ordained monks and nuns should not give up their three robes. [86] As for our body, since we need it for the practice of Dharma we should not bring harm to it in order to accomplish a minor purpose. If we deprive our body of proper nourishment and let it become weak, we will be unable to practise Dharma intensively during the day and the night. We should not forget that if we take full advantage of this precious human life and follow a systematic practice of the three higher trainings we will be able to fulfil the wishes of all living beings swiftly.

[87] To clarify this point further, Shantideva says that if we have not developed the pure intention of great compassion we should not try to give our body to others. If we do so, the only result will be that harm and injury will be received by ourself and others. Yet much benefit will be gained if the body is given by someone whose mind is sufficiently tamed, who sees great purpose in such giving and can give his or her body with the pure intention of benefiting others.

One of the supreme ways of benefiting others is through giving Dharma teachings, but before we can practise such giving we need to understand the mind of the intended recipient. [88] Dharma should never be taught to someone who lacks respect either for us or for Dharma itself. Teaching such a person will not benefit him or her and will only create downfalls, or obstacles, for ourself. The way to approach such a person is to satisfy his needs through material gifts and then, when his faith in ourself and in Dharma has been cultivated, introduce him to the pure teachings. Shantideva next gives a detailed account of the circumstances in which it is improper to teach Dharma. Because teaching should only be given to those who have the proper attitude we should never teach anyone whose dress, manner or bearing demonstrates disrespect. This would include those who cover their heads though they are not sick, those who have not put down their umbrellas, canes or weapons, and those who defiantly wear turbans. Of course, there are many things we must take into account when deciding whom to teach and whom not to teach.

However, once we have taken stock of the situation and have developed rapport with a potential student, we should make sure that the teaching situation takes place in an atmosphere of respect and accords with Buddha's injunctions.

[89] When trying to discriminate between proper and improper teaching situations we should take into account the general expectations and preconceptions of the society in which we live. For example, in many societies it is considered shameful for a man to remain alone with an unaccompanied woman unless that woman is somehow related to him. In such societies, therefore, it would bring great disrespect to Dharma for a male Teacher to give Dharma to an unaccompanied woman. It is not enough for our own intentions to be good; we must be aware of how our actions are affecting others. We must be especially careful that our behaviour does not bring Dharma into disrepute for this would cause untold harm to others.

As far as the contents of our teachings are concerned, we should try to determine the capacity and inclination of our listener's mind. If a student has a small disposition, we should not force the profound and vast teachings of Mahayana upon him. On the other hand, although we should have equal respect for the teachings of both the Hinayana and Mahayana, [90] we should not lead someone into the Hinayana path if he or she has a strong desire to receive Mahayana teachings. And, of course, under no condition should we ever forsake the Bodhisattva way of life. We should remember that the best way to guide others is by our own example and practice.

[91] It is also important to observe good hygiene. We should not spit wherever we like, or throw our cleaning implements, such as the sticks used in India for cleaning

teeth, on the ground without covering them up. Neither should we defecate or urinate on the banks of rivers, near water or in any place frequented by others.

[92] When eating we should not fill our mouth or eat noisily or keep our mouth open. When sitting we should not stretch our legs or rub our hands together meaninglessly. [93] For reasons similar to the ones mentioned earlier, we should not sit alone on the same seat as another's partner, nor in the same vehicle, nor in the same room. As long as such behaviour is not offensive to anyone else, however, and does not cause delusions to arise, it is permitted. In brief, we should not act in ways that displease worldly people. If we are unfamiliar with the local customs and do not know if our actions are considered offensive or not, we should ask for advice and abandon doing anything contrary to accepted habits.

Shantideva now gives advice concerning the movement of our hands and arms. [94] If someone asks us for directions we should not point with one finger but show the way respectfully with our fully outstretched right hand. [95] We should not wave our arms about aimlessly or violently. If it is necessary to attract another's attention we should do so quietly and in an appropriate manner.

[96] Even going to sleep is an action that can be done with mindfulness and alertness. When Buddha Shakyamuni lay down prior to his departure from this life, he did so on his right side with his body outstretched, his left hand down at his left side and his right hand under his right cheek. It is very beneficial if we fall asleep in the same position. If we can do this with proper mindfulness and alertness, with our mind focused on virtue, our entire sleep will be virtuous. Otherwise, if we go to sleep with a negative mind, the period we spend sleeping will be filled with non-virtue. Therefore,

before we fall asleep we should generate a beneficial state of mind and make the firm decision to arise early.

[97] In short, we should follow to the limit of our ability the practices taught by Buddha concerning the boundless conduct of the Bodhisattva. In the beginning of our practice, however, the most essential thing is to tame our mind for only this will enable us to benefit all sentient beings.

## HOW TO PREVENT OUR PRACTICE FROM DEGENERATING

[98] When we take the Bodhisattva vows as described in the third chapter we should try very hard not to break them, for the consequences of doing so are severe. Therefore, before we take the vows, it is strongly advised to check whether we can keep them or not. If we take the vows and do break them, however, there are ways of restoring them and avoiding harmful results. For instance, if we break one of the eighteen root vows, we can purify this transgression by applying the four opponent powers and by retaking the Bodhisattva vows at another ceremony. If we break any of the forty-six secondary vows, we can purify them by reciting the *Sutra of the Three Superior Heaps* (Skt. *Triskandhasutra*) three times during the day and three times at night after first going for refuge and generating bodhichitta.

[99] Whenever we engage in actions of body, speech or mind, whether for the sake of ourself or others, we should take care not to contravene the teachings of Buddha. [100] Because there is no precept taught by Buddha that is not practised by a Bodhisattva, we should keep all such vows and precepts purely by remaining mindful and alert in all our actions. [101] We should always remember that the chief

practice of a Bodhisattva, either directly or indirectly, is to benefit others. Whatever merit we may accumulate from any of our actions, even offering one stick of incense, should be dedicated to the enlightenment of all sentient beings.

[102] As for the Mahayana Spiritual Guide who is wise in the meaning of the teachings and who practises the Bodhisattva way of life, we should follow him or her continuously and not forsake him even at the cost of our life. Why is such a Guide so important? Because ultimately he or she leads us to the goal of the Bodhisattva's way of life, the full enlightenment of Buddhahood, and temporarily he teaches us what we do not know and provides us with the methods that keep what we do know from degenerating. If we follow such a Spiritual Guide sincerely, the actions of our body, speech and mind become extremely pure.

There are many texts we can read to enhance the practices that we have discussed. [103] The best method for following our Spiritual Guide is expounded in the biography of Shri Sambhava, which forms part of *Stalks in Array Sutra* (Skt. *Gandavyuhasutra*). [104] Having read this and other Buddhist scriptures we should acquaint ourself well with the advice they contain. As for information concerning the Bodhisattva vows, we can read the *Akashagarbha Sutra*. [105] If we wish to study the Bodhisattva practices extensively, we should read *Compendium of Trainings* (Skt. *Shikshasamuchchaya*) and *Compendium of Sutras* (Skt. *Sutrasamuchchaya*) by Shantideva over and over again. [106] The protector Nagarjuna also wrote two works, which have the same titles, and our practice will be greatly enhanced if we study these as well. A detailed explanation of the Bodhisattva vows and the method for purifying downfalls can be found in the book *The Bodhisattva Vow*.

[107] To summarize, then, everything that is forbidden in Buddha's teachings and in the commentaries to them should be abandoned and everything that is recommended should be practised. The Bodhisattva way of life should be followed in this manner in order to guard the minds of worldly people and to prevent their faith from decreasing. Thus we should keep our precepts and follow our practices as purely as possible.

## IN CONCLUSION, THE NECESSITY OF FOLLOWING THE MEANING AND NOT MERELY THE WORDS OF THE PRACTICE

[108] As mentioned before, whenever we perform any action through the doors of our body, speech and mind, we should use the wisdom of alertness again and again to check whether we are transgressing our precepts or if our mind is under the influence of delusion. This is the supreme method for maintaining mindfulness and alertness and ensuring that they do not decrease.

[109] In all situations the most important thing to remember is that the conduct of Bodhisattvas is something we must actually follow. There is no purpose or value in learning the mere words of a teaching if we do not put that teaching into practice. As Shantideva asks, 'Will a sick man receive any benefit merely by reading a medical treatise?'

This concludes 'Guarding the Mind with Alertness', the fifth chapter of the text *Meaningful to Behold*, a commentary to Shantideva's *Guide to the Bodhisattva's Way of Life*.

# *Patience*

## EXPLANATION OF THE FOUR REMAINING PERFECTIONS: PATIENCE, EFFORT, CONCENTRATION AND WISDOM

This has four parts:

1. How to practise patience
2. How to practise effort
3. How to train in the concentration of tranquil abiding
4. How to develop the wisdom of superior seeing

### HOW TO PRACTISE PATIENCE

The subject matter of the sixth chapter of Shantideva's *Guide* is the perfection of patience. The explanation of how to practise patience has two parts:

1. The method of meditating on patience
2. The method of practising patience

### THE METHOD OF MEDITATING ON PATIENCE

Because patience is the opponent force overcoming the delusion of anger, this section has two parts:

1. The faults of anger
2. The benefits of patience

Geshe Potowa

## THE FAULTS OF ANGER

Shantideva begins his discussion of patience by stating:

[1] Whatever merit we have accumulated throughout thousands of aeons through virtuous deeds, such as venerating the Three Jewels and practising giving, can be destroyed in a single moment by generating anger towards a Bodhisattva.

Because bodhichitta is an internal quality it is difficult to tell who is and who is not a Bodhisattva. It can easily happen that a famous Dharma practitioner is not a Bodhisattva while someone dwelling among a group of poor and needy people is in fact such a high-minded being. If, as Shantideva has said, a moment of anger towards someone who has developed bodhichitta can destroy aeons of virtue, it is therefore advisable not to generate anger towards anyone.

Our anger can arise towards many different objects and if it arises towards someone who has high Dharma realizations it will counteract and destroy the merit we have accumulated over thousands and thousands of lifetimes. Similarly, if we generate anger towards our mother or father or others from whom we have received great kindness, there will be no limit to the destruction of our merit. Even anger directed towards someone who is our equal will destroy the roots of virtue collected over many previous lifetimes.

Perhaps on one particular day we created a great wealth of merit by making lavish offerings to the Three Jewels or by being generously charitable to many people. However, if the virtuous merit of those actions was not properly dedicated and on the following day we became angry with someone, all the virtue accumulated from the previous day's practice would be destroyed. Thus the delusion of anger harms us severely. An alcoholic drink possesses the potential power to intoxicate us but if it is boiled it will lose this potential. In the same way, the practice of virtue creates the potential power for us to attain the fruit of happiness, but anger can destroy this potential completely. Nevertheless, as explained in the earlier chapters, if we remember to dedicate our accumulated merit for the attainment of enlightenment and the benefit of all sentient beings, that merit is safe and cannot be destroyed by anger.

[2] There is no evil greater than anger. It is a force capable not only of negating the effects of whatever positive actions we have done in the past but also of preventing us from attaining goals we have set for ourself, whether attaining full enlightenment or merely improving our mind. The opponent to anger is patience, and if we are seriously interested in advancing along the path of spiritual development there is no greater practice than this.

The destruction of virtue is one of the invisible faults of anger and therefore something we must accept on faith. There are, however, many visible faults of this delusion, and the value and importance of developing patience will become obvious once we look at these more manifest shortcomings. [3] When we are overcome by hatred we immediately lose all peace of mind and even our body becomes uncomfortable. We are plagued by restlessness and the food we eat seems unpalatable. We find it nearly impossible to fall asleep and whatever sleep we do manage to get is fitful. Anger transforms even a normally attractive person into an ugly red-faced demon. We grow more and more miserable and, no matter how hard we try, we cannot control our feelings.

One of the most harmful effects of anger is that it robs us of our reason and good sense. [4] Wishing to retaliate against those who have harmed us, we expose ourself to great personal danger merely to exact our petty revenge. We lose all freedom of choice, driven here and there by an uncontrollable rage. Sometimes this blind rage is even directed at our loved ones and benefactors. In a fit of anger, forgetting the immeasurable kindness we have received from our friends, family and Teachers, we might strike out against and even kill the ones we hold most dear. [5] It is no wonder that a person habitually controlled by anger is soon avoided by all who know him. This unfortunate victim of his own hostility is the despair of those who formerly loved him and eventually finds himself abandoned by everyone.

It is by displaying the red face of anger towards others that we transform them into our enemies. It is generally assumed that anger arises in response to meeting someone we do not like but in truth the situation is often the exact reverse of this. It is the anger already within us that transforms the person we meet into our imagined foe. Someone who is anger-prone lives within a vision of paranoia surrounded by enemies of his own creation. The false belief that everyone hates him can become so overwhelming that he might even go insane, the victim of his own delusion.

It often happens that in a group one person always blames the others for what goes wrong. Yet it is generally the person who complains who is actually at fault for whatever disharmony arises. The story is told of an old woman who used to argue and fight with everyone. She was so disagreeable that eventually she was expelled from her village. When she arrived at another town the people there asked her, 'Why did you leave your home?' She replied, 'Oh, all the people in that village were wicked; I left there in order to escape from them.' The townspeople thought this was very strange. 'This can't be true,' they said. 'The old lady herself must have been quite wicked.' Fearing that she would cause them nothing but trouble they threw her out of their town as well. Finally this angry old woman was evicted from so many different villages that she was unable to find anywhere to live.

It is very important to recognize the true cause of whatever unhappiness we feel. If we are forever blaming our difficulties on others, this is a sign that there are still many problems and faults within our mind. Why is this? If we were truly peaceful inside and had our mind under control, nothing that happened would be able to disturb that peace, and no one we met would ever appear to be our enemy. To one who has subdued his or her mind and eradicated the last trace of anger, all beings are like friends. A Bodhisattva, for instance, whose sole motivation is the welfare of others, has no enemies. Very few people wish to harm someone who is a friend of all the world. Moreover, even if someone did harm or abuse this high-minded being, the Bodhisattva could remain at peace. With his mind dwelling in patience, he would remain calm and untroubled, able to smile at his assailant and even treat him with respect. Such is the power of a well-controlled mind. Therefore, if we sincerely want to be rid of all enemies, the wisest course of action is to uproot and destroy our own anger.

We should not think that this is an impossible task or an unreasonable goal. Skilled doctors are now able to cure illnesses that were fatal only a short time ago, and have eradicated other diseases completely. Just as scientists and physicians fought and finally overcame these diseases, so we can eradicate the disease of anger infecting our mind.

Methods to gain release from this crippling delusion are available to all of us. They have proved their effectiveness whenever people have sincerely put them into practice and there is no reason why they cannot work for us as well. Imagine what the world would be like if we all conquered our anger! The danger of a third world war would evaporate; armies would become unnecessary and soldiers would have to look elsewhere for work. Machine guns, tanks and atomic bombs – instruments useful only to the angry mind – could be put away as all conflicts, from wars between nations to quarrels between individuals, came to an end. Even if this universal harmony is too much to hope for, imagine the freedom and peace of mind each of us individually would enjoy if we exorcised this hateful demon within us.

To summarize, one who is constantly filled with anger will not find any happiness either in this life or in lifetimes to come. Therefore, [6ab] without forgetting that anger is our main enemy and the creator of so much of our suffering, we should strive continuously to defeat it.

## THE BENEFITS OF PATIENCE

Once we have contemplated the many faults of anger we should employ the force of mindfulness to keep us from forgetting them. [6cd] We should also realize that if we overcome our anger we will always find happiness in this life and in future lifetimes. If we truly wish to gain happiness, therefore, we should rid our system of the poison of anger. This is only a brief explanation of the benefits that follow from practising patience. An extensive explanation is given later in this chapter.

## THE METHOD OF PRACTISING PATIENCE

As with all the other perfections, the practice of patience is primarily a training of our mind. The remainder of this chapter, therefore, is a discussion of the various meditation practices that help us to eliminate the delusion of anger from our mind and replace it with the virtuous attitude of patience. The explanation of these practices has five parts:

1. Preventing the cause of anger
2. Meditating on the patience of voluntarily enduring suffering
3. Meditating on the patience of definitely thinking about Dharma
4. Meditating on the patience of not retaliating
5. An extensive explanation of the benefits of patience

## PREVENTING THE CAUSE OF ANGER

What are the methods for overcoming and finally destroying our anger? There are two allied approaches for accomplishing this aim. The first is to gain as clear a recognition as possible of the many faults and disadvantages of anger, as already discussed briefly, identifying the poisonous delusion, and not any external force, as our true enemy. This recognition is necessary if we are to channel our efforts in the right direction. The second approach is to gain a deep understanding of why we become angry, and then work to counteract and eliminate the causes we have uncovered.

The root cause of anger, as of all the other delusions, is our innate self-grasping: the ignorant view that holds on to ourself and all other phenomena as inherently existent. If we cut through this ignorance there will no longer be any basis left for unhappiness or dissatisfaction. Yet self-grasping is a deeply entrenched habit of mind and it requires a great deal of time and effort to gain the profound realizations required to uproot it completely. However, there are other more immediate causes for the arising of anger and, since these can be dealt with right away, it is worth concentrating on them during the early stages of our practice.

Anger is a response to feelings of unhappiness, which in turn arise whenever we meet unpleasant circumstances. [7] If we are prevented from fulfilling our wishes or forced to deal with a situation we do not like, in short, whenever we have to put up with something we would rather avoid, our uncontrolled mind immediately feels unhappy. This uncomfortable feeling eventually turns into anger and we become even more disturbed than before. For example, someone who wants very much to be with his lover will become extremely resentful of anyone or anything that prevents him from doing so. If she refuses to see him or leaves him for someone else, his unhappiness can easily turn into rage. Therefore, aside from innate self-grasping, frustration of our desires is the main reason for anger to arise.

To overcome anger we have to learn new ways of responding to frustration. Since it is unreasonable to expect that we can fulfil all our desires, we must cultivate a more realistic and balanced approach to the problems of life. The methods of training our mind in this more realistic approach are included within the practice of patience. [8] The more clearly we understand that the sole function of anger is to make us miserable, the more motivated we will be to train ourself in patience and defeat this enemy. But how can we prevent the cause of anger, the unhappy mind, from arising?

[9] If we contemplate the benefits of the patience involved in voluntarily enduring suffering, we can maintain a peaceful mind even when we are experiencing suffering and pain. If this happy state of mind is held and maintained through the force of our mindfulness, there will be no chance for an unhappy mind to arise. On the other hand, if we allow our mind to dwell on unhappy thoughts there will be no way for us to fulfil our wishes and our merit will be threatened.

As indicated before, the objects in relation to which an unhappy mind arises are our unfulfilled wishes. [10] Thus if there is a method whereby our wishes can be fulfilled, then there is no reason for the unhappy mind to arise. And if there is absolutely no way we can fulfil those wishes, if this is completely beyond the realm of possibility, then there is also no reason for becoming unhappy. What would be the benefit in that? As Shantideva says, 'What is the use of being unhappy about something if it cannot be remedied?' If we can train our mind well so that we can look at frustrating situations in a more realistic manner, we can liberate ourself from a lot of unnecessary suffering. Just as water cannot flow in a stream that has been blocked, anger cannot arise in a mind that no longer entertains unhappy thoughts.

What usually causes the unhappy mind to arise? [11] When our family, our friends or we experience suffering or are spoken to harshly, these unwished-for circumstances make us unhappy. Furthermore, if our enemies obtain wealth, praise or a good reputation we become unhappy because we do not want these things to occur. In both cases the unhappiness we feel can easily lead to anger. Thus we should examine carefully if it is sensible or not to become unhappy in such situations. If we realize that it is not sensible or realistic to behave in this manner, we can begin to familiarize our mind with a more workable approach to the circumstances of everyday life. The sections that follow outline the meditations that can familiarize our mind with this more realistic approach.

## MEDITATING ON THE PATIENCE OF VOLUNTARILY ENDURING SUFFERING

In general there are three spheres of activity involved in the practice of patience: (1) learning how to endure suffering with acceptance and joy, (2) definitely thinking about Dharma and (3) refraining from retaliation. At first glance these practices may seem a bit strange and even unnatural, but if cultivated with the proper understanding they can liberate our mind from one of its most obsessive delusions and confer great peace and joy. It is therefore worth persevering in these practices even though initially they may seem unusual.

Concerning the first practice of patience, learning how to deal with and accept inevitable suffering, we should remember that [12ab] wherever we find ourself within samsara, only a few circumstances bring happiness while the causes of misery are plentiful. This is the very nature of samsara – its sufferings are infinite while its joys are limited. Moreover, all the suffering we encounter is the result of actions we ourself have done in the past. If we do not experience this suffering then who should? Since this is the case we should learn to endure what is unavoidable rather than fight against the inevitable.

If we learn the proper way of enduring what is unpleasant, unhappy thoughts will never arise to bother us. We can avoid the many hindrances, including anger, that disturb both our everyday life and our practice of Dharma. If, however, we are impatient with our suffering we will only make ourself more miserable. For example, perhaps our body is attacked by a disease. If we have a method for enduring and accepting the pain, for instance, by seeing it as a means of exhausting negative karma, we may discover that the pain actually subsides. However, if we refuse to deal realistically with the discomfort, cursing our illness or letting ourself become depressed, then not only might our physical pain increase but we will also experience the additional suffering of mental torment. Our anger has only made matters worse, creating the causes for further suffering in the future. It is surely the thief who steals our wealth of virtue.

There are many benefits of meditating on the patient acceptance of suffering. In addition to maintaining a calm and peaceful mind in the face of distressing circumstances, we will be able to gain a clear and dispassionate view of just how unsatisfactory our samsara really is. [12cd] There is a certain mental stability to be had merely from recognizing that every experience of pain or discomfort is the fault of our being caught up in samsara – the fault of being born, living and dying in a state of unknowing and confusion. This recognition, which cannot dawn on a mind consumed with anger, is the basis for developing renunciation: the spontaneous and continuous wish to attain complete and utter freedom from every trace of dissatisfaction in life. Without firm renunciation there is no way to reach any of the higher goals along the spiritual path and thus no way to experience the boundless happiness of liberation and enlightenment. If this precious mind of renunciation can be generated through our practice of patient endurance, then it is certainly worth putting up with whatever discomfort we may have to experience, and to do so joyfully.

We should not be discouraged by the difficulties involved in practising patience. [13] Shantideva cites the people of Karnapa in ancient India and certain ascetics who endured the tremendous pains of combat and self-mortification merely to engage in sport and propitiate certain deities. Nowadays as well there are many famous examples of athletes – boxers, weightlifters, football players and others – who inflict extraordinary physical punishment upon themselves in the pursuit of their professions. It is easy to think of many other people who voluntarily endure great suffering merely to earn some money or enhance their reputation. If for limited goals they can bear such tremendous difficulties, why can we not accept the difficulties and inconvenience involved in our pursuit of complete human perfection – the attainment of enlightenment for the welfare and benefit of all? Why should we be so easily discouraged by discomfort?

[14] By acquainting our mind with the patience of voluntarily enduring suffering our problems and troubles will eventually disappear. All conceptions of the mind depend upon familiarity; once we become familiar with something it can be accomplished without any difficulty. If we first learn to be patient with the small sufferings of heat, cold, abuse and slander, we will gradually learn to endure the greater sufferings and pains we encounter. [15] Shantideva points out that through the force of familiarity we can learn to put up with the trivial sufferings of animal or insect bites, hunger, thirst, skin infections and the like. If we are unfamiliar with these, their pain is difficult to endure, but once we have become used to experiencing them it is not very difficult to put up with them. In a similar manner, we

can learn to deal with all the other sufferings we now find so unendurable.

What sufferings should we learn to endure? [16] Shantideva advises us always to be patient with heat, cold, wind and rain, disease, bondage and beatings. Why? Because if we do not learn to put up with these comparatively small harms, the pain associated with each of them will increase.

Shantideva gives the following analogy to explain how we can increase the strength of our patient endurance. [17] When a courageous man is wounded in battle and sees his own blood, the sight makes him roar defiantly and his courage and strength increase. On the other hand, a weak-minded person will become discouraged merely by the sight of another person's blood. He can become so weak that he may even faint! [18] Since both of these men have human forms and both saw human blood, why is the brave man encouraged and the weak-minded man discouraged? The difference is due to the force of familiarity. The more we become familiar with the patience of enduring suffering, the more the strength of that patience will increase. Thus we should hold on to our mind firmly. Whenever we experience suffering we should recall Dharma and thereby prevent this suffering from harming us.

[19] Whenever a wise person of the Mahayana tradition encounters difficulties or adverse circumstances he or she endures these hardships without letting the suffering disturb his peaceful mind. We should realize that our deadliest enemies are anger and the other delusions. When battling these enemies with the appropriate forces we should learn to put up with all the hardships we will inevitably encounter.

[20] The person who bears all suffering and overcomes the enemy of anger as well as the other delusions is truly worthy

of being called a 'hero' or 'heroine'. Yet we usually reserve this title for someone who kills an ordinary enemy in battle. Such a person is not really a hero because the enemy he killed would have died naturally in the course of time anyway. What he did was not much different from killing a corpse. But those internal enemies, the delusions, will never die a natural death. If we do not exert effort in ridding our mind of these persistent foes, they will keep us locked in the prison of samsara as they have done since beginningless time.

[21] From the Dharma point of view, suffering does not have to be a negative experience. In fact, it has many positive qualities. If we meditate on our own suffering and that of samsara in general, many benefits can arise. We can generate the mind of renunciation and dispel our arrogance and false pride. If we want to make our suffering experiences worthwhile and meaningful, we should use them to develop renunciation. Furthermore, if we learn how to be patient with our own suffering and then meditate on the suffering of others, compassion for all the unfortunate beings still trapped in samsara will arise effortlessly. Renunciation and compassion are two of the most important Dharma realizations and it is our suffering that enables us to attain these realizations. The person who never learns how to face up to the truth of suffering and deal with his or her problems, however, not only feels helpless and unhappy but is also prevented from ever gaining any Dharma realizations at all.

## MEDITATING ON THE PATIENCE OF DEFINITELY THINKING ABOUT DHARMA

This, the second of the three types of patience, is explained in four parts:

1. Because the angry person and the anger are both dependent upon causes, there is no choice
2. Refuting the assertion that the cause of anger is independent
3. The necessity of abandoning anger
4. Summary

## BECAUSE THE ANGRY PERSON AND THE ANGER ARE BOTH DEPENDENT UPON CAUSES, THERE IS NO CHOICE

[22] When a person is afflicted by jaundice he experiences great physical suffering. What caused this? The disease. If someone hits a person on the head with a stick, pain also arises. Who caused this pain? The wielder of the stick. If pain is experienced in both cases, why do we get angry with the person who wielded the stick and not with the disease?

We may answer that it is not appropriate to generate anger towards a disease because it has no independent power to cause us suffering. We know that a disease and the suffering that it produces depend upon many other circumstances and conditions. Therefore, anger is not an appropriate response to have towards it. But if this is the case, it is also inappropriate to become angry with someone who harms us. Why? Because he too has no power or independent choice to cause us harm; he acts solely under the power of his delusions. If we are to get angry at all, we should direct our anger at these delusions. If we do not become angry with the disease of jaundice neither should we become angry with animate beings.

[23] Without choice people suffer from sicknesses. In a similar manner, the mental disturbance of anger arises whether someone wants to become angry or not. We might think that

there is a difference between sickness and an enemy's wrath insofar as disease has no wish to harm us while an enemy most certainly does. What we must realize, however, is that the enemy who wishes to harm us does so without freedom; he or she is completely under the control of his or her anger. [24] Without considering beforehand, 'Now I will become angry,' he experiences the arising of anger without having any control over it. Moreover, the anger itself comes into being without first thinking, 'Now I will produce myself.'

[25] All shortcomings, non-virtues and so forth arise through the force of circumstances and conditions. They do not govern themselves. [26] The assembled conditions that bring forth suffering have no thought to produce a suffering result. Nor does the resultant suffering think, 'I was produced by assembled conditions.' Therefore, the angry person, the anger itself and all things in general are completely without volition; they exist solely in dependence upon their causes and conditions. If we train our mind to see the interdependent nature of all phenomena we will be able to eliminate the cause of much of our anger.

## REFUTING THE ASSERTION THAT THE CAUSE OF ANGER IS INDEPENDENT

In the previous section Shantideva discussed the senselessness of indulging in anger by pointing out that there is no choice or volition involved in our experiences of harm. This is so because all things, including our state of mind, are dependent arisings, that is, they come into existence in dependence upon causes and circumstances, and do not have an independent, or self-existent nature of their own. There are certain non-Buddhist schools of philosophy, however, that do assert that some of the factors bringing us help and harm are permanent, unchanging and independently existing. A more detailed refutation of these schools is presented in the ninth chapter. What follows is a brief refutation of such wrong views in terms of the appropriate way of dealing with anger-provoking situations. Shantideva's arguments are presented in three parts:

1. Refuting the Samkhya school's assertion of an inherently existent general principle and self
2. Refuting the Vaisheshika school's assertion of an inherently existent self
3. Recognizing all beings as illusions, and thus the inappropriateness of generating anger towards them

## REFUTING THE SAMKHYA SCHOOL'S ASSERTION OF AN INHERENTLY EXISTENT GENERAL PRINCIPLE AND SELF

The Samkhya school asserts the existence of a general principle that possesses certain unique characteristics. They claim, for example, that this general principle is the cause of the environment, the beings living therein and the objects of our senses. Although it is the cause of all these things, the general principle itself is said to be causeless, independent and permanent. Furthermore, according to this school the self is also independently existent, while the general principle is the cause of all other knowable things.

Shantideva now points out the many contradictions that arise from such assertions. [27] If the general principle and the self were, as the Samkhyas assert, causeless and unproduced, they would not arise in dependence upon the thought, 'Now I will come into existence in order to cause harm.' Thus it would still be the case that there is no volition involved in our experience of harm. In fact, however, neither the general principle nor the self could exist in the way the Samkhya asserts. [28] If the general principle were independent it could not produce anything, and if the self were independent it could not utilize or experience anything that was produced. How can an effect be produced from something that is supposedly permanent? Moreover, if the self were permanent, whenever it saw a form or heard a sound it would do so eternally. If changes do occur in its experiences, the assertion that it is permanent is obviously incorrect. For all these reasons, then, Shantideva refutes the existence of a permanent general principle and an independent self.

## REFUTING THE VAISHESHIKA SCHOOL'S ASSERTION OF AN INHERENTLY EXISTENT SELF

The Vaisheshika school asserts the existence of a permanent self, which is thought to be material in nature. [29] Shantideva says that it is futile to assert this view because if the self were permanent then, just like space, it would never perform any action or function. When the Vaisheshika school claims that even though the self is permanent it is still able to produce fruit when it meets with other circumstances, Shantideva says that this is an impossibility. First of all, how can something that is permanent ever meet with circumstances and conditions? And even if it did meet, how could it ever change? Something is called 'permanent' precisely because it never changes. [30] If the self were permanent it would remain as it was whether it met with conditions or not. Therefore, how could there be any effects attributed to it? Can anything be produced by something that is permanent? No, all such assertions are groundless and self-contradictory.

## RECOGNIZING ALL BEINGS AS ILLUSIONS, AND THUS THE INAPPROPRIATENESS OF GENERATING ANGER TOWARDS THEM

Despite what the Samkhya, Vaisheshika and other schools assert, [31] all effects arise from other causes, and these causes also arise from previous causes. All causes and effects arise in dependence upon other conditions. Therefore they completely lack any independent or inherent existence. Even though all things seem to exist from their own side, they are in reality like illusions. If we can remember to look at things in this light whenever difficulties present themselves, our anger and indeed all our delusions will vanish. Keeping such thoughts in mind when encountering anger-provoking situations is part of practising the patience of definitely thinking about Dharma.

## THE NECESSITY OF ABANDONING ANGER

[32] It might be argued that if everything is like an illusion, who is there who should restrain what anger? Surely, all such restraint would be inappropriate in a world of illusions. But this objection is not correct. Although all things are like illusions in that they lack self-existence, suffering is still experienced. Severing this stream of suffering depends upon the efforts we exert in restraining such delusions as our anger. Although things lack independent existence – in

fact, because they lack independent existence – cause and effect operate to bring suffering results from non-virtuous actions and beneficial results from virtuous ones. Therefore it is never appropriate to indulge in anger because this only plants the seeds for future misery.

## SUMMARY

[33] Whenever we are harmed by an enemy or even see our friend committing an improper action against us, we should think, 'It is only because of his delusion that he harms me; he has no freedom of action.' If we can think in this way and realize that all things arise from conditions, we can prevent anger from arising and remain in a happy frame of mind no matter what we experience.

[34] If everything that arose did so according to its own nature and choice, no sentient being would ever have to experience any suffering. Why? Because no one chooses to suffer and everyone wishes to be happy. If things happened solely because of our own choice and volition, who would choose to experience suffering? Clearly there must be another explanation of the situation. Because the minds of sentient beings have been conditioned since beginningless time by ignorance, and because these unfortunate beings have not yet attained the wisdom that sees the true nature of reality, they have no choice but to experience the ever-changing sufferings of samsara.

This concludes Shantideva's discussion of the second of the three types of patience: definitely thinking about Dharma.

## MEDITATING ON THE PATIENCE OF NOT RETALIATING

This third type of patience is explained in three parts:

1 Reflecting with attention on the methods for developing compassion
2 Overcoming the cause of anger
3 Contemplating our own faults when undesirable situations arise

## REFLECTING WITH ATTENTION ON THE METHODS FOR DEVELOPING COMPASSION

We have already discussed the many visible and invisible faults of anger, but how can we keep from retaliating when someone harms us? The difficulties involved in practising this type of patience can be overcome if we combine it with a method for generating compassion. For example, if someone harms us we should not only think, 'He is hurting me only because he is deluded' but also, 'He is hurting himself, too.' When we train our mind to see things in this way, compassion will spontaneously arise and all impulses towards anger and retaliation will subside.

[35-6] The ways in which people bring harm to themselves are numerous and extremely varied. Out of obedience to their teachers or for the sake of fulfilling their own purposes, some people lie naked on a bed of thorns and nails, while others burn themselves and still others hurl themselves off high cliffs. In their search for sexual partners, possessions and wealth, some people become so obsessed that they deprive themselves of food. If we remember what people do – including even the murder of their parents!

– while controlled by greed, we can begin to imagine the tremendous suffering these poor, deluded people are heaping upon themselves. When we think of the immediate and future harm their delusions will inflict upon them, we can better understand why they often harm us as well. If we contemplate this deeply, not only will we overcome the wish to retaliate, but we will also be able to generate great compassion for those who would disturb our peace.

[37] Under the influence of anger a person who normally cherishes himself more than anything else in the world is even capable of committing suicide. If the force of his delusions can drive him to such desperate measures, we can certainly see how it can cause him to inflict pain on others. [38] Anger can so totally rob a person of his or her freedom of action that it is unreasonable for us to express hostility towards anyone under its sway. If we cannot generate compassion for such an unfortunate person, at the very least we should be able to refrain from getting angry at him.

The ability to practise the patience of non-retaliation requires a great deal of prior mental preparation. Without such preparation it is unreasonable to expect that we can remain unruffled when someone interferes with us. If we have trained our mind well beforehand, however, we will find that we can avoid getting angry or needing to suppress our anger forcibly even in situations of great provocation.

As Shantideva has emphasized before, there is no greater evil than anger. It destroys our own and others' virtues and leads to nothing but unhappiness. In the future, whether we are reborn as an animal or a human being, our body will be ugly. We are all aware that there are certain types of animals, and certain people as well, that instinctively arouse fear and loathing in others. Being reborn with a repulsive form, having a temperament that is quick to anger and being disliked by others because of our fearful appearance are all karmic results of an angry mind. On the other hand, the attainment of an attractive body and a pleasing appearance is the karmic result of the practice of patience.

## OVERCOMING THE CAUSE OF ANGER

[39] When we receive harm from another we should examine whether it is the inherent nature of our adversary to be harmful or whether it is just a temporary fault. If the former were true and being harmful were the very nature of that person, there would be no reason to generate anger towards him. When we burn ourself we never blame the fire because we know that it is the very nature of fire to burn. On the other hand, [40] if the harmfulness of our adversary were only a temporary fault, arising in response to temporary circumstances and conditions, there would certainly be no reason for us to become angry with him. When rain falls from the sky we do not become angry with the sky because we realize that rain is not part of its inherent nature. Rain falls from the sky only as the result of such changing and temporary circumstances as the amount of heat and moisture in the air, the effect of wind and so forth. Therefore, if the harmfulness of our adversary is not part of his essential nature, whose fault is it that he harms us? It is the fault of delusion itself.

[41ab] Let us imagine that someone is about to attack us. He picks up a stick and hits us with it. Should we not get angry with him? After all, he has harmed us. At this point someone might argue, 'Don't get angry with the man; get angry with the stick. After all it was the stick that was the immediate cause of your pain.' Such an argument is hardly

convincing. We would certainly retort, 'The stick didn't hit me by itself. Without the man who wielded it, it would have had no power to hurt me. It's the man himself I should be angry with.'

[41cd] If this is the line of reasoning that keeps us from getting angry at the stick, we should apply it to the man as well. We should realize that he was manipulated by the power of his anger in exactly the same way that the stick was manipulated by the power of his hand. With scarcely any control over his mind, he was at the mercy of his delusions. Therefore, if being harmed is going to provoke anger in us at all, we should direct our wrath against the actual cause of our pain, the delusion of anger itself.

It should be noted that we are concerned here with our own internal, mental reaction to experiences of pain and discomfort. No suggestion is being made that we should passively let ourself be beaten up or harmed merely for the sake of practising patience. If there is a way open for us to prevent this man from hurting both us and himself, then certainly we should stop him. The question here, however, is: 'What should we do with our mind once the harm has been received?' The entire practice of patience, and indeed of Dharma as a whole, is to provide protection for the mind because ultimately it is our mind that determines whether we are happy or miserable.

## CONTEMPLATING OUR OWN FAULTS WHEN UNDESIRABLE SITUATIONS ARISE

Another powerful method for overcoming anger and refraining from retaliation is to see all undesirable situations as a reflection of our own faults and shortcomings. [42] If we are the object of someone's abuse, for instance, we can remember the teachings on actions and their effects and think, 'I wouldn't be suffering this harm now if I hadn't abused someone similarly in the past.' The same approach can be used with regard to sickness, injury or any other problem. Our ability to use this way of thinking effectively depends upon our familiarity with the karmic law of actions and their effects. Once our understanding of and conviction in this law becomes firm – once we realize that we always reap the fruit of our own actions, receiving good for good and evil for evil – we will be able to remain inwardly peaceful and calm even in the most adverse circumstances. We can view the harm we receive with a sense of relief, seeing our pain as the repayment of a long-standing debt. This is certainly preferable to becoming angry and upset, which only incurs the future debt of more pain and anguish.

[43] Whenever we receive physical harm from another we should remember that there are two immediate causes for the suffering we experience: the weapons used against us, and our own contaminated body. It is only when these two factors meet that suffering arises; therefore to which object should we direct our anger? If we direct it towards our attacker or the weapon he uses, why do we not similarly direct it towards our own body? And if we never generate anger towards our own contaminated body, why should we direct it towards the attacker and his weapon? We should realize that since suffering arises because of our own past creation of non-virtue, we ourself alone are to blame for whatever misery we experience.

[44] Our present body is fragile and delicate, unable to bear even the slight discomfort of a thorn prick. Greater suffering than that arises from the harm received from

weapons but if we had not first received such a contaminated body we would now be free from all experiences of misery. Lacking wisdom and driven by our craving and ignorance we have created the karma to take this contaminated body, the cause of so much suffering. Realizing this, why should we ever become angry with others or hold them responsible for our troubles? [45] Although we childish beings wish for happiness and freedom from suffering, because of our delusions of attachment, anger and so forth we happily create the causes that lead to suffering results. Thus the harm we receive is the result of our own deluded actions and it is completely inappropriate to blame our suffering on others. What reason then is there for us to become angry?

To illustrate the above points Shantideva, in lines harking back to verses seven and eight of the fifth chapter, points out that [46] just as the guardians and forests of razor-sharp leaves in the hell realms are produced by our own actions, so is it the case with all our suffering. Our misery is not created by others but is solely the result of our own karma, so to whom should we direct our anger? The torment of the hell realms is not something unrelated to our mind or a punishment imposed from without. As with all our experiences of suffering, it is the creation of our own deluded mind. If we wish to avoid experiencing these unbearable sufferings the proper course of action is to abandon all faults and delusions in this very life. If we can gain control over our mind in this way, there is nothing in samsara for us to fear.

[47] Next Shantideva investigates closely who actually suffers and who benefits when we receive harm from someone else. When someone becomes angry with us and causes us harm, we serve as the object provoking that anger. If we were not present, his anger would not arise. The harm

we receive is the ripening fruit of our own karma, our own actions done in the past, and in relation to it we should practise patient endurance. If we practise patience in this way we will experience happiness and peace of mind not only in this life but in future lives as well. Looked at in this way as an object of our patience, the person who harmed us is seen as the source of our happiness. If we overcome our narrow-mindedness and take a comprehensive view of the situation, we will understand that his harmful actions are in fact a source of great benefit.

But what will our attacker experience from generating anger and harming us? Because we provided an object for his anger, he will find unhappiness in this life and plant the seeds for a future hellish rebirth. In fact, therefore, we have harmed him and he has benefited us! If this is so, why should we become angry with him? [48] By giving harm he has allowed us to practise patience, a practice that, if done properly and with the correct motivation, can purify us of accumulated non-virtue and bring us great merit. On the other hand, what we have done for him by serving as his object of anger is allow him to create much non-virtue impelling him towards the lower realms. [49] To become angry with such an unfortunate, ill-destined benefactor is surely the behaviour of an unruly, distorted mind.

If our true goal in life is to seek liberation from suffering and the full experience of enlightenment, then material wealth is of no consequence. Only the inner wealth of accumulated virtue is important. The enemy who allows us to practise patience and thereby accumulate an inexhaustible wealth of virtue is a treasure trove of incalculable value. Without him how could we develop and cultivate the virtuous mind of patience? Whenever we are harmed, abused, criticized and so forth the opportunity arises to create great accumulations of merit. Our adversary, therefore, should be seen as what he really is: a great benefactor who fulfils all our wishes.

When Atisha lived in Tibet there was an Indian servant who constantly abused this great Teacher. Atisha's disciples said to him, 'This man is obviously a great disturbance; he should leave at once.' But Atisha explained to them, 'Oh please do not say that. This man is very kind to me; he serves as my object of patience. Without him how could I ever practise this perfection?'

The practice of non-retaliation is a very unusual one for most of us because it goes against our deeply ingrained habit patterns. It is not unusual, therefore, if our mind comes up with many objections to this practice. Shantideva anticipates many of these objections and answers them in the following verses.

[50] *Even though I practise patience when someone harms me, won't I be reborn in the lower realms for acting as his object of anger?*

No, this is not the case. If we contemplate that an enemy is beneficial to us, and practise patience in relation to the harm he gives us we will not be accumulating any non-virtue. Therefore, because we have not created the cause we will never experience a suffering result.

*Then the person who harms me will also not receive suffering results from his action. After all he created the virtuous and beneficial circumstances for my practice of patience.*

This is also not true. Karmic results are experienced only by the person performing the action. There is no way for the person who harms us to receive the fruit of our virtuous practice of patience. Because his actions were not virtuous, how will he obtain a happy result from them?

[51] *Then perhaps if someone harms me, the best thing I could do would be to retaliate. Surely this would be of benefit to him because then I would be his object of patience.*

There are several reasons why this is a mistaken notion. First of all, if we retaliate to harm we will be breaking our Bodhisattva vows, weakening our bodhichitta and causing our practice of patience to degenerate. Secondly, there is no certainty at all that if we retaliate with harm to the harm we receive our adversary will practise patience. It is much more likely, since he was the one who initiated the trouble, that he will only react with more anger; and even if he did practise patience, this would not keep our own Bodhisattva vows from degenerating.

[52] *There is a good reason for becoming angry and retaliating when someone harms my body with a weapon. My body experiences suffering and therefore, because my mind holds on to this body strongly as its own, it is proper for my mind to become upset and wish to retaliate.*

This line of reasoning is illogical. If it were true, why do we get angry when someone speaks harsh words to us? [53] These unpleasant words do not give harm to our body or to our mind, so why do we wish to retaliate?

[54] *Because other people hearing these harsh and slanderous words will dislike me.* The dislike that people might feel towards us has absolutely no power to bring us harm either in this life or in future lifetimes. So there is no reason to become upset.

[55] *If people dislike me and I receive a bad reputation, this will prevent me from obtaining a good position and wealth. To avoid this I must respond and retaliate to the harm I receive.*

If we retaliate to harm and abandon the practice of patience we will create even greater obstacles to our pursuit of position and wealth. The practice of patience never hinders such attainments; in fact, it helps us gain them. If we do not retaliate to harm we will naturally receive a good reputation, a respected position and wealth, either in this life or in future lives.

Furthermore, there is absolutely no purpose in generating anger in our pursuit of material gain because, no matter how much we might acquire, it will all be left behind when we die. The only things that will remain and travel with us into the future are the imprints of the evil delusion of anger we have placed upon our consciousness. [56] It is far better to die today than to live a long life filled with such non-virtue.

No matter how long we live, it is certain that one day we will all experience the pain of death. [57] If one person dreams of experiencing one hundred years of happiness and another dreams of experiencing one moment of happiness, when they awake their dream experiences amount to the same thing – [58] neither of them will have received anything. Similarly, whether we live for a long time or a short time, our situation when confronting death is the same; the only thing that will help us is the strength of our virtuous actions. [59] We may live a long life and have the good fortune to obtain wealth and possessions, but when death comes it will be like being robbed by a thief. Empty-handed, without any wealth and with nothing to wear, we will go naked into the future.

[60] *Isn't it important for me to acquire material wealth now so that I can support my life and thereby have the opportunity to purify my defilements and accumulate merit?*

As stated before, [61] if we commit non-virtue in our quest for material wealth and thereby allow our good qualities to degenerate, there is no purpose at all in living for a long time.

[62] *Perhaps I should not retaliate if a person hinders me from accumulating material wealth, but if he gives me a bad reputation I should retaliate. Otherwise those who have faith in me will lose it.*

That line of reasoning is very weak. If we retaliate when we are abused, why do we not retaliate when someone else is the object of abuse? Will that not cause other people to lose their faith in him as well? [63] It makes no sense to be patient when someone else is abused, and impatient when we are the object of abuse. All abuse is related to the arising of mistaken conceptions and therefore there is no reason to respond to it with anger.

*Perhaps I can practise patience if I alone am the object of harm but if someone else abuses the Three precious Jewels then I should certainly retaliate. Surely there can be no fault in this.*

[64] Because the Buddhas are completely beyond all harm it is inappropriate to generate anger towards someone even if he or she insults the Three Jewels, destroys holy images or abuses Dharma in any other way. It is clear that anyone committing such senseless actions must be completely under the influence of his delusions. Such a powerless being should not be the object of our anger; he should be the object of our compassion.

[65] Even if those who are close to us, such as our Spiritual Guide, family and friends, are harmed, we should still refrain from retaliating or becoming angry. We should realize that all such harm is the ripening fruit of past deeds. Of course, if it is within our power and we can do so without getting angry, we can certainly try to prevent others from causing harm. Practising patience does not mean that we should let others commit non-virtue without intervening. It only means that we should guard our own mind from the delusion of anger.

[66] The pain and harm we receive comes from two sources: animate and inanimate objects. Why is it that our

anger is particularly generated towards the animate objects? If we are patient with one type of harm, we can certainly learn to be patient with both. [67] If one person harms another out of ignorance and the latter out of ignorance becomes angry with him, which of the two would be at fault and which would be without fault? Whether it is hurting someone else or retaliating with anger, both actions arise from the confusion of ignorance. To respond with anger is therefore inadvisable.

[68] We should contemplate that everything we experience is dependent upon causes and conditions. Both we and our antagonists have created the karma to interact as we do. Therefore there is never any reason for us to get angry with others. [69] Once we have seen the truth of this, we should work towards what is meritorious. We should generate the wish that all beings learn to live harmoniously with love for one another.

Attachment to loved ones is often the cause for our anger to arise as we often retaliate on their behalf. Shantideva discusses this situation by giving the following analogy. [70] If a house is on fire, the dry grass around it can carry that fire to other houses. If the grass is not cut, the fire will spread and consume those houses and the possessions therein. [71] In a similar way, when those to whom we cling are harmed, the dry grass of attachment carries their harm to us as we burn with the fire of anger and thereby consume our wealth of merit. To prevent this from happening we should abandon all objects of attachment.

*But if I abandon my relatives and friends I will continuously experience suffering.*

Such suffering should be endured. [72] If a prisoner is about to be executed but, because of the intervention of others, he is pardoned and is sentenced instead to having his hand cut off, he will certainly rejoice. Even though he has to experience the suffering of losing his hand, he will feel very fortunate that his life has been spared. In a similar fashion a person experiencing the sufferings of the human realm, such as being separated from the objects of attachment, should consider himself fortunate that he is spared the far worse miseries of hell.

*But I cannot bear the pain of abuse and divisive speech.*

[73] If we cannot bear this slight suffering, how will we ever be able to endure the unbearable sufferings of hell? And if we cannot bear the sufferings of hell, why do we continue to become angry and thereby create the causes for such an unfortunate rebirth? [74] In the past, because of our confusion about the law of cause and effect and because our mind was polluted by the poisons of anger and attachment, we experienced great suffering in the fires of hellish existence. None of these suffering experiences brought us any benefit. [75] But now we have obtained this precious form. We have the unique opportunity, by enduring comparatively insignificant suffering, to work for the benefit of others and thereby attain the supreme state of enlightenment. Realizing this we should voluntarily endure whatever hardships we may encounter with a happy and peaceful mind.

Anger is often related to jealousy and we should try to overcome both delusions. [76] If someone who is our rival is praised, instead of becoming jealous we should be happy and rejoice. [77] If we can do this sincerely we will experience happiness both now and in the future. Not only are the Buddhas delighted by such actions, but rejoicing in another's good fortune is a supreme method for gathering a circle of friends. [78] If we dislike seeing others happy, then it would absurdly follow that we should not pay wages to the people who work for us for this also makes them happy. Yet we know full well that if we do not pay these wages we will encounter many difficulties. The workmen will not do their job correctly or at all, and our own present and future happiness will decrease. Rejoicing in the praise that others receive, however, is similar to paying fair wages to those in our hire for this is both pleasing to them and in our own best interest.

[79] When someone praises us and talks about our good qualities we become happy. Because everyone else enjoys receiving such praise, we should be happy when this happens. What prevents us from being pleased when others receive the pleasure of praise? [80] Having generated the altruistic aspiration to benefit all sentient beings, and then having taken the Bodhisattva vows to confirm this aspiration, why should we ever become angry when, through their own efforts, others find a small measure of happiness? [81] Since we have promised to lead all sentient beings to the state of Buddhahood, a state in which they will receive worship and praise from countless beings, why do we begrudge them the temporary pleasures they find? To become angry with them in this way is ridiculous!

[82] Parents are responsible for the welfare of their children, but when the children are eventually able to look after themselves and seek their own livelihood the parents are pleased. They are happy at their children's accomplishment and feel no jealousy. The same should be true for us. [83] If we wish to lead all sentient beings to fortunate states of existence, liberation and enlightenment, there is no reason to become jealous and angry when they find a little happiness for themselves. If we do become angry on such occasions, how can we ever claim to be practising the Bodhisattva's

way of life? As long as our mind is filled with jealousy and malice we will never be able to develop the precious bodhichitta. When jealousy, hatred and the other delusions arise, our bodhichitta automatically degenerates. If we are truly interested in following the Bodhisattva path, therefore, we should do everything in our power to defeat these delusions quickly and completely.

Jealousy is one of the most senseless and purposeless of all the delusions. [84] Suppose someone gives our rival some money. The jealousy and unhappiness we feel about this will not do anything to change the situation. Whether that person gives money to our rival or not, there is no way in which we are going to receive that money. So why should we be jealous? Furthermore, [85] becoming jealous on the one hand yet wishing to obtain wealth and possessions on the other are contradictory states of mind. Why? Because the root cause for receiving wealth, possessions and any other pleasurable objects is our own accumulation of virtue. This virtue is collected by practising giving and rejoicing, developing faith in the teachings, and so forth. When jealousy, anger and selfishness arise, however, they immediately destroy these virtues and thereby destroy our chances for future happiness. Thus if we are really interested in obtaining wealth and so forth in the future, we should guard our mind well.

[86] If we do not feel remorse or regret for the non-virtue we have committed and instead allow jealousy to arise towards others' virtue, we are surely absurd! [87] There is no reason to be happy and joyful when our enemy meets with suffering. How does such a jealous reaction hurt our enemy or benefit ourself? Even if we were to think, 'How wonderful it would be if my rival were to suffer', this would never

harm him. [88] Moreover, when he is harmed, how does that ever bring us happiness?

*But if my enemy suffers I will be satisfied.*

Thoughts like this never fulfil our wishes. On the contrary, there is no greater harm that we could create for ourself than indulging in such low-minded and petty behaviour. [89] Such vengeful thoughts do nothing but drag us down into the three lower realms. Just as a fisherman hooks a fish and cooks it over a fire, we are caught by the hook of our anger and boiled by fearsome karmically created guardians in the burning cauldrons of hell.

*If I don't retaliate when others harm me, what will people think? The fame, reputation and praise I receive will certainly decrease.*

[90] To answer this doubt we have to examine the value of fame, reputation, praise and the like. How do these benefit us? Will others' opinions help us to develop our minds, ensure our long life or prevent us from becoming sick? Since they can do none of these things, why should we be unhappy when our praises are left unsung or our reputation suffers?

[91] If our only interest is in obtaining the transient pleasures of a good reputation, wealth and sense gratification, there is no fault in behaving in the same heedless way we have always done and continuing to neglect our spiritual training. But anyone who desires ultimate happiness and has even an inkling of how far the mind can be developed will never be satisfied with such insubstantial pursuits. A good reputation, wealth and a respected position in society are, it is true, generally quite beneficial. Like all experiences of pleasure, they are the result of our own skilful and virtuous actions of the past. Yet if our attachment to these fortunate conditions forces us to become angry when they are threatened, they will cease to be beneficial and will become instead

only the cause of more suffering. We should understand that it is not external circumstances that make us happy but the way our mind relates to them. Therefore we should abandon attachment to these things and, having obtained this precious human life, practise the essence of Dharma and remove the delusions from our mind.

[92] For the sake of receiving fame and reputation, we may sacrifice large amounts of money and even our life. Yet what is the benefit of sacrificing all that is precious to us for a few dry, empty words? Who will gain happiness if we die in the process of seeking fame and glory?

Those who become elated when praised or miserable and angry when criticized were referred to by Buddha as 'the childish ones'. [93] Children at the beach love to make sandcastles. When the surf eventually sweeps away these piles of sand, they weep with disappointment, 'My castle is gone!' Similarly, if we allow our mind to be swept here and there by the changing waves of praise and criticism, we are as foolish as these children.

[94ab] When the mere sound of a few words of praise reaches our ears, why do we become so happy? After all, the sound itself has no mind. It has no intention to praise us. [94cd] *I should be pleased because the person who praises me is happy to do so. Therefore I should also be happy.* [95] As for the person who praises us, his pleasure will not be the cause of our future happiness or benefit. His pleasure is entirely in his own mind and we will not receive any part of it.

[96] *But it is right to be pleased at another's pleasure. Hasn't it been said that we should rejoice when sentient beings are happy?* This is very true. It is important to contemplate this point deeply so that we can be pleased when seeing our enemy's happiness as well. It is senseless to have the falsely

discriminating mind that is happy when our friends are praised but jealous when our enemies are made happy. [97] And to savour the praise that we ourself receive is like the behaviour of a small child.

[98] Although a good reputation, a high position and wealth are generally considered beneficial, they can in fact hinder our attainment of enlightenment. They can easily distract our untamed mind from the necessary meditations on the path. Our renunciation can easily decline and jealousy can arise towards others as the result of thinking about reputation and the like. Such distractions bring interruptions to others and cause our own virtues to decrease. Through being attached to a good reputation and so forth we will descend to the lower realms and remain caught in the swamp of samsara.

A person who is trying to practise Dharma purely is better off without these obstacles and distractions. Who helps us break attachment to these diversions? It is our enemy. He prevents us from gaining a good reputation and thereby benefits us in our desire to gain liberation and enlightenment. [99-101] He is our greatest Teacher because he shows us how to practise patience. He helps us cut our attachment to reputation and fame, to sever the rope binding us to samsara. He prevents us from creating the causes to be reborn in this swamp of suffering and instead helps us create the causes for the attainment of full enlightenment. By seeing him as our Spiritual Guide who benefits us in so many ways, we should abandon all anger that we might feel towards this best friend of ours.

[102] *Why should a Dharma practitioner think of an enemy as his best friend? When someone harms me he can be interrupting my Dharma practice, preventing my accumulation of merit and*

*hindering my practice of giving and the other virtues. Not only is he not my friend at such times, but it is right for me to retaliate against him.* This is wrong. The opportunity to practise patience – one of the most important elements of the spiritual path – arises because of the kindness of an enemy. [103] By giving us a chance to practise patience, this bothersome person helps us create extensive merit. But if we retaliate, this opportunity will be lost. [104] The fruit of patience can only grow from its cause, the enemy. Without this cause, the fruit will never arise. It is therefore mistaken to think that an enemy can interrupt our Dharma practice. After all, [105] a beggar is not an obstacle to someone who wishes to practise giving, nor is an Abbot an obstacle to someone who wishes to take ordination. Far from being obstacles they are absolute necessities.

In general, patience is a stronger virtue than giving because the object of patience is more difficult to find than the object of giving. [106] There are many poor people but where is the enemy who will actually teach us patience? [107] We should think about the rarity of finding such an object for our patience and recognize the enemy as a treasury from which inexhaustible wealth can be received. He is a true Teacher on our path towards the unsurpassable state of enlightenment. [108] Therefore we should constantly remember the kindness of the enemy, the one who would provoke our anger, and feel joy at having found him. It is he who has made our practice of patience possible, and whatever virtue or positive energy arises from this opportunity should first be dedicated to him.

[109] *But I have no reason to venerate my enemy. He has no intention for me to practise patience.* If such an objection is valid, we have no reason to venerate the sacred Dharma. It does not have the intention to bestow virtue upon us either.

[110] *This is not the same thing at all. My enemy harbours harmful thoughts against me, which the sacred Dharma does not.* It is precisely because of the harmful intentions of our enemy that we have the opportunity to practise patience. If, like the doctor who only wishes to benefit his patient, our enemy only tried to do us good, we would never have the opportunity to train our mind in non-retaliation.

[111] Even though our enemy has no intention of helping us with our practice, he is still worthy to be an object of our veneration like the sacred Dharma. [112] Buddha Shakyamuni said that there are two fields for the cultivation of virtuous crops: the field of enlightened beings and the field of ordinary sentient beings. If we have faith in the former and strive to benefit the latter, our own and others' purposes will be fulfilled. [113] These two fields are similar in that they both yield benefit and both are to be cultivated if we wish to attain enlightenment.

*If this is so and the two fields of merit are equally valuable then why do we make offerings and prostrations to the Buddhas and not to sentient beings?* [114] By presenting the above arguments, Shantideva has no intention of saying that the qualities of the enlightened beings and those of ordinary beings are the same. However, these two are similar in that they are both causes of our attainment of enlightenment, and as such are equally worthy of our veneration and respect.

In general, if we give material goods, protection from fear or Dharma teachings to others, this is called the practice of giving. However, because a Bodhisattva regards all sentient beings as infinitely precious and is grateful for the benefits he receives from them, he views his deeds of giving as offerings to them. He recognizes that by acting as the objects of his virtuous practices, such as giving and patience, these beings allow him to reap the fruits of the path. Thus, along with the Three Jewels, they are his field of merit.

[115] Buddha has stated that there is immeasurable merit to be gained from venerating someone who has developed the mind of limitless love. Why is that? Such a person is concerned with the welfare of numberless beings and therefore any service we do for him or her has these infinite beings as its indirect object. Because their number is limitless, so is the merit gained from our veneration. Similarly, it is more beneficial to give assistance to the mother of many children than to someone without dependents. The more beings who gain from our giving, the greater the fruits of our actions for ourself. Similarly, having faith in the Buddhas is a powerfully beneficial mental action because the good qualities of the enlightened beings are so plentiful and profound. [116] For these reasons, therefore, sentient beings and Buddhas are seen to be equal by someone following the Bodhisattva's way of life. If we have faith in the enlightened beings and a mind of limitless love for all sentient beings, the fruit of Buddhahood will be quickly attained. Yet we must bear in mind that Buddhas are endowed with vast and profound qualities that are not possessed by any sentient being whatsoever.

[117] The qualities of a Buddha are so extensive that if someone shared even a small fraction of them he or she would be worthy of extreme veneration. While sentient beings in general do not share the profound qualities of a Buddha, [118] they do share the role of being our field of merit. Because we rely upon this field for our cultivation of full enlightenment, surely it is proper to venerate all sentient beings as we would a Buddha.

Through the blessings of the compassionate Buddhas who show the path, many sentient beings attain enlightenment and many have the opportunity to study their teachings. [119] How are we able to repay this infinite kindness? The perfect way to repay a Buddha who is solely concerned with the welfare of all living beings is for us to generate love and compassion towards them as well. [120] In his previous states of existence while following the Bodhisattva path, Buddha Shakyamuni gave up his life many times for the benefit of sentient beings. Therefore we should never harm those who have been the objects of his loving care. Whenever we are harmed, we should refrain from retaliating and try instead to give as much happiness, benefit and love as we can to our adversary. If we learn to do this, all the infinite Buddhas will be pleased.

How can we train our mind to be able to do this? [121] We should remember that the Protector Buddha Shakyamuni gave up his family, his kingdom, his body and his very life for the sake of sentient beings, and looked upon them all with great loving kindness. If such a one as Buddha gazed upon all others with boundless love, then ignorant beings like ourself should also respect them and offer what we can to them. We should act as if we were their servant. How is it possible to harm those who have been and still are the objects of all the Buddhas' love and compassion? We should seize these thoughts with the power of mindfulness and meditate until we have become completely familiar with them. If we do this we will be able to generate love and compassion towards everyone, even towards those who give us harm.

[122] If we are Dharma practitioners, there is no sense in relying upon Buddha yet continuing to harm sentient beings. This would be the same as acting kindly towards a mother but turning and striking her children. In the same way that we harm a mother by harming her children, we displease the

Buddhas by having evil intentions towards sentient beings. To give another example, [123] someone who is ablaze with fire finds no pleasure in receiving food and delicacies. Similarly, if we harm sentient beings and then offer elaborate gifts to the compassionate Buddha, these offerings will never please him.

Shantideva summarizes the conclusions we should draw from the above considerations by making the following heartfelt prayer:

[124-125] In the past I have committed many non-virtuous actions against sentient beings and greatly displeased the Buddhas. Today I openly confess all these non-virtues and pray that you Buddhas and Bodhisattvas will forgive me. From now on in order to please and delight you I will endure whatever harm sentient beings might give to me and practise patience. I will serve sentient beings in the same way as a servant serves his master. Others may kick me or stamp on my head but I will never retaliate, even if my life is at stake. In your presence I now make these promises and pray that you will take delight in me.

One of the most powerful methods for developing and maintaining the mind of enlightenment, or bodhichitta, is the meditation known as exchanging self with others, which will be explained in detail in the eighth chapter. [126] The compassionate Buddhas have fully accomplished this exchange and, abandoning all selfishness, cherish sentient beings more than themselves. There is no doubt that they have cultivated this realization completely. Therefore, because Buddha Shakyamuni has become completely familiar with exchanging himself for others, everyone we encounter is in the nature of the Protector Buddha himself. If we recognize that sentient beings are, in this way, no different from enlightened beings and if we venerate and cherish them as they deserve, we will quickly attain the fruit of enlightenment. We should continuously make the appropriate offerings to sentient beings and generate boundless love and compassion for them.

## AN EXTENSIVE EXPLANATION OF THE BENEFITS OF PATIENCE

[127] Anyone who practises patience when harmed and who respects all sentient beings as if they were Buddhas pleases all the Tathagatas and dispels the misery of the universe by accomplishing the state of Buddhahood. For this reason we should always practise the three types of patience: voluntarily enduring suffering, definitely thinking about Dharma and refraining from retaliation.

[128] If there is a trusted minister who causes much harm to many people, he may be vulnerable to retribution when far from his own kingdom but no one would dare attack him in his own country. [129] This is because he has the support and the protection of a powerful king. In the same way, if we are presented with the opportunity to harm apparently insignificant beings, we must refrain from doing so [130] because they have the support of all the Buddhas and Bodhisattvas and the guardians of hell as well. [131] A powerful and angry king can only harm others during this lifetime; he cannot cause them to experience the torments of the lower realms. [132] Even if we please such a powerful king he can only reward us with the temporary benefits of wealth and title in this life; he is unable to create causes for our enlightenment.

However, if we displease sentient beings and the Buddhas who protect them, we will encounter many problems during this lifetime and will have to experience unbearable suffering in the future. And if we please sentient beings we will not only find happiness now but will be creating the causes for attaining the unsurpassable happiness of enlightenment.

What does it mean to show the same respect for sentient beings as we do for a Buddha? It is not appropriate to make prostrations to sentient beings, but whenever we encounter them we should remember that they are the objects of the Buddhas' love and therefore try to please and love them and satisfy their needs. As has been explained in the first chapter, all sentient beings have been our mother many times in the beginninglessness of samsara. All these mothers are therefore proper objects of our loving kindness, compassion, patience and so forth.

[133] If we remember the kindness of all sentient beings and try to please and satisfy them as much as possible, we will find happiness even in this lifetime. Others will respect us, our fame will spread widely, and we will find abundant wealth and possessions. Eventually, as a result of our virtuous actions, we will obtain the fruit of supreme Buddhahood. [134] And if Buddhahood is not immediately attained, wherever we are reborn in samsara we will reap the benefits of practising patience. We will be endowed with a beautiful form and surrounded by a circle of devoted servants and disciples. We will also have good health, popularity and a long life. It is even possible to win the great pleasures of the glorious chakravatin kings, rulers over entire universes!

Whenever we experience troubles, disturbances or sickness we should contemplate the faults of not enduring this misery and of the unhappy mind that arises when we are impatient with our suffering. Then we should apply the appropriate opponent force by meditating upon the patience of voluntary endurance. Whenever we have difficulty in understanding or applying the teachings we have received, we should contemplate the faults of distrusting the profound and widespread methods of Dharma and then apply the opponent force: meditation upon the patience of definitely thinking about Dharma. Finally, whenever someone harms us we should remember the many faults of anger and of causing sentient beings displeasure, and seek to abandon these faults by relying upon the patience of non-retaliation. By practising patience in these various ways we should extract the greatest possible meaning from our precious human life and waste no more time binding ourself to the samsaric wheel of suffering and dissatisfaction.

This concludes 'Patience', the sixth chapter of the text *Meaningful to Behold*, a commentary to Shantideva's *Guide to the Bodhisattva's Way of Life*.

*Geshe Sharawa*

# *Effort*

#### HOW TO PRACTISE EFFORT

This chapter has four main parts:

1 An exhortation to practise effort
2 Recognizing effort
3 Overcoming the opponent to effort
4 Increasing the force of effort

#### AN EXHORTATION TO PRACTISE EFFORT

[1] Once we have familiarized ourself with the practices of patience and the other perfections, we should strive with effort to attain the full enlightenment of Buddhahood. If our practices are not accompanied by the force of such effort, the fruit of enlightenment will never be attained. If the wind is not blowing a candle flame will remain motionless, and if we lack the energy of effort our collections of merit and wisdom will remain incomplete. If we lack energy we will be unable to develop or increase any of the good qualities to be gained on the path. Even when performing a worldly action, nothing will be achieved if we do not apply effort to the task.

At first the interest may arise within us to practise Dharma and we may strive enthusiastically to develop our mind.

But then, because we mistakenly expect to receive immediate realizations, we grow disheartened when this does not happen. We may, in fact, be tempted to abandon our entire Dharma practice. Such an unfortunate result comes about because of our unrealistic expectations and the laziness of being easily discouraged. Under the powerful influence of these faults it is nearly impossible to gain any Dharma understanding. If we want our practices to be successful we should exert effort in them continuously until our goal is achieved.

Laziness deceives us and causes us to wander aimlessly throughout samsara. If we can break free from the influence of laziness and immerse ourself deeply in Dharma practices, we will quickly attain release from the cycle of suffering and dissatisfaction. Attaining enlightenment is like constructing a large building: it demands great sustained effort over a long period of time. If we allow our efforts to be interrupted by laziness, we will never see the completion of our work.

There was once a Tibetan Yogi named Drugpa Kunleg who went to the great central temple in Lhasa to see its famous statue of Buddha Shakyamuni. In the presence of this statue he said, 'You and I were once exactly the same. We both experienced unbearable sufferings and were reborn in hell many times. Through the power of your effort you attained enlightenment, but under the spell of laziness I continue to wander in samsara. Now it is time for me to prostrate to you.'

Buddha Shakyamuni was not always an enlightened being. He had to listen to Dharma, reflect upon the teachings and follow the practices unceasingly with effort before he finally attained supreme Buddhahood. The Buddha-to-be experienced many problems trying to find Dharma and a qualified Spiritual Guide to teach it to him. Even when he found such a Guide he had to sacrifice his wife, his family, his kingdom and all his possessions in order to receive just one verse of the teachings. Then, in order to receive further instructions, he had to endure the rigours of extreme ascetic practices and accept the pain of having thorns driven into his flesh.

The great Yogi Milarepa also had to endure much hardship and pain for the sake of Dharma. For many years he served his Teacher Marpa like an animal and patiently endured all the difficulties that arose so that he could receive the precious teachings. If we are seriously interested in developing our mind, even though we need not become ascetics we must be prepared to practise in the same enthusiastic way as Buddha Shakyamuni and Milarepa did. Without being discouraged by the hardships that arise or distracted by our desire to associate with family and friends, we should strive diligently to complete all the practices along the path.

It is important to realize that spiritual development proceeds gradually with results coming only after we have exerted effort in training our mind. To study Dharma and expect immediate realizations is the same as planting a seed and expecting to harvest the fruit at the same time. If we are truly interested in achieving the results of our practices, tireless effort must pervade all that we do.

## RECOGNIZING EFFORT

[2] Effort is defined as the mind that takes delight in performing what is virtuous. It is the chief opponent to laziness. Effort does not mean working hard at worldly activities but rather engaging diligently in eliminating delusion and practising virtue.

There are four types of effort: (1) armour-like effort, (2) effort of non-discouragement, (3) effort of application, and (4) effort of non-satisfaction. All four types of effort are the same in that they are minds that delight in virtue but their functions are different. The first effort principally overcomes external interferences from conditions that are unfavourable to the practice of virtue. The second effort overcomes internal interferences such as discouragement and depression. The third effort principally functions to actually engage in the practice of virtue. The fourth effort principally functions to progress in and complete the practice of virtue without being satisfied with what has been achieved so far. If we apply these four types of effort to our practices, there is no doubt that we will achieve our goals quickly.

## OVERCOMING THE OPPONENT TO EFFORT

A major way of developing the perfection of effort is by eliminating all opponents to it. The method of overcoming the opponent force obstructing effort is explained in two parts:

1 Recognizing the opponent, laziness
2 How to overcome laziness

## RECOGNIZING THE OPPONENT, LAZINESS

In general, laziness is a mental state that is attracted to what is non-virtuous and not to the performance of virtue. There are three types: the laziness of indolence, the laziness of attraction to what is meaningless or non-virtuous and the laziness of discouragement.

The laziness of indolence is an attraction to mental and physical quietness and the pleasures of sleep. It implies a habitual love of ease and a settled dislike of activity. The next type of laziness, being attracted to what is meaningless or non-virtuous, includes what most people think of as effort. It is a mind that is drawn to and distracted by worldly actions and meaningless activity, such as gambling, drinking, smoking and general worldly nonsense. The last type of laziness is that of discouragement. It refers to harbouring thoughts of our own inability or worthlessness with regard to Dharma practices. Because of such discouragement we lose all pleasure in our practice. Without abandoning these three types of laziness and developing the mind of effort, it is impossible to attain the supreme citadel of enlightenment.

## HOW TO OVERCOME LAZINESS

This section has three parts corresponding to the three types of laziness:

1 Overcoming the laziness of indolence
2 Overcoming the laziness of being attracted to what is meaningless or non-virtuous
3 Overcoming the laziness of discouragement

### OVERCOMING THE LAZINESS OF INDOLENCE

How to overcome the first type of laziness is explained in three parts:

1 Examining the cause of indolence
2 Contemplating the faults in this life of indolence

3 Contemplating the suffering in future lives caused by indolence

## EXAMINING THE CAUSE OF INDOLENCE

[3] When overcome by the laziness of indolence we do not practise either virtue or non-virtue. Instead we wish to remain undisturbed and are attracted to a life of ease, particularly to the pleasures of sleep. In such a state we never develop aversion to or disillusionment with the many faults and disadvantages of samsara. The only things that interest us are the supposed pleasures of the world.

Once we recognize that attraction to a life of ease is the cause of indolence we should abandon it by contemplating the faults of such attachment. If we meditate on impermanence and familiarize ourself with the fact that death is certain but that the time of death is most uncertain, our attachment to the transitory pleasures of this world will decrease. Furthermore, if we think about the many faults and miseries of samsara we will realize how foolish we are to expose ourself to future suffering merely for the sake of a brief taste of pleasure.

## CONTEMPLATING THE FAULTS IN
## THIS LIFE OF INDOLENCE

Shantideva now addresses the mind governed by indolence and chastises it strongly as follows:

> [4-5] Just as deer and birds caught in the hunter's snare will eventually be killed, under the influence of delusion beings are enmeshed in the net of samsara.

Don't you see that in the past all beings have been devoured by the Lord of Death and that you too will come to the same end? Regardless of their age, health or any other consideration, the Lord of Death is systematically slaughtering all those around you. If you realize this, why don't you practise Dharma instead of pursuing worldly desires and indulging in sleep? You are like a buffalo who stupidly continues to eat his grass unconcerned that all around him are being taken to slaughter.

As Shantideva says, how can we continue to engage in meaningless activities while death is creeping ever closer to us? [6] Although the Lord of Death is trying to kill us and prevent our travelling along the path to the city of liberation, we feel no fear but continue to be addicted to the pleasures of sleep, food and our petty attachments. [7] Soon the time of death will come and then it will be too late to abandon laziness. We should awake from this indolent stupor and practise Dharma right now!

[8] Our life is full of the tasks we have set for ourself: some have not yet been started, others have just begun, and still others are partially completed. Yet no matter what state our worldly affairs are in, death will descend upon us suddenly. Completely unprepared, we will be struck with terror and it will be too late to feel regret. Think of what will happen when death finally comes. We will be filled with anxiety. [9] There will be much crying as the relatives around our deathbed give up all hope for our recovery. [10] Fearful visions, the reflection of our past non-virtue, will appear before our mind and we will be enshrouded in a deep feeling of gloom. If our rebirth is to be in one of the suffering lower realms, we will

experience a small sample of that agonizing pain. We will be so frightened that we will lose control and cover ourself with our own excrement. Remember, this is not fiction. Without any doubt death will come some day and, if we do nothing to rid our mind of delusion, it will be as fearful as described. Therefore we must overcome our indolence and begin our practice of Dharma immediately.

## CONTEMPLATING THE SUFFERING IN FUTURE LIVES CAUSED BY INDOLENCE

[11] A live fish on hot sand experiences unbearable torment. If the misery we will experience while still alive is as unendurable as this, how unimaginable will our suffering be if we are reborn in hell! There we will have a large, extremely sensitive body tormented by fire and boiled alive. Without a doubt we have accumulated enough causes to experience such hellish suffering over and over again. If we do nothing to counteract them, we will definitely experience their miserable results. [12] If we are honest with ourself and acknowledge this fact, how can we remain under the control of laziness and neglect practising Dharma for a brief life of ease?

Imagine a person who has committed many murders and is finally caught and now on his way to be executed. When he thinks about the punishment he will receive, what joy or happiness will he find in the beautiful jewels or the delicious food that someone might give to him? In the same way, how can we who have accumulated much karma to be reborn in hell confidently enjoy whatever small ease we may have?

There are four unrealistic wishes that many of us harbour. [13] We want to gain swift enlightenment without having to apply any effort, and we want to be happy without having to create virtuous causes. Furthermore, unwilling to endure the slightest discomfort we wish to vanquish all suffering, and while living in the mouth of the Lord of Death we wish to remain like a long-life god. No matter how much we might desire these wishes to be fulfilled, they will never be granted. If we do not arouse the energy to train our mind diligently, all the hopes we have for happiness are in vain.

[l4ab] The fully endowed human body we now possess is like a boat that can carry us across the ocean of samsaric suffering and take us to the island of enlightenment. If we extract the meaning and value of this precious life we will certainly reap great benefits. However, if this rare opportunity is wasted, how will we ever be able to find such a precious human form again? Just as a boat without a diligent helmsman will never go anywhere, if the boat of our precious human life is not guided by the power of Dharma, how will it ever cross the ocean of suffering by itself? In an attempt to impress upon the mind the seriousness of the situation, Shantideva declares:

> [14cd] Do not squander this life under the influence of laziness. You fool, this is not the time to sleep!

## OVERCOMING THE LAZINESS OF BEING ATTRACTED TO WHAT IS MEANINGLESS OR NON-VIRTUOUS

[15] Whenever we are drawn to trivial amusements and idle speech or completely distracted by spectacles or business affairs, this is a sign that our mind has been overcome by laziness: the laziness of being attracted to worldly desires and non-virtuous actions. It is senseless to abandon the supreme

joy that springs from the practice of Dharma and instead be so happy to create the causes of suffering. Why is attraction to such trivial pleasures as singing, dancing and the like a cause of suffering? Because these trivialities litter the path that leads to sublime happiness with many obstacles. If we desire everlasting happiness we should practise Dharma, and if we want something to abandon we should give up those worldly activities that lead to nothing but unbearable suffering.

This advice should not be taken to mean that there is no place within the spiritual life for relaxations such as music, or that pursuits such as business are incompatible with Dharma. As has been emphasized throughout Shantideva's *Guide* and this commentary, it is our motivation that determines the virtue or non-virtue of a particular action. With the proper motivation, such as the wish to benefit others, there are many so-called worldly activities we can engage in without having to worry that we are wasting our time or creating the causes for future suffering. What is being stressed in this section on the second type of laziness is that many of the amusements and occupations of daily life are mindless or valueless diversions. Our motivation to indulge in them is often nothing more than a small-minded selfishness, and some of our accustomed activities are actually harmful to others. It is our attachment to this type of behaviour that constitutes laziness because all effort channelled in this direction distracts us from the higher purposes of our precious human life.

## OVERCOMING THE LAZINESS OF DISCOURAGEMENT

Sometimes we dishearten ourself by thinking, 'I can't practise Dharma; I am hopeless and always fail in whatever I do.' If we indulge in such thoughts there will be no way to take delight in the performance of virtuous acts. How can we abandon this laziness of discouragement? [16] First of all we should uplift the mind by reinforcing our armour-like effort. Then, as we work to complete the two collections of merit and wisdom, we should remain buoyant and flexible, controlling our mind with the rope of mindfulness and the hook of alertness. Then, as will be explained more fully in the eighth chapter, we should try to realize the equality of self and others and exchange the two in our thoughts.

[17] We should not discourage ourself by thinking that we lack virtuous qualities and are therefore unsuited to attain enlightenment. Such thoughts are self-defeating. The Tathagata, who never spoke falsely, has said that [18] even flies, gnats, other insects and animals possess Buddha nature and therefore have the potential to attain enlightenment. Although at present they do not have the opportunity to listen to, think about or practise the teachings, the very fact that they have a mind that is capable of limitless development means that they too can become Buddhas. [19] Therefore, how can we who have been born human, who know the benefits of virtue and the faults of non-virtue, who have taken the Bodhisattva vows and so forth, fail to attain Buddhahood if we continue to travel the spiritual path? Recalling what Buddha said and realizing our own good fortune we should abandon all self-defeating thoughts and the laziness of discouragement completely.

To encourage our mind further we can recall that in the past many people in India, Tibet and numerous other countries attained full enlightenment through their practice of Dharma. They were human beings just like ourself and the Dharma they followed is the same Dharma we are practising now. If we think about this we can fill our mind with the energy of effort and be confident that one day we too will achieve the supreme goal.

[20] When we hear about the great sacrifices that Bodhisattvas in the past have made while travelling the path we may become discouraged. The thought of giving up our flesh as they did fills us with great fear, and we do not even want to contemplate such a ghastly experience. This fear, however, only arises because we are unable to discriminate between great and small suffering. [21] During countless aeons in the past we have been cut and mutilated by weapons and burned innumerable times. Despite this intense suffering, no meaning or benefit was derived from those existences. The suffering was senseless and our lives were completely wasted. None of the pain we received brought us any closer to enlightenment and still we have not awakened. But the problems that arise in our pursuit of Dharma are very different. [22] If we can endure them and persevere with our practice, our experiences will have great meaning and value. Furthermore, these problems and sufferings are totally insignificant when compared to the torments of the three lower realms. The difficulties some Dharma practitioners encounter concerning food, clothing and shelter are nothing when we think of the suffering caused by the delusions. Remembering that we are working for the greatest possible goal, full enlightenment, we should have the fortitude to endure the problems we encounter along the way.

[23] When a doctor is trying to cure a severe illness he or she may have to prescribe unpleasant medicine or painful remedies for a short period of time. And the patient, from his side, prepares himself to endure these painful measures because he is anxious to get rid of his disease. The same

should be true of us. In order to remove every trace of delusion from our mind and attain the most exalted goal possible we should be prepared to endure the comparatively small problems and hardships we encounter. If we are serious in our wish to dispel the suffering of all living beings, this is a very small sacrifice to make.

[24] Buddha is known as the 'Supreme Physician' because he can cure the chronic diseases of our mind. Unlike worldly physicians he does not employ painful methods when leading sentient beings to the cessation of their suffering. He requires no other medicine than renunciation, bodhichitta and the wisdom realizing emptiness to treat the ailments that continuously afflict all sentient beings. Even if an ordinary doctor is skilful he cannot guarantee that the disease he has cured will not be replaced by another in the future. Yet Buddha's superior medicine of renunciation, bodhichitta and the realization of emptiness eradicates all physical and mental illnesses completely and ensures that they will never arise again.

The main cause of all suffering is our self-grasping ignorance. Meditating on emptiness with the force of perfected concentration uproots this ignorance and thereby cures all ordinary sicknesses, which arise from that same main cause. A Bodhisattva who has gained a realization of emptiness is able to cut his or her body into many pieces in order to benefit others. Because of his skill in meditation on the true nature of reality he experiences no pain, and, should a disease arise, the power of his meditation will dispel it immediately.

Earlier Shantideva mentioned the fear that arises when ordinary beings like ourself contemplate sacrificing their bodies for others. Now Shantideva points out that [25] Buddha never suggested that we give up our body or anything else as long as our mind has not been trained and prepared to do so. Training is gradual and at first the practitioner should give ordinary things like food and clothing until his or her mind becomes progressively accustomed to the practice of giving. Through the force of constant familiarity, after some time we will be able to emulate the great Bodhisattvas and give even our own body without difficulty. [26] When that time comes we will be able to give our flesh in the same way as we are now able to give away food, and such supreme giving will cause us no suffering.

[27] At present we experience suffering when our body is cut only because we grasp it as inherently 'mine'. In addition we have a large accumulation of non-virtuous imprints on our mind and these give rise to pain whenever our body is struck. The Superior Bodhisattva possesses a direct realization of the non-inherent existence of his or her body. Therefore, even if it is wounded he does not experience physical suffering. [28] Due to his collection of merit his body is comfortable, and due to his profound skill and wisdom of realizing emptiness his mind is joyful. Through the power of his great compassion he experiences no dissatisfaction no matter how long he remains in samsara for the sake of others. [29] The strength of his bodhichitta dispels all of his previous non-virtue and allows him to accumulate a wealth of merit and wisdom. For all of these reasons, therefore, the graduated path of the Bodhisattva excels that of the Hearer – the practitioner working only for his own liberation from suffering.

Through the strength of his bodhichitta the Bodhisattva destroys all problems and discouragement as he travels through samsara leading others from their suffering. [30] Having mounted the horse of bodhichitta he gallops from joy to joy until he reaches the city of enlightenment. His path is so excellent and noble that no intelligent being could possibly be discouraged from following it. Buddha did not show a rough, uncompromising way to enlightenment; his path does not demand such ascetic practices as fire-walking and self-mortification. Instead, he shows a comfortable and happy path leading to a joyful result. Therefore, we should never let ourself become discouraged by thinking that there is no way for us to attain enlightenment. If we apply the proper effort there is nothing to prevent our reaching this goal.

## INCREASING THE FORCE OF EFFORT

This has four parts:

1 Recognizing the four powers that increase the force of effort
2 An extensive explanation of the four powers
3 Practising earnestly with mindfulness and alertness
4 Using suppleness of body and mind to engage in virtuous conduct

## RECOGNIZING THE FOUR POWERS THAT INCREASE THE FORCE OF EFFORT

[31] Our effort in following the path of Dharma will be increased if we employ the four powers of (1) aspiration, (2) steadfastness, (3) joy, and (4) rejection. These four can be briefly explained as follows. In order to enter the Bodhisattva's way of life and benefit others we need to

engage in those virtuous practices that Shantideva has been describing throughout the text. Actually engaging in these practices depends upon developing beforehand a powerful wish or motivation. This is what is meant by the power of aspiration. Once it has been developed, we should not waver in our practice or turn away from it but complete it with the power of steadfastness. The delight we take in generating effort along the path is due to the power of joy. If continuous practice tires our body or mind, we should relax from our efforts by employing the power of rejection (sometimes called the 'power of relaxation') and then continue once our strength has returned. 'Rejection', here, refers to the rejection or elimination of our tiredness through rest. It does not refer to the rejection of our effort, which, in fact, is sustained by means of the power of rejection.

[32] These four powers increase and complete the practice of effort. They are like a vast assembly of soldiers who conquer the opposing forces of laziness. To attain enlightenment we must complete all the practices of effort, and to do so we must cultivate these four powers. Just as a king uses his army to vanquish the enemy and gain victory, so does effort defeat the enemy of laziness – one of the greatest obstacles on the path to enlightenment – by employing the four powers of aspiration, steadfastness, joy and rejection.

## AN EXTENSIVE EXPLANATION OF THE FOUR POWERS

1 The power of aspiration
2 The power of steadfastness
3 The power of joy
4 The power of rejection

## THE POWER OF ASPIRATION

[33] At the very moment of generating bodhichitta the Bodhisattva promises to eradicate the limitless non-virtue and faults accumulated by himself and all others, even though this task may take an ocean of aeons. However, when those of us who are trying to emulate the widespread deeds of a Bodhisattva look at our situation realistically, it conforms to Shantideva's following bleak description:

[34] At the moment I do not possess even the smallest fraction of a Bodhisattva's ability and because of this I am the abode of much suffering. When I realize that the vast non-virtue I have committed will lead me only to the unbearable suffering of the lower realms, why does my heart not crack immediately from fear?

The root of all our problems is self-grasping, which must be abandoned if we are to find happiness. However, when we look at our past actions we realize that we have not been diligent in trying to abandon this delusion even for five minutes. As Shantideva says:

[35] For the sake of myself and others I must develop the excellent qualities of a Buddha but so far I have not realized even the smallest part of them. Although I have occasionally attained a precious human life, I have squandered these rare opportunities in meaningless activities. Since beginningless time I have wandered throughout samsara experiencing only suffering.

[36] Miraculously we have attained this precious human rebirth once again and it would be strange indeed if we were to waste it yet another time. But what have

we done with it so far? What meaning have we extracted from it?

> [37-38] Have I performed extensive offerings to the Buddhas? Have I practised pure virtue? Have I made extensive gifts, with pure motivation, to others? Have I received any Dharma realizations, abandoned non-virtue or practised virtue? Have I fulfilled the needs of the poor and those who hunger for Dharma? Have I granted fearlessness to people who are frightened by those in authority, robbers, adversaries, wild animals and so forth? Have I confessed all my non-virtues and accumulated a wealth of virtue? No, I have done none of these things.

We should take a good look at how our life has been spent. Since the agonies of our birth we have encountered the sufferings of sickness, ageing, not getting what we want and receiving what we do not want. [39] Our time has been spent encountering one difficulty after another and our life has slipped by without providing meaning for ourself or for others. Why have we so thoroughly wasted this precious opportunity? It is because in both our past and present lives we have lacked the aspiration to practise Dharma. We have not cultivated the wish to tame our mind and be rid of delusions, and have instead allowed ourself to be sidetracked by pursuits that are ultimately meaningless.

We may not be materially poor but if we do not have the aspiration to develop our mind we are poor in Dharma. This is a much worse poverty than lacking wealth and possessions and can cripple even the richest king. Because we have lacked this aspiration to practise Dharma during our previous lives, we are deprived of Dharma in this present life.

Likewise, if we do not cultivate the wish to practise now, we will have no opportunity to meet with Dharma in the future. [40] Buddha Shakyamuni has stated that the root of all virtue is correct aspiration; therefore what intelligent person would neglect aspiring to practise Dharma?

The power of aspiration is developed in two ways. First of all we should contemplate the many advantages and benefits of cultivating an aspiring mind. Then, in analytical and placement meditation, we should contemplate the fact that all suffering arises from non-virtuous actions and that all happiness arises from what is virtuous. If we meditate clearly on these two related points we will be motivated to abandon all actions that are unskilful and practise only what is beneficial. Because it is the teachings of Dharma that help us discriminate between what is to be abandoned and what is to be practised, our meditations on actions and their effects will naturally develop within us an aspiration to practise Dharma.

[41] To understand the infallible law of actions and their effects we should try to determine what factors lie at the source of our physical pain, mental unhappiness, frustration, fear and torment of separation. These experiences of suffering stem solely from our past non-virtuous actions. [42] Someone who performs skilful and virtuous deeds is sustained by happiness wherever he is reborn [43] but the evil-doer, despite his search for happiness, must face the weapons of suffering no matter where he finds himself.

[44] A transcendent experience of happiness awaits those Bodhisattvas who become completely familiar with the practice of virtue. They are born from the cool heart of a vast and fragrant lotus in Sukhavati, the Pure Land of Buddha Amitabha. There they are sustained and nourished by the sweet voice of the Buddhas, which has sixty excellent

qualities. By hearing and contemplating the meaning of these sweet sounds, the fortunate Bodhisattva is nourished by the food of his concentration on emptiness, and the magnificence of his body is thereby enhanced.

When Amitabha generates light from his heart, the lotus opens and from its centre the Bodhisattva, adorned with all the major signs and minor indications of a Buddha, is born. He or she then resides in the Pure Land, experiencing great bliss and not even hearing the word 'suffering'. The cause for gaining such a fortunate Pure Land rebirth is the practice of virtue.

[45] What experiences await the person who commits heavy non-virtue, who takes another's life, for example? He is reborn in hell where the henchmen of the Lord of Death rip his skin open with sharp weapons. Then they pour molten copper into his mouth and thrust flaming swords into him, cutting his body into a hundred pieces. The ground of this hell realm is red-hot and the unfortunate victim of his own non-virtue is scorched even when a severed part of his body touches it. The cause of all this graphically depicted torment is nothing but the person's past non-virtuous actions. [46ab] If we contemplate the difference between the happiness that arises from virtuous actions and the suffering that arises from non-virtuous actions, we will be able to generate a powerful aspiration for virtue and respect for the authentic practice of Dharma.

## THE POWER OF STEADFASTNESS

[46cd] We develop the power of steadfastness by cultivating self-confidence in our practice and in our meditation on virtue. This was stated by Buddha in the *Vajradotsa Sutra*, a section of the *Flower Garland Sutra* (Skt. *Avatamsakasutra*).

[47] We cultivate self-confidence by examining beforehand what has to be done, according to our capacity, and then completing whatever we have started. [48] If there is a virtuous action that we are unable to complete at present, we should postpone attempting it until a later time. Confidence in our ability will grow if we are realistic about what we can do and approach each action we undertake with a steady mind.

Many faults and disadvantages arise if we continually abandon the actions we have started. It is very unskilful to neglect one path in favour of another, only to abandon that path in order to begin a third. This erratic type of behaviour places negative imprints on our mind, leading to a future inability to complete our Dharma practices. Both now and in the future we will experience an increase in our dissatisfaction and will discover that whatever good we do will take a long time to complete and will yield only meagre results. This is an important point because nowadays many students practise like this. They jump from one meditation to another and therefore never accomplish anything. If we want to achieve results from a practice, then once we have started it we should complete it with self-confidence and thereby weaken the power of delusion. Because such self-confidence encourages us to practise Dharma, helps us to abandon non-virtue and increases the power of the opponents to evil, this attitude of mind is anything but a delusion.

Self-confidence in the practice of virtue can be generated by cultivating the following thoughts:

> [49-51] I alone will practise all that is virtuous. Those who are powerless and under the control of karma and delusion are unable to benefit themselves or attain their own purposes. Worldly people are completely unable to

make their lives meaningful. Therefore, I will practise what is virtuous for the benefit of all sentient beings. While others are engaged in inferior and menial tasks in which they encounter many difficulties, how can I sit here at peace and do nothing? I must and will benefit them, but without ever succumbing to the poison of self-importance.

As is the case with most positive qualities, self-confidence is strengthened if we think about its benefits and the faults of its absence. What are the disadvantages of lacking self-confidence? Shantideva explains them with the following analogy. [52] When crows encounter a dying snake they act as if they were brave eagles and attack it. Similarly, when our self-confidence deteriorates, a host of evils, non-virtue and faults will descend upon us like a flock of crows. [53] If we lack the confidence to practise Dharma we will easily become discouraged. Separated from effort in this way, we will be far removed from the methods for overcoming delusion and therefore will never attain liberation or even happiness. On the other hand, if we develop strong self-confidence no obstacle will have the power to overwhelm us as we strive to complete our Dharma practices.

[54] Therefore, steadfast in our pursuit of virtuous actions, we should strive to conquer our enemy: poisonous delusions. If this enemy is not overcome, it will be victorious. To be defeated by our negative karmic downfalls, yet still wish for liberation is but a joke. Therefore, Bodhisattva Shantideva declares:

> [55] I, the Son of the lion-like Conqueror, will overcome all delusions and not let a single one overwhelm me. In this way I will remain self-confident.

[56] Any sentient being who manifests self-importance or is under its influence is not victorious over the enemy, delusions, because he or she is under their control. In general, someone who is victorious over his enemies cannot be overwhelmed by them. If we are under the sway of delusions, we are not victorious over the real enemy. [57] By following such pride we will fall to the lower realms. Even if we are eventually reborn as a human, the imprints of this delusion will ripen as a life of poverty, devoid of happiness. We will be like a slave, forced to eat the food of others and burdened with a bad reputation. [58] Stupid, ugly and weak we will be disrespected by everyone.

The person who is full of his own self-importance and puffed up by conceit is interested only in himself. What could be more pathetic than this? Such a haughty person gains no victory over delusion; instead, he is defeated by it. What reason, therefore, does he have for his inflated opinion of himself? [59] By contrast, a person who applies opponent forces to the delusion of self-importance and thereby defeats the fearsome enemies of attachment, anger and pride is a true conqueror and worthy of the title 'hero' or 'heroine'.

If we destroy the delusions of pride and so forth we will be able to benefit sentient beings and bestow upon them the fruit of enlightenment. Once our delusions are destroyed they are unable to cause us any more harm. As Shantideva says:

[60-2] Like a lion dwelling amongst foxes, when I find myself in a crowd of delusions I will be protected from their harm in a thousand ways. When great danger and turmoil arise, the first things I protect are my eyes. In the same way, I will protect my mind from the host of

mental disturbances and distractions. When I contemplate the way delusions harm me, I think it would be far better for me to be burned, or to have my head cut off and my life taken away from me than ever to bow down to them.

## THE POWER OF JOY

Whenever we engage in the practice of Dharma we should do so joyfully. If we let ourself become depressed by the physical and mental problems that might arise, our ability to practise continuously in the future will be hindered. For example, if we enter a month-long meditation retreat and find that our mind is filled with problems, it is unlikely that we will be motivated to do such a retreat again. Many of these problems and difficulties arise because we do not know how to practise in a reasonable manner and instead push ourself beyond our limits. The result of such an extreme method of practice is nothing but unhappiness.

If we can maintain a sense of joy, not only will we experience inner happiness and peace but the fruits of our practice will ripen swiftly. As a result we will relish the opportunity to practise even more. [63] Just as a sportsman enjoys his sport and is not content to give it up, so should we practise Dharma: never tiring of it and only wishing to do more.

[64] In their search for happiness worldly people exert much effort in business ventures although it is far from certain that they will be successful. Perhaps the ventures will be profitable but it is also possible that their only results will be frustration and dissatisfaction. In spite of this uncertainty, these people pursue their work with joy and enthusiasm. When we practise Dharma there can be no doubt about

its result; it is certain to be happiness. If people can be enthusiastic about something whose results are dubious, why do we not take great pleasure and joy in practising something that will never betray us?

This is an important point to consider. We should investigate deeply to see if the activities we habitually engage in bring us the results we expect or not. [65] In general, we are highly motivated to pursue the five objects of desire: pleasing forms, sounds, smells, tastes and tactile objects. Yet, as Buddha Shakyamuni said, all of these objects are like honey smeared on a razor's edge or like a beautiful flower that is in fact poisonous. If we approach these five objects with the great attachment they normally evoke, we should be prepared to continue experiencing the sufferings and dissatisfaction of samsara endlessly.

If we eat something that looks attractive but is actually poisonous we may not experience anything adverse immediately. At first it may even taste quite sweet, but after we swallow this poisonous food it becomes the cause of much pain. In the same way, if we use attractive objects with much attachment and desire, we may experience some pleasure at first but this will quickly fade, only to be replaced by dissatisfaction, desperation and suffering. Our attraction to these transitory pleasures will close the door to liberation and open the gates that lead to the three lower realms.

In another analogy Buddha Shakyamuni compared objects of desire to a fire. We can find relief from the cold by sitting in front of a fire, but if we overestimate it as a source of pleasure and reach out and touch it we will be severely burned. With great delight a moth is drawn to a candle flame, but is soon charred and consumed by it. Similarly, holding on with attachment to the small pleasures derived from attractive objects deprives us of the certain happiness of enlightenment and exposes us to disappointment and misery.

It is very helpful to keep the above analogies in mind and meditate on the many faults and disadvantages of samsaric desires. Once we become dissatisfied with pursuing sensual objects, which give momentary pleasure but lasting suffering, we can ask ourself, as Shantideva does:

> [66] Why do I not enter the path to liberation wherein is contained no word of suffering and which confers both temporary and ultimate happiness? Throughout my Dharma practice I will be like the elephant who, tormented by the heat of the midday sun, plunges into a cool and refreshing pool.

Thinking in this way of the much sought-after relief from suffering offered by Dharma we should approach our spiritual practices not with a heavy heart but with great enthusiasm and joy.

## THE POWER OF REJECTION

For our Dharma practices to be fruitful they must be balanced and realistic. Cultivating an extreme approach of either over-zealousness or indolence is self-defeating. An important way to ensure that our practices are balanced is to employ what is known as the 'power of rejection'. This has several applications. In general it means that when we are engaged in a virtuous practice we should occasionally take a break from it in order to overcome (that is, 'reject') our tiredness and then return to our practice when refreshed. It also means postponing our entrance into more advanced practices, such as giving away our body the way a Superior

Bodhisattva can do, in favour of engaging in easier and more manageable practices, such as giving material aid to the needy. There is no benefit in pushing ourselves into the higher practices before we are ready for them. For example, there are nine stages of progressive development through which we must pass when trying to cultivate a fully concentrated mind. It is impossible to meditate on the later stages and gain worthwhile results until we have practised the initial levels. Temporarily postponing higher practices until we are ready for them is a facet of the power of rejection.

[67] Occasionally our strength may weaken or tiredness may set in. At such times it is a sound practice to leave whatever activity we are engaged in and relax. Then, when we are ready to continue, we can resume our practice with renewed vigour. If we do not know how to practise Dharma properly and push ourself too hard, we are following the path of 'crazy virtue'. This phrase indicates lack of skill and points out that even supposed Dharma practices, if carried out incorrectly, can be the cause of mental disturbance. Thus it is extremely important to know when to apply the power of rejection.

A third aspect of this power is knowing when to leave our attainments behind. We should not be attached to any stage of realization we may achieve, no matter how enjoyable or even blissful it may be. Instead, by reminding ourself that our goal is the full awakening of Buddhahood, we should give up such attachment and progress to the next stage of development along the spiritual path. Thus the power of rejection also refers to knowing when to turn away from what we have accomplished and seek higher attainments.

This concludes a more detailed discussion of the four powers that increase the force of our effort.

## PRACTISING EARNESTLY WITH MINDFULNESS AND ALERTNESS

[68] When a seasoned and skilled warrior fights in battle he protects his body from the weapons of his enemy and uses all his ability to strike back. In the same manner, the skilful Dharma practitioner protects himself from the weapons of delusion and binds that treacherous enemy tightly so that he can strike back with the appropriate remedy. With the rope of mindfulness and the hook of alertness, this brave practitioner strikes back at the delusion conscientiously.

To continue with the warfare analogy, [69] if in the heat of battle a soldier drops his sword he will pick it up again immediately in fear of his life. Similarly, if a Dharma practitioner ever loses his or her mindfulness, he should recollect the sufferings of the lower realms and instantly retrieve his weapon. If the rope of mindfulness is allowed to go slack, the strength of our virtues will decrease and our three doors of body, speech and mind will be open to attack by the host of delusions and negativities that cause us so much suffering both now and in the future.

It is important for us to try to overcome even the smallest taint of delusion by applying the appropriate opponent force immediately. [70] Just as the poison on the tip of an arrow, though small in quantity, can spread throughout our entire body because of the circulation of blood, so too a seemingly small and insignificant thought of delusion can easily multiply until it permeates our entire mind. To keep this from happening it is extremely important to secure the forces of mindfulness and alertness. Shantideva provides a very striking analogy illustrating how vigilant we should be in employing these two forces:

[71] Imagine how careful a man would be if he had to carry a jar full of hot mustard oil for a long distance while pursued by someone holding a sword who walks directly behind and threatens to kill him if he spills even a single drop! Dharma practitioners should be just as careful.

When we are engaged in meditation it is very beneficial to remember this example and keep our concentration focused on one object without letting our mindfulness deteriorate.

[72] If a poisonous snake were to crawl into our lap we would certainly remove it as quickly as possible. Likewise, whenever the poisonous snake of laziness makes its way into our mind we should remember the fearful suffering it exposes us to and cast it away immediately. In fact, whenever any delusion or non-virtuous thought appears in our mind we should chastise ourself in the following way:

> [73ab] You evil-doer! By entertaining such thoughts as this in the past you have wandered throughout samsara, continuously experiencing its miseries. And look, you are still acting in the same way!

[73cd] Regarding all delusions in such a critical manner, we should try to prevent ourself from falling under the influence of non-virtuous thoughts, and make the strong determination not to let such a mind arise again.

In the fourth chapter the story was told about the famous Geshe, or Teacher, Ben Gungyel. He was famous for the constant mindfulness he employed while guarding his mind. From morning until night he would keep a close watch on his mind, checking to see whether the thoughts that arose were virtuous or non-virtuous. Whenever a negative thought arose, he put a black stone on the ground in front of him; whenever a virtuous thought arose, he placed a white stone there. At the end of the day he would add them up. If he discovered that there were more white stones than black he would shake his own right hand vigorously, offer praises and address himself by the title 'Venerable Geshe'. However, if the black stones predominated he would chastise himself: 'You rogue, you scoundrel, you charlatan! Don't you fear death? How can you be so confident when your mind is so treacherous?' Then he would exact from himself the promise not to repeat those non-virtuous actions of mind again.

Geshe Ben Gungyel practised intensively like this for a long time. His method of abandoning non-virtue and strengthening virtue was praised by many Teachers and scholars at that time. If we are serious in our desire to tame our mind and achieve something meaningful with our life, we too should practise as he did. We should try to determine whether our daily thoughts are predominantly virtuous or non-virtuous and then use methods to strengthen the positive mind and eliminate the negative. It is wise to take the responsibility of calculating our virtuous and non-virtuous deeds now because when we die the Lord of Death will be doing the calculating and then it will be too late for us to do anything about it. [74] In summary, we should try to abandon non-virtue as much as possible by acquainting ourself with the power of mindfulness. With this thought in mind we should seek a Mahayana Spiritual Guide and practise whatever he or she teaches us.

## USING SUPPLENESS OF BODY AND MIND TO ENGAGE IN VIRTUOUS CONDUCT

[75] By remembering the fourth chapter's instructions on conscientiousness and then abandoning laziness by means of effort, we should try to make our body and mind very supple in the performance of virtuous actions. [76] Just as the wind blows a piece of cotton to and fro, our mind – equipped with the joy of practising virtue – should be in full control of our body and speech. If we can practise like this, we will swiftly fulfil all our aims and wishes. The essential message of this chapter is that we should realize how harmful all forms of laziness are. They keep our virtuous deeds from expanding and allow our non-virtuous actions of body, speech and mind to increase effortlessly. Buddha Shakyamuni said that no one who is lazy can practise Dharma purely. Therefore we should always strive to generate effort and thereby overcome this poisonous delusion. All factors opposed to the development of effort should be abandoned and we should employ the four powers of aspiration, steadfastness, joy and rejection to bring our effort to its full development. All forms of sloth and sluggishness should be left behind. We should not discourage ourself with thoughts of inadequacy. By meditating on impermanence, death and the suffering of the lower realms, we should aspire to take full advantage of our precious and unique human existence. Contemplating the many shortcomings and faults of samsara as a whole, we should put aside all worldly distractions and our attachments to transitory pleasure.

Even someone who has inferior qualities can attain enlightenment if he or she cultivates the perfection of effort. Now that we have attained this precious human life and have met with the peerless teachings of Dharma, there is no reason why, if we develop effort, we cannot attain enlightenment as well. We should school ourself in this way of thinking and then decide, from the depths of our heart, to abandon all forms of laziness. Then, if we cultivate the four powers properly, we will be able to bring the perfection of effort to completion.

This concludes 'Effort', the seventh chapter of the text *Meaningful to Behold*, a commentary to Shantideva's *Guide to the Bodhisattva's Way of Life*.

# Concentration

## HOW TO TRAIN IN THE CONCENTRATION OF TRANQUIL ABIDING

This chapter has four parts:

1 Why we need to attain tranquil abiding
2 Exhortation to abandon the opponents to tranquil abiding
3 How to abandon the opponents to tranquil abiding
4 How to attain tranquil abiding

### WHY WE NEED TO ATTAIN TRANQUIL ABIDING

[1] Having developed effort in the manner explained in the previous chapter, we should place our mind in concentration and try to develop the state of tranquil abiding (Skt. shamatha), a state in which we have full control over our mind, free from any disturbing interferences.

What are the disadvantages of not placing our mind in single-pointed concentration? No matter how much we might attempt to practise the other perfections, if we have not developed concentration our mind will be continually distracted by delusions. We will be trapped between the fangs of the wild beast of conflicting emotions. Instead of controlling our delusions, they will be controlling us. In

Geshe Chekhawa

such a state whatever we do, whether it is reciting prayers, visualizing Deities or practising other virtues, will lack strength and be unable to produce significant results. If we are seriously interested in attaining enlightenment we should discover which objects enable us to develop renunciation, bodhichitta and the correct view of reality, and then focus in meditation single-pointedly on them. There is no benefit in meditating upon anything else.

At the present time our mind is not sharply focused on objects of virtue. Because our mind is not mixed intimately with such objects, our meditations do not proceed or progress very well. If we could always retain a firm state of concentration, however, all our Dharma practices would naturally increase and it is certain that we would receive their fruits. Thinking about how advantageous this would be, we should strive diligently to develop deep concentration and attain the peaceful state of tranquil abiding.

Normally, when we try to meditate on a virtuous object, such as our precious human rebirth, impermanence or emptiness, our mind does not stay tranquilly placed on that object. Instead it is constantly distracted elsewhere. At such times the mind is like a candle flame blown about by the wind. Such a flickering light does not allow us to see things clearly. Similarly, for as long as our mind is blown about by distractions we cannot focus on our object of meditation clearly. If we could construct a protective screen of concentration around our mind, the focus of our meditation would become immovable and we would have an undisturbed view of any virtuous object we chose. Therefore, we should follow the methods outlined below for the development of concentration.

[2ab] The way to prevent our mind from becoming distracted is, first of all, to dwell in solitude. Separated from our family, friends and acquaintances, we achieve physical solitude. More importantly, by opposing and abandoning all our disturbing thoughts we achieve mental solitude. In such a quiet state we can begin to develop the much-needed concentration of mind.

## EXHORTATION TO ABANDON THE OPPONENTS TO TRANQUIL ABIDING

[2cd] For reasons mentioned above, Shantideva urges us to forsake our worldly life and completely abandon the disturbing thoughts of our mind.

## HOW TO ABANDON THE OPPONENTS TO TRANQUIL ABIDING

This has six parts:

1. Recognizing the causes of our attachment to worldly life
2. Recognizing the opponent to our attachment
3. How to generate the opponent to attachment
4. The faults of worldly associations
5. The benefits of living in solitude
6. How to abandon disturbing conceptions

## RECOGNIZING THE CAUSES OF OUR ATTACHMENT TO WORLDLY LIFE

[3] Why are we attached to our mundane existence? Before any attachment arises we grasp at a strong feeling of I. From this arises thoughts such as 'my friend', 'my family' and 'my possessions'. We look at all these things as if they were inherently and independently existent and, as a result, we become attached to what we think is inherently ours.

As described above, the origin of all attachment is our ignorant self-grasping. Since this is so, we might think that in order to develop tranquil abiding we first need to abandon self-grasping. But this is not the case. By contemplating the faults of being attached to our family, possessions and so forth we can temporarily abandon our grasping attitude. This will be enough for our purpose of developing concentration. The full eradication of self-grasping only comes with developing wisdom, and this in turn depends upon first cultivating tranquil abiding. It is sufficient at this point to apply temporary remedies to the problem of our attachment; the final cure can then be applied later.

## RECOGNIZING THE OPPONENT TO OUR ATTACHMENT

[4] The ultimate opponent to attachment and indeed to all the delusions is the wisdom of superior seeing observing emptiness, the true nature of reality. This wisdom, which is endowed with the force of tranquil abiding (a mind that has overcome all forms of mental sinking and excitement), can uproot self-grasping and all other delusions completely. Therefore, as stated before, if we are to develop the tranquil abiding upon which the full force of wisdom

depends, we must seek ways to abandon temporarily the gross attachment we have towards worldly life. If we do not apply these temporary measures we will never be able to win complete cessation of our suffering or help others win their freedom.

## HOW TO GENERATE THE OPPONENT TO ATTACHMENT

This has two parts:

1 Abandoning attachment to sentient beings
2 Abandoning attachment to inanimate things

## ABANDONING ATTACHMENT TO SENTIENT BEINGS

Of the two types of objects to which we can become attached, animate and inanimate, Shantideva now discusses the former. What are the disadvantages of becoming attached to our friends, family, pets and the like? We must remember that both the subject and the object of our clinging attitudes are transient, impermanent and changing every moment. [5] If, for the sake of our attachment to other transient beings, we commit non-virtuous actions we will create the cause to be reborn where we will not be able to see any beautiful or pleasing objects for thousands of lifetimes. Thus our obsession with what we find beautiful is the cause for us not to be able to encounter anything beautiful again for a long time. [6] The result is nothing but unhappiness and the inability to maintain a balanced mind focused on virtue. Furthermore, even when we are fortunate enough to meet with attractive objects, our exaggerated attachment to them causes us much discomfort and suffering.

[7] Having strong attachment to loved ones interrupts our ability to gain a correct understanding of emptiness and also obstructs our development of renunciation and bodhichitta. In all these ways, then, it closes the door leading to liberation. Inevitably attachment will cause us great torment when the unsympathetic Lord of Death separates us from our family and friends and we are forced to depart for our next life completely alone.

[8] With our mind interested only in the affairs and attachments of this lifetime we waste this rare opportunity of our precious human life. Although the objects of our attachment are transitory, they nevertheless have the power to obstruct our path to freedom. For the sake of people who are as impermanent as ourself, we give up the chance to gain Dharma realizations and the achievement of everlasting enlightenment. [9] Behaving in such a near-sighted and childish fashion we do nothing but bring ourself steadily closer to rebirth in one of the lower realms. Therefore what is the benefit of depending solely upon the family and friends to whom we are attached?

We spend much of our time, because of our attachments, trying to please others whose attitudes are as childish as our own. [10] For instance, if we fulfil someone's wishes, he immediately heralds us as his dearest friend. However, if we should thwart his wishes in some small way shortly thereafter, he suddenly views us as his worst enemy. [11] Furthermore, if we give worldly people some advice or urge them to practise Dharma they can easily take offence and say, 'What is the use of that?' If we do not listen to what they have to say they easily become angry, disparage Dharma and proceed to the lower realms. This type of behaviour is what Buddha meant when he called worldly people childish.

As pointed out in the sixth chapter on patience, we too are deserving of being called childish. We are elated when receiving a little praise, some small gain or a slight increase in our reputation. If we fail to receive these, however, we immediately become depressed and extremely unhappy. [12] As with other worldly people, we become jealous of our superiors, competitive with our equals and arrogant towards those lower than ourself.

Why does Shantideva point all this out? He wants to make it clear that there is no benefit in remaining attached to worldly people. Instead of remaining confused and allowing ourself to be distracted by worldly concerns, we should devote ourself to seeking a place of solitude in which we can settle our mind, develop tranquil abiding and progress along the path to enlightenment. [13] If we do not do this but continue to let ourself be distracted by meaningless activities and petty attachments, we will reap only confusion. As a result we will commit non-virtuous deeds, engage in self-praise and disparage others, and waste our time in discussing the transitory pleasures of samsara despite its unsatisfactory and suffering nature. If we look at our lives closely we will agree with Shantideva when he says:

> [14-15a] Although I have devoted myself to meaningless relationships for so many years, what benefits have I gained from them? If I calculate correctly I see that I have gained nothing worthwhile from others, and they too have gained nothing from me. Since there has been no benefit on either side, I should certainly flee from those who distract me as soon as possible.

The conclusion is to live in solitude. [15b-d] If afterwards we should meet with our family and friends again, we should be pleased and happy and greet them with a smile, but we should avoid becoming over-involved with them. Then, without attachment, we should return to the solitary life. It should be noted, however, that this type of life is recommended specifically for those who are engaged in developing single-pointed concentration. It should not be taken as blanket advice that anyone who aspires to practise Dharma must run away to live in a barren cave.

[16] Once we are comfortably dwelling in solitude we should fulfil whatever desires we may have for food or clothing in the same way as a bee takes pollen from a beautiful flower. Without becoming attached to the flower the bee takes what it needs and returns to the hive. In the same way we should seek food and clothing from others and then, without developing a clinging attitude towards the people we have met or the places where we have been, we should return to our place of quiet and avoid getting into relationships with anyone.

## ABANDONING ATTACHMENT TO INANIMATE THINGS

Attachment to material possessions and the like is a further obstacle to be abandoned in our quest for tranquil abiding. We can counter this clinging attitude by training our mind in the following manner. Consider first of all that [17] if we are attached to our wealth, fame and reputation, and develop pride in the respect these attributes elicit from others, the delusions of pride and attachment will only lead us to rebirth in the lower realms where we will have to experience terrible fears. [18] We should understand that our thoroughly confused mind is unable to discriminate between what is beneficial and what is harmful to it.

Therefore, it runs uncontrollably towards objects of attachment, heedless of the thousand-fold misery that must be endured for their sake in lifetimes to come. [19] It is a wise person who remains unattached to wealth, fame and the like, because it is our clinging to these delights that gives birth to all our fears.

[20] A further consideration is that all our possessions and everything we have striven for in this life must certainly be left behind when we depart alone for our next life. Therefore, by remembering death and realizing that we can take nothing with us when we go but the imprints on our mind, we should abandon attachment to the fleeting pleasures of this life.

A final consideration concerns our attitude towards receiving praise. There is really no reason why we should be happy when people say good things about us or unhappy when criticized. Why is this? Because no praise that we ever receive will have the power to elevate us or increase our good qualities and no blame can make us fall. Moreover, [21] there will always be some people who will praise us and others who will despise us. So what pleasure can there be in being praised, and what displeasure from being despised?

## THE FAULTS OF WORLDLY ASSOCIATIONS

The following doubt may now arise: 'Isn't it inappropriate to abandon sentient beings and seek solitude? If we are supposed to be following the Bodhisattva's way of life, shouldn't we try to benefit these beings by remaining among them?' This is a mistaken conception. We must admit that at present our mind is uncontrolled. Since this is the case, [22] how can we hope to be able to fulfil all sentient beings' wishes and please them? Each of them has different, and often conflicting, inclinations and intentions, and even Buddha could not please them all. Is there any need to point out that someone as confused as we are certainly will not be able to do so?

Temporarily, therefore, we should give up the wish to associate with worldly people and engage instead in those practices, namely the development of tranquil abiding and meditation on emptiness, that will actually increase our ability to help others. Then, when we attain a state of realization, the time will come when we can mix with and benefit many people. This is the same approach taken by someone who wishes to become a medical doctor. Before he or she can be of greatest service to others she must withdraw to a medical school for a period of intense training during which she equips herself for the task ahead. Only after she has prepared herself in this way is she confident and able to aid others in the relief of their suffering.

If we continuously associate with worldly people now we will find not only that we are unable to benefit them effectively but that, because of their delusions, they will do nothing but create heavy non-virtuous karma in relation to us. [23] If we adopt an ascetic lifestyle and live simply, they will scorn us and say, 'You are nothing but a beggar, you miserable being!' On the other hand, if we possess material wealth they will say to us, 'You cannot be much of a Dharma practitioner; look how attached you are to the good life!' If we remain among people who are so hard to please, how will they ever see anything but faults in us?

[24] Childish, worldly people are only interested in their own welfare. If we do not fulfil their wishes they become unhappy. Our association with them, therefore, exposes us to the danger of becoming like them ourself and having our Bodhisattva practices degenerate. Buddha has said that these

childish beings do not know how to benefit others and it is therefore unwise for us to associate with such foolish people or to depend upon them.

## THE BENEFITS OF LIVING IN SOLITUDE

Once we have become deeply convinced of the need to leave our worldly attachments behind, we should turn our mind towards the setting within which we can develop concentration properly. Shantideva describes the longing a Dharma practitioner has for a place of solitude in the following manner, and we should pray to be able to find and live in such a place as well:

> [25-28] Having left the childish people of the world behind, where will I dwell? In solitude where there is no one to interrupt my Dharma practice. The trees, birds, deer and other forest dwellers will never hinder me but rather will benefit me by serving as objects of my renunciation and bodhichitta, which will increase daily. I will receive nothing unpleasant from these forest folk.
> 
> When will I dwell in a cave where there is no foundation for clinging to arise? In empty shrines or at the foot of trees, unattached to family and not looking back – when will I come to dwell like that?
> 
> When will I dwell in that place not owned by others, which causes no arguments and allows me to meditate for as long as I like: a clean open place where I can dwell without attachment to my body and possessions? When will I be able to live without fear, with nothing but a begging bowl, a cooking pot and some poor clothes of no use to others, and not desiring anything? If I abide

in this way, I will not even have to protect or hide my body. There is no danger from thieves or robbers since I will possess nothing that anyone else would want.

If we generate the aspiration and pray to be able to dwell in this way it is certain that one day we will be able to do so. If the circumstances do not come about in this life, they definitely will in a future life. At the present moment our attachment to both animate and inanimate objects would make dwelling in solitude very difficult for us. However, once we abandon this attachment, living in solitude will bring us much happiness and contentment.

In the past, great Indian and Tibetan Yogis such as Milarepa spent much of their lives in seclusion. Compared with us, who spend our life in comfortable homes surrounded by luxuries, who has the greater happiness? Without a doubt Yogis like Milarepa experience bliss that is a thousand times greater than anything we ever experience. Their unsurpassed happiness is due to their inner calm and their complete lack of attachment to external objects, while our suffering and dissatisfaction is due to our complete submersion in attitudes of attachment and aversion to external objects.

When we realize the many advantages of dwelling in a place of solitude we should make heartfelt prayers to be able to practise in such surroundings. It can be very helpful for those who are interested to read the biographies of Buddha and other great meditators to learn how they lived and practised in solitude. Until 1959 there were many practitioners living in the remote areas of Tibet, and many meditators at this very moment are following this way of life and dwelling peacefully in seclusion. We should rejoice in their practices and pray to emulate them.

There are many stories that could be told about the great practitioners of the past, but I will only make a few remarks here about the great Tibetan Yogi Kachen Yeshe Gyaltsen, the tutor to the eighth Dalai Lama. When he was an ordinary monk in Tashi Lhunpo Monastery he received many teachings on Sutra and Tantra from his Spiritual Guides. He then developed the strong desire to meditate and decided to do so in the same caves as Milarepa used centuries before.

On one occasion he travelled to Kyirong, a district in which Milarepa spent much time in various retreat caves. Yeshe Gyaltsen was looking in particular for a cave called Kar, which was situated at a great altitude on the side of a snow mountain beyond dense woods. There was such danger from heavy snows around Kar that it was accessible only during a few months each summer. Consequently it was a place where few people ever went.

When Yeshe Gyaltsen arrived in Kyirong he asked one of the villagers he met where he might find Milarepa's cave called Kar. The villager was startled and asked, 'What do you want to know that for?' When Yeshe Gyaltsen explained that he meant to meditate there, the villager laughed derisively and said, 'Anyone who wants to stay in such a place had better have a body of copper and a heart of iron. Are you like this?' Yeshe Gyaltsen once again asked for directions, and once again the villager laughed and repeated his taunts. Finally, however, he told the would-be meditator how to reach the cave he was looking for.

People in the surrounding area came to know that Yeshe Gyaltsen was last seen heading to Kar, and when many months had passed without his being seen again, they feared the worst. When summer came a few of them made their way up the treacherous route leading to the cave and were surprised to discover the Yogi sitting happily at peace following his practices. When the people in the surrounding villages heard about Yeshe Gyaltsen's unusual abilities they developed great faith and devotion towards him and soon his place of meditation became a pilgrimage site. So many people came to pay homage to him, in fact, that after a while he had to leave and find another place to practise.

In this manner Yeshe Gyaltsen travelled between the former caves of Milarepa and meditated in them for many years. In later years when the eighth Dalai Lama asked him to give his autobiography, Yeshe Gyaltsen replied, 'My practice of Dharma was even harder than that of the great Yogi Milarepa. While he ate nettles and begged for food in the towns, I endured all my problems and pains in strict solitude.' Eventually he was recognized as an incarnation of Milarepa himself. This is just a brief story from the life of one Yogi, but there were many like him throughout India and Tibet.

To strengthen our resolve to live and meditate in solitude we should first contemplate impermanence and death. This will increase our desire to practise Dharma. If we meditate upon the certainty of our death, the utter uncertainty of when it will actually occur, and the fact that at the time of death the only thing of benefit to us will be our practice of Dharma, our determination to practise purely will be greatly enhanced. [29] It is a good idea to visit a cemetery or cremation site occasionally to further our abandonment of attachment towards our body. When we see or think about the corpses and bones they will remind us that one day we too will become like them. Then we should aspire to meditate in a secluded place and follow spiritual practices until death interrupts us. We should think how our death in a lonely cave will pass completely unnoticed. [30] Our flesh will fall from our bones and become so rotten that not even animals who normally like flesh will come near it.

If we abandon worldly life and dwell solely on the thought, 'When will I be able to practise like this?' it will be impossible for us not to gain realizations. However, if today we were to move into an isolated cave we would find it impossible to achieve any results from our practice and would instead encounter great difficulties. Why is this? Because at present we only have one foot in Dharma; the other is firmly planted in the distractions of worldly life. Although we may have some small wish to practise Dharma and attain enlightenment we also hanker after the pleasures of samsara. Therefore there is no way for us to receive realizations quickly. Why are we so split between these two opposing desires? Because we lack the proper recollection and meditation on the fears of death. If we develop death awareness we will not waste our human potential on worldly affairs, but will instead be motivated to follow Dharma purely.

We should try to look at our human situation as realistically as possible. [31] Although our body arose as an integrated unit, eventually our bones and flesh will separate from one another and decay. The same is even more true of relationships – our friends and acquaintances will soon be parted from each other and from ourself.

[32] At birth we came into this world alone. Until now we have been inseparable from our body, but when the signs appear telling of the approach of the Lord of Death, we will realize that we have to depart from this life alone, without even our present body to accompany us. If such separation is in store for our very body and mind, is there any need to speak of our inevitable separation from family and friends? It does not matter how long we have spent living together

with our loved ones; we are born alone and will depart from this life alone. All the suffering we experience must also be endured alone. No one can share it with us. What, then, is the use of being attached to others and referring to them as 'my husband', 'my wife', 'my friend' and so on? These beings do little to benefit us and only serve to interrupt our journey to enlightenment. What use are such obstacle-making friends?

[33] We should try to go through life in the way a traveller passes from place to place. He does not become attached to the guest house in which he will only stay a night or two for he realizes that he will soon be on his way somewhere else. Similarly, even though we may be surrounded by luxuries, it is certain that some day we will have to depart alone and empty-handed. Our body is nothing more than a guest house and our mind, like the traveller, must soon vacate it and move elsewhere.

[34] Eventually the henchmen of the Lord of Death will call for us, and our body will be carried off to the cemetery by four pallbearers. All our relatives will gather around. They will be stricken with grief and many tears will fall. Since this is certain to happen, it is much wiser to entrust ourself to solitude beforehand. [35] If we abide in this way we will encounter no objects to arouse our anger or attachment while we are still alive and we will be left alone by our friends and enemies alike. When we do die there will be no one to get upset, for our friends and relatives will long since have regarded us as dead. [36] At the time of death we will not be disturbed by loved ones mourning over us or enemies planning to cause harm. There will be no one to distract us from concentrating on the precious Three Jewels and from meditating upon the path. By thinking deeply about all these reasons [37] we should make up our mind to dwell in

solitude – happy, content and with few problems. We should work to pacify all mental disturbances so that we can achieve perfect single-pointed concentration through the practice of tranquil abiding.

## HOW TO ABANDON DISTURBING CONCEPTIONS

[38] Once we have given up our obsessive attachment to our family and friends, and hatred of our enemies – both of which disturb our peace of mind and hinder the attainment of tranquil abiding – we should let ourself be motivated solely by bodhichitta and settle our mind single-pointedly on the chosen object of meditation. Gradually we should develop our practice until we gain a clear realization of emptiness and thereby subdue the poisonous mental delusions. For us to accomplish this highest of aims we must cut our attachment to objects of desire and worldly activities. Otherwise, instead of progressing to liberation and enlightenment we will be exposing ourself to the unwanted consequences of our negative actions. As Shantideva says:

> [39] Desires give rise to extreme misfortune in both this and future lives. In this life we will experience killing, bondage and flaying and in the next the hellish suffering of the lower realms.

In this section dealing with disturbances Shantideva gives a detailed discussion of the many faults of attachment and the way in which our deluded desires bind us to a life of endless searching, dissatisfaction and misery. Because attachment to sexual pleasures is one of the most universal forms of desire, Shantideva especially emphasizes the bondage of obsessive sexual longing. Because his original audience consisted of monks, Shantideva focused on a man's longing desire for a woman and presented as an antidote a description of the unclean nature of a woman's desire-provoking body. However, as Shantideva himself makes clear, this discussion should not be understood to imply that one sex is by nature unclean while the other is pure, or that sexual longing is only experienced by men. Bearing all this in mind, readers should make whatever changes may be necessary – in viewpoint, gender, and so forth – for a more personal interpretation of the following material.

[40] Some men, out of longing desire for sexual pleasure, will do almost anything to possess a woman, from sending messengers and go-betweens to the woman's parents, all the way to committing adultery with another man's wife. They do this regardless of the dangers involved and the damage to their reputation. [41] To fulfil their wishes and intentions men spend a lot of money, engage in many non-virtuous acts and sacrifice their wealth and their very lives. What is the goal of all this trouble? What meaning does it have?

The ultimate aim is to engage in the sexual act with a woman. But let us examine the nature of the body that is the object of so much desire. [42] It is a collection of marrow, bone, flesh, skin, blood, pus, lungs, liver, intestines, excrement, urine and so forth. This collection contains not a single pure part, nor is it autonomous or inherently existent. After seeing the faults and impurities of such a filthy collection, how can we still be so obsessively attached to it? Why do we not strive instead to break free from the vast ocean of samsaric dissatisfaction and attain the perfect bliss of full awakening?

How strange are a man's desires and how fickle! [43] In ancient India, whenever a man encountered a woman her face was hidden by a veil. Even at the marriage ceremony her face would be covered and she would be very bashful. Afterwards, when the husband finally saw the face of his wife, a great desire would arise to have sexual intercourse with her. If this unveiling of a woman's face can have such a magnetic effect on a man, [44] why is he not similarly attracted when, after her death, her face is unveiled by vultures? Why does he not want to copulate with her then? Her body is still there but the man only wants to run away from it.

[45] Lecherous men cherish a woman's body so much that if another man were merely to look at her, great jealousy would arise. If this is the case, why do we not protect her when the vultures are tearing her to pieces with their beaks? It is senseless to protect her body so jealously now when eventually it will become the food of wild animals and birds. [46] Why go to the trouble of offering flower garlands, sandalwood and ornaments of gold and silver to something that will shortly be devoured by others? [47] Moreover, why are we frightened by her motionless skeleton when we see it lying in the cemetery but not afraid now when we see her zombie-like body moving about like a walking corpse controlled by momentary impulses? Such contradictory behaviour is very strange.

[48] It is also strange that we are attached to her body when it is covered with skin and clothed, but repulsed by it when it lies exposed on the charnel ground.

*But then she is dead. That's what makes the difference.* Yet it is the body we are attached to and that is the same at both times. [49] When we kiss a woman we drink the saliva from her mouth. Why is it that we like this spit that arises solely from the food she has eaten but not her urine and excrement, which arise from the same source? [50] Furthermore, we like a woman's body because it is soft and smooth to the touch, but we are not attached to a cotton pillow that has the same qualities. In fact there is more reason to like a pillow than a woman because, unlike her, a pillow does not give off foul odours. [51] But we are so confused that we cannot tell the difference between what is clean and what is unclean. If we find our pillow uncomfortable one night we are liable to get angry with it, but we never become upset with the discomfort of sleeping next to the impure body of a woman.

*But the object of my attachment, a woman's body, is not really unclean.* Let us examine its nature. [52] The body is a cage of bones tied together with muscles and plastered over with the mud of flesh. On the inside it is full of impurities, so how can we say that it isn't unclean? If it is so impure, why do we long to embrace her so? Are we so attached to filth? [53] Is not the obvious impurity of our own body, which we experience daily, enough for us? Are we so enamoured of things defiled that we must copulate with other bags of filth?

*The example of the cotton pillow is ridiculous. I am not interested in that:* [54] *I like to touch the flesh of a beautiful female body.* If that is the case, why aren't we attached to her dead body? It is still a body of flesh and, for a while at least, still smooth and beautiful.

*But a dead body is devoid of mind. I like a woman because she possesses a mind.* [55] All right, but since her mind is intangible, why do we engage in meaningless copulation?

We should remember that it is not only a woman's body that is unclean; a male body is likewise polluted. We should understand this and not think it is otherwise. [56] It is not so strange that we do not realize the unclean nature of another's body, but that we fail to recognize the unclean nature of our own body is certainly peculiar. Thinking about this well, we should try to counteract the uncontrolled attachment we feel towards others.

*It is the beautiful shape of the female body that attracts me. That is why I indulge in sexual intercourse.* [57] But a fresh young lotus and a water lily both have extremely beautiful shapes when they unfold their petals in the sunlight. Why do we not become attached to them instead of to this cage of filth?

[58] If we do not want to touch a place that has been defiled by excrement or vomit, why are we so avid to touch those places on her body that emit such filth? All of this excrement and vomit comes from her body, which itself is the result of much impurity. [59] It came from her father's sperm and mother's ovum and spent many months inside a damp and unclean womb. The essence of her body, its cause and what it produces are all unclean. Since there is not a single aspect of it that is not impure, why are we so anxious to embrace it? [60] Not even a particle of desire arises in us for the small insect that emerges from a pile of dung. Why then are we so attached to a body made up of thirty-six different kinds of impurity?

[61] We do not disparage our own body for its impure nature and go so far as to develop strong attachment to another's impure collection. This is so nonsensical! Can we not see the impurity of the body? Look what it does to whatever we put into it. [62] Such delicacies as savouries, cooked rice and vegetables are all clean before they are eaten, but if they are put into our mouth and then spat out again they will defile the ground on which they land.

[63] If there is still any doubt as to the body's impurity, go to a cemetery and examine a corpse. [64] If we were to peel the skin from our object of attachment it would smell so foul that intense revulsion would arise. Yet still we enjoy the fleshly delights of the female body!

*Now be quiet for a minute; I want to say something. When a woman anoints her body with scented perfumes, powders and other toiletries, it is truly beautiful to behold.* No, why be quiet? Your statement is ridiculous. [65] These fragrant perfumes and delicate scents have nothing to do with her body. They arise from other sources such as sandalwood and so forth. Are we attached to her body because of the things she puts on it? If she did not use these aids and neglected to wash for a while, we would soon see what her body is really like. [66] Then it would emit the foul odours that are natural to it. If a woman's body is so unclean and foul, is it not a good idea not to be attached to her?

*Oh no. If she washes herself, anoints herself with perfume and adorns herself with jewels, and then dresses in fine clothing, she is wonderfully appealing. Haven't you seen such beautiful women as this?* [67] But is this beauty her own or not? Surely it has been contrived temporarily: this beautiful appearance is nothing but a fabrication. She took soap and water and washed her foul odours away. Then she oiled her hair and powdered and decorated her face. Afterwards she covered herself in fine garments and sparkling ornaments so that we would behold her as beautiful. But if we prepared a wooden dummy in the same way it would also appear beautiful. What is her body's nature without such fabrications as these? [68] If she were to remain in her natural state for some time without attending to herself as described, what would we see? Just a frightening, naked, filthy body with long dishevelled hair, dirty nails and yellow, foul-smelling teeth.

Shantideva has spent a lot of time describing the basically unclean nature of the body and he has done so not out of morbidity but to help us counter the faults of attachment. As he says, if we are full of attachment and self-cherishing and constantly run after the objects of our desire, [69] this is like polishing and sharpening a weapon that will eventually kill us. There is no reason to engage in activities that will do nothing but harm us, yet this is precisely what people all over the world are constantly doing. They are deeply confused about what is virtuous and what is non-virtuous, clean and unclean. [70] They are afraid when they see the pile of human bones in a cemetery but have not the slightest aversion for or fear of the graveyard cities full of moving bones. This is quite odd and shows how perverse their thinking really is.

[71] Furthermore, its basically impure nature is not the only disadvantage of the desirable body of others. We should realize that in order to engage in the sexual act we tie ourself ever tighter to the unsatisfactory aspects of samsara. As stated before, we forfeit our wealth, act non-virtuously and work with great difficulty merely to possess the object of our desire. Because of all this we encounter many problems during this lifetime and create the cause to descend to the lower realms where we will experience even more suffering.

[72] When we were young it was difficult to amass wealth and when we grew a bit older we had to exert much effort to find a wife. When we finally did get married the effort required to make ends meet left us little time to enjoy her company, and sometimes all her company did was make us miserable. This is the story of many people's lives.

[73] Those under the influence of desire have to work hard every day and put up with many difficulties just to support themselves and their family. When they come home at night they are often too exhausted to have intercourse and spend the evening lying motionless like a corpse. [74] Others, desirous of food, clothing and material gain, travel to far-off lands and even join the army. While away they undergo the

suffering of being separated from the woman they desire and have no opportunity to engage in sex with her. No one wants to be separated from what he or she finds attractive but that is just what our attachment often leads us to experience.

[75] Many people are so confused about how they should earn the material wealth they desire that they sell themselves to others and are forced to perform heavy menial labour. In order to support a wife and family it is usually necessary to work and earn wages. In such a situation there is no freedom, for we are under the power of our employer or benefactor and driven here and there by the wind of their actions and desires. [76] Some very unfortunate people are so destitute that they literally become the slaves of others, lacking all freedom of choice. When it is time for the wives of these poor men to give birth they are so lacking in basic necessities that they are forced to have their children in the most miserable of conditions, perhaps even outdoors at the foot of a tree.

[77] Desire turns people into fools. Some are so deceived by the lure of material gain and the longing for fame that they go off to war and thereby risk their very lives. Others are driven by their attachments to become the slaves of others and must endure great suffering and pain. [78] Lusting for women, material gain and the like, some turn to theft and other crimes, and then have to face the torment of being caught by the authorities and imprisoned, or of being mutilated, impaled, stabbed and burnt.

[79] We should take a close look at all the various torments that are involved in collecting material gain and the like, protecting it and eventually losing it. We should realize that guarding wealth is fraught with infinite problems and leads only to frustration and desperation. Anyone who allows

himself to be distracted by his attachment to wealth, family and so forth will never have the opportunity to break free from the cycle of samsaric suffering and attain the peace and happiness of full enlightenment.

There are so many faults in being attached to worldly life and, no matter how hard we strive, there is but little profit to be gained. [80] Our situation is similar to that of a horse that is forced to draw a cart. If it dares to pause for a brief moment to eat a mouthful of grass, it has to endure a beating from its impatient owner. [81] We have such a rare and precious opportunity to do something special with our life that it is a great shame to squander it solely for the sake of gratifying the petty desires of this life. There are many animals who are more skilled than ourself in finding desirable objects and avoiding pain and danger. What a waste to employ our humanity in endeavours that even an animal can do! While we are still human we should try our hardest to extract some meaning from our existence.

What good is the wealth that we try so hard to amass? [82] No matter how much we collect it will all eventually perish. Moreover, if we let ourself become attached to this wealth, we will certainly fall to the lower realms of existence. From time without beginning we have worked hard to amass samsaric pleasures but what meaning has all that work had for us? [83] If we had spent the same energy on Dharma practices as we had on samsaric pleasures, surely we would have been enlightened by now. However, because we involved ourself in worldly affairs and non-virtue, we now find ourself in this meaningless situation. The hardships we had to put up with while chasing worldly pleasures were greater than the hardships of attaining Buddhahood; the struggles we had to go through to find samsaric happiness were without meaning and they still have not come to an end. [84] If we look at the hellish suffering that follows from attachment to this life we will see that it is a million times greater than the sufferings we experience in this life from weapons, poison, fire, treacherous places and enemies.

[85] When we contemplate the faults of samsara correctly and develop disillusionment with it all, we will generate the wish to abide in solitude and strive to develop deep concentration through the practice of tranquil abiding. What kind of solitude should we look for? It should be a place that is free from disputes and the objects that arouse our disturbing thoughts. [86] The fortunate one who has the opportunity to develop bodhichitta (the object of the Yogi's concentration as described later in this chapter) lives in a peaceful forest cooled by the sandal-scented moonlight. In a house made of flat stones and fanned by peaceful, silent forest breezes, he thinks about renunciation, the mind of enlightenment and emptiness; and, for the sake of others, meditates according to the methods for developing tranquil abiding.

[87] Living in abandoned houses, at the foot of trees or in caves and having left behind the pain of clinging to and guarding our possessions, we can dwell free from all cares and be completely independent. [88] We can use whatever we possess freely without attachment and without getting into relationships with others. This happy and contented life is spent in pursuit of spiritual realizations, and even the powerful lord of the gods, the great Indra, cannot find as happy and joyful a life as this. Reflecting in this way, we should entrust ourself to the life of a solitary seeker after truth.

## HOW TO ATTAIN TRANQUIL ABIDING

This, the main subject matter of this chapter, has two parts:

1 A general explanation of the stages of tranquil abiding meditation
2 Explanation of the particular use to which tranquil abiding is to be put: meditating on equalizing and exchanging self with others

## A GENERAL EXPLANATION OF THE STAGES OF TRANQUIL ABIDING MEDITATION

The actual methods for developing tranquil abiding are not taught in Shantideva's root text. What follows has been extracted from the works of Maitreya and Asanga and included in this commentary in response to the great interest in meditation in general, and single-pointed concentration in particular, expressed by many westerners. Despite this widespread interest, few people possess a flawless understanding of the methods for calming and concentrating the mind, and, as a result, there are very few who meditate properly. The following instructions are offered with the hope that they will contribute a little to the understanding of whoever is interested.

Why is it important to attain a state of tranquil abiding? Only when our mind has achieved this imperturbable state can we focus single-pointedly on the various objects of meditation and gain the necessary realizations of the spiritual path. For example, one of the temporal results of spiritual practice is the attainment of miracle powers, such as clairvoyance. Such powers can definitely be developed and are of great use in bringing benefit to others. As the great Pandit Atisha said, 'Lacking clairvoyance yet wishing to benefit others extensively is like a bird without wings trying to fly.' However, there is no way that we can achieve such heightened states of awareness if we fail to develop tranquil abiding beforehand.

All the realizations of the Hinayana path leading to personal liberation, and of the Mahayana path leading to full enlightenment, spring from the mind that has achieved tranquil abiding. If we have the motivation of renunciation and take emptiness, (the true nature of reality, taught in the following chapter) as our object of tranquil abiding meditation, we can cut through self-grasping and attain complete cessation of all suffering. If, in addition, we develop the precious bodhichitta, we can remove all the obstructions to omniscience and attain the complete awakening of Buddhahood. Without tranquil abiding, none of these ultimate goals can possibly be reached.

Once we have developed tranquil abiding our mind becomes as immovable as Mount Meru, the hub of the universe, and can be placed single-pointedly upon any object of virtue we choose. When we enter into meditation our mind mixes completely with its object and we therefore gain an unparalleled understanding of it. At the present time, even though we may meditate on Dharma, our mind and its object never become one; they always remain separate. This is why we do not develop realizations. The mind and its object of meditation are like two mountains that never meet. If we attain tranquil abiding, however, all such faults will be overcome and the fruit of whatever we practise, be it Sutra or Tantra, will fall easily into our grasp. All our practices of virtue will grow stronger and more powerful, and we will be able to develop our mind limitlessly. By reflecting again and again on these many benefits, we should strive with joy and enthusiasm to attain tranquil abiding.

The general explanation of tranquil abiding meditation will be presented in four parts:

1. The six necessary conditions for attaining tranquil abiding
2. The nine mental abidings
3. The five obstacles to attaining tranquil abiding
4. The eight opponents to the five obstacles

## THE SIX NECESSARY CONDITIONS FOR ATTAINING TRANQUIL ABIDING

Those who wish from the depths of their heart to develop the actual state of tranquil abiding must, at the outset of their practice, gather six necessary conditions that will ensure success. As Atisha said in his *Lamp for the Path* (Skt. *Bodhipathapradipa*), if we do not gather all these necessary conditions it will be extremely difficult to develop tranquil abiding even if we sit in meditation for many years. When wishing to perform mundane actions, such as preparing a cup of tea, we cannot hope to be successful if we complete only one of the many necessary causes, such as having the hot water but no tea leaves. If this is true for ordinary activities, how much more necessary it is when seeking such an extraordinary state as tranquil abiding!

The first condition for successful tranquil abiding meditation is a suitable place, or environment, in which to do the practice. Such a place should have the following five qualities:

(1) It is a place where it is easy to obtain whatever we need such as food and clothing.
(2) If possible the retreat site should be one that has been blessed by the presence in the past of Yogis or even Buddhas. If we cannot find such a place we should seek a solitary site where there is no danger from wild animals, thieves, robbers, disputes and fighting.
(3) The environment of the retreat site is healthy and free of sickness, and the water supply is clean.
(4) There should be one or two spiritual friends living nearby who hold the same views as ourself and who are observing pure moral discipline.
(5) It is a quiet place free from the sounds of people during the day and animals at night.

The above constitute the external preparations necessary for a successful retreat. The internal preparation, which is the most important one of all, is knowing all the methods for meditating on tranquil abiding. Once we have gained this knowledge by receiving instructions from a well-qualified Teacher, it is not too difficult to find a retreat site with all the proper external conditions.

This completes the first general condition, that of place. Second, we should have little desire for material things, such as food and clothing. We should abandon the mind that thinks, 'How wonderful it would be to have such-and-such.' Third, we should have contentment, being satisfied with whatever we possess no matter what its quality. Fourth, we should give up all activities that do not relate to the practice of tranquil abiding. These include such things as writing letters, reading unrelated books, seeing friends and so forth.

Fifth, it is essential to keep pure moral discipline, specifically refraining from the ten non-virtuous actions of body, speech and mind discussed in chapter five of this commentary. Lastly, we should abandon all disturbing conceptions. These include all thoughts that, instead of being directed at the object of tranquil abiding meditation, are distracted by any of the five objects of desire: attractive sights, sounds, smells, tastes and tactile objects.

It is said that if we study and understand thoroughly the techniques of tranquil abiding meditation, have all six necessary conditions just described and then practise continuously with effort, it is possible to attain a perfect state of tranquil abiding within six months.

After we have found a suitable retreat site, we should prepare a proper meditation cushion and sit in the correct posture. Normally the quality of our chair or cushion is not very important but if we wish to attain tranquil abiding we must have a comfortable seat or our meditation will be disturbed. The cushion should be raised a little at the back to allow us to assume the correct posture easily and hold it for a long time. As a further aid in making our seat more stable and firm, we can draw a swastika – the ancient Indian symbol of immovability and auspiciousness – and place it on the ground directly beneath the centre of the cushion. On top of this drawing we can lay two strands of couch grass symbolizing long life, and two of kusha grass symbolizing the clarity of wisdom, so that they are lying side by side with their tips pointing towards the front. If we are not able to prepare these there is no harm in doing without them; they are helpful but not at all essential.

In Tantric close retreats, once our meditation cushion has been prepared we are not allowed to move it for the duration of the retreat. When practising to develop tranquil abiding, however, we can rearrange our cushion to suit varying situations. For example, if our mind becomes too excited it is a good idea to sit facing a wall. If we are disturbed by sluggishness and mental sinking it is helpful to sit in a bright part of the room and thereby refresh our mind. In brief, we should be aware of our state of mind and arrange the meditation conditions accordingly.

The next important consideration is the proper meditation posture. There are seven parts to this posture, comprising the legs, hands, back, head, eyes, shoulders, and the teeth, tongue and lips. It is best if our legs are crossed so that our feet rest on the opposite thighs with soles pointing upwards. This is the full vajra posture, but if this is not possible we can assume the half-vajra posture, where one foot rests on the opposite thigh while the other is on the ground, or any other comfortable cross-legged position.

We should place our right hand upon the left, palms up, at a distance of four fingers' width below the navel, with our thumbs gently touching each other just above the navel. Our back should be straight and our head slightly inclined forwards, our eyes opened slightly and gently gazing down along the line of the nose. Our shoulders should be level. Our mouth should be gently closed with the lips resting together in the usual manner. In order to prevent too much saliva from forming we can keep our teeth resting gently together – making certain that our jaw is not clenched – and place the tip of our tongue against the back of the upper teeth.

This is the best of all meditation postures for it helps to prevent sleep, mental dullness, distractions and other obstacles to concentration, and it also helps in the development of mental clarity. This manner of sitting is sometimes known as the 'seven-point posture of Vairochana' after the Buddha who blessed it and who is often depicted in this position. If we familiarize ourself with this posture we will be planting imprints on our mind to become like this Buddha.

The great Yogi Marpa the Translator was renowned for the depth and stability of his meditative concentration. A master of the seven-point posture, he once declared, 'If all the qualities of the great Tibetan meditators were gathered together, they would be unable to challenge my meditation posture.' This was not said out of pride but from a profound realization of the importance of this posture in the practice of Tantra. Remembering all the excellent qualities of this manner of sitting, we should receive a personal demonstration from a qualified meditation master and accustom ourself to this best of all meditation postures.

Having seated ourself on a properly prepared cushion in the manner described, we should first attend to our motivation: the state of mind in which we are entering the meditation. If we discover that our mind is full of wild, uncontrolled thoughts, we should try to eliminate them. We can overcome strong attachment, anger and all other types of mental disturbance by paying attention to our breath in the following manner. Breathe normally through the nostrils, without haste or noise, and mentally count 'one' on completion of the first cycle of the incoming and outgoing breaths. (If we like we can also visualize all our non-virtues, delusions and disturbances in the form of thick, black smoke that flows out of our mind with the out-breath and disappears in the far distance. When we breathe in we can visualize the blessings of all the Buddhas entering our nostrils in the form of pure, white light, which then dissolves into our entire body and fills us with inspiration. This visualization, however, is not essential and can be practised or omitted at our discretion.) This manner of breathing and counting can then be maintained for twenty-one cycles. If this is not sufficient to calm the mind, the process can be repeated until the noise of our mental disturbances has been reduced. Once our mind is free from such gross disturbances we can seek the actual object of tranquil abiding meditation, which can be a visualized Deity, a seed-letter, the thought of renunciation or love and so forth.

The importance of cutting the flow of disturbing thoughts in meditation cannot be overestimated. To meditate properly means to prevent the mind from wandering distractedly, and to place it so that it remains focused on a single object. If we have no object of meditation the mind becomes like a bird that wishes to land but cannot find any ground on which to do so. And if we have an object but our mind wanders elsewhere and everywhere, this is like a bird, who after landing on the ground, is unable to stand firmly in one place. It is therefore essential that we abandon mental distractions, and we can do this by means of the breathing meditation outlined above.

When these gross distractions have been pacified we should turn our mind towards the chosen object of tranquil abiding meditation. For example, we can select the form of a Buddha and use it as the object upon which to develop single-pointed concentration. If we choose the form of Buddha Shakyamuni, we should select a well-made statue or painting and examine it in great detail from head to toe and back again. When we become acquainted with a general image of Buddha in this way and can bring it to mind in visualization, we have found the object of meditation. We should hold this object (the visualized image) comfortably, neither too loosely nor too tightly. When we are able to maintain our grasp on this object well, we have attained the first mental abiding described below. We should then continue in this fashion until we are able to hold the object for approximately five minutes. At that point we will have achieved the second of the nine mental abidings.

At the beginning of our practice we should apply great effort in attaining these first two stages purely. Together they form the basis for the remaining stages, and for this reason they are emphasized strongly. The following instructions explaining how the nine mental abidings are related to one another, and how we should develop them are drawn from the teachings of Buddha Maitreya and the Superior Bodhisattva Asanga.

## THE NINE MENTAL ABIDINGS

**(1)** *Placing the mind.* As explained above, having found the object and being able simply to hold it, without yet being able to maintain it, is called the concentration of 'placing the mind'. This initial stage is attained through the force of listening, primarily by listening to or reading instructions concerning tranquil abiding meditation. Owing to the force of listening to instructions from our Spiritual Guide, we can place our mind on an object of meditation. At this stage we will recognize and experience many disturbing thoughts as they arise.

**(2)** *Continual placement.* We attain this stage by continually familiarizing ourself with the practice of the first mental abiding. When we are able to hold the object for about five minutes, we have reached this second mental abiding. The force we employ to gain this level of concentration is that of contemplating, or reflecting upon, the teachings we have heard. At this stage some of our mental disturbances are pacified and others, after they arise, appear to slow down a little and become exhausted.

The practitioner who has gained these first two mental abidings still has more distractions than concentration and so must work to abandon these distractions and strengthen his hold on the object of meditation. Therefore the particular type of attention he employs is called 'tight attention'.

(3) *Replacement.* When we are still at the second stage we are unable to return our mind immediately to its object once it has been distracted from that object. But with the third mental abiding we have the ability to bring the mind back immediately after it has wandered away from its object. Both this and the following mental abiding employ the force of strong mindfulness.

(4) *Close placement.* The power of our mindfulness at this stage is so strong that, for the duration of the meditation session, the mind never loses its object. At this level of concentration the force of mindfulness is complete.

(5) *Controlling.* At the fourth stage the force of mindfulness can cause the mind to become too collected and there is a danger of the meditator experiencing subtle mental sinking. Therefore, at the fifth stage we apply the force of alertness, thereby uplifting the mind. At this level of concentration there is no longer any danger of the mind experiencing gross mental sinking.

(6) *Pacifying.* Having overly uplifted the mind while on the previous level the meditator may now face a slight danger of subtle mental excitement. However, this can also be countered by the force of alertness, which is completed with the sixth mental abiding. During this stage neither gross nor

subtle mental sinking can affect the mind as it concentrates on its object of meditation.

(7) *Completely pacifying*. Because the powers of mindfulness and alertness are now complete, the mind has achieved a state of balance. It is neither overly uplifted in response to mental sinking nor overly collected in response to mental excitement. While there is no longer a great danger from either of these hindrances, it is still possible to develop very slight subtle sinking or excitement. However, these subtle obstacles are immediately overpowered by the force of effort.

From the third to the seventh mental abidings our concentration is very strong but mental sinking and excitement still occur in one form or another. Therefore the type of attention we employ during these stages is called 'interrupted attention'. As will be explained in the next section, it is extremely important for us to recognize and discriminate between the gross and subtle forms of mental sinking and excitement, and apply the appropriate remedies.

(8) *Single-pointedness*. At this stage we can, with just a little effort, maintain concentration on the object of meditation throughout the entire session without any danger at all from any form of mental sinking or excitement. The concentration we have now achieved is called 'single-pointedness' of mind and, because we are able to stay on the object without any faltering, our attention has become uninterrupted. Both the seventh and the eighth mental abidings are attained through the force of effort.

(9) *Placement in equipoise*. In all the previous stages of concentration we required effort to place our mind on the object of meditation. At this final stage, however, such effort is no longer needed and we can keep our mind focused on its object for as long as we wish. This level of concentration

is attained through the force of complete familiarity, and the attention we employ is called 'spontaneous'.

Having achieved this ninth mental abiding our mind can remain effortlessly placed on virtue for as long as we wish, during which time all problems, obstacles, heaviness and dullness will be overcome. We will have attained a state of continuous mental suppleness, which will cause beneficial energy to suffuse the body. This energy destroys all the physical obstacles and feelings of heaviness and discomfort that would prevent us from engaging in continuous Dharma practice. As a result we attain great physical suppleness and our body feels as light as cotton. This leads to our attainment of great physical bliss, after which we gain the ability, during our meditation sessions, to perceive nothing but our chosen object of contemplation. No other phenomena appear to our mind. We feel as though our body had completely dissolved into the object of meditation.

When our body has apparently dissolved in this way we achieve great mental suppleness. At that time, because of the intensity of the bliss we experience, it seems as if our mind were no longer abiding on its object of meditation. Because this is the meditator's first experience of this special bliss, which greatly increases the vibration of his mind, he no longer feels he can keep his mind focused on its proper object. As a result, the feeling of bliss declines a little, but this is not a fault. When the experience of bliss becomes more stable the meditator attains an unchangeable bliss of concentration, which is called 'immovable suppleness'. When we achieve such suppleness of mind, we attain actual tranquil abiding.

After we have attained tranquil abiding there are two paths we can follow: mundane or supramundane. If we are solely interested in obtaining clairvoyance, the other miracle powers, rebirth as a form realm god and so forth, we are following the former path. However, if we are primarily concerned with attaining enlightenment and therefore use our power of tranquil abiding to develop renunciation, bodhichitta and superior seeing into the true nature of reality, we are following the supreme, supramundane path leading to Buddhahood.

In order to progress through the nine mental abidings and achieve tranquil abiding we have to overcome specific obstacles by employing specific opponent powers. These obstacles and their opponent counter-measures are the subject matter of the next two sections.

## THE FIVE OBSTACLES TO ATTAINING TRANQUIL ABIDING

(1) *Laziness.* Laziness is the greatest obstacle to our meditation and is the main reason why we have not yet developed tranquil abiding. In this context laziness is the feeling that meditation is too difficult to accomplish. We are reluctant to practise and take no pleasure in meditating single-pointedly. With such an obstacle we do not even bother to train our mind in tranquil abiding and are thus greatly deceived.

(2) *Forgetfulness.* This refers to losing the object while we are trying to meditate on it, or being unable to remember the instructions we have received from our Spiritual Guide.

(3) *Mental sinking and mental excitement.* There are two types of mental excitement: gross and subtle. Gross mental excitement occurs when the mind is distracted by an object of attachment and consequently loses its object of meditation completely. (When the mind is distracted from the object of

meditation by something other than an object of attachment this is called 'mental wandering'.) Subtle mental excitement occurs when only part of the mind is distracted by an object of attachment and thus the object of meditation is not completely lost.

There are also two types of mental sinking. Gross mental sinking occurs when we are holding the meditation object with the rope of mindfulness. If our single-pointed concentration is strong but the clarity and intensity of it diminish greatly, we have fallen under the influence of gross mental sinking. Subtle mental sinking occurs when our concentration and the clarity of this concentration are both strong, but the intensity decreases slightly. Generally, mental sinking only occurs when we are actually concentrating on the object of meditation but due to internal wandering, the clarity or intensity of our concentration decrease slightly.

It is often very difficult to recognize mental sinking. As a result there is a danger of mistaking it, especially in its subtle form, for a state of deep concentration. If we cannot discriminate between an actual state of concentration and one polluted by mental sinking, there will be no way to attain tranquil abiding and we will encounter many problems in our meditation. Some people think that mental sinking and dullness are the same thing, but in fact the latter is the cause of the former. Dullness is heaviness of body and mind leading to sleep and is a facet of ignorance.

**(4) *Non-application*.** During our meditation sessions the various forms of mental excitement and sinking are apt to arise again and again. If we neglect to employ the appropriate counter-measures when this happens, this is known as 'non-application of the opponent'. To let the various hindrances to meditation arise without doing anything about them is the same as standing idly by while a thief enters our house and steals our possessions. Mental sinking and excitement are thieves that take from us the riches of tranquil abiding. If we do not apply the proper opponents to them, they will keep us in spiritual poverty forever.

(5) *Unnecessary application.* There are times during our meditation sessions when we are in no danger from either mental sinking or mental excitement. If at such times we continue to apply counter-measures, this is called the fault of 'unnecessary application' of the opponent. Such faulty application only serves to interrupt our single-pointed concentration. The situation is like that of a loving daughter who, out of respect, always carries out her mother's wishes faultlessly. If the mother nevertheless continues to chastise and rebuke her, this will only interfere with the daughter's feelings of love and compassion for her.

These five obstacles are overcome by means of the following eight opponent forces.

## THE EIGHT OPPONENTS TO THE FIVE OBSTACLES

(1) *Faith.* This is an attitude of mind that takes pleasure in meditating upon tranquil abiding. It is developed by thinking again and again about the excellent qualities of tranquil abiding, as explained before.

(2) *Aspiration.* This is the strong intention, derived from faith, to attain tranquil abiding.

(3) *Effort.* Effort arises from aspiration and is what urges us to strive enthusiastically and persistently to attain tranquil abiding.

**(4) *Suppleness.*** This is lightness of body and mind, the fruit of effort. These first four opponents all counter the obstacle of laziness.

**(5) *Mindfulness.*** This is the mental factor that keeps the mind from forgetting and that holds the object of meditation continuously. It is the opponent to the obstacle of forgetting the instructions we have received and losing the object of meditation.

**(6) *Alertness.*** This is an aspect of wisdom that works as a spy, keeping watch to see if and when an obstacle to concentration arises. It counters mental sinking and excitement by recognizing these obstacles, watching to see if they are about to attack, and urging the opponent forces into action should these hindrances actually appear.

We need great skill to apply alertness properly. If we never apply it we will be unable to recognize the interruptions to our concentration, and if we apply it too continuously we will harm the flow of our concentration. Therefore we must use it in a balanced manner, neither too much nor too little. The following analogy demonstrates the type of balanced approach that is required. Imagine that we are walking along a path in the company of someone we suspect is plotting to murder us. One part of our attention will be directed in front of us on the path we are following, while another part will be occasionally directed towards our suspected enemy. In a similar fashion, while we are developing concentration the main part of our mind is holding the object of meditation, but occasionally a part of our mind looks to see whether or not the obstacles of mental sinking and excitement are arising.

**(7) *Application.*** When the spy of alertness has recognized the enemies of sinking or excitement it urges the general of

*Geshe Chilbuwa*

application to give the order to its army of opponent forces to attack. The way in which this army is deployed depends on which obstacle is to be overcome.

If *subtle mental sinking* arises we must tighten the intensity of our concentration. However, as when adjusting the strings on a guitar, this should be done with a sense of proportion. If we tighten our concentration too much we will be in danger of mental excitement, and if we relax it too much we will be in danger of gross mental sinking.

If gross mental sinking arises we should try to refresh and uplift the mind. For example, if we are meditating upon the visualized image of Buddha Shakyamuni and gross sinking occurs, we should pay more attention to the details of the visualization. If this does not concentrate the mind we should temporarily abandon the object of meditation and look around our room at shiny objects, the sunlight and so forth, or meditate upon such things as the good fortune of having attained a precious human rebirth and the benefits of tranquil abiding. These methods should uplift the mind, but if they do not there is a more forceful technique that can be applied. We visualize the mind situated at the heart in the aspect of a small bundle of white light. Then we forcefully recite the syllable 'PHAT' (pronounced 'Peh') while visualizing this white light rising quickly up through our body and out of the crown of our head. The mind, in the form of this light, flies high up into space and becomes inseparable from it. This technique is very effective for energizing the mind and overcoming gross mental sinking.

If *subtle mental excitement* arises we should realize that this is due to our mind holding the object of meditation too tightly. Therefore relax the grip of the mind slightly and then continue to meditate. If this remedy is not successful and the mind wanders away from its object completely, then gross mental excitement has occurred.

If *gross mental excitement* arises we should try to settle the mind by meditating on such topics as impermanence, death, the faults of samsara and so forth, and try to arouse disillusionment with the unsatisfactory state of samsara. If this method fails we should practise the breathing meditation described earlier in this chapter until our mind is again calm and the gross distractions have subsided. Then we can bring the object of meditation to mind again and continue our practice.

**(8) *Non-application.*** If there is no danger from either mental sinking or mental excitement and our concentration is proceeding well, we should refrain from employing any of the opponent forces. It is enough to remain naturally in concentration. To apply counter-measures at such a time would only create interruptions.

It is extremely important to study the methods for attaining tranquil abiding with an experienced Spiritual Guide. Then we should gather the six necessary conditions, find a secluded retreat site, sit in the correct seven-point posture and generate a pure motivation. Then we should abandon the five obstacles by applying the eight opponent forces, and progress through the nine mental abidings by means of the six forces and four attentions. In short, we should practise according to the complete set of instructions we have received.

Conditions for the complete practice of tranquil abiding thus described are not easily arranged. It is rare nowadays to find both a suitable place and enough time – six months or more – to devote to such meditation. This does not mean, however, that we have to neglect training our mind in concentration. Without worrying about all six conditions or attaining the advanced mental abidings, we should concentrate instead on finding and focusing upon the object of meditation. During our daily practices we can limit our attention to the first two mental abidings and try to develop our ability to hold the meditation object for increasing lengths of time. Once we have reached the second mental abiding we can think about arranging all the proper conditions for a complete tranquil abiding retreat. Having prepared ourself beforehand in this way, we will have a much greater chance of success when we actually try to develop tranquil abiding.

## EXPLANATION OF THE PARTICULAR USE TO WHICH TRANQUIL ABIDING IS TO BE PUT: MEDITATING ON EQUALIZING AND EXCHANGING SELF WITH OTHERS

This has two parts:

1 How to meditate on equalizing self and others
2 How to exchange self with others

### HOW TO MEDITATE ON EQUALIZING SELF AND OTHERS

This has five parts:

1 A brief explanation of the meditation
2 The meaning of equalizing self and others
3 The actual meditation on equalizing self and others
4 The benefits of meditating on equalizing self and others

5 How we are able to develop the mind in this meditation

## A BRIEF EXPLANATION OF THE MEDITATION

[89] Once we have meditated on the qualities of a solitary life as explained before, we should abide in seclusion, forsake the wild disturbances of the mind, and meditate on bodhichitta. [90] The first thing we must do is meditate on equalizing self and others. How is this accomplished? By realizing that just as we seek nothing but happiness and wish to avoid pain, so do all other living beings. As this is the case we should protect other beings in exactly the same way as we now protect ourself. Just as we have cherished ourself, so should we now train our mind to cherish others by understanding that we are all equal in wishing to experience pleasure and be free from all torment.

## THE MEANING OF EQUALIZING SELF AND OTHERS

What does it mean to say that self and others are equal? We can understand this through the following analogy. [91] The body has various parts – arms, legs and so forth – but they are all equally cherished and protected. In the same way there are many different types of beings in this universe – humans, gods, animals and so forth – but their wish to be happy is exactly the same as ours. They are all objects to be cherished and protected in the same way as we protect ourself. In this respect they are no different from us. The happiness and suffering of others are in no way different from our own happiness and suffering. If we meditate deeply on this and develop the mind that seeks the happiness of others and their separation from suffering *to the same degree* as we now work to gain our own happiness and avoid our own suffering, this is the true meaning of meditating on equalizing self and others.

Such a good mind and kind heart are an incomparable treasure not possessed by many other beings. At the moment we have all the circumstances and conditions for developing this precious mind, which, if cultivated, is wonderful and rare. Kings and queens do not possess a mind like this, though they are revered and command a lofty position. Even Indra and Brahma, the highest of the celestial beings, do not possess such a treasure. If they do not have such a mind, how can we expect ordinary beings of this world to possess it?

## THE ACTUAL MEDITATION ON EQUALIZING SELF AND OTHERS

The mind that sees the equality of self and others is so rare because it is counter to our ordinary selfish, egocentric way of relating to the world. Therefore it is not surprising that many objections automatically arise when we contemplate adopting this altruistic outlook. As before, Shantideva anticipates these objections and answers them.

*The suffering I experience doesn't harm others and their suffering doesn't harm me. Therefore there is no reason why I should work to dispel others' suffering in the same way as I work to dispel my own. I should only be interested in overcoming my own problems.*

[92] It is true that the suffering we experience does not harm others and vice versa, but the suffering of others itself is no different from our own. If our body is cut and suffering arises, we call it 'my suffering' only because we cherish this body and cannot bear to see it harmed. [93] If we were to

cherish others in the same way as we cherish ourself, we would not be able to bear it when they experienced suffering. [94] If we reflect on this clearly we will see why we need to dispel others' suffering as we would our own and bring them the happiness we wish for ourself. After all, we are all sentient beings and we all dislike misery.

To someone who has not familiarized his or her mind over a long period of time to Dharma, and particularly to someone who is not used to such forms of reasoning, these teachings on equalizing self and others may appear to be very unusual. It is not surprising if this way of training the mind seems so strange. These teachings are concerned with the practices and experiences of high-minded Bodhisattvas and are supported by a wealth of logical reasoning. They are, therefore, not something that can be understood quickly by the untrained mind. If someone has the sincere desire to study these teachings deeply, he or she should remain with a qualified Spiritual Guide for a long time and undergo a gradual training that will lead to a first-hand experience of the truth behind the mere words of this teaching.

What is the principal cause preventing us from accepting that others' suffering is no different from our own? The main hindrance is our deeply ingrained habit of holding tightly to the 'I' and identifying it with our body while identifying the body of another being as 'other'. Having made such a strong identification we cling to these appearances as being true. It is this clinging to appearances that makes it difficult to listen to teachings on equalizing and exchanging self with others.

What we need to ask ourself is: 'Are self and other always as different as they appear?' Let us examine this. The colour yellow and the colour blue are always different. It is impossible for a clear cognition of blue to be a clear cognition of yellow. When our eye consciousness is perceiving one, that same consciousness is not perceiving the other. We all know this. But self and other are not like this at all. They are not as distinct and exclusive as they appear. Despite this, we hold 'I' strongly in relation to ourself, and label as 'other' those who are separate from us. Because we insist on making such hard and fast distinctions between ourself and others, we are drowning in the ocean of samsara. Why? Because of our falsely discriminating attitude we feel jealousy, attachment, anger and so forth towards these 'others', and in dependence upon these deluded states of mind we create heavy non-virtuous karma that leads to nothing but suffering and dissatisfaction.

If we think clearly we will see that self and other are not like yellow and blue. Rather, these two are more like 'this mountain' and 'that mountain'. If we happen to be on an eastern mountain then the one to the west is called 'that mountain'. But when we travel to that western mountain we refer to it as 'this mountain' and the one we just left – which formerly was 'this mountain' – now becomes 'that mountain'. This raises some important questions. Is the eastern mountain both 'this' and 'that' mountain? If that is so, then the same is true for the western mountain. If the two mountains are always different, which one is truly 'this' and which is truly 'that' mountain? Is it not merely a matter of point of view, something that is changeable? If we examine self and other well, we will find that they are also like this.

Self and other can also be likened to tall and short. For example, an eight-year-old boy is *both* tall and short. Compared to a young man of twenty he is short but compared to a child of three he is tall. Therefore we cannot say that he is always one or the other. Tall and short are not always different phenomena in the way as yellow and blue are. Similarly, self and others are not always as different as two colours. It is mistaken to cling to the false conception that they are so distinct.

If we think about these examples and different lines of logical reasoning and, furthermore, if we reflect upon the many disadvantages of our self-cherishing attitude and upon the many virtues of cherishing others, there is hope that we will be able to practise the meditation on equalizing self and others and accomplish the actual exchange of the two. If we do not prepare our mind in this way, however, it will be very difficult, if not impossible, to be successful. Since the ability to develop the precious mind of bodhichitta depends upon seeing the equality of two things we are accustomed to viewing as completely different, we should exert great effort in this training.

[95] Ourself and others are the same in that both wish for happiness. If this is so, then what is so special about us that we are only interested in our own happiness? [96] Also, since both self and others are equal in wanting to be free from suffering, why are our efforts limited to dispelling only our own misery?

[97] *As I said before, there is no reason for me to protect others from their misery. It causes me no harm.* But then why do we work to eliminate the sicknesses of old age coming in the future or even the discomforts of tomorrow and the day after tomorrow? These future sufferings will do us no harm today.

[98] *But if such misery is not prevented now I will experience it in the future.* This is a misconception. The self of this life will not experience the suffering of future lives. This life and future lives are completely different. The same is true

concerning tomorrow's suffering. It is wrong to think that the suffering of tomorrow will be experienced by the self of today. Why? Because by the time tomorrow's suffering is experienced, the self of today will have perished. When we see a person we saw last year we cling to last year's person as being today's person but such grasping at permanence is a completely mistaken conception.

[99] *But surely whatever suffering there is should be dispelled by the one who is actually experiencing the suffering. It is not at all appropriate for someone else to dispel it.* Is it not suitable for the hand to help dispel the suffering of a thorn in the foot? According to your objection, because the foot's suffering is not the hand's suffering, the hand has no reason to protect the foot.

*I maintain that it is not suitable to relieve the suffering of others because there is no relationship with them. The same is not true of your examples.* [100] *It is appropriate to relieve the sufferings of our foot and of our future lives because we grasp on to these as 'my foot's suffering' and 'my future life's suffering'.*

It is completely unjustified to cling to the independent existence of the self and the independent existence of others. It is important to stop this grasping at independent existence because this has been the root cause of our floundering in the swamp of samsaric suffering since beginningless time.

*The reason I say the suffering of the foot should be dispelled by the hand and that the suffering of our future lives should be avoided by our present life is that these pairs are of the same collection and continuum. The same is not true of self and others.*

[101] Yet there is no independently existent, or self-existent, collection or continuum as you imply. A collection consists of many parts upon which we impute the mental label 'collection'. In the same way a continuum consists of

many earlier and later moments upon which we impute the label 'continuum'. To take an example, a mala or rosary is a collection of one hundred and eight beads and a string, and upon this collection we impute 'mala'. Similarly, upon a collection of soldiers preparing for or engaging in battle we impute 'army'.

Normally we cling very strongly to the independent existence of things, saying 'my mala' when in fact there is no independently existent mala there at all. This mala was just designated upon its parts by a process of mental labelling. If we examine this collection of parts closely and search for a true mala among them, we can never find such a thing. In the same way a true, independent, self-existent army cannot be found no matter how hard we search among the milling soldiers.

[102] There is no independent, self-existent possessor of suffering. Furthermore, the suffering that is experienced has no self-existence either. Therefore who is there who has control over it? Who owns it? Nevertheless, even though neither the person nor the suffering he or she experiences has the slightest independent existence, we should still try to dispel that imputedly existing suffering. Moreover, because there is no inherently existing I that owns the suffering, there can be no difference at all between the suffering of self and that of others. Both our own and others' suffering are real by imputation and both must be dispelled simply because they are painful.

If there is no inherently existent self or others there is no reason to distinguish between them so sharply and with such certainty. What is the point of clinging to our own and others' supposed inherent existence and then, on the basis of this false assumption, feel that 'our suffering' is to be abandoned while 'their suffering' can be tolerated? [103] How

## CONCENTRATION

can anyone argue, 'There is no need to dispel the misery of others'? If we are interested in preventing suffering at all, we should be as interested in overcoming others' misery as we are in overcoming our own. And if we are not interested in dispelling others' suffering, neither should we be interested in getting rid of what bothers us.

[104-5] *It is too much of a burden to cherish others as we do ourself. These others have limitless suffering. Why should I want to take on more suffering than I already have?* If a Bodhisattva had to experience more suffering in the course of helping other sentient beings overcome their misery, he or she would gladly endure it. The kind-hearted Bodhisattva accepts whatever he can for the sake of benefiting others. But do not be concerned that such a being will have more suffering from his practices. When he sees someone in misery his own great compassion protects him from experiencing any problems or suffering. Whatever difficulties he may encounter he will endure with a happy mind. His true delight is in working continuously for the sake of all living beings.

There is a story that illustrates the joy a Bodhisattva takes even when encountering great difficulties. [106] During the time of a previous Buddha, the Tathagata Ratna Pemachandra, there was a Bodhisattva monk named Supushpachandra. At the time of this story he was meditating with seven thousand other Bodhisattvas in a forest called Samantabhadra. By his powers of clairvoyance he saw that if he went to the realm of the king Viradatta and taught Dharma, ten thousand people would attain liberation. But he also saw that if he did this King Viradatta would have him killed. He told his fellow Bodhisattvas that he would soon depart for that kingdom and teach the people there and that he would lose his life doing so. They implored him, 'Don't go and give up your life. Stay here. Think of the welfare of all sentient beings, not just those ten thousand.' However, Supushpachandra did not listen to their entreaties. He went to the kingdom, taught Dharma and led the beings there to liberation and enlightenment. As foreseen, the king became angry and jealous of his influence over his subjects and had him murdered. The Bodhisattva was so intent on dispelling the suffering of others that he willingly sacrificed his own life for their sake. He had fully understood the equality of self and others and thus was able to perform such an outstanding deed of compassion.

## THE BENEFITS OF MEDITATING ON EQUALIZING SELF AND OTHERS

[107] Because he or she has become strongly acquainted with meditating on equalizing of self and others, the fearless Bodhisattva is pleased to dispel the misery of others. Just as a wild goose plunges with delight into a beautiful lotus pool, if there is benefit to be had the Bodhisattva will happily plunge into the fires of the lowest hell realm for the sake of others. The unshakeable inner strength of a Bodhisattva comes from his meditation on equalizing self and others. He will gladly lead others out of their misery according to each person's individual capacity. Though neither Bodhisattvas nor Buddhas can remove suffering from others as we can pull a thorn out of someone else's foot, they are ready to do everything within their power to lead others along the path to the complete cessation of suffering, even if it means sacrificing their own life. [108] If a Bodhisattva's efforts result in rescuing another from the ocean of samsaric suffering, then he or she experiences great happiness no matter what it may have cost him. Helping others is the Bodhisattva's supreme wish.

For a Bodhisattva there is no point in seeking his own self-liberation alone. [109] Whenever he engages in beneficial actions designed to free others, he does so without pride or arrogance and is completely devoid of pretension. He performs his beneficial actions with no thought for the fruit he will receive from them; all his deeds are totally unconditional. For example, if he practises giving he dedicates the merit of this action to others, wishing that the benefits ripen on them. Whenever he practises Dharma in any way, he dedicates the positive results in the same manner. The Bodhisattva has no self-interest but does whatever he does solely for the welfare of others. All his inner strength to perform his deeds of love and compassion arises from meditating on equalizing self and others.

If we meditate well on equalizing self and others we will be able to exchange our attitude of self-cherishing for the altruistic attitude of cherishing others. By accomplishing this exchange completely we will complete the practice of the precious bodhichitta and speedily attain supreme enlightenment. Therefore, by contemplating the many advantages of meditating on equalizing self and others we should think:

[110] Just as I now protect myself from even the slightest unpleasant thing, so too will I always act towards others with a compassionate and caring mind.

## HOW WE ARE ABLE TO DEVELOP THE MIND IN THIS MEDITATION

At this point grave doubts may arise about the feasibility of this selfless practice. *I cannot develop the mind that holds 'I' while identifying with the bodies of others. How can I think of another's eyes as my eyes? And how can I hold on to others' sufferings as if they were my own? How can I seek happiness for others as I now seek my own welfare? This is impossible!*

It is not our fault if we think like this; it is only the talk of someone without experience. At present we have strong familiarity with self-grasping and our experiences are based solely on that. [111] Because of our acquaintance and familiarity we cling to the collection of our father's drops of sperm and our mother's ovum – from which arise our bones and flesh respectively – as if it constituted an inherently existent I. [112] If we developed familiarity with a correct way of thinking, however, there would be no trouble in identifying I with the bodies of others.

In fact, our body does belong to others. As was explained in the fourth chapter, this body is on loan to us as if it came from someone else. Togme Sangpo, in a section of his *Thirty-seven Practices of All Bodhisattvas* (Tib. *Leg len so dun ma*) referred to earlier, says that our body is like a guest house and our mind is merely a traveller lodging there for a short while. If the Lord of Death comes now, we will have to vacate this guest house and depart alone. If our body really did belong to us as we instinctively feel, we would be able to take it with us when we leave this world at the time of death.

[113] If we acquaint ourself with the above ways of looking at our situation and remember the advantages of cherishing others and the many disadvantages of the self-cherishing attitude, it will not be too difficult to see the equality and eventually the interchangeability of our own and others' bodies. Understanding the disadvantages of self-cherishing is a powerful weapon to keep the self-grasping mind from arising. If we then concentrate on the advantages of cherishing others and actually develop the type of mind

that cares about others the way we now care about ourself, no problems will arise to interfere with us. By receiving the complete set of teachings on how to meditate on equalizing self and others from a fully qualified Spiritual Guide, and then by striving to put these teachings into practice as much as possible, it is definitely possible to attain these bodhichitta realizations. All it requires is the proper motivation and continuous effort.

## HOW TO EXCHANGE SELF WITH OTHERS

Once we have equalized self and others we can begin to practise the actual exchange of self with others. This has four parts:

1 A brief explanation of the exchange
2 The way to exchange self with others
3 Completing the exchange by means of reflection
4 Completing the exchange by means of action

### A BRIEF EXPLANATION OF THE EXCHANGE

Once we recognize that the root of all suffering and faults is our self-cherishing attitude, we should strive with all our energy to abandon it; and when we see that an ocean of excellence is derived from cherishing others as if they were our very self, we should strive to practise in this way.

How is it possible to cherish limitless sentient beings? Through accustoming the mind by means of constant familiarity. [114] For example, we have many different limbs and parts of our body. Owing to the force of strong familiarity they are all cherished alike as parts of our body. In the same way, if we accustom the mind to cherishing others, then all embodied beings can be regarded as the very limbs of our life.

## THE WAY TO EXCHANGE SELF WITH OTHERS

This has four parts:

1. Gaining familiarity with cherishing others
2. Abandoning self-cherishing
3. Reflecting on the disadvantages of self-cherishing and the advantages of cherishing others
4. Summary

## GAINING FAMILIARITY WITH CHERISHING OTHERS

[115] As stated before, it is owing to the power of familiarity that we posit 'I' on our non-self-existent body. Similarly, through the power of familiarity we can hold this I in respect of the bodies of others as well. [116] If we acquaint ourself with cherishing others we can prevent pride, conceit and arrogance from arising no matter what we do on others' behalf. The Bodhisattva so closely identifies himself with others that his actions on their behalf never have an ulterior motive. When we feed our body we never expect anything back from it in return; we feel it is only natural and appropriate to take care of what we identify as our own. The Bodhisattva's actions with respect to others are done with a similar lack of expectation and with the same sense of appropriateness. As we train our mind in the Bodhisattva's way of life we should do everything for others that we would do for ourself. [117] Just as we protect ourself from even the

slightest unpleasantness or loss of reputation, so too should we develop a compassionate and caring mind for others and strive to protect them as well from even the smallest suffering.

The great Bodhisattvas have always done everything they could to benefit others and protect them from even the most insignificant suffering. [118] The Superior Bodhisattva Avalokiteshvara, out of his great compassion, sought to alleviate peoples' fears by blessing his own name. He proclaimed, 'If frightened sentient beings recite my name three times they will be free from all their fears.' Whether the cause of fear is great or small, whether it is brought about by having to address a large crowd or because we are frightened of violence, this compassionate blessing was and still is effective. This is only one small example of how a high-minded Bodhisattva cherishes others and wishes to protect them.

*I agree that it would be good to attain the realization of exchanging myself with others, but it is so extremely difficult to do!* [119] While at the beginning of our practice it might indeed be difficult to attain this other-cherishing mind, we should not be discouraged and turn away from this practice for that reason. By training ourself ceaselessly in the practice it is definitely possible to attain this elevated mind. Take the following example. There is a person whom for many years we regarded as our enemy. Now this year he becomes such a close friend that to be separated from him for even an hour brings us unhappiness. What caused such a startling change? It was entirely due to the power of familiarity. If we can learn to cherish an enemy we certainly can learn to exchange self with others.

[120] If we truly want to be free from this ocean of samsara and be able to protect others as well from this round of suffering, we should practise the holy secret: exchanging self

with others. These teachings, along with those on emptiness, are not appropriate for everyone. Those who lack Dharma experience can easily misunderstand the meaning and intent of these profound subjects. For this reason Shantideva referred to exchanging self with others as a 'holy secret'. Other great Teachers of the past felt the same way about this method of Mahayana mind training. Atisha kept these teachings very secret and only gave them to a few select disciples. Eventually, however, the Kadampa Geshe Chekhawa gave these instructions to many students, and wrote a famous text on mind training dealing primarily with this holy secret. A commentary to this text *Training the Mind in Seven Points* can be found in the book *Universal Compassion*.

The best method for realizing this exchange of self with others is to reflect for a long time on the many disadvantages of our self-cherishing attitude and on the many advantages of cherishing others. As mentioned before, the source of all our suffering, without exception, is the self-cherishing mind. Furthermore, all of our happiness derives from one source, cherishing others. Take this precious human life for example. The great Indian Teacher Chandrakirti wrote in his *Guide to the Middle Way* (Skt. *Madhyamakavatara*) that the main cause of being reborn as a human or god is the practice of moral discipline. How did we practise moral discipline in a previous life so that we now possess the fruit of a fully-endowed human form? By cherishing the lives of others we abstained from killing. By cherishing others' possessions we abstained from stealing. By cherishing other people and their spouses we refrained from the various types of sexual misconduct. By cherishing others and not wishing to deceive them, cause disharmony among them, disturb their peace or waste their time we refrained from the four non-virtuous actions of speech: lying, divisive speech, hurtful speech and idle chatter. Also, because we cherished others we viewed ourself as low and held others as supreme, and thereby kept our mind free from covetousness and malice. Finally, because we cherished the instructions we received from others we took Dharma teachings to heart and abandoned wrong views.

Therefore it is clear that all the virtuous actions of body, speech and mind, the entire practice of basic moral discipline, derived from cherishing others; and because of these virtuous actions we achieved this perfect human rebirth. Furthermore this human form of ours is endowed with certain additional attributes and these also are the result of cherishing others. Attractive features derive from the practice of patience, refraining from retaliating against others. Long life is the result of protecting others' lives and refraining from killing. People who are popular and well loved are reaping the fruit of loving and cherishing others in previous lives. Some people always seem to have good health and this is the result in particular of caring for the sick. Thus we can see that all happiness, without exception, arises from the attitude of cherishing others.

## ABANDONING SELF-CHERISHING

All the fearful aspects of samsara, from the greatest down to the smallest, arise from the self-cherishing attitude. [121] Why are we frightened when we see a poisonous snake or scorpion, for example? Because we are so full of attachment and cherishing towards our own body. It goes without saying that the fears of the lower realms are due to this self-centred state of mind.

If we did not cherish our own body we would have no attachment for it and we would be able to give it away to others freely. There would then be no basis upon which trouble could arise for us. It would no longer matter to us whether we were harmed or not because the body would no longer be cherished. Therefore, when we realize it is our self-cherishing that gives rise to so much trouble and fear, we should revile it as our worst enemy.

Because we are so attached to our body and the wish to sustain it, we are anxious to dispel all the sufferings of hunger, thirst, cold and sickness that this body encounters. We are not anxious like this when it is the body of another that suffers, but when our own body is in discomfort we react very strongly. [122] To alleviate our hunger, for example, we kill birds, fish, deer and the like. We steal from others and wait in ambush to harm them. [123] We tell lies, and, for the sake of profit and gain, may even kill our own beloved father and mother! We even go as far as to steal the property of the precious Three Jewels of refuge, thereby creating vast negative karma in so many ways. The result of all this non-virtue is that we proceed to hell and are surrounded by its unceasing fires for many aeons. Even in this human life we have to experience such miseries as imprisonment, a short life filled with much sickness and the like. Who is the creator of all this misery? If we make a careful analysis we will see that it is our cherishing attitude towards our own body. [124] If we are wise we will view such self-cherishing as our most hated foe.

## REFLECTING ON THE DISADVANTAGES OF SELF-CHERISHING AND THE ADVANTAGES OF CHERISHING OTHERS

[125ab] 'If I give up my wealth, possessions, clothing and so forth to others, how will I ever be happy? What will I eat? What will I wear?' The self-cherishing mind that thinks like this is following the terrifying path of the frightful spirits. A spirit is usually an object of our fear but the true object of fear lurks within us in the guise of our self-cherishing attitude. People fear spirits because they are afraid they will do them harm; but if we banished our self-cherishing attitude, we would not be afraid even if a whole army of ghosts appeared before us.

From exalted kings down to the lowliest of insects, all living beings are beset by fear caused by their self-cherishing attitude. If we are worried by inauspicious omens we should realize that selfishness is the worst omen of all. The Kadampa Geshes gave the self-cherishing attitude the nickname 'devil with the head of an owl'. Fear, anxiety, dissatisfaction and suffering will arise continuously until this inner devil of self-cherishing is completely exorcised.

[125cd] 'If I use and enjoy my wealth, possessions, clothing and so forth for myself, what will I be able to give to sentient beings?' The mind that thinks like this selflessly cherishes others and is following the joyful path of the fortunate Deities. A Deity is an exalted being who grants blessings and empowerments. If we depend upon the Deity of cherishing others, we need not devote ourself to any other celestial being; this Deity of selflessness will fulfil all our wishes both in this world and in the worlds to come.

Shantideva expands on this theme by presenting three pairs of contrasting destinies. [126] First, if for our own sake we harm others, then temporarily we will suffer hardship in this life, and eventually we will have to bear the pain of hellish torment. However, if for the sake of others we are harmed, then temporarily we will attain rebirth as a human or god, and ultimately we will achieve the supreme state of complete Buddhahood. [127] Second, holding ourself in high esteem and seeking only selfish ends we will fall into the lower realms, and when we are eventually born as a human we will have a low social position, an unattractive body and a foolish mind. However, if we shift our concern away from ourself and begin to hold others in high esteem we will attain a fortunate rebirth, acquire respect and find ourself in pleasant company and surroundings. [128] Lastly, if we employ others with the selfish motive of gaining profit only for ourself we will eventually be reborn in a low social class and experience much servitude. However, if we employ ourself so that others may prosper we will gain rebirth with a good form and exalted status. [129] To summarize, whatever joy there is in this universe arises from cherishing and desiring the happiness of others, and whatever suffering there is arises from cherishing our own happiness. Is it possible to think of one instance of misery that cannot be traced to the demon of self-cherishing?

Self-cherishing derives from self-grasping as will be explained further in chapter nine. First we grasp at an independent self-existent I. Following from this we cling to 'my body', 'my house', 'my wife', 'my husband' and so forth. As a result we become painfully attached to the people and things strongly conceived to be 'mine'. Because Arhats – those beings who have attained the liberation of nirvana by abandoning self-grasping completely – do not develop such self-cherishing, they have overcome all suffering.

[130] As Shantideva says, there is no need to speak at length about the differences between the self-cherishing and the other-cherishing attitudes. All we have to do is look at the childish beings who work solely for their own benefit and see how they are born again and again in the realms of samsara where they have to experience suffering unceasingly. Compare them with the Buddhas who have conquered the demon of self-cherishing and are solely concerned with the welfare of others. By contrasting the misery and dissatisfaction of the former with the unsurpassed bliss and happiness of the latter we will quickly become convinced of the superiority of cherishing others.

[131] We may have the intention deep in our heart to attain enlightenment, but if we do not engage in the practice of exchanging self with others there is no hope of our attaining it. And if we do not work towards Buddhahood, thinking that it does not matter if we stay in samsara or not, we will never find true happiness. Even if we are reborn as a king or queen, as long as we remain in samsara it is impossible to experience pure, unchanging joy.

If we do not abandon the self-cherishing attitude but continue to work with selfish motives, then, as explained before, we will experience suffering in the future. [132] Yet this is not the only unsatisfactory result of self-cherishing; if we do not abandon selfishness even our wishes in this present life will remain unfulfilled. For example, if there is an employee so unconcerned with the welfare of his employer that he refuses to give him proper service, and if there is an employer who is so unconcerned with the welfare of his employee that he refuses to give him proper wages, then neither of them will receive what he wants from the other.

[133] If we allow our mind to be pervaded by the self-cherishing attitude, the great value and potential of this precious human existence – and the future states of existence as well – will be lost. We will be throwing away all the excellent qualities of this life. Furthermore, if our self-cherishing causes us to harm others, such confused actions will gain us nothing but unbearable pain. We must understand fully and deeply that, whatever universe we may inhabit, all harm inflicted upon us by humans, non-humans, wild animals and the like, and all fears and misery as well as all unfree states of existence are, without a single exception, produced from our self-cherishing attitude. [134] If holding ourself as most precious is the cause of so much torment, how can we be complacent while this worst of all demons dwells within us? What need do we have of such a fearful and devilish spirit?

[135] If we pick up a stick that is on fire and do not immediately throw it away, there is no way to prevent our hand from being burnt. Similarly, if we are unable to give up our self-cherishing attitude – the mind that considers ourself to be the most precious of all – then there is no way for us to abandon suffering. [136] Therefore, if we have a sincere desire to overcome all our own and others' problems we should give up our self-cherishing and consider others as precious as we now consider ourself.

## SUMMARY

[137] Once we have exchanged self with others as explained above we should cultivate the thought, 'Now I am under

the complete control of others; I no longer have the choice to do anything for my own sake alone.' We should make certain that our mind understands the new situation. We must keep it aware that from now on it must work for nothing else but the benefit of others. This new attitude should pervade all that we think, say and do. [138] For example, our eyes are now completely at the disposal of others; therefore we should no longer look at things for our own purpose or benefit, nor stare angrily at others with a threatening glance. [139] Holding others to be more precious than ourself, we should steal whatever belongs to the self – whatever we wear, eat or own – and give it away to others. We should cultivate the attitude that regards everything we use as belonging to others and be like a servant who uses his master's clothing, food and possessions without ever forgetting that they belong to another. It is very important for those intent on travelling the Mahayana path, and in particular for those who have received the Bodhisattva vows, to reflect upon this attitude continuously and consider it well.

## COMPLETING THE EXCHANGE
## BY MEANS OF REFLECTION

This section has five parts:

1. A brief explanation
2. Meditation on jealousy towards a superior
3. Meditation on competitiveness towards an equal
4. Meditation on pride towards an inferior
5. The results of this meditation

## A BRIEF EXPLANATION

In the following sections Shantideva presents a radical, but very effective, method for training the mind in the exchange of self with others. Normally our self-cherishing attitude leads us to categorize people into three groups: those who are inferior to us in certain ways, those who are our equals or rivals and those who are better than us. Having established these categories, we feel haughty towards those in the first group, competitive towards those in the second, and jealous of those in the third. All of these states of mind cause us immediate and long-term suffering and are therefore deluded. Shantideva now shows us how we can turn these deluded states of mind against themselves and thereby increase the power of our bodhichitta.

In the previous sections Shantideva explained very clearly the ways in which selfishness, instead of bringing us the happiness we desire, only leads to dissatisfaction and misery. Furthermore, he has contrasted our miserable state of self-cherishing with the bliss of a Buddha, a being whose mind spontaneously and continuously works for the welfare of others. If we contemplate these points deeply we will be motivated to destroy the demon of self-cherishing and win the state of Buddhahood for the benefit of all. Such a motivation is the precious bodhichitta, and once it has developed in our mind we are worthy of the title 'Bodhisattva'.

Now Shantideva demonstrates how a Bodhisattva – or a practitioner training in the Bodhisattva's way of life – can strengthen his or her bodhichitta by completing the exchange of self with others described earlier. Using his powers of imagination and empathy [140] the practitioner exchanges places with those considered lower than, equal to or higher than himself, and from this new stance looks back at his former self, towards whom he then generates the appropriate feeling of jealousy, competitiveness or pride. All this is done without a trace of the crippling conception of undecided doubt, the mind that thinks 'It is impossible for me to do this.' With a strong determination and a conviction that this practice is indeed possible, the Bodhisattva engages in the exchange and cultivates thoughts of jealousy and so forth. There is no danger here of these attitudes giving rise to delusion because they are only directed at himself. In fact, by aiding the practitioner to identify strongly with others and cherish them as he would himself, these attitudes actually increase the power of his virtuous mind.

It is important to remember that the exchange taking place here is not a physical one; we are not giving up our present form and taking on the body of another. Rather, we are transplanting our cherishing attitude from the place in which it currently resides – the self – and cultivating it in a new field – the thoughts, feelings and concerns of others. To make this exchange more evident Shantideva literally transposes the grammatical elements of the next several stanzas so that 'I' is now used to refer to someone else, while 'he' (or 'she') refers to the practitioner of the exchange: the would-be Bodhisattva, that is, ourself.

## MEDITATION ON JEALOUSY TOWARDS A SUPERIOR

In order to perform this first of three related meditations we should exchange places with someone inferior to ourself in some respect (for example, prestige, education or wealth) and identify with him or her as completely as possible. Having done this, we then look back at our former self (the supposed Bodhisattva) with such jealous thoughts as the following:

> [141-2] He (or she) always receives honour and veneration for his good qualities but I receive nothing at all. He has great wealth and many possessions but I am destitute. He receives much praise but I am despised. He is happy but I suffer. I have much heavy work and many tasks to perform while he is able to relax comfortably and remain at rest. His reputation has spread throughout the world but all I am known for is my inferiority.

Still identifying with this 'inferior' person, we should realize that the only reason why a Bodhisattva has enviable qualities is his or her strong effort in practising virtue. If inferior beings were to practise in the same way they could also attain good fortune. Then, in order to alleviate whatever discouragement we might feel from being in a lower position, we should think:

> [143] This Bodhisattva may be superior to me, but there are many Bodhisattvas greater than him. Furthermore, although there are many beings higher than myself, there are also many who are lower. Therefore there is no reason for me to feel so disheartened.

After cultivating such thoughts we should investigate to see if this superior Bodhisattva (who is really our former self) is living up to his or her exalted rank:

> [144-146] It is true that my morals, views and conduct have deteriorated, but this is not my fault. I have no freedom in this matter; it is the force of my delusions that has caused this degeneration. If that superior

Bodhisattva were truly compassionate he would restore whatever has deteriorated in me. Such a Bodhisattva should work hard so that I and all similar beings can generate good qualities and achieve realizations; and while working for our sake he should willingly bear any problems and hardships he might encounter.

But this so-called Bodhisattva is doing nothing to help us! Although he has the ability he neglects to aid us. Therefore what right does he have to be so scornful? Have we ever received any benefit from him?

Despite the fact that we poor beings, because of our degenerated morals, are dwelling within the jaws of the lower states of existence, this supposed Bodhisattva has no compassion for us. All he does is develop false pride in his attainments. He even goes as far as presuming to contend with and disparage the wise!

The specific purpose of meditating on jealousy in this way is to counter the false pride we usually feel in relation to our inferiors. By identifying with those who are lower – and by bringing to mind the discrepancy between our bodhichitta vow to help others and our selfish behaviour – all such deluded pride will evaporate.

## MEDITATION ON COMPETITIVENESS TOWARDS AN EQUAL

Now we should change places with someone of the same rank, ability or intelligence as ourself, identify with him or her so strongly that we label that person 'I', and then look back at our old self, the Bodhisattva, with intense competitiveness as follows:

[147-150] This Bodhisattva is my equal but, in order to outshine him, I will defeat him in many ways, including debate. I will proclaim all my own qualities throughout the world but his I will hide so that no one hears of them. Also, I will hide all my own faults while declaring his openly. I will make sure that I receive veneration from others and that he receives no praise at all. I will have fame, possessions and material gain, but he will have nothing. I will take great pleasure in seeing him receive problems, abuse and the like for a great length of time, and will seek to make him the laughing-stock of all, an object of ridicule and blame.

By meditating in this way in relation to our rivals we will be specifically enhancing the power of our effort, in addition to gaining further familiarity with the exchange of self with others.

## MEDITATION ON PRIDE TOWARDS AN INFERIOR

Finally we should exchange places with someone who is clearly superior to us in some way, and look down upon our former self in the following manner:

[151-154ab] That deluded being is trying to compete with me, but how can he begin to compare with my learning, wisdom, family and wealth? May my superior qualities and realizations be known to all beings and, as a result, may they develop such bliss that their hair pores tingle with delight! In this way may all beings be conjoined with happiness. As for that lowly Bodhisattva, whatever possessions, good qualities, food and clothing he might have I will take away by means of my superior powers and use for my own and others' benefit. Since he is working for our sake I will leave him just enough to sustain his life; the rest we will use for ourselves. I will curtail his happiness and comfort, burden him with all our suffering and afflict him with our problems.

Such a meditation specifically counters our laziness of discouragement and motivates us to work enthusiastically for the benefit of others.

## THE RESULTS OF THIS MEDITATION

What is the reason for meditating in the three ways just described? Why should we exchange places with someone else in our imagination and then cultivate jealousy, competitiveness or pride towards ourself? The main purpose of such meditations is to stabilize and increase our actual ability to exchange self with others and thereby destroy our self-cherishing attitude. From such an exchange an unusually strong mind of great compassion emerges, and from this we develop an unusually strong bodhichitta motivation. In fact, the bodhichitta developed through this approach is generally more powerful than that cultivated in the meditation on the sevenfold cause and effect described in chapter one of this commentary.

As with all the other instructions described in this text, none of the above-mentioned meditations will be of any use to us if we neglect to put them into practice. There is very little benefit to be gained from merely reading about such practices. In fact, because these specific methods of exchanging self with others may sound unusual to many people, a superficial reading may do nothing more than rouse our doubts and derision.

If we wish to derive real benefit we must study these meditation instructions carefully, acquaint ourself with all the supporting reasons that prove their necessity, validity and effectiveness, and then meditate upon them deeply. We should dispel any doubts or misunderstandings we may have by receiving personal guidance from a well-qualified Teacher who has already trained his or her mind in these meditations. Most importantly we should practise with the motivation of benefiting all beings and bringing them temporary and ultimate happiness.

## COMPLETING THE EXCHANGE BY MEANS OF ACTION

[154cd-155] From beginningless time we have received continuous harm from our self-cherishing attitude. Addressing our own mind we should now think, 'For countless aeons you have thought only about your own welfare, yet what have you received as a result? Only misery, pain and problems.'[156] Contemplating deeply the truth of this so that all the shortcomings of the self-cherishing attitude appear clearly before us, we should dedicate our practice to the benefit of others. If we entrust ourself to the non-deceptive teachings of Buddha, in the future we will experience the excellent results of our own practice and understand the excellent qualities of Buddha's words.

[157] If we had practised this exchange of self with others in the past we would not be experiencing our present suffering and dissatisfaction. By now we would be well on our way to the supreme, blissful attainment of full enlightenment. What is preventing us from accomplishing

this exchange? It is our lack of familiarity with cherishing others. Such familiarity can be developed. For example, at present we identify completely with our body and hold it as I. But in fact this body is not ours; as stated earlier it is only a collection derived from our parents' sperm and ovum. [158] Just as we have come to hold the germ cells of others as I, likewise, through the power of familiarity, we can learn to cherish others as we now do ourself. There is nothing to interfere with this worthwhile accomplishment but our own laziness and lack of motivation.

[159] It is important to examine our behaviour closely to see if we are working for the benefit of others or not. Then, according to our capacity, we should use our possessions and wealth in the service of others without letting the self-cherishing attitude pollute our thoughts. We should think:

[160] I am happy, but others are sad. I have a high position, but others are lower. I give benefit to myself, but not to others. What is the point of being concerned only for my own happiness like this? Why do I not feel jealous of myself and express true love to others?

Having reflected upon these questions well, we should make the following strong determination:

[161] Why should I continue holding on to my faulty attitudes? I must instead separate myself from my happiness, give it to others and take their suffering upon myself. I should examine all my actions for faults and constantly ask myself why I am acting in this way.

[162] Whenever someone harms us we should transform the experience, viewing the harm not as the other person's fault but solely as our own. We should even pray that the

karmic effects of that harmful action ripen on us. And if we have inflicted even the slightest harm on someone else we should declare it, without any reservations, in the presence of many others.

[163] If others have fame and renown we should spread their good reputation even further and cause it to increase. At the same time we should work towards decreasing our own fame and concealing whatever good reputation we may have. Considering ourself to be the servant of others, we must employ ourself in their benefit. [164] We should recognize ourself as being full of faults and avoid indulging in even the slightest self-praise. Our good qualities are not to be displayed to even a few people but to be kept in strictest secrecy.

In brief, we should think:

[165] For the sake of myself I have caused much harm to others. In the future may all that harm return and descend upon me.

[166] Our manner should not be domineering, conceited or self-righteous. Rather, we should bring to mind the image some societies have of a newly married bride and behave in a similarly bashful, timid, and restrained fashion. We should refrain from all non-virtuous activities and, if our mind rebels against this discipline, we should harness it by means of mindfulness and alertness. If our thoughts continue to be selfish, then there is nothing left to do but threaten this self-cherishing mind with destruction:

[167-169] If you, mind, do not act virtuously as advised, then, since you give rise to all my misfortune, there is nothing for me to do but annihilate you.

In the past, because I lacked understanding, I let myself fall under your influence. As a result I suffered constant defeat and torment. But now I clearly see that you are the source of all my problems, so I will not let myself be governed by you ever again. I will uproot you completely, and wherever you go I will destroy you.

If the self-cherishing mind arises again, we should think:

[170-172] You don't belong to me any more; I have sold you to others. You are working for them now, so don't be discouraged and get on with it!

If I hadn't sold your services to others it is certain that you would have delivered me up to the guardians of hell. You have done that to me countless times in the past and have caused me innumerable problems. Recalling all the grudges I have against you, I am determined to overcome you completely.

[173] If we have a strong wish to find happiness both now and in the future, we should not remain happy with the self-cherishing attitude or continue to treat it like a friend. Similarly, if we want to find protection for ourself from suffering, the best thing to do is protect others from suffering. As long as we continue to cherish our own body and behave selfishly on its behalf we will encounter unceasing difficulties and problems and be constantly frustrated in the fulfilment of our wishes. [174] To whatever extent we have self-cherishing desires, to that extent we will suffer from dissatisfaction when those desires are left unfulfilled.

[175] It is impossible to satisfy all the wishes of the self-cherishing mind. We could receive wealth equal to the

expanse of this universe and still remain unsatisfied. There is no way to satiate our desires, for our craving knows no limit. The story is told of the ancient king Manthada who conquered the entire earth and, still not satisfied, took half the celestial kingdom of the god Indra. There are countless other examples from history and our own experiences that demonstrate this truth clearly; selfish desires are a bottomless pit.

[176] When we are unable to fulfil our insatiable desires, our mind becomes flooded with disturbing thoughts and delusions. As a result, whatever virtue we have deteriorates and much suffering ensues. However, the person who is content with what he or she has does not experience the pain of dissatisfaction and instead receives inexhaustible happiness. Of all forms of wealth, that of contentment is found to be supreme.

There was once a beggar in India who found a precious gem. Being a spiritually minded person he wanted to practise generosity by giving this gem away but he could not find a suitable object for his generosity among his beggar friends. Although they were poor and had scant food and clothing, they were content with what they possessed. Finally, after looking throughout the city for an appropriate recipient, he gave the jewel to the king. When asked why he bestowed his gift upon the person who was undoubtedly the richest man in the kingdom, the beggar replied, 'In my eyes this king, because he is not content with his wealth, is really a beggar and therefore the most worthy object for the practice of giving. I have found no one poorer in contentment than this supposedly rich man who thinks solely of receiving things from others just as a hungry cat thinks solely of mice. So I gave the jewel to him.'

## CONCENTRATION

[177] It is necessary to give up our self-cherishing attitude towards our body, refrain from following our attachment and thereby avoid opening the door of discontent. A person who feels no attachment to beautiful, external objects will discover a beautiful mind within. Remaining content is the best wealth; not to grasp at what is attractive is the best of all possessions.

Once we have seen the faults of our self-cherishing attitude we should abandon it completely. These are easy words to say but they are difficult to put into practice. For example, we may have a clear perception of our body's faults and impurities yet still grasp it strongly as 'mine'. Depending on the customs of our native country, this body will eventually be consigned to the earth, consumed by fire or eaten by wild animals. [178] Despite the fact that it is destined to become dust, ashes or even food, this body – which cannot even move from here to there without depending on the force of the mind – is deeply cherished as 'mine', and for its sake we commit actions that will lead us into the agonizing miseries of the lower realms of existence. If we see this clearly, why do we still hold on to and cherish this body so strongly?

We should examine these points closely. [179] Whether we live or die, what is the use of grasping at this mere machine as I? As it is not different from a clod of earth, why do we not abandon the foolish pride of saying 'my body'? [180] Because of our mind's attachment to this body we experience much suffering without any purpose. What is the point of feeling attachment or anger for something that is like a piece of wood and which, no matter how it is served, will never repay us in the future? [181] Although we spend a lifetime caring for this body and guarding it strongly, in due time it will be eaten by vultures. [182] Since the body itself is neither pleased when cared for nor angry when devoured, why do we feel so attached to it? Likewise, though our body may be praised by some for its beauty and abused by others for its ugliness, the body itself does not care, so why should we? Why do we become so attached to it? Why do we trouble ourself so much?

In objection to this line of questioning someone might say, [183] 'Although my body has no awareness, I still want it; it and I are friends. I want and care for this body because my mind knows when it is praised or abused and I become pleased or hurt as a result.' To such an objection Shantideva replies, 'If what you say is true, why aren't you pleased or displeased every time someone praises or abuses the body of another? After all, your mind knows this too.'

Once we have considered all the above-mentioned points well and have reflected deeply upon the many faults and disadvantages of our present contaminated body, we should make the following strong determination:

> [184ab] In order to benefit all sentient beings, I will give up my body without any attachment and accustom myself to this selfless thought.

Does this mean that we should give up our body right now and neglect looking after it completely? No, this is not the implication at all. Our present form, although it is impure and lacking in many ways, should be conceived of as the boat we need in order to cross the ocean of samsara and arrive at the jewel island of enlightenment. [184cd] Thus it is important that we care for it properly so that we are able to work for the benefit of others. What we must give up is the selfish attitude with which we use our body in the vain pursuit of ephemeral samsaric pleasures.

[185] Thus our mind should not be directed towards meaningless and childish behaviour but rather should follow the path of the wise Bodhisattvas. Remembering the teachings on conscientiousness, we should turn away from sleep, dullness, mental sinking and mental excitement, and all other hindering states of mind. [186] Like the compassionate Sons and Daughters of the Conqueror, Buddha, we should increase the power of all mental factors that oppose our delusions. If we do not make constant effort throughout the day and the night in this way, when will our misery ever come to an end? When will enlightenment ever be reached? Contemplating in this way we should strive to attain tranquil abiding, the essence of meditative concentration, and train our mind in the exchange of self with others.

[187] To summarize, in order to dispel the obstructions to both liberation and full enlightenment we should withdraw our mind from all mistaken paths and place it in continuous concentrated equipoise on a perfect object of meditation.

This concludes 'Concentration', the eighth chapter of the text *Meaningful to Behold*, a commentary to Shantideva's *Guide to the Bodhisattva's Way of Life*.

*Je Tsongkhapa*

# *Wisdom*

**HOW TO DEVELOP THE WISDOM OF SUPERIOR SEEING**

This has five parts:

1. Showing why those who wish to attain liberation need to develop the wisdom realizing emptiness
2. The presentation of the two truths
3. Showing the reasons why those who seek only personal liberation need to develop the wisdom realizing emptiness
4. An extensive explanation of the reasons that establish emptiness
5. Encouraging the practitioner to strive to develop this wisdom

**SHOWING WHY THOSE WHO WISH TO ATTAIN LIBERATION NEED TO DEVELOP THE WISDOM REALIZING EMPTINESS**

[1] For those practising the Mahayana path Buddha taught all the method aspects of Dharma, such as developing bodhichitta, giving, moral discipline and so forth. He did this for the sake of their being able to cultivate the wisdom realizing emptiness, which can eliminate the obstructions to omniscience that block the attainment of the highest goal,

Buddhahood. Even those who wish merely to overcome their own suffering and attain a state of liberation need to cultivate this wisdom. For other than the wisdom realizing emptiness there are no means by which we can eradicate the root of our own and others' suffering.

The root of all suffering is our grasping at a self of persons as well as of other phenomena, together with the imprints of such a wrong awareness. In order to sever this root it is necessary to develop the wisdom realizing emptiness supported by the conditions of the mind of enlightenment and the six perfections. However, it is the wisdom aspect that is primarily instrumental in this process; therefore much effort should be given to its development. How is this to be done? We have to realize that the two truths – conventional truth and ultimate truth – do not contradict but mutually assist each other.

We need to be able to posit and establish an object's conventional nature without refuting its ultimate nature, and vice versa. When these two natures are seen to be non-contradictory we have understood the union of the two truths. To gain this understanding it is essential that the practitioner develop both the method aspect of the path in order to comprehend conventional truth and the wisdom aspect of the path that comprehends ultimate truth.

Even if we strive for many aeons cultivating method and wisdom as separate and unrelated practices, we will never achieve the result of Buddhahood. If we meditate without developing both practices of method and wisdom we are like a bird trying to fly without using its wings. Those who wish to attain the perfect view must, like a bird with two sound wings, strive to develop an understanding that realizes the two truths. Therefore in his ninth chapter Shantideva extensively presents the nature of these two truths, the respective understandings of which are like two wings propelling us towards enlightenment.

## THE PRESENTATION OF THE TWO TRUTHS

This has five parts:

1. The distinctions between the two truths
2. The definition of the two truths
3. The distinctions between the individuals who assert the two truths
4. The distinctions between their varying degrees of mental capacity
5. Refuting the argument that it is not necessary to realize emptiness in order to attain liberation

## THE DISTINCTIONS BETWEEN THE TWO TRUTHS

[2] There exist two types of objects that can be known: conventional truths and ultimate truths. All phenomena other than emptiness are conventional truths and all emptinesses are ultimate truths. For example, the person as well as the aggregates of body and mind are conventional truths, whereas the emptiness or lack of inherent existence of the person and the aggregates is an ultimate truth. These two truths, however, are not different in the same way as the right and left horns of a bull are different. With regard to any phenomenon, its conventional and ultimate truths are the same entity although they are nominally distinct. As long as they are considered to be fundamentally distinct entities the perfect view is lacking. In many Sutras and other

scriptures it has been shown by many logical reasonings that the two truths are not fundamentally distinct entities. Thus it is important for us to understand these reasons.

## THE DEFINITION OF THE TWO TRUTHS

Some scholars have misunderstood Shantideva's statement in the second verse of his ninth chapter that ultimate truths are not objects that can be experienced by mind. They have inferred from this that ultimate truths are not knowable phenomena. Others have also concluded that ultimate truths are neither existent nor non-existent. However, in his works on Madhyamika philosophy Je Tsongkhapa clearly refutes all such views and presents the nature of ultimate truths in exact accordance with the meaning intended by Shantideva. Those interested should consult these works of his, and other authentic commentaries such as the book *Ocean of Nectar*.

An ultimate truth is defined as that which is realized by a direct valid cognizer to which all dualistic appearances have subsided. A conventional truth is defined as that which is realized by a direct valid cognizer to which dualistic appearances have not subsided. What is meant by dualistic appearance is the appearance of an object together with the appearance of its inherent existence.

'Inherent existence' has a very specific meaning in Buddhist thought. It refers to an object's supposed existence from its own nature or from its own side. In fact, however, such a mode of existence is utterly non-existent. It is only conceived by a mind that mistakenly grasps at what is known as 'true existence'.

According to Shantideva and the Madhyamika-Prasangika school to which he belongs, all the following terms refer to this falsely conceived mode of existence and all are to be understood as synonyms: inherent existence, true existence, existence from its own side and independent existence.

It is this false mode of existence, phenomena existing from their own side without being merely imputed by mind, that is the very object to be refuted by emptiness. Thus whenever any of these synonymous terms are used in this chapter they refer to a mistaken idea of the way things actually exist – a mistaken view responsible for all of our suffering in samsara – and it will be Shantideva's purpose to refute any person or school (Buddhist or non-Buddhist) holding such a wrong view.

To return to the discussion of the two truths, consider the following example. For sentient beings two things appear in the visual perception of a conventional truth such as a jug: the jug itself and the inherent existence of the jug. However, in a direct perception of the ultimate truth of the jug – its lack of inherent existence – both the appearance of the jug as well as the appearance of its inherent existence have subsided, and one is left contemplating the bare emptiness of inherent existence alone. Thus when Shantideva states that ultimate truths are not objects that can be experienced by the mind, he means that ultimate truths cannot be experienced by a direct perceiver in which dualistic appearance has not subsided. They can only be experienced by direct perceivers in which dualistic appearance has subsided.

## THE DISTINCTIONS BETWEEN THE INDIVIDUALS WHO ASSERT THE TWO TRUTHS

[3] There are two types of individual who assert the two truths: Yogis who recognize all phenomena as being empty

of inherent existence, that is, those who hold the views of the supreme Madhyamika-Prasangika school; and the common Yogis, or 'proponents of things', who propound that all things are inherently existent, that is, those who subscribe to the views of the Madhyamika-Svatantrika, Chittamatra, Sautrantika and Vaibhashika schools.

## THE DISTINCTIONS BETWEEN THEIR VARYING DEGREES OF MENTAL CAPACITY

The views of the common Yogis who assert that all things are inherently existent are refuted by the logical reasonings presented by the Yogis who hold the Prasangika viewpoint, such as Shantideva. [4abc] Furthermore, Yogis holding the Prasangika view include those with many levels of insight; therefore those with higher levels of understanding surpass and go beyond those with lesser degrees of realization. (It should be noted that a Yogi is someone who has achieved the concentration of the union of tranquil abiding and superior seeing.) But why is it necessary for Shantideva to mention the different levels of understanding of Yogis? He does so in order to point out that the Prasangika system that he represents is superior to and cannot be contradicted by any of the other philosophical schools.

At this point I would like to explain briefly why Buddha taught the four different philosophical systems. Buddha taught two Hinayana systems of tenets, Vaibhashika and Sautrantika, and two Mahayana systems, Chittamatra and Madhyamika. These systems present emptiness in different ways, but Buddha's final view is the view presented by the Prasangika school, which is a division of the Madhyamika school. According to this view, emptiness is the mere absence of inherent existence, and so a phenomenon's emptiness is its lack, or emptiness, of inherent existence. Inherent existence is the object of negation of emptiness. This means that in order to realize emptiness it is necessary to negate inherent existence. Through understanding that there is no inherent existence we come to understand emptiness. Thus to gain a correct realization of emptiness it is extremely important to recognize exactly what needs to be negated. We must gain a clear understanding of what inherent existence, the object of negation, means, for only then will we be able to refute it. Because we are so habituated to our ordinary way of perceiving the world it is extremely difficult for us to gain an understanding of the Prasangika view immediately. Our mind must be trained gradually so that we steadily approach the ultimately correct view. It is for this purpose that Buddha taught the four distinct systems of tenets.

Let us examine this question of inherent existence in terms of our sense of self, or I. In dependence upon our aggregates of body and mind all of us grasp at a self. However, not every apprehension we have of I is what is meant by self-grasping. In apprehending the self or I two distinct aspects of the mind are functioning. One, which is valid, apprehends the conventionally existent mere I; and the other, which is invalid, apprehends the I as inherently existent. The latter is the mind of self-grasping. At present these two modes of existence of the self, one being true and the other false, appear mixed together and it is extremely difficult to tell them apart. At certain times, however, the falsely conceived self does appear more distinctly to us. For example, when we are in danger of falling from a high cliff we do not cling to the idea that our body will fall or that our mind will fall. We only think, 'I will fall.'

At such times as these there appears a vividly appearing I, independent of the body and mind. If this I existed it would be an inherently existent I. However, the mind that conceives such an I is a wrong awareness and the object it grasps is entirely non-existent. This mind is an example of self-grasping, and the I that it holds so strongly is an object of negation of emptiness. In a similar fashion the vivid appearance of all other phenomena as inherently existent should be understood as objects to be negated in realizing emptiness.

Now we might wonder whether the self or I exists at all. It exists, but in a way that can be distinguished as separate from the false sense of I only by a very sharp and penetrating intellect. Furthermore, we might think that the false conception of our self only occurs at particular times, such as when we are about to fall from a cliff, but this is not so. For us at present there is not a single moment in which this grasping at an inherently existent self does not arise. Even insects have self-grasping. If we place our hand out in front of an ant, for instance, it stops and turns away. What is it thinking? It thinks, 'Someone is harming me.' At that time it does not cling to either the body or mind but to a vividly appearing 'me' that is independent of the body and mind. This clinging mind is the ant's self-grasping.

According to the Prasangika view the object of negation of emptiness is the inherent existence of phenomena. The lower Buddhist schools present a different object of negation. Although the schools below the Prasangika differ in their presentation of the mode of existence of phenomena, they all agree that it is possible to achieve liberation from samsara through realizing subtle selflessness of persons. With the exception of some Vaibhashikas, they assert that subtle selflessness of persons is the person's emptiness of being self-supporting and substantially existent. Thus, according to these schools the object of negation of the subtle selflessness of persons is a self-supporting, substantially existent person. However, the Prasangikas say that this is the object of negation of *gross* selflessness of persons and that the subtle selflessness of persons is in fact the person's emptiness of inherent existence. Moreover they assert that in order to gain even personal liberation it is not sufficient to realize that the person is empty of being self-supporting and substantially existent; it is necessary to realize that the person is empty of inherent existence.

Shantideva's teachings are in accordance with the Prasangika view and consequently he deals extensively with the Prasangikas' presentation of subtle selflessness of persons but not with the lower schools' presentation. Since there are many texts written from the point of view of the lower schools, I would like to explain briefly the difference between gross and subtle selflessness of persons in order to avoid any confusion.

Gross selflessness of persons (which the lower schools call subtle selflessness of persons) is the person's lack of being self-supporting and substantially existent. In order to understand what is meant by this we must understand the object that is being negated: namely a self-supporting, substantially existent person. This is a person that is able to appear to the mind without depending upon the appearance of any of the person's aggregates. In fact we never perceive a person without at least part of the person's aggregates appearing to us. This indicates that the person is empty of being self-supporting and substantially existent.

Although our I is dependent upon our aggregates, through the force of habitual self-grasping we hold the opposite view.

It seems to us that our aggregates depend upon the I. We habitually regard our aggregates of body and mind as our possessions and conceive of an I that owns and controls them. Thus we talk of *my* body and *my* mind. In this way we grasp an I that is independent of the aggregates and can appear to the mind without depending on the appearance of the aggregates. If such an I existed it would be a self-supporting, substantially existent person. Such a person is the object of negation of gross selflessness of persons, and the mind that conceives it to exist is gross self-grasping of persons.

Subtle selflessness of persons is the person's emptiness of inherent existence. What is the difference between this and gross selflessness of persons? The difference lies in the object of negation. Gross selflessness of persons is the negation of the existence of a person that is able to appear to the mind without depending upon the appearance of his or her aggregates. Subtle selflessness of persons is the negation of more than this; it is the negation of the existence of any kind of inherently existent person. According to the Prasangikas, there is no inherently existent person to be found even within the aggregates. Although the lower schools negate the existence of a self-supporting, substantially existent person they all accept the existence of an inherently existent person. A mind that conceives a person to be inherently existent is subtle self-grasping of persons.

The realization of gross selflessness of persons is very helpful but it is necessary to progress to the realization of subtle selflessness of persons before liberation can be attained. It is therefore very important to differentiate clearly between gross and subtle selflessness. In Buddhist literature we may find the object of negation of gross selflessness of persons and the object of negation of subtle selflessness of persons described in the same words, so great care is needed when interpreting the meaning. For example, when Khedrubje, one of the principal disciples of Je Tsongkhapa, explained the object of negation of the subtle selflessness of persons of the Chittamatra system he described the self-supporting, substantially existent person as 'the vividly appearing I that does not depend upon any part or collection of the aggregates'. Exactly the same phrase has also been used by scholars and meditators to describe the inherently existent person that is the object of negation of the subtle selflessness of persons of the Prasangika system. Even though the words used are the same, the meaning is quite different. Therefore it is important not to rely on mere words but to gain a true inner experience of the meaning based on scriptural authority, logical reasoning and skilful analysis. If I were to explain in detail the difference between a self-supporting, substantially existent person and an inherently existent person, it would take many pages. Those who wish to know clearly the difference between the two should consult Je Tsongkhapa's *Essence of Good Explanations* (Tib. *Leg she nying po*) and Jangkya's *Clear Explanation of Tenets entitled 'Beautiful Ornament of the Mountain of Buddha's Doctrine'* (Tib. *Thub ten lhun poi dze gyen*).

Although it is hard for those who have not studied emptiness to distinguish between the non-existent and the existent I, once emptiness is understood these two will be seen to be quite distinct from one another. The four major systems of Buddhist philosophy identify the existent I in different ways. Since all the major schools agree that the person is empty of being self-supporting and substantially existent, they accept that the person is merely imputed in dependence upon his or her aggregates. However, the lower schools use the words 'merely imputed' in a different way to the Prasangikas. For the lower schools the words mean simply that a person appears to the mind due to the appearance of the person's aggregates. For instance, we say we see Peter when in fact we see Peter's body. In this case due to seeing Peter's body we say we see Peter. If we study and understand this well, we will realize that Peter is merely imputed in dependence upon his aggregates such as his body. Here 'merely' is used to exclude a person existing separate from the person's aggregates. However, all the lower schools accept that there is an inherently existent person that can be found within the person's aggregates. The various lower schools differ in their identification of this existent person.

Generally the followers of the Vaibhashika school, on searching for the person or I among the aggregates of body and mind, come to the conclusion that no single aggregate is the I. Instead they identify the mere collection of the five aggregates as the existent I. Among the two sub-schools of the Sautrantika system – those who follow scriptural authority and those who follow reason – the former have a view similar to the Vaibhashikas, whereas the latter consider the mental consciousness alone to be the existent I. The adherents of the Chittamatra school see serious contradictions in the views of both the Vaibhashikas and Sautrantikas. When they search for the existent I within the five aggregates, they say the aggregates of form, feeling, discrimination and compositional factors are not the existent I. When they search within the aggregate of consciousness, they realize that the six consciousnesses – the five sense consciousnesses and mental consciousness – are not the existent I, and also the deluded mind is not the I. Finally they posit a consciousness-basis-of-all (Skt. alayavijnana) and consider this to be the existent I. The Svatantrikas, who together with the Prasangikas constitute the Madhyamika school, refute all the preceding viewpoints and assert a non-truly existent mental consciousness to be the existent I.

In fact none of these schools is completely faultless in its assertions. None of them has been able to identify the existent I correctly. Nevertheless, the Sautrantikas are closer to the correct view than the Vaibhashikas, the Chittamatrins are closer than the Sautrantikas, and the Svatantrikas are closer than the Chittamatrins. But only the highest school, that of the incomparable Prasangikas, correctly realizes the nature of the existent I. According to them all the other schools have failed to make a correct identification. The Prasangikas show that no I can be found among the aggregates either individually or collectively. How, then, do they assert the I to exist? They accept the existent I to be the I that is merely imputed by conception in dependence upon any of the person's aggregates. Other than this, no I exists. It follows that the existence of an I is entirely dependent upon conceptual thought; there is nothing that exists inherently as an I. Nevertheless, the I that is imputed by conception is said to be existent provided that the basis upon which it is imputed is appropriate. By convention, any of the person's aggregates can act as a valid basis for imputing the person, so a person who is merely imputed on this basis is conventionally existent.

The Prasangikas assert that all phenomena exist in a similar fashion: namely, as mere conceptual imputations. For them all phenomena are like an elephant we see in a dream. Where was that large elephant that we dreamt of last night in our small bedroom? Was it in our room? Or was it in our mind? The elephant existed in neither place; it merely appeared to our mind. In this case it is clear that the elephant did not exist inherently but was merely imputed by our conception. In the same way, all the phenomena we perceive, even when we are awake, are also merely imputed by conception.

Among the Buddhist systems of thought it is the Prasangika school that is free from contradiction and is representative of Buddha's real intention. Protector Nagarjuna, Aryadeva, Buddhapalita, Chandrakirti, Shantideva, Atisha and Je Tsongkhapa were all proponents of this view. Through studying the different Buddhist systems of tenets it is possible for those with sharp faculties to comprehend the highest Prasangika view and develop the correct understanding of emptiness.

## REFUTING THE ARGUMENT THAT IT IS NOT NECESSARY TO REALIZE EMPTINESS IN ORDER TO ATTAIN LIBERATION

Apart from the Prasangikas all the other Buddhist schools maintain that it is unnecessary to realize that all phenomena are devoid of inherent existence in order to attain liberation. In the following sections Shantideva sets out to refute this tenet in particular and in doing so continues to examine and reveal other fallacies in the tenets of the proponents of things. Thus this section has two parts:

1 A refutation of the proponents of things in general
2 A refutation of the Chittamatrins in particular

# A REFUTATION OF THE PROPONENTS OF THINGS IN GENERAL

A proponent of things is a proponent of tenets who asserts that phenomena are truly existent. The Buddhist schools of the Vaibhashika, Sautrantika and Chittamatra all belong to this category. All the lower schools state that there is no proof for the Prasangika assertion that all phenomena are empty of inherent existence. However, Shantideva points out the means whereby the Prasangikas are able to establish their viewpoint for their critics in the lower schools. In all the schools it is commonly accepted that such things as a magician's illusions and dream images are unreal and false. It is by referring to such examples as these, since they are commonly regarded as false, that the Prasangikas are able to prove to their opponents that all phenomena lack inherent existence.

*Proponent of things:* If you maintain that all phenomena lack inherent existence, it follows that the six perfections also lack inherent existence. If this were the case, then since they would be non-existent, what would be the purpose of practising them?

*Prasangika:* [4d] Although giving and the other perfections are empty of inherent existence, without making any investigation of their true nature it is necessary to practise them in order to be able to accomplish the resultant state of Buddhahood. Conventionally they exist as conceptual imputations and as long as they are not further analyzed they function effectively as means by which the path may be travelled and the goal attained. Hence there is no contradiction in stating that the six perfections are to be practised although they lack any inherent existence.

*Proponent of things:* But surely you see with direct perception that, for example, fire burns wood. In our tradition whatever we see with such immediate perception is said to be truly existent, so there is no point in arguing that such objects are non-truly existent.

*Prasangika:* Your objection arises because you have not understood clearly the nature of the two truths. [5] With direct perceptions, Yogis of the Madhyamika school and those who are proponents of things see that fire burns wood. The difference is that you see such things and immediately conceive them to be inherently existent without recognizing their illusion-like character. We, on the other hand, regard them as non-inherently existent and realize their illusory nature. It is precisely on this point that the Madhyamikas and the proponents of things have a ground for argument.

*Proponent of things:* [6] In this case, if forms and so forth are not truly existent, it is a contradiction to say that they can be seen by valid direct perceivers.

*Prasangika:* Direct perceivers of such things as forms are valid cognizers in terms of conventionally existent objects but are not valid cognizers of their ultimate mode of existence. Forms exist, but they are merely imputed by conception and are established by worldly convention.

In reality, the human body is impure but it is conventionally accepted by the people of the world as something very clean and pure. In a similar manner phenomena are completely empty of inherent existence although they appear to the minds of worldly beings as having inherent existence. Thus the manner in which things appear and the manner in which they exist are not in harmony.

Things exist in a different way from their appearance. For example, the illusory figure of a woman created by a magician is not a real woman, but to those in the audience whose eyes have been affected by the magician's spells this illusion appears and is taken for a real woman. This woman is thus said to be false. In the same way, beings whose minds are affected by grasping at inherent existence behold and apprehend inherently existent phenomena whereas, in fact, no such phenomena exist. In this way phenomena are likewise said to be false and deceptive. Their manner of appearance and existence do not correspond to one another.

*Proponent of things:* To deny the inherent, true existence of things is surely a denial that they exist or have any nature at all. Your assertion, therefore, is in contradiction with Buddha's statement that all conditioned, or produced, phenomena do have a nature, an impermanent nature.

*Prasangika:* There is no contradiction at all. [7abc] Buddha specifically taught that things have a gross and a subtle impermanent nature in order to lead people gradually to the higher view that they are empty of inherent existence. When he turned the first Wheel of Dharma at Sarnath he did clearly state that all conditioned phenomena are impermanent. This is true. However, he did not mean that their momentary arising and perishing was a truly existent process. It is only conventionally that they arise and perish.

*Proponent of things:* [7d] But it is incorrect to say that conventionally conditioned phenomena are impermanent – that is, in a state of momentary change – because such change is not witnessed by worldly people. Not being seen by them, impermanence would not meet your criterion for being established as a conventional truth. When worldly people see an object in the morning and then later in the day they do so without perceiving any visible signs of change. They assume that such things, therefore, are non-momentary and permanent.

*Prasangika:* [8] Although worldly people see things in this way, this is a mistaken awareness. We never say that for something to be a valid conventional truth it must be seen by worldly people. That is not our criterion. The impermanent nature of conditioned phenomena, for example, is established by the conventional valid cognizers of Yogis who have gained insight into the subtle momentary nature of things. Thus there is no contradiction between the Yogis' understanding and our statement that things exist merely conventionally.

*Proponent of things:* But isn't this view of yours in contradiction with Buddha's statement that by beholding impermanence we see reality?

*Prasangika:* When Buddha made this statement he was talking to individuals who believed that forms are permanent and that the body is pure and clean. In comparison with their point of view it was quite correct for him to say that to see impermanence is to see the truth. In the world the body is regarded as something pure and clean but in reality it is not. If it were, then the view of the worldly people would harm the Yogi's realization that the nature of the bodies of ordinary men and women is impure.

*Proponent of things:* If all phenomena have no true existence, then Buddha too must have no true existence. In this case, when there is no true Buddha, how can merits accrue from making offerings to him?

*Prasangika:* [9ab] In the same way as you receive merits, which you consider to be truly existent, from paying respect to a Buddha whom you consider to be truly existent, so do we receive merits we consider to be like an illusion from paying respect to a Buddha whom we consider to be like an illusion. Whether we regard Buddha as inherently existent or not, if from our side we devote ourself to him with much faith and veneration, merit will always ensue.

*Proponent of things:* [9cd] If sentient beings lack true existence and are like an illusion, then how do they take rebirth after death? When the magician's illusory woman ceases she never comes into existence again.

*Prasangika:* Sentient beings are not the same as illusions in all respects. We are only comparing them to illusions in order to illustrate the fact that they lack inherent existence in the same way as illusions do. A magician's illusory woman does not exist as a woman from her own side; it is we who conceive her to be a real woman. In a similar manner, sentient beings do not exist inherently, from their own side, but exist only through conceptual imputation. In this way alone they are similar to illusions.

[10ab] Whenever the causal conditions necessary to produce an illusory woman are gathered together, the illusory woman will appear. Likewise, for as long as sentient beings have the necessary causes and conditions for taking rebirth in samsara, they will continue to take rebirth. In this way the appearance of both is dependent upon a particular set of causes and conditions.

*Proponent of things:* But there is still a great difference. The magician's woman is manifested and then remains for a very short time, whereas sentient beings have been in existence since beginningless time. Therefore we can say that the former is false and unreal whereas the latter are truly and inherently existent.

*Prasangika:* [10cd] Their difference in duration is no proof at all for establishing one to be truly existent and the other to be false. If this were a valid criterion, then it would follow that an illusion or a dream of long duration would be more true than one of shorter duration. This is clearly not the case; all illusions and dreams are equally false.

*Proponent of things:* If sentient beings are like illusions there can be no evil in killing them. This would be so since there is no evil in killing an illusory woman created by a magician.

*Prasangika:* [11] The reason why there is no actual evil committed when we kill a magician's woman is because she has no mind; but if we cause any harm to someone who has a mind then evil will automatically be accumulated. Likewise, if we benefit someone with a mind, merits will result. Nevertheless, it should be pointed out that in killing a magician's woman, for example, we are not completely free from evil and the necessity of having to experience an unfortunate result. We do not accumulate the actual karma of killing but we do accumulate a certain degree of negative karma through the force of our malicious intention to kill and cause harm.

*Proponent of things:* Why, if both a magician's woman and sentient beings are alike in not being truly existent, does one come to be endowed with a mind whereas the other does not?

*Prasangika:* [12] A magician's woman has no mind because her causes – the mantra used as a spell, the magical substance and the pieces of wood and stone – do not have the ability to produce mind. All various types of illusions differ according to their various causes. [13ab] There exists no single cause that alone has the ability to give rise to a variety of different results.

*Proponent of things:* [13cd-14ab] You Madhyamikas assert that the emptiness of samsara is the natural state of nirvana. Therefore sentient beings would be endowed with the state of nirvana since this would be their ultimate nature. In this case there would be a common point between samsara and nirvana. It would likewise follow that Buddha in his state of nirvana would also be in samsara, in which case what would be the purpose of practising the Bodhisattva way of life in order to attain Buddhahood?

*Prasangika:* [14cd] Although we call the emptiness of true existence of samsara 'natural nirvana', this is not the same as the actual state of nirvana attained by Arhats and Buddhas. We would never accept that there is anyone who is both in samsara and nirvana. Only through the elimination of the cause of samsara, ignorance, will samsara be destroyed and nirvana realized. For as long as its cause is present there will be no possibility of liberation from samsara. Even in the case of illusions, if their causes are not severed they will continue to appear and they will only cease when their causes cease. [15ab] Once the causes of samsara are destroyed it will not occur even conventionally.

## A REFUTATION OF THE CHITTAMATRINS IN PARTICULAR

For both Mahayana systems of tenets, that is, the Chittamatrins and the Madhyamikas, sense consciousnesses of ordinary beings are regarded as mistaken minds. For the Chittamatrins this is so because the objects of sense consciousness appear to exist externally while for the Prasangikas it is so because these objects appear to be inherently existent. Thus for different reasons they both arrive at the same conclusion. Because the Chittamatrins deny external existence (that is, that things have any nature other than the nature of mind) and the Prasangikas deny inherent existence (that is, that things exist from their own side or nature without merely being imputed by mind), they both regard sense consciousness as mistaken.

*Chittamatrin:* [15cd] If, as you assert, all phenomena have no true existence, it follows that the mistaken sense consciousnesses are non-existent. In which case what consciousness is able to behold the illusion-like objects such as form? Since there would be no consciousness, the illusion-like objects would also cease to be existent.

*Prasangika:* [16ab] But for you, do forms and so forth exist in the way that they appear to consciousness or not? If they do then you would have to assert that they are external objects, for this is the way in which they appear. Once you have said that they are externally existent it would be meaningless for you to say that they are like an illusion. But if they do not exist in the way that they appear it follows that they could not be truly existent, for to be truly existent means to exist and appear in the same way. In your system, to be non-truly existent means to be non-existent: therefore you yourself would also have to say that the illusion-like forms are non-existent. In this case there could be no such thing as the apprehension of form.

*Chittamatrin:* [16cd] It is true that form does not exist in the way that it is apprehended by eye consciousness because the eye consciousness sees it as existing externally. Therefore it is not an externally existing object but it nevertheless exists in another way. It exists as the nature of the mind itself. However, it is not actually mind because it lacks the characteristics of mind; yet neither is it something by nature separate from mind. It therefore cannot be expressed as being either mind or separate from mind; in this sense we say that it is 'inexpressible'. It is like the elephant we see in a dream. This has a similar quality of inexpressibility because it too can be said to be neither mind nor entirely other than mind.

When we are watching a film the pictures appear to be existing from the side of the screen; but in fact they are only being projected upon the screen by the projector behind us. This we can all understand. Similarly when we see a blue patch of colour, the blue appears vividly to be existing from its own side. In this case too the blue is not existing externally from its own side but is existing as the same entity as the subjective perception of blue. The same is true for all objects of sense consciousness. According to us there is no blue other than the blue-appearing-to-the-consciousness-apprehending-blue. When we realize the blue to be devoid of any external existence, we realize emptiness with regard to blue.

(The view of reality presented by the Chittamatra school is very close to the view put forth by the Prasangika school. Hence to gain an understanding of their tenets is extremely helpful. Of course, their beliefs are not in exact accordance with the Prasangika system and finally are to be set aside.)

*Prasangika:* [17ab] If the illusion-like forms that appear to the mind have no external existence then, since there can be no object condition, how can the mind arise? If, according to you, it does arise, then by what valid cognizer is it beheld and established?

*Chittamatrin:* The eye consciousness that apprehends form has two aspects: an other-cognizing aspect that is only conscious of objects distinct from consciousness, and a self-cognizing aspect that only apprehends the consciousness itself, and which we call a 'valid self-cognizer'. A self-cognizer is always a non-deceptive consciousness and is the mind that establishes the existence of the eye consciousness of form and so forth.

The refutation of the Chittamatra position attacks this concept of self-cognizers and is presented in four parts:

1 Refuting self-cognizers by scriptural authority
2 Refuting self-cognizers by reasoning
3 Refuting the Chittamatrins' proofs of the existence of self-cognizers
4 Refuting the assertion that all imputed existents must have as their basis something truly existent

## REFUTING SELF-COGNIZERS BY SCRIPTUAL AUTHORITY

*Prasangika:* [17cd-18ab] If a cognizer of form is able to be conscious of itself, this will contradict scriptural authority. In *Gone to Lanka Sutra* (Skt. *Lankavatarasutra*) as well as in *Ratnachudapariprrcha Sutra* Buddha stated that just as the blade of a sword cannot cut itself likewise the mind cannot behold itself. If you assert that consciousness is self-cognizing, you are in fact asserting the existence of a consciousness that does not depend upon an object of consciousness. In such a case both the subject and the object would be exactly the same thing, that is, one state of consciousness, and it would be impossible to make a subject-object distinction. If such a consciousness were possible it would have to be truly, independently existent and such a mode of existence is refuted by much logical reasoning.

## REFUTING SELF-COGNIZERS BY REASONING

*Chittamatrin:* [18cd] Take a lamp for example. It is able to illuminate clearly both itself and other external objects. In a similar way the mind is able to be conscious of both itself and other phenomena.

*Prasangika:* [19ab] This is not a valid analogy because the light of a lamp does not illuminate itself at all. If the lamp were to illuminate itself, then by the same token why could we not say that darkness obscures itself? However, if darkness obscures itself it would be impossible to ever behold it, whereas darkness is something that is quite visible.

*Chittamatrin:* [19cd] Then let us take another example. A piece of clear crystal is able to appear as blue when placed upon a blue object which is other than it. Its appearing as blue is thus dependent upon something other than it. Lapis lazuli, on the other hand, does not need to depend upon anything else in order to appear as blue; by its very nature it appears as blue. [20ab] Similarly eye consciousness and so forth are necessarily related to objects that are other than consciousness, whereas self-cognizers exist as consciousness without being related to objects other than consciousness.

*Prasangika:* [20cd] But again your example is not valid. It is surely evident to everyone that the blueness of lapis lazuli does not exist without depending upon anything else; it is dependent upon other causes and conditions. It does not create its own nature.

*Chittamatrin:* [21a] Returning to the previous example, we concede that the lamp does not illuminate itself but nevertheless its nature is that of illumination.

*Prasangika:* [21bcd] In a similar way, you should assert that the mind does not know itself but is merely of the nature of conscious illumination. So what does apprehend consciousness? Is consciousness apprehended by a consciousness substantially different from itself? If this were so then we would need an endless series of substantially different consciousnesses to be conscious of one another. If neither of these alternatives is possible, then what apprehender of consciousness can there be? [22] If no apprehension of consciousness can be established it must follow that consciousness cannot be an object of knowledge and therefore must be non-existent. In this case it would be utterly pointless to discuss whether consciousness is self-illuminating or not. To do so would be just like trying to describe the features of the daughter of a childless woman.

## REFUTING THE CHITTAMATRINS' PROOFS OF THE EXISTENCE OF SELF-COGNIZERS

*Chittamatrin:* [23ab] If eye consciousness and so forth do not have a self-cognizing aspect, then in the future how would it be possible to remember them? We do not simply remember the object but are also able to recollect the consciousness that apprehended it. From this fact it is clear that in addition to apprehending an object other than itself consciousness also beholds itself. Because of the process of memory we are thus able to establish the existence of self-cognizers.

*Prasangika:* [23cd] This is not a valid proof. The consciousness of the object is remembered simply owing to its having had a relationship with the object itself. For example, there is a particular type of rodent that has the habit of biting people and other animals during the winter but the poison emitted at the time of biting does not immediately take effect; it is only felt in the following spring. In this way a man may experience the biting of the rodent without being conscious of the poison entering his system. Later, at the beginning of spring, he starts to feel some pain. At this time he realizes it is spring and remembers that the previous winter he was bitten by this particular rodent. In dependence upon these factors he then correctly draws the conclusion that he was poisoned when the rodent bit him. In a similar way the recollection of the consciousness that experienced a particular form, for example, is implicit in the recollection of its object, the form.

*Chittamatrin:* If you do not accept memory as establishing the existence of self-cognizers, here is another argument. [24ab] When someone looks into the distance and is able to see a tiny object, such as a needle, it goes without saying that he will be able to see a mountain that is close by. Similarly, once we have attained tranquil abiding and other conditions, it is possible clairvoyantly to see the minds of other people that are far away. If this is so, there should be no difficulty in seeing our own mind that is so close to us.

*Prasangika:* [24cd] When someone applies a certain magical eye lotion to his eyes he is able to see clearly treasure vases that are buried deep beneath the earth but he is unable to see the eye lotion itself. Similarly, just because the mind is very close it does not follow that it can be beheld by itself.

*Chittamatrin:* But if you refute the existence of self-cognizers how can consciousness be established as existent? In this case you would be refuting awarenesses of forms, sounds and so forth.

*Prasangika:* [25] We have no intention of refuting the existence of eye awareness, ear awareness and other awarenesses. We are only refuting self-cognizers; in doing so it does not follow that we are refuting the other awarenesses as well. There is no need to abandon them because they do not cause us suffering in samsara and are still possessed by Arhats. The mind that has to be abandoned is the conceptual grasping at truly existent forms, sounds and so forth. This is to be rejected because it is the fundamental cause of suffering in samsara.

At this point the Chittamatrins begin a new argument concerning what they consider to be truly existent forms.

*Chittamatrin:* [26ab] Illusion-like forms are neither external objects other than the mind nor are they the mind itself. Therefore, they are what we call 'inexpressible'.

*Prasangika:* [26cd] Nevertheless you assert that forms are truly existent phenomena. In this case, since they are true they should exist in the manner in which they appear to the eye consciousness that beholds them and thus be the externally existent objects they appear to be. If this is so then why do you claim that form is not other than mind? On the other hand, if form does not exist in the way it is beheld by the eye consciousness, then it makes no sense for you to say that form is truly existent.

Thus to deny the external existence of objects and to assert the true existence of these same objects and consciousnesses are both mistaken views. [27ab] Just as the objects of consciousness, forms and so forth, are like illusions and lack any true existence, similarly the consciousnesses themselves are like illusions and lack any true existence.

## REFUTING THE ASSERTION THAT ALL IMPUTED EXISTENTS MUST HAVE AS THEIR BASIS SOMETHING TRULY EXISTENT

According to the Chittamatra school, phenomena are either substantial existents or imputed existents. A substantial existent is an object that can appear to the mind without the mind having to refer to objects other than it. Colours, jugs and so forth are examples of substantial existents. An imputed existent is an object that is apprehended in dependence upon objects other than it being apprehended. The person, for example, is an imputed existent because it cannot be apprehended without the mind also apprehending either the body or the mind, which are objects other than it. Similarly, samsara cannot be apprehended independently of the living beings experiencing samsara being apprehended. Thus it too is an imputed existent. In the Prasangika school, however, such a distinction is not made; for them all existent phenomena are imputed existents.

*Chittamatrin:* [27cd] Samsara and all imputed existents must have as their basis of imputation something truly and really existent. Otherwise they would become utterly abstract and non-functional, just like space.

*Prasangika:* [28ab] But if samsara had as its basis something truly and really existent, how could we ever achieve liberation from such a state and how could we ever be born into such a state? Thus it is impossible for samsara to depend upon a truly existent basis.

[28cd] If, according to your way of thinking, the mind were something truly existent, then it could not possibly be related to or dependent upon any objects; it would become

an isolated, independent cognition of itself. In this case it could never become defiled by any obstructions. [29] Being free from all obstructions it would follow that all beings with mind were already Tathagatas, fully enlightened Buddhas. Therefore, what benefit is there in trying as you do to prove that all phenomena are of the nature of the mind alone?

At this point the Chittamatrins raise the following objections to the Prasangika assertion that things are not truly existent but are merely like illusions.

*Chittamatrin:* [30] How through realizing that all phenomena are like illusions can delusions be eliminated? The magician who has manifested an illusory woman is still able to have desire for her although he realizes that she is devoid of being a real woman. Likewise, even though we may see all phenomena as like illusions, what is there to prevent attachment and other delusions from arising?

The refutation of this objection is in three parts:

1 The reason why a magician can have desire for the illusory woman he manifests
2 The reason why meditation on emptiness can abandon all delusions and their imprints
3 Showing that excellent results will come from abandoning grasping at true existence and its imprints

## THE REASON WHY A MAGICIAN CAN HAVE DESIRE FOR THE ILLUSORY WOMAN HE MANIFESTS

*Prasangika:* [31] For as long as a magician has not eliminated grasping at the true existence of his illusory woman he may still have desire for her, because when he sees her the tendency to perceive her lack of true existence is very weak. Although the magician realizes intellectually that the woman is his own manifestation and is thus unreal, nevertheless she appears to him as a real woman, and because of his instinctive tendency to apprehend her as truly existent he instinctively has feelings of desire for her.

## THE REASON WHY MEDITATION ON EMPTINESS CAN ABANDON ALL DELUSIONS AND THEIR IMPRINTS

*Prasangika:* [32] It is only through developing familiarity with the view of emptiness over a long time that we will be able finally to abandon all traces of grasping at true existence. Furthermore, through realizing that the emptiness of true existence itself is also empty of true existence we come to realize the emptiness of emptiness. In this way we are able to abandon the conception that emptiness has true existence. In practice, once we have realized that phenomena lack true existence we then proceed to meditate, from among the sixteen emptinesses, upon the emptiness of emptiness. Through this meditation we can swiftly overcome dualistic appearance. Thus it is important to concentrate upon this meditation once we have gained an initial insight into emptiness.

[33-4] When, in dependence upon perfect reasoning, we realize the emptiness of true existence, how for such a mind could the true existence of the emptiness of true existence ever be maintained? Since the lack of true existence has been established, there is no basis upon which such a misconception could possibly occur. Through continuing to meditate upon this reality for a long time, eventually the state of the

resultant Dharmakaya, in which there is no conceptual activity at all, will be realized.

## SHOWING THAT EXCELLENT RESULTS WILL COME FROM ABANDONING GRASPING AT TRUE EXISTENCE AND ITS IMPRINTS

It should be noted that when Shantideva is applying the Prasangika dialectic to the other schools, such as the Chittamatrins, he is not doing so in the hope of achieving an immediate conversion to his way of thinking. In fact, the reasoning used is stated and defined in terms acceptable only to someone who has already accepted or is at least sympathetic to the view of the Prasangikas. For a Chittamatrin who is firmly convinced of his or her own standpoint, the initial function of the Prasangika critique is to force him to reconsider the validity of his own premises and in so doing gain familiarity with the Prasangika position. Only when that person has actually discovered the inconsistencies in his own system will the full force of the Prasangikas' consequential reasoning be effective in establishing an understanding of emptiness in his mind.

Furthermore we should not think that Shantideva is only arguing with and trying to refute the positions of particular adherents of certain strictly defined schools of philosophy. His dialectic is equally applicable in our own contemplation and meditation. As we progress in the analysis of phenomena, searching for their ultimate nature, we are liable to arrive at certain conclusions similar to the traditional viewpoints stated in the philosophies of the Samkhyas, the Chittamatrins and so forth. At these times the critical examination by the Prasangikas becomes especially relevant in seeing whether our own internally formed convictions are justified or not. It becomes a means whereby we are able to weigh our insight in the light of further possibilities and thus proceed to an even deeper and more far-reaching understanding.

*Other schools:* If Buddha has no conceptual mind then how can it be possible for him to consider teaching Dharma to sentient beings? It is contradictory to maintain, on the one hand, that Buddha has no conceptions, and on the other that he teaches Dharma.

*Prasangika:* There is no contradiction. [35] Wishfulfilling trees and jewels have no conceptual mind but are nevertheless able to fulfil the hopes of the men and gods who pray to them. Similarly, although Buddha has no conceptions, through the force of his having made prayers when he was a Bodhisattva, and through the force of the merits accumulated by his disciples, he manifests in a physical form and performs the deed of turning the Wheel of Dharma for the benefit of sentient beings. In reality he has no conceptual mind although he manifests as though he had one.

*Other schools:* But these prayers were made a long time ago when Buddha was a Bodhisattva. Now that he has attained the state of Buddhahood how can such prayers have any effect upon him?

*Prasangika:* [36] There is no fault here. For example, if a Brahmin with certain mantric powers consecrates some special substances and places them in a reliquary, they will have the power to eliminate the negative effects of poison and so forth not only while the Brahmin is alive but also after his death. [37] Likewise, in dependence upon the collections of merit and wisdom, the Bodhisattva creates the 'reliquary' of a Buddha. Although he himself eventually passes beyond sorrow into nirvana he is still able to bestow temporal and ultimate benefits on sentient beings.

The point is that although the Bodhisattva who made the prayers to become a Buddha and who accumulated the collections of merit and wisdom has ceased to exist, nevertheless the continuum of his or her consciousness continues to exist and finally becomes the Dharmakaya mind of a Buddha. In this way the effects of a Bodhisattva's deeds are able to become manifest at the time of Buddhahood.

*Other schools:* [38ab] Nevertheless, if Buddha has no conceptual mind, what would be the point of making offerings to him? Since he could have no conscious acceptance of our gifts, how could there be any merit resulting from the act of offering?

*Prasangika:* [38cd] Although Buddha has no conceptual mind, it has been taught in the scriptures that whether we make an offering to a living Buddha or to a reliquary that only contains his remains, the merit accumulated will be the same. [39] Likewise whether our offering is accompanied by our thinking of it as truly existent or by our understanding of its non-true existence, we will receive merit according to our degree of faith. We receive merit from making offerings to an illusion-like Buddha in the same way as you receive merit from worshipping a Buddha whom you consider to be truly existent.

## SHOWING THE REASONS WHY THOSE WHO SEEK ONLY PERSONAL LIBERATION NEED TO DEVELOP THE WISDOM REALIZING EMPTINESS

The Prasangikas assert that the realization of emptiness is necessary not only to attain full enlightenment but also to attain mere liberation from samsara. In the following debate this view of the Prasangikas is challenged by a proponent of Hinayana (that is, Vaibhashika or Sautrantika) tenets.

*Hinayanist:* [40ab] By gaining a direct perception of the four noble truths that Buddha taught when he turned the first Wheel of Dharma, we are able to attain Arhatship and find freedom from samsara. Therefore why is it necessary to understand the emptiness of true existence?

*Prasangika:* [40cd] Let alone the attainment of Buddhahood, it is definitely necessary to realize emptiness even in order to attain personal liberation. It has been clearly stated in the *Perfection of Wisdom Sutras* (Skt. *Prajnaparamitasutra*) by Buddha himself that without the path of realizing emptiness we are unable to realize the goals of either the Hinayana or Mahayana. (Shantideva cites such scriptural authority to the Hinayanists because he wishes to put himself in a position to prove that the Mahayana Sutras are indeed the word of Buddha, which the Hinayanists deny.)

*Hinayanist:* The citations you are using to establish your point are from the *Perfection of Wisdom Sutras*, which are Mahayana texts. [41] But we do not accept that the Mahayana scriptures are the word of Buddha, so it is of no avail to try to prove your points on the basis of their authority. In fact, what reasons do you have to substantiate your claim that such texts are the word of Buddha?

*Prasangika:* For that matter, how are your own scriptures established as the word of Buddha?

*Hinayanist:* Our Sutras are clearly the word of Buddha because both of us accept them as such.

*Prasangika:* Nevertheless those Sutras were not established as the word of Buddha for you before you accepted

Je Phabongkhapa

the validity of your tradition. You only accepted them as such on the basis of certain reasons. [42] These reasons are equally able to establish the Mahayana Sutras as the word of Buddha. Also, just because two people accept something as true, this is no real proof. If it were, then since many people believe the Vedic scriptures to be true, it would follow that they are true.

*Hinayanist:* [43] There is much dispute about the Mahayana scriptures; thus their credibility is put into question.

*Prasangika:* The Hinayana scriptures are greatly disputed by the followers of the non-Buddhist schools yet you do not question their credibility. Moreover, among the eighteen sub-schools of the Vaibhashikas themselves there is argument as to whether Sutras that preach the existence of the intermediate state between death and rebirth are the actual teachings of Buddha. Therefore if you can reject the validity of the Mahayana Sutras on the grounds that they are under dispute, you should equally reject the validity of your own scriptures.

[44] For you the criterion for a Sutra being considered as the word of Buddha is if it can be included within the Tripitaka: the three sets of scripture. Most of the Mahayana Sutras teach all of the three higher trainings; therefore they too can be included in the Tripitaka. If you accept the teachings of the first turning of the Wheel of Dharma as the word of Buddha why do you not accept the teachings of the second and third turnings as well? [45] Just because the *Perfection of Wisdom Sutras* teach that all phenomena are empty of true existence, does this mean that they cannot be the word of Buddha? You may not recognize them as Buddha's teaching, but in fact they fulfil your criterion of Buddha's word

and give a complete explanation of the meaning of the three higher trainings.

On the basis of not accepting the *Perfection of Wisdom Sutras* as the word of Buddha, why do you then regard all Mahayana texts as corrupt? And since *Sutra Interpreting the Intention* (Skt. *Samdhinirmochanasutra*) definitely does fulfil your criterion for being the word of Buddha, why do you not accept all the other Mahayana Sutras as being the word of Buddha?

***Hinayanist:*** If the *Perfection of Wisdom Sutras* were the word of Buddha his immediate successor, the great Kashyapa, should have known about them. But since he never spoke of them it is clear that he did not know of them. Therefore they cannot be the word of Buddha.

***Prasangika:*** [46] Just because the great Kashyapa and yourselves do not know of the Mahayana Sutras, this is no reason for their not being the word of Buddha. Surely no one would accept such reasoning.

[47] After Buddha's passing away, the monk Arhats were those who upheld and were responsible for the propagation of Buddha's teachings. They became like the root of the teachings. However if, as you maintain, they had not understood that all phenomena are devoid of true existence, it would be extremely difficult to maintain that they were actual Arhats. It is impossible for there to be an Arhat, a being liberated from samsara, who still clings to true existence.

***Proponent of things:*** [48a] Simply by meditating on the sixteen characteristics of the four noble truths, such as impermanence, it is possible to abandon suffering and attain liberation. It is quite unnecessary to realize the emptiness you talk about in order to become an Arhat.

*Prasangika:* [48bcd] This is a mistaken view. Through meditating on the sixteen characteristics of the four noble truths as presented by you it is only possible to overcome the manifest delusions temporarily. You seem to think that by abandoning these manifest delusions nirvana will be immediately attained. This is impossible because one who has only temporarily abandoned these manifest delusions still bears the karmic potential power to be born in samsara again.

*Proponent of things:* [49ab] The abandonment of delusions that we attain through meditating on the sixteen characteristics of the four noble truths is not temporary but final, and it includes the abandonment of all impurities as well. Such Arhats are free from craving, the principal cause for being born in samsara; thus there is no chance of their being born in samsara again.

*Prasangika:* [49cd] For you there are two kinds of confusion: deluded and non-deluded confusion. If you can talk of a non-deluded confusion then why not of a non-deluded craving? Such a craving would then have to be possessed by your so-called Arhats. Although temporarily they may not have the craving derived from grasping at a self-supporting, substantially existent self, they still have the craving derived from grasping at a truly existent self.

For as long as we have not realized that pleasant feelings are empty of true existence then on the basis of them this craving will occur. [50] According to you, Arhats have pleasant feelings and they apprehend these as truly existent. Therefore they must be subject to the craving that arises in dependence upon them. [51] For as long as phenomena are conceived of as truly existent there is no way in which craving will not be derived from such conceptions. In the same way as those meditating on the absorption without discrimination temporarily lack feelings and discriminations only to experience them again as soon as their absorption ends, so will your supposed Arhat come to re-experience the arising of gross delusions although he has temporarily overcome their manifestation. This will always be the case for those who have not abandoned grasping at true existence.

Therefore we should strive to realize the emptiness of true existence not only in order to attain Buddhahood but also in order to attain nirvana.

We may wonder what is the purpose of all these arguments between the different schools: the Hinayana schools, the Chittamatrins and the Prasangikas. There are two main purposes: firstly to recognize that it is only the ultimate view of the Prasangikas that is able to cut the root of samsara, and secondly to refute the other views that contradict this view and thus hinder us from recognizing it. However if the only correct view is that of the Prasangikas, why did Buddha not teach it alone? Why did he teach all the other views as well?

Teaching four different schools of tenets clearly illustrates Buddha's skilful means. A wise doctor will never simply prescribe the same medicine for all his or her patients. He will treat them according to their individual complaints. Similarly, in turning the different Wheels of Dharma, Buddha was teaching in accordance with the different capacities and inclinations of his various disciples. Just as a doctor needs to cure each of his patients according to a specific course of treatment, so the Buddhas guide sentient beings to enlightenment in a manner that is suitable to their individual dispositions. Otherwise, if they taught only one view, the Prasangika view, this would be like a doctor giving all his patients the same medicine.

Buddha Shakyamuni's intention is gradually to lead all his disciples to the highest viewpoint of the Prasangikas, and to do this he first taught the views of the Vaibhashikas, the Sautrantikas, the Chittamatrins and the Svatantrikas. These systems are like rungs in a ladder that progressively ascend to the Prasangika view. This is the reason why Buddha taught these different systems, although his ultimate intention is the Prasangika view. Therefore, if we wish to attain perfect enlightenment it is necessary to study and meditate on this view sincerely.

*Prasangika:* [52] Superior Bodhisattvas do not fall into either the extreme of attachment or the extreme of fear. Here, the extreme of attachment, which can also be called the 'extreme of samsara', refers to being attached to the true existence of phenomena and as a result circling in samsara under the power of actions and delusions. The extreme of fear, which can also be called the 'extreme of solitary peace', refers to being fearful of the sufferings of samsara and as a result seeking nirvana for ourself alone. Avoiding both these extremes, Superior Bodhisattvas out of their great compassion take birth in the places of samsara. They do so in order to work extensively for the benefit of sentient beings who, because of their confusion, are experiencing great suffering. The ability of Superior Bodhisattvas to continue to take birth among beings in samsara and to work for their benefit without falling into either of the two extremes is the fruit of their meditation on emptiness. Both extremes are avoided because their meditation on emptiness is motivated by great compassion.

[53] Grasping at true existence is the very root of samsara. Until we have negated its conceived object, true existence,

it will be impossible to cut the root of samsara and attain nirvana. All the obstructions, both the delusion-obstructions and the obstructions to omniscience, are overcome by realizing that all phenomena are empty of true existence. Therefore why do those who wish to attain enlightenment as quickly as possible not meditate on emptiness?

[54] For these reasons it is quite incorrect to reject this sacred emptiness of true existence. In the following verses we will continue to establish this emptiness and in this way be able to develop further conviction in the precious view that realizes it. It is necessary for anyone who wishes to attain either Buddhahood or nirvana to strive for and meditate on, without any doubts at all, this perfect view of emptiness.

*Other schools:* You are right, but I do not want to meditate upon emptiness because it frightens me.

*Prasangika:* [55] But isn't the grasping at a self the creator of all the fears in samsara? If so, it would make more sense to be afraid of that than of meditation on emptiness. It is completely inappropriate to be afraid of emptiness because through meditating on it all the fears of samsara will be eliminated. So why be afraid of it? [56] If there really were such a thing as a truly existent I it would be right to be afraid of certain things, but since there is no such truly existent I, who is the truly existent fearer? If you think well you will realize that it does not exist. Make an effort to gain a correct understanding and you will gain freedom from all fears.

## AN EXTENSIVE EXPLANATION OF THE REASONS THAT ESTABLISH EMPTINESS

As has been stated repeatedly, emptiness refers to the lack of true or inherent existence of all phenomena. Thus the wisdom realizing emptiness sees that, despite appearances, everything lacks a self. The reasonings that support this view are discussed in two parts:

1 An extensive explanation of the reasons that establish selflessness of persons
2 An extensive explanation of the reasons that establish selflessness of phenomena

## AN EXTENSIVE EXPLANATION OF THE REASONS THAT ESTABLISH SELFLESSNESS OF PERSONS

This is discussed in three parts:

1 Refuting the conceived object of the innate self-grasping of persons
2 Refuting the conceived object of the intellectually-formed self-grasping of persons
3 Refuting arguments against these refutations

Delusions are of two types: intellectually-formed and innate. Intellectually-formed delusions are only present in the minds of those who have been influenced by views other than those that are instinctively their own. We may listen to a Chittamatrin expounding his or her doctrine that other-powered phenomena are truly existent and then, being convinced by his arguments, consciously adopt his viewpoint. Such a view of true existence would be called an 'intellectually-formed delusion'. Nevertheless, all of us, independently of any external indoctrination, have a natural, instinctive tendency to regard ourself and the objects of our world as truly existent. Such a deluded attitude is an innate delusion. Among the beings of this world intellectually-formed delusions are generally present only in human beings whereas all sentient beings have innate delusions.

## REFUTING THE CONCEIVED OBJECT OF THE INNATE SELF-GRASPING OF PERSONS

Before being able to negate the conceived object of innate self-grasping of persons, it is first important to recognize the nature of this grasping. Innate self-grasping of persons is the innate mind that conceives persons to be inherently existent. When someone speaks to us we automatically think, 'He is speaking to me.' We never think that he is speaking to our body or to our mind. At these times we feel that he is speaking to an I unrelated to the body and mind. Such a vividly appearing I unrelated to the body and mind is the conceived object of the innate self-grasping of persons. This is a subtle object of negation eliminated by the view of emptiness. Some people may think that this vividly appearing I is the gross object to be refuted by the realization of selflessness of persons but in reality, here, this is not the case. If you have doubts about this you should read carefully the explanation given on pages 402-410. The purpose of all the following lines of reasoning that establish the selflessness of persons is to eradicate this vividly appearing I.

Everything that appears to the minds of ordinary people is apprehended as truly existent. In reality, though, such true existence is utterly non-existent. If the I were truly existent in the way it appears, then, upon investigation, it should be found. To be found it would have to exist in one of three places: in one of the individual aggregates of body and mind that constitute an individual, in the collection of these aggregates, or somewhere other than these two places. However, if we make a careful analysis we will discover that the I cannot be found in any one of these places.

Why can it not be located in one particular aggregate? [57] The teeth, hair or fingernails are not the I; nor are the bones, blood, mucus or phlegm the I. Lymph and pus are also not the I. [58] The body's fat or sweat are not the I. Neither the lungs, liver, nor any of the other internal organs are the I. Excrement or urine are not the I. [59] The flesh or skin, the body's warmth or inner winds are not the I. The cavities of the body, such as those within the abdomen, are also not the I. Also none of the eye, ear, nose, tongue, body or mental consciousnesses are the I. Individually each of these parts cannot be the I because in that case it would follow that a person has as many Is as he or she has parts. Some people may think that the brain is the I but from our own experience we can see that this is not true. When we refer to the brain we say my brain; we think of it as belonging to the I and therefore it obviously cannot be the I.

Many people feel that the mere collection of all these parts is the I. We have shown that there is no I to be found among any of the parts that form this collection; therefore how can the collection itself be the I? It is also clear that the I cannot be found anywhere other than among the five aggregates. Thus by making such an investigation we will realize that the I cannot be found. Thus because it exists merely as an imputation dependent upon the collection of aggregates it is proved to be empty of any true existence whatsoever.

All emptinesses are included in either the category of selflessness of persons or the category of selflessness of phenomena. The emptiness of an inherently existent person is called 'subtle selflessness of persons' and the emptiness of inherent existence of phenomena such as the aggregates is called 'subtle selflessness of phenomena'. Both types of emptiness are subtle emptinesses.

The explanation of the emptiness of phenomena will be given later in the chapter; now we will continue to explain the means whereby we can gain an understanding of the subtle non-true existence of the person. For example, if at dusk we see a striped rope, we may easily mistake it for a snake and consequently become frightened of it. At that time we do not apprehend a striped rope at all. Just as we grasp the rope as a snake, so we grasp a person as inherently existent. Both the snake and the inherently existent I are the conceived objects of their respective conceptual minds. The striped rope and our aggregates are similar in acting as the bases for such misconceptions. Grasping the snake, we become afraid; and likewise by grasping an inherently existent I we become subject to the fears of samsara. By realizing the non-existence of the snake we cease grasping at there being a snake; and likewise by realizing the non-existence of an inherently existent I we cease grasping at that as well. Having in this way caused our wrong awarenesses to cease we are released from the fears that they respectively produce.

The wrong awareness does not apprehend a striped rope but only a snake that has been imputed upon the rope; likewise our innate self-grasping of persons does not apprehend our aggregates of body and mind but only an inherently existent, vividly appearing I. Both of these wrong conceptual minds in turn give rise to fear. In order to eradicate these wrong conceptual minds it is necessary first to recognize their respective conceived objects – the snake and the inherently existent I – and then realize that they are utterly non-existent. Once we understand that the inherently existent I is non-existent, then by continually meditating upon its non-existence all grasping at an inherently existent I can be completely uprooted. Since such grasping is the root of all suffering in samsara, through abandoning it we also come to abandon all suffering.

This is something we have to reflect upon carefully. If we examine these examples and see what they mean, this will eventually lead us to a recognition of the subtle object negated by emptiness. The snake that we apprehend on the basis of the rope and the inherently existent I that we apprehend on the basis of the aggregates are very similar; both are merely apprehended by the mind and have no existence at all. Once we have recognized the inherently existent I, we have recognized the subtle object to be negated. It is then easy to realize emptiness. First we must recognize exactly what has to be negated; only then can its emptiness be determined. Initially we may have some difficulty in performing this investigation and see many contradictions in what is being taught. However, if we reflect seriously for a long time the mind will eventually become like clear space, free from all clouds of confusion.

## REFUTING THE CONCEIVED OBJECT OF THE INTELLECTUALLY-FORMED SELF-GRASPING OF PERSONS

This is explained in two parts:

1 Refuting the permanent self asserted by the Samkhya school
2 Refuting the permanent self asserted by the Vaisheshika and Naiyayika schools

## REFUTING THE PERMANENT SELF ASSERTED BY THE SAMKHYA SCHOOL

The Samkhyas posit the existence of a self that possesses five characteristics: consciousness, cognition, experience, intention and permanence. Such a view does not arise innately in beings. Rather, it is an example of a view of self speculatively fabricated by the intellect. Thus in terms of the outline given above it is a conceived object of intellectually-formed self-grasping of persons. The refutation by the Prasangika Shantideva of this conceived object – his proof that such a supposedly permanent entity is a totally fictitious creation of the mind – is presented in the following debate.

*Prasangika:* [60] If the conscious self that apprehends sound is permanent, then whether there is any sound present or not there will always be a conscious apprehender of sound. Yet how is it possible for a conscious apprehender of sound to occur when its object is no longer present? [61] If a subjective consciousness could exist without having an object of consciousness, it would follow that a piece of wood could also be a subjective consciousness. Without there being an object to be conscious of, it is quite impossible for anything to be established as a consciousness.

*Samkhya:* [62a] We are free from this fault. The conscious apprehender of sound is permanent; when there is no sound present, at that time it apprehends visual forms and other such objects. Therefore although there is no sound it still has an object of consciousness, namely visual forms.

*Prasangika:* [62b] Then why does the apprehender of visual forms not apprehend sound? It follows that it should because the conscious apprehension of sound is permanent.

*Samkhya:* [62c] When visual forms are apprehended, no sound is heard because there is none in the vicinity.

*Prasangika:* [62d] At the time when there is no sound in the vicinity how can there be a conscious apprehender of sound? If there is no apprehender of sound at that time it would contradict your assertion that the apprehending self is permanent, because at first it apprehends sound and then it changes into a consciousness that does not apprehend sound. If it were really permanent it could never be subject to any change. [63ab] Furthermore, it would never be possible for there to be a conscious apprehender that perceives both sounds and visual forms, because the apprehension of visual form and the apprehension of sound are mutually exclusive states of consciousness.

*Samkhya:* [63c] Take for example one particular man: he is apprehended as a son by his father and as a father by his son. In this way he can be considered both as a son and as a father, although he is only one individual. In the same way the conscious self can be considered both an apprehender of sound and an apprehender of visual form, depending upon which particular object it is conscious of at the time. In this way these two distinct apprehenders can be regarded as being of one nature.

*Prasangika:* [63d] Your example is unable to prove your point. The one person is discerned as both a father and a son merely through conceptual imputation. He is father or son totally in dependence upon the minds viewing him as such. Thus he is established as a dependent phenomenon and therefore cannot possibly have any true existence. According to you, however, sounds, visual forms and the conscious self are truly existent. They are thought to exist from their own side quite independently of the conceptual imputations we might have of them.

[64] In your school an ultimately existent general principle having the nature of a balanced state of three qualities (activity, lightness and darkness) is asserted. It is this general principle that forms the nature of all phenomena that are manifested from it, such as sounds, visual forms and so forth. All these manifestations are said to be of one nature since they are all of the nature of the partless general principle from which they have originated. Thus, for you, father and son, fire and water, pillar and jug all become of one nature. Therefore you maintain that two unrelated and distinct entities can be of one nature. In this case you must affirm that the apprehender of sound and the apprehender of visual form are likewise of one nature, but who has ever seen this to be so? If this were true it should be evident but it has never been witnessed by a valid mind.

*Samkhya:* [65a] The self is like an actor who is constantly forsaking one role and assuming another. When the conscious self apprehends visual form it ceases to apprehend sound.

*Prasangika:* [65b] In that case it would follow that the self is impermanent because, just like an actor, it changes its role and aspect.

*Samkhya:* [65c] There is no mistake because although the aspects change its nature remains one and the same. Hence the apprehender of sound has the same nature as the apprehender of visual form.

*Prasangika:* [65d] So you assert that two unrelated phenomena – the apprehenders of sound and of visual forms – can be of one nature. But such a proposition has never been heard of before.

*Samkhya:* [66a] The particular aspects of an apprehender of sound and an apprehender of visual form are in fact false and untrue; it is their nature that is one, true and permanent.

*Prasangika:* [66b] But if the particular aspects are untrue, what reason is there for saying that their nature is true?

*Samkhya:* [66c] Their nature is true and the same in the sense that they are both merely conscious apprehenders.

*Prasangika:* [66d] In that case it would follow that all sentient beings are one and the same because they are all the same in being merely conscious apprehenders. [67] Furthermore, it would follow that both animate and inanimate phenomena are one and the same because they all have the nature of the partless general principle.

*Samkhya:* Although the particular aspects of the various apprehenders are false, nevertheless their general character is the same and true.

*Prasangika:* If all the particular instances are false then how can their general basis, the general principle, be maintained as something true? It is impossible to prove this. Furthermore, there is no way in which false results – the manifestations of the general principle – can arise from a true cause, the general principle itself. If the cause is true the result must also be true, and if the cause is false its results must also be false.

## REFUTING THE PERMANENT SELF ASSERTED BY THE VAISHESHIKA AND NAIYAYIKA SCHOOLS

In addition to being permanent, the self asserted by these schools is regarded as being material.

*Prasangika:* [68ab] The material self that you assert cannot be the self because it is devoid of any mind in the same way as a jug is devoid of mind.

*Vaisheshika and Naiyayika:* [68c] Although the self is material, it has a relationship with the mind and hence is able to know objects.

*Prasangika:* [68d-69] There is a contradiction here. On the one hand you say that the self is permanent and on the other you claim that it can come into relationship with something other than itself and thereby know and experience objects. Prior to forming this relationship the self experiences no objects, but in dependence upon meeting the causal condition of the mind it changes into a knower and experiencer of objects. If the self can change its status in this way it cannot possibly be permanent as you claim. If it really were permanent it would be impossible for it to change in any way. But if it never changes, how can it form a relationship with the mind and become a knower of objects? In short it follows that you are asserting a self that would be unable to do anything; in which case it would be like asserting space to be the self. It is pointless to talk of a self that would be incapable of causing any benefit or harm.

## REFUTING ARGUMENTS AGAINST THESE REFUTATIONS

So far Shantideva has refuted the existence of a supposedly truly existent, permanent self, whether grasped at innately by all beings or intellectually by proponents of different schools. Now these other schools present arguments supporting their own views and Shantideva refutes these as well.

*Non-Buddhists:* [70] If the self were not permanent, then in the following moment it would perish. In which case, how could you maintain a relationship between the self who commits an action and the self who experiences the result of that action? If the self perished the moment after the action had been committed how could it survive to experience the fruits of its actions? It would follow that the self who committed the action would never experience the results of its actions. (This would destroy one of the basic convictions of Buddhist thought: the workings of karmic cause and effect, whereby a non-virtuous action leads to a suffering result and a virtuous action to an experience of happiness.) For this reason we assert that the self is permanent.

*Prasangika:* [71] It is meaningless for us to argue about this because we both assert that the person who commits the action and the person who experiences the results are of different aspects. Although you maintain the existence of a permanent and unchanging self of the person, nevertheless this is revealed in a variety of different aspects at different times. You say that this self underlies and gives cohesion to the various aspects assumed but is itself immutable. Thus we both accept that at the time of experiencing the fruit the person who committed the causal action no longer remains. There is no fault in such an assertion but as soon as you claim that there is such a fault it immediately becomes applicable to your own position, not mine. [72] At the time when the causal action is being committed, it is impossible to see the person experiencing its results.

*Non-Buddhist:* Well then, how, in your system, is the committer of an action regarded as being the experiencer of the result of that action?

*Prasangika:* According to us, both the committer of the action and the experiencer of the result are merely imputed by conception upon one continuum of a collection of aggregates. This continuity allows for a relationship between the committer of the action and the experiencer of its results, but we would never say that the cause of something – the person who did the act – could exist at the time of its fruit.

[73] Furthermore, neither the mind of the past nor the mind of the future can be the self because the former has

ceased to exist and the latter has yet to come into being. The mind arising in the present moment cannot be the self, because upon investigation the self cannot be found at all. [74] When, for instance, we peel away the layers of the hollow trunk of a plantain tree we will never discover anything substantial. Similarly, upon careful analysis, no self or I will ever be found. If someone thinks that he or she has discovered a truly existent self it will never be able to stand up to our logical analysis.

*Other schools:* [75] If sentient beings have no true existence, for whom can we develop any love and compassion?

*Prasangika:* Sentient beings have no true existence; however, we do assert the conventional existence of love, compassion, bodhichitta and so forth leading to the goal of Buddhahood. Compassion and these other qualities are to be developed for sentient beings who are imputed as truly existent by a confused mind.

*Other schools:* If sentient beings exist in this way, then why does the snake that is imputed onto a striped rope also not exist? What difference is there? It too is an imputation of a confused and ignorant mind.

*Prasangika:* Although the way in which they are imputed is similar, nevertheless sentient beings do exist whereas such a snake does not.

*Other schools:* But how can there be any difference? You say that they are both merely imputed by the confused mind and devoid of true existence.

*Prasangika:* The difference lies in the fact that the conceptual mind that imputes sentient beings is a valid mind whereas the conceptual mind that imputes a snake onto a rope is not a valid mind. Why is the former a valid mind? Because it arises in dependence upon a valid basis of imputation for a sentient being. The conception of the snake, however, is non-valid because at that time it is not depending upon a valid basis of imputation for a snake. The aggregates of body and mind are a valid basis upon which a sentient being may be imputed because they are fit to perform the functions and so forth of a sentient being. A striped rope is not a valid basis upon which to impute a snake because in no way can a rope perform the functions of or act as a snake.

We may wonder in what way a process of valid imputation takes place. Imagine a person called 'Peter'. Firstly, at his birth, upon the collection of his five aggregates (the basis of imputation for Peter) his parents designated the name 'Peter'. Because of this, everyone, including Peter himself, comes to think, 'He is Peter' or 'I am Peter'. The conceptual minds that arise in dependence upon the aggregates of Peter are valid cognizers and therefore Peter is established as existent. He exists merely through conceptual imputation, and not in a truly existent manner; that is, he is not findable among his bases of imputation either individually or as a collection.

All sentient beings exist in the same way. In the case of the snake imputed upon the rope there exists no such valid basis of imputation and hence the conceptual mind apprehending a snake is a non-valid cognizer. In this way the snake cannot be regarded as existent. Therefore, although the sentient being imputed upon the aggregates of body and mind and the snake imputed upon the rope are similar in being mere imputations and non-truly existent, they are shown to differ in terms of being existent or not.

*Other schools:* [76] But if nothing is truly existent, then from meditating on compassion and so forth who will finally attain the goal of Buddhahood?

*Prasangika:* Although it is true that the cause, compassion, and the result, Buddhahood, lack true existence, nevertheless through meditating on conceptually imputed compassion directed at conceptually imputed sentient beings we will definitely attain a conceptually imputed Buddhahood.

*Other schools*: But since sentient beings appear as truly existent to our compassion, and since this compassion is therefore a mistaken mind, should it not be rejected in the same way as the mistaken mind of self-grasping?

*Prasangika:* [77ab] In order to remove completely the suffering of sentient beings it is essential to meditate on compassion for them. Therefore compassion is never to be rejected. However, because self-grasping causes the delusions of ignorance, attachment and anger, and thereby all suffering to increase, it is definitely to be abandoned. We must recognize that it is not compassion itself that grasps at sentient beings as being truly existent. Compassion merely focuses on sentient beings and their suffering. Thus even a mind without ignorance can have compassion. It is ignorance that grasps at the true existence of sentient beings and so forth. Thus it is the self-grasping ignorance – not compassion itself – that must be abandoned.

*Other schools:* [77c] But there are no means to abandon this self-grasping in such a way that it will never recur.

*Prasangika:* [77d] It is only that you do not know of one. Sincere and continuous meditation on the emptiness of true existence is the supreme method whereby self-grasping can be completely eliminated.

# AN EXTENSIVE EXPLANATION OF THE REASONS THAT ESTABLISH SELFLESSNESS OF PHENOMENA

This is explained in three parts:

1 Explaining selflessness of phenomena by means of the four close placements of mindfulness
2 Refuting arguments concerning the two truths
3 Explaining the reasoning that establishes selflessness

## EXPLAINING SELFLESSNESS OF PHENOMENA BY MEANS OF THE FOUR CLOSE PLACEMENTS OF MINDFULNESS

This has four parts:

1 Close placement of mindfulness of body
2 Close placement of mindfulness of feelings
3 Close placement of mindfulness of mind
4 Close placement of mindfulness of phenomena

### CLOSE PLACEMENT OF MINDFULNESS OF BODY

This has four parts:

1 Establishing the non-true existence of the body as possessor of its parts
2 Establishing the non-true existence of the parts of the body
3 Therefore it is inappropriate to be attached to this dream-like non-truly existent body
4 Through this, establishing the non-true existence of the person

## ESTABLISHING THE NON-TRUE EXISTENCE OF THE BODY AS POSSESSOR OF ITS PARTS

To ordinary people like us the body appears as truly existent and we grasp at, hold on to and assent to this true existence. In reality, the body has no true existence at all. In what way do we cling to it as truly existent? Instead of regarding it as a phenomenon merely imputed by conception we apprehend it as something existing by its own nature, from its own side. Such confused minds that apprehend phenomena as truly existent are the very root of samsara, and in dependence upon them self-grasping of persons arises. So far we have not had the opportunity to meet a Spiritual Guide and to examine thoroughly this state of affairs. We have continuously experienced the body as something truly existent according to the way in which we falsely apprehend it. Now we should try to examine clearly the way in which we grasp this body as being truly existent.

At times when we think, 'My body is very attractive' and so forth, we are not thinking that our hand or our head is beautiful. We are instinctively apprehending and grasping at a vividly appearing body that is separate from and unrelated to its parts. In this way we apprehend a truly existent body. In fact the body does not exist in the way in which we apprehend it, and it lacks or is empty of this apparent true existence. If the body really were truly existent then it would have to be findable either within one of its parts, as a collection of its parts or as something other than these two alternatives. Upon investigation a truly existent body is never to be found in any of these three possible places.

[78] None of the individual parts of the body is the body. The feet and legs are not the body, nor are the thighs and

waist. The stomach and back are not the body, nor are the chest and shoulders. [79] The ribs and hands are not the body, nor are the armpits and back of the neck. They are all parts of the body, but none of them is the body itself. If the individual parts were the body, it would follow that one person would have many bodies.

The collection of the parts is also not the body because the body is merely imputed in dependence upon this collection. The collection is the basis of imputation and the body is the imputed phenomenon; but the collection itself is not the body. The body cannot be found separate from the individual parts and their collection. In this way it is shown that the body is merely imputed by the conceptual mind and in no way exists inherently, from its own side.

*Other schools:* We maintain that the body does exist as a phenomenon separate from its parts.

*Prasangika:* [80] Does this body exist partially among all its different parts or does the entire body exist in each part? In the former case there is nothing wrong in maintaining that the body's parts exist in the hands, legs and so forth, but other than these parts where would a separate body as a possessor of these parts exist? It cannot be within its parts or separate from them. Therefore it is seen to be merely imputed in dependence upon them. [81] In the latter case, if the entire body existed in each part, the absurd consequence would follow that the hands and all the other parts are individually bodies. Therefore, there would be as many bodies as there are parts.

[82] Upon such an investigation it will be seen that a truly existent body is not to be found either inside or outside the body. Therefore how can there be a truly existent body

among the hands and the other parts, and how can there be a truly existent body separate from them? Thus it is proved that there is no truly existent body at all.

[83] In reality there is no truly existent body, but because our confused mind apprehends the parts of the body as truly existent, we then apprehend a truly existent body. For example, at dusk we can easily mistake a pile of stones shaped like a man for a real man. Similarly, within the hands and other parts there is no truly existent body, but nevertheless we mistakenly apprehend them as being a truly existent body.

[84] For as long as the causes for mistaking a pile of stones for a man are present, we will mistakenly apprehend a man. Likewise, for as long as we continue to grasp the hands and so forth as truly existent, we will continue to grasp at a truly existent body.

## ESTABLISHING THE NON-TRUE EXISTENCE OF THE PARTS OF THE BODY

*Prasangika:* [85] Just as the body is merely imputed upon the collection of its limbs and other parts, so is the hand, for example, merely imputed upon the collection of its parts: the fingers, nails, palm, joints, knuckles and so forth. In this way the hand also lacks true existence. Likewise a finger lacks true existence because it too is merely imputed upon its parts: the collection of joints, nails and so on. The joint too is only imputed upon the collection of its parts and hence also lacks true existence. [86] The individual parts of the joint are merely imputed upon the collection of particles that make them up and so they also lack true existence. The particles in turn are merely imputed upon their directional parts

– north, east, south and west – and are therefore not truly existent; likewise even the parts of the directions can be further divided. Thus a lack of truly existent parts is revealed, empty like space.

## THEREFORE IT IS INAPPROPRIATE TO BE ATTACHED TO THIS DREAM-LIKE NON-TRULY EXISTENT BODY

[87ab] Having analyzed the body in this way not even the slightest part can be found to have true existence. Therefore, what wise and intelligent person would develop attachment to this illusory, dream-like body? It is completely inappropriate to become so attached.

## THROUGH THIS, ESTABLISHING THE NON-TRUE EXISTENCE OF THE PERSON

Since a person's body lacks true existence, it is impossible for a person to be truly existent. [87cd] In which case, how can there be such a thing as a truly existent male and a truly existent female body? There can be no such thing. Therefore, there is no reason to have so much attachment and desire for the bodies of the opposite sex.

Once we have developed insight into the non-true existence of the body, to abandon grasping the body as truly existent we should cultivate constant mindfulness of this point. This form of meditation is called a practice of the 'close placement of mindfulness of body'.

## CLOSE PLACEMENT OF MINDFULNESS OF FEELINGS

This has four parts:

1 Refuting the true existence of the nature of feeling
2 Refuting the true existence of the cause of feeling
3 Refuting the true existence of the object of feeling
4 Refuting the true existence of the subjective experiencer of feeling

## REFUTING THE TRUE EXISTENCE OF THE NATURE OF FEELING

This has three parts:

1 Refuting the true existence of painful feelings
2 Refuting the true existence of pleasant feelings
3 Explaining the yoga of meditating on the non-true existence of feelings

## REFUTING THE TRUE EXISTENCE OF PAINFUL FEELINGS

At present all the contaminated feelings we have act as a cause for our wandering in samsara because whenever such a feeling occurs we naturally regard it as truly existent. From pleasant feelings desirous attachment arises and from painful feelings aversion and hatred arise. Because of these delusions we then engage in non-virtuous actions, thereby accumulating evil which ripens as further suffering. Therefore we are unable to abandon suffering until we have eliminated clinging to our feelings as truly existent.

*Other schools:* How can you say that pleasant and painful feelings are not truly existent?

*Prasangika:* [88ab] If painful feelings were really truly existent it would be impossible to experience any pleasant feelings at all. For if a painful feeling truly existed it would be impossible for it to be changed by any causes and conditions. In this case how could a pleasant feeling ever come to be experienced? Surely a painful experience would not allow for a pleasant experience to occur. However, we can all see that we are able to experience pleasant feelings; thus we have an indication that painful feelings cannot be truly existent.

## REFUTING THE TRUE EXISTENCE OF PLEASANT FEELINGS

*Prasangika:* [88cd] If pleasant feelings were truly existent it would follow that the pleasant feeling that arises from eating some tasty food would be unable to change. The eater of the food would have to experience this pleasant feeling continuously. Therefore, upon encountering the death of his child it would be impossible for the father to experience any misery because at such a time the pleasant feeling of the taste of the food would be giving him truly existent, and therefore unchangeable, pleasure.

*Other schools:* [89ab] When he is tormented by the sorrow of his child's death, pleasant feelings will still occur but will be suppressed by the painful feelings and therefore not experienced.

*Prasangika:* [89cd] How can there possibly exist a feeling that is not experienced? If a feeling is not experienced there is no ground for calling it a feeling.

*Other schools:* [90a] When a strong pleasant feeling occurs there is still a very subtle painful feeling taking place. The presence of a pleasant feeling does not imply the absence of all pain.

*Prasangika:* At such a time would you really say that there is a painful feeling? If there is a subtle painful feeling in what way does a strong pleasant feeling overcome it? If there is the presence of pain is it not absurd to speak of an intense feeling of pleasure taking place? As long as there is any pain surely there can be no real happiness?

*Other schools:* [90bc] The strong feeling of pleasure dispels the gross feeling of pain, and the subtle pain that remains becomes the nature of a subtle pleasant feeling.

*Prasangika:* [90d] So now you say that it is in fact the nature of pleasure. How then can you still maintain that it is painful?

*Other schools:* [91ab] We concede then. When tasty food is eaten and a pleasant feeling occurs, at that time there is no unpleasant feeling at all because the tasty food is acting as a condition in dependence upon which pleasure is being produced. Thus tasty food is a cause that inherently produces the pleasant feeling.

*Prasangika:* [91cd] But, depending upon the person, one food can act as the condition for both pleasant and painful feelings. Therefore, in the instance you cite it is a cause of pleasure merely through conceptual imputation. In the same way as the cause is merely a conceptual imputation it follows that the resultant feelings themselves are also merely conceptual imputations. In this way feelings are established as having no inherent existence.

## EXPLAINING THE YOGA OF MEDITATING ON THE NON-TRUE EXISTENCE OF FEELINGS

[92] To abandon grasping at feelings as truly existent it is necessary to meditate on the wisdom that realizes them to be empty of true existence. This is the direct antidote for such grasping. The superior seeing that arises from the analysis of emptiness, together with tranquil abiding, is the food that nourishes the body of the Yogi's realization. Furthermore, such a concentration also sustains and nourishes the gross physical body of the meditator. For these reasons we should strive to meditate on the perfect view of emptiness.

## REFUTING THE TRUE EXISTENCE OF THE CAUSE OF FEELING

This has three parts:

1. Refuting a truly existent meeting between a sense power and an object
2. Refuting a truly existent meeting between an object and a consciousness
3. Thus establishing the non-true existence of the contact that arises from the meeting of an object, sense power and consciousness

## REFUTING A TRULY EXISTENT MEETING BETWEEN A SENSE POWER AND AN OBJECT

(Here Shantideva is presenting an argument against those who assert partless particles.) The cause of feeling is the mental factor contact. Contact is the initial mental response to the meeting of a consciousness, a sense power and an object. This contact can be shown to lack true existence because its cause – the meeting of a consciousness, a sense power and an object – lacks true existence. [93] Firstly, if the meeting of a sense power (which possesses subtle form) with an object were a truly existent meeting, then would the meeting of the partless particles of the sense power with the partless particles of the object be truly existent? If this meeting is truly existent then it must be under one of two conditions: either with space separating the partless particles or with no space separating the two. In the former case, if there is space between them how can you maintain that they have met? In the latter case, if there is no space between them at all then it follows that the two particles must become completely one. This is necessarily so because, being partless, a meeting must be a total meeting of all aspects; a partial meeting – the top part of one particle meeting the bottom part of another, for example – would imply that one part of the particle is met with and another part is not. In which case the partless nature of the particle could no longer be maintained.

If two partless particles are said to become one upon a total meeting, what is there that meets with what? [94] Furthermore, they could never become one, because in order to do so one would have to dissolve into the other. This is impossible because they are equal in size and neither of them contains any empty space. Without dissolving into each other there can be no mixing of the two partless particles and therefore no possibility of their meeting on all sides. [95] Simply stated, if two things are partless how could they ever meet? If you ever come across such a phenomenon it would be most interesting to see it, but actually it is quite impossible.

# REFUTING A TRULY EXISTENT MEETING BETWEEN AN OBJECT AND A CONSCIOUSNESS

[96] There can be no truly existent meeting between consciousness and form because consciousness has no material qualities. If a truly existent meeting were to take place with a truly existent particle of form, what meets would have to become of one nature with what it meets. In this case consciousness would have to become form. The reason for this is as follows: if form were truly existent, its mode of existence would be inherent and unalterable. A meeting with it could not be a meeting with only one aspect of it because in this case its mode of existence would alter and become twofold: namely a mode of existence of being-met-with and another mode of existence of not-being-met-with. As this is clearly unacceptable, any meeting would have to be total. Such a total meeting would necessarily imply a oneness and thus a oneness of entity. Therefore, a meeting with consciousness would entail the consciousness becoming one entity with the form and therefore of a material nature. In this case it would cease to be consciousness and to talk of a meeting would thus be absurd.

Moreover, as we have already refuted the true existence of a collection, there cannot be a truly existent collection of material particles. In which case there cannot be a truly existent meeting with it.

## THUS ESTABLISHING THE NON-TRUE EXISTENCE OF THE CONTACT THAT ARISES FROM THE MEETING OF AN OBJECT, SENSE POWER AND CONSCIOUSNESS

*Prasangika:* [97] In the above sections we have refuted a truly existent meeting between a sense power and an object as well as between a consciousness and an object. In this way it can be seen that the condition that gives rise to contact has no true existence. If the contact that in turn gives rise to a feeling has no true existence how can we consider the feeling to have any true existence?

It is impossible for a falsely existent cause, that is, a non-truly existent cause that appears in one way but exists in another, to give rise to a truly existent result, that is, a result that both appears and exists in the same way. If the cause is falsely existent, its result will likewise be falsely existent; the two must bear the same mode of existence. In this way, through understanding that the cause of feeling, contact, lacks true existence, it can thus be proved that the resultant feeling must also lack true existence. Therefore, what purpose is there in exhausting ourself for the sake of experiencing pleasant feelings? There is really no point in this at all.

*Other schools:* We are primarily engaged in making an effort to dispel all truly existent painful feelings. It is for this reason that we exhaust ourself.

*Prasangika:* [98] This is also unnecessary. To whom could a truly existent painful feeling cause any harm? Since a truly existent painful feeling is non-existent it could not possibly harm anyone. When it is understood that there is no truly existent feeling it becomes clear that there can also be no truly existent person to experience any feeling. In seeing these reasons why do we not proceed to abandon our craving for feelings? If we fully understood the non-true existence of feeling we would definitely cease to crave. Craving arises from clinging to feelings as truly existent, and from this arise all other delusions such as attachment and hatred that lead us into the realms of samsara. Through realizing the non-true existence of feelings and the person experiencing feelings we will be able to stop grasping at them as truly existent and thereby begin to sever the root of samsara.

## REFUTING THE TRUE EXISTENCE OF THE OBJECT OF FEELING

[99] All objects of consciousness, from visual forms to tactile objects, that give rise to feelings, are like dreams and illusions, and are utterly devoid of true existence. They do not exist in the way they appear to the consciousnesses that apprehend them. Since these causes of feeling lack true existence, it is proved once again that the resultant feeling itself has no true existence.

## REFUTING THE TRUE EXISTENCE OF THE SUBJECTIVE EXPERIENCER OF FEELING

[100] The mind that experiences feeling also has no true existence. If the subject-mind were truly existent, feelings could never be experienced because such a mind arising simultaneously with the feeling it is claimed to experience could have no relationship with its object. The mind and the feeling would be phenomena inherently distinct from one another and thereby incapable of maintaining any kind of relationship with one another. Furthermore, a mind that arises prior to a feeling cannot possibly experience that

feeling because the feeling has yet to come into existence. Likewise a mind that comes into existence after the feeling cannot experience it because the feeling has already ceased to exist. Feeling cannot experience itself because the possibility of self-cognizers has already been refuted above. Other than these, no truly existent consciousness can experience feeling because, being truly existent, it would be unable to form any relationship with anything else. [101] If the consciousness that experiences feeling were truly existent it would follow that the person who experiences these feelings would also be truly existent. This is clearly impossible since such a truly existent person has already been extensively refuted above.

We have now established that the nature, cause, object, subjective consciousness and the person experiencing feelings are non-truly existent, so it is clear that feelings can have no true existence. What truly existent feelings can harm or benefit the collection of the aggregates? It is inappropriate to submit ourself to the control of our feelings and the craving that results from them because none of these things have any true existence. To abandon grasping at feelings as truly existent it is necessary to realize their non-true existence by means of intelligent analysis and then proceed to familiarize ourself with this fact thoroughly. Such a meditation is called a practice of the 'close placement of mindfulness of feelings'.

**CLOSE PLACEMENT OF MINDFULNESS OF MIND**

This has two parts:

1 Establishing the non-true existence of mental consciousness

2  Establishing the non-true existence of the five sense consciousnesses

## ESTABLISHING THE NON-TRUE EXISTENCE OF MENTAL CONSCIOUSNESS

[102] We can prove that mental consciousness lacks true existence because, upon investigation, it cannot be found in the six powers, in the six objects of consciousness, or in the collection of the two. Thus, a truly existent mental consciousness cannot be found either inside or outside the body, nor can it be found anywhere else. [103] Mental consciousness is neither the body nor is it other than the body. Finally our analysis leads us to conclude that there is not the slightest part of mental consciousness that is truly existent. This emptiness of true existence of the minds of sentient beings is called the 'natural state of nirvana'.

## ESTABLISHING THE NON-TRUE EXISTENCE OF THE FIVE SENSE CONSCIOUSNESSES

[104] The five sense consciousnesses, that is, eye, ear, nose, tongue and body consciousnesses, are also found to lack true existence. If they were posited as being truly existent many contradictions would appear. If a sense consciousness had true existence it would have to exist in this way either prior to, simultaneously with, or subsequent to its object. If it existed prior to its object, what object would it be conscious of? At that time the object would not yet have come into existence. If a sense consciousness and its object arise simultaneously, then in dependence upon what object does the consciousness arise? Prior to the arising of consciousness

*Vajradhara Trijang Rinpoche*

the causal condition of an object must first be established. Otherwise no causal relationship would be able to exist between a consciousness and its object. [105ab] But if the consciousness is truly and *independently* existent, how could it possibly arise subsequently *in dependence upon* the condition of an object?

[105cd] In this way we can understand that all six consciousnesses are empty of true existence. To abandon grasping at the six consciousnesses as truly existent it is necessary to realize their non-true existence by means of intelligent analysis and then proceed to acquaint ourself with this fact thoroughly. Such a meditation is called a practice of the 'close placement of mindfulness of mind'.

## CLOSE PLACEMENT OF MINDFULNESS OF PHENOMENA

In the same way as we have shown person, body, feelings, and mind to be non-truly existent, so all phenomena can be understood to exist in this way. If a car, for example, were truly existent, upon thoroughly investigating all its parts and the collection of its parts we should be able to find a truly existent, independent car. But such a car is never found. Neither any one part nor the collection of all the parts is found to be the car. If each of the parts were the car it would follow that there would be as many cars as there are parts. In this case, since none of the individual parts is the car, how can the collection of them all together be the car? The collection of the parts of the car is not the car because it is the basis of imputation for the car. The car is the phenomenon imputed in dependence upon the collection of these parts. As we previously saw in our example with Peter, the parts are first collected and then the name, in this case 'car', is given to this collection. The car is none of the parts nor the collection of its basis of imputation; it is merely a conceptual imputation existing in dependence upon a valid basis. In this way it lacks true existence. All phenomena exist in precisely the same way.

To abandon grasping at phenomena as truly existent it is necessary to realize their non-true existence by means of intelligent analysis and then proceed to acquaint ourself with this fact thoroughly. Such a meditation is called a practice of the 'close placement of mindfulness of phenomena'.

## REFUTING ARGUMENTS CONCERNING THE TWO TRUTHS

*Other schools:* [106] If all phenomena are not truly existent, it follows that they cannot exist conventionally, in which case the presentation of conventional truths becomes invalid. If there are no conventional truths, then ultimate truths (their ultimate nature) cannot be established either. If all conventional truths are merely imputed by the deceptive mind of grasping at true existence, how can they be conventional truths? If this is the case how can you say that sentient beings are able to pass beyond sorrow into nirvana?

*Prasangika:* [107] There is no contradiction here. According to our system, to exist conventionally does not mean to be imputed by a deceptive awareness grasping at true existence. All conventional truths are imputed by a valid conceptual mind that arises in dependence upon a valid basis of imputation. First there must be a valid basis of imputation and then, by a valid mind that subsequently arises in dependence upon this basis, a conventional truth is apprehended and thereby established. Without such imputation by a valid mind we cannot speak of something being a conventional truth.

[108] According to the Madhyamika-Prasangika school, the subjective conceptual mind and the object that it apprehends and imputes are established in mutual dependence upon each another. Thus neither of them has any true, independent existence. Each distinct phenomenon is posited merely through the force of what is validly known in the world. All phenomena are merely imputed by conception; there is not even the tiniest particle that truly exists.

*Other schools:* [109] When an analytical mind concludes that all phenomena are non-truly existent, surely it is unable to realize that it is non-truly existent itself? Therefore, is there another analytical mind that realizes the original analytical mind to be non-truly existent or not? If there is not, then that original analytical mind would be truly existent, which would be untenable in your system. If another analytical mind is needed then it would follow that yet another would be needed to realize the non-true existence of that one, and so on. In this case the process would be endless and this would be clearly absurd.

*Prasangika:* [110] No further analytical mind is needed in order to establish the non-true existence of the original analytical mind. From the standpoint of the analytical mind that realizes all phenomena to be empty of true existence, not a trace of true existence is established. Since the true existence of all phenomena is directly negated, the true existence of the analyzing subject is implicitly negated as well. Therefore it is unnecessary for another analytical mind to negate the true existence of the original analytical mind. This non-true existence of both subject and object is also called the 'natural state of nirvana'. Furthermore, through meditating for a long time on emptiness we will finally attain the actual state of nirvana in which we are free from all delusions.

In our system, therefore, the non-true existence of subject and object can be validly established. We can prove our assertions. This is not the case for the proponents of lesser tenets. [111ab] For example, Chittamatrins find it extremely difficult to establish the true existence of the apprehending consciousness and the object of consciousness because they cannot find any valid reasons to prove this.

*Chittamatrin:* [111c] Because consciousness apprehends truly existent forms and other objects, this is proof for us that those forms are truly existent.

*Prasangika:* [111d] But really what reason is this for asserting the true existence of the objects of consciousness? Consciousness and the objects of consciousness are posited as such in dependence upon one another. Therefore both can be clearly seen to be empty of true, independent existence.

*Chittamatrin:* [112a] The mind immediately and directly perceives that its objects are truly existent; therefore that consciousness must be truly existent.

*Prasangika:* [112bcd] Then please tell me what mind it is that realizes consciousness to be truly existent. We have already refuted the existence of self-cognizers. If you claim that there is another consciousness that can establish the true existence of consciousness then you will succumb to the fault of having to admit an endless process of such cognizers.

*Chittamatrin:* All objects of consciousness are truly existent because this is established by valid cognition.

*Prasangika:* [113] How can this possibly be so? Consciousness and objects of consciousness are established in mutual dependence upon each other. In this way it is clear that they have no true existence. 'Longness' is established in dependence upon 'shortness', and 'shortness' in dependence on 'longness'; the far mountain is established as such only in dependence upon its relation to the near mountain and vice versa. If a man has no child he cannot be established as a father, and without a father we cannot speak of a child being born. Thus father and child are mutually dependent phenomena and have no true, self-existence. Likewise consciousness is only established as such in dependence upon its having an object to be conscious of, and an object of consciousness is only established as such in dependence upon a consciousness being conscious of it. Therefore, consciousness and objects of consciousness are mutually dependent phenomena and have no true, independent existence at all.

*Chittamatrin:* [114] Because a truly existent sprout arises from a seed, it is a perfect indication that the seed also truly exists. Likewise because a truly existent consciousness arises from an object of consciousness, does this not act as a perfect indication to prove the true existence of the object of consciousness?

*Prasangika:* [115] It is correct to say that a consciousness, substantially distinct from the sprout, is able to realize that the sprout had a seed as its cause through the indication of the sprout itself. But what consciousness can cognize a truly existent consciousness that, according to you, is a perfect indication for the existence of truly existent objects of consciousness? We have already refuted the possibility of self-cognizers performing this function and other than this you cannot assert the possibility of a substantially distinct consciousness.

# EXPLAINING THE REASONING THAT ESTABLISHES SELFLESSNESS

This has three parts:

1 The reasoning of vajra fragments
2 The reasoning of dependent relationship
3 The reasoning that refutes inherent production of existents and non-existents

## THE REASONING OF VAJRA FRAGMENTS

This has five parts:

1 Refuting production from no cause
2 Refuting production from a permanent cause that is other
3 Refuting production from a permanent general principle
4 A summary of the refutation of production from no cause
5 Refuting production from both self and other

## REFUTING PRODUCTION FROM NO CAUSE

The non-Buddhist Charavaka school claims that such things as the rising of the sun, the flowing of water downhill, the roundness of peas, the sharpness of thorns, the colours on a tail feather of a peacock, and the smoothness of the stem of the lotus flower are produced without cause but simply arise from their own nature. Taking these things as examples they proceed to assert that all things have no cause but come into existence merely from their own nature.

*Prasangika:* [116] This is clearly incorrect because even worldly people can see with direct perception that most internal and external phenomena, like crops for example, have causes. In the same way it can be inferred that the rising of the sun, the flowing of water downhill and so forth are also produced from a variety of different causes.

*Charavaka:* [117a] But what created the variety of different causes?

*Prasangika:* [117b] Each cause is created from its own various causes.

*Charavaka:* [117c] But how is a distinct cause able to produce a distinct result? What is the specific cause for the sharpness of a thorn or the colour in a tail feather of a peacock?

*Prasangika:* [117d] All of these particular phenomena are produced from a specific potentiality latent in their preceding causes. Within the seed of the thorn lies the latent potentiality to produce sharpness. In this way all things are derived from their previous causes. Briefly stated, we can say that all things are produced from causes because they are occasional phenomena, that is, they come into existence at one point in time and perish at another point.

## REFUTING PRODUCTION FROM A PERMANENT CAUSE THAT IS OTHER

This has three parts:

1. Refuting what is meant by the god Ishvara
2. Refuting that Ishvara is the cause of everything with the reason he is permanent
3. Refuting permanent partless particles as the cause of everything

## REFUTING WHAT IS MEANT BY THE GOD ISHVARA

The non-Buddhist Naiyayika and Vaisheshika schools assert a god Ishvara who has five qualities: divinity, purity and worthiness of veneration, permanence, partlessness, and being the creator of everything. Thus these schools maintain that Ishvara is the cause of all beings as well as the worlds they inhabit.

*Prasangika:* [118ab] If Ishvara is the creator and cause of all these things, firstly could you please tell me who or what Ishvara is?

*Naiyayika and Vaisheshika:* [118c] We assert that the four great elements of earth, water, fire and wind are Ishvara, since it is through the increase in the elements that all things increase and through the decrease of the elements that all things decrease.

*Prasangika:* [118d] But we maintain exactly the same thing: the increase and decrease of things are due to the increase and decrease in the elements. So what is the purpose of your adding the name 'Ishvara' to these elements? [119] Furthermore, earth and the other elements are by nature impermanent, multiple, unmoved by consciousness, non-divine, walked upon (and thus not venerated) and unclean. Therefore how can you say that they are Ishvara? They clearly do not bear the five characteristics by which you define him. [120ab] You cannot state that space is Ishvara because it is inanimate and is incapable of producing effects. Likewise you cannot assert a permanent self to be Ishvara because we have already refuted such a thing above.

*Naiyayika and Vaisheshika:* [120c] The creator god Ishvara is really unknowable, so we cannot be subject to criticism on this point.

*Prasangika:* [120d] Then what is the purpose of talking about something that is unknowable and indescribable? If your Ishvara is unknowable, this seems to us a perfect indication of his non-existence.

## REFUTING THAT ISHVARA IS THE CAUSE OF EVERYTHING WITH THE REASON HE IS PERMANENT

*Prasangika:* [121a] If all suffering and happiness are the results of previous actions, please tell us exactly what it is that Ishvara creates.

*Naiyayika and Vaisheshika:* [121b] Ishvara produces the self, the atoms of earth and so forth, as well as his own subsequent continuum.

*Prasangika:* [121cd] Ishvara cannot possibly create such things because he is permanent. Whatever is permanent has no ability to create any effects at all. As for other phenomena, all states of consciousness such as the apprehension of blue are caused by the objects of which they are conscious. [122] And from beginningless time all happiness and suffering have been produced by virtuous and non-virtuous actions respectively. We cannot find any object that is produced by a permanent god. In this case what is it that you claim Ishvara creates? According to you today's suffering and happiness are directly created by the permanent god Ishvara. Moreover, being permanent, the god Ishvara has no beginning. If Ishvara – the direct cause – has no beginning, would it not absurdly follow that today's suffering and happiness – the result – are also without a beginning? If the direct cause of something has no beginning how can you say that that thing itself has a beginning?

[123] Also, in order to produce his creation Ishvara has to remain independent of any other conditions, otherwise he would no longer be autonomous and the creation would no longer be entirely dependent upon him. Why then do the results of suffering and happiness not arise continuously without any interruption? This would follow because their production would not be dependent upon any other conditions and thus would not be able to be interrupted by any other conditions. According to you there are no phenomena other than those created by Ishvara. In this way he has created all conditions. So, when he creates an effect, upon what cause and conditions does he depend? Because he is autonomous it would follow that he can depend upon nothing.

[124] If you were to say that he did depend upon other substantial causes and circumstantial conditions in order to produce his creation, then the main cause for the creation would become those other substantial causes and circumstantial conditions and not Ishvara. In this case how could you say that it is Ishvara who produces all living beings and the worlds in which they live? For without these causes and conditions it would be impossible for Ishvara, even if he existed, to manifest creation. As long as these causes and conditions were assembled together they would have the power to produce everything. In this case Ishvara would become an other-powered being.

[125] The god Ishvara can have no wish to produce the effect of suffering; this is something produced by our own actions. But if this is so you can no longer maintain that Ishvara is the creator of all possible effects. Alternatively, you would have to maintain that he is responsible for the unsought suffering of the beings he created.

Moreover, if all effects were wished for by Ishvara, it would follow that creation depends upon the wishes of Ishvara. These wishes are impermanent whereas Ishvara is permanent; now it seems that creation is not produced by the permanent Ishvara but by impermanent wishes. Therefore how can you say that Ishvara is the cause of everything?

## REFUTING PERMANENT PARTLESS PARTICLES AS THE CAUSE OF EVERYTHING

The non-Buddhist Vaisheshika school asserts that all living beings and the worlds in which they live are produced from permanent partless particles. [126ab] This is clearly unacceptable since Shantideva has already refuted the existence of such particles above in verse 86.

## REFUTING PRODUCTION FROM A PERMANENT GENERAL PRINCIPLE

The non-Buddhist Samkhya school, the followers of Rishi Kapila, maintain that all knowable phenomena can be classified into twenty-five categories: the self, the general principle, the intellect and the I principle; visual forms, sounds, smells, tastes and tactile objects; eye, ear, nose, tongue and skin; speech, arm, leg, anus and genitalia; mental faculty; earth, water, fire, wind and space. Among these twenty-five the general principle is considered to be solely a cause, or nature, and not a result or manifestation. This is because it is the source of all the other categories except the self and is itself not caused by anything. The intellect, the I principle, forms, sounds, smells, tastes and tactile objects are both causes as well as results because they are produced by the general principle and are also a cause for their own effects. The remaining sixteen categories – the five faculties of the eyes and so forth, the five physical faculties of speech and so forth, the mental faculty, and the five elements of earth and so forth – are considered to be only results and not causes. Finally the self is regarded as neither a cause nor a result. It is an experiencer and user of objects.

[126cd] The general principle is the root nature or fundamental cause of all results, but it is compared to a man with legs who is blind because although it is capable of manifesting results it is unable to experience or use them. The self, on the other hand, is compared to a man with sight who is lame because it is able to experience and use the objects but unable to manifest them.

According to this non-Buddhist school the terms 'nature' and 'cause' are synonyms. A difference is made, however, between general nature and nature. The intellect and its accompanying six categories are natures but not general natures. Only the general principle is called the 'general nature' since it is the general and principal cause for all phenomena. The terms 'general nature', 'general cause' and 'general principle' are synonyms. Furthermore, the general principle is recognized as possessing five characteristics: permanence, partlessness, materiality, invisibility and being the creator of all.

The process of creation and manifestation occurs in the following way. Initially it occurs to the self that it would like to experience an object; immediately the general principle then commences to issue forth manifestations. The self then proceeds to experience and make use of the various objects such as visual form, sound etc. Both the external objects and the self appear to the intellect, which then falsely conceives them to be one. It does not realize that all external phenomena are the manifestation of the general principle and therefore, because of this confusion, sentient beings continue to wander in samsara.

To attain liberation from samsara the Samkhyas present the following solution. Firstly we must receive instruction from a Samkhya Spiritual Guide in which the process of manifestation from the general principle is clearly explained. In this way we come to understand that all manifestations are produced from the general principle. Through meditation on this truth we proceed gradually to separate ourself from attachment to objects. Next, through depending upon a firm concentration we cultivate the clairvoyance of divine eye. When the divine eye is led to behold the general principle the latter becomes like an embarrassed mistress when seen by the wife, and as a consequence it gathers all of its manifestations back into itself. Thus all visual forms, sounds and so forth disappear and the permanent self remains alone and inactive, free from the experience of objects. For the Samkhya school this is liberation.

[127] You Samkhyas regard the nature of the general principle as a balanced state of the three qualities of lightness (Skt. sattva), activity (Skt. rajah) and darkness (Skt. tamah) – also understood as the three feelings of indifference, pleasure and pain in a state of equilibrium. You say that all unbalanced states of these three qualities are the various types of manifestation of the general principle and are regarded as the world. In this way you assert the general principle to be the cause of the world.

The refutation of this view has four parts:

1 Refuting a general principle that is the cause of all manifestations
2 Refuting a permanent general principle

3 Refuting an effect existing at the same time as its cause
4 Refuting the claim that the Madhyamika school is at fault

## REFUTING A GENERAL PRINCIPLE THAT IS THE CAUSE OF ALL MANIFESTATIONS

[128] If the general principle is partless, it is contradictory to say that its nature is an equally balanced state of the three qualities of pleasure, pain and indifference. In this case, having three qualities as its nature, it can hardly be singular. However, you also maintain that it is not multiple. Therefore, it seems that it is neither singular nor multiple, in which case it must be non-existent since everything that exists is necessarily either singular or multiple.

The individual qualities themselves also cannot be singular in nature because you say that each one is made up of the three qualities as well. Pleasure, for example, is said to be a compound of the qualities of pleasure, pain and indifference. But if these qualities truly exist in the nature of the partless general principle they too would have to be partless. As with the general principle the qualities that you speak of can be neither singular nor multiple and therefore must be non-existent. [129ab] As soon as the existence of these qualities is denied, the existence of a general principle, the nature of which is a balanced state of the three qualities, is also refuted. Furthermore, it follows that, if these qualities cannot be established, it is impossible to establish their manifestations such as visual form and sound.

[129cd] It is also absurd to say that clothing and other gross manifest objects have the nature of the qualities of

pleasure, pain and indifference because they are material and have no mental qualities. Since pleasure, pain and indifference are mental phenomena, whatever has them as its nature must also be a mental phenomenon. [130] In addition you say that all the manifestations of the general principle truly exist within the nature of their cause, but we have already refuted the possibility of truly existent things, so this claim is also invalid. Also, clothing and other such manifestations cannot arise from the general principle because we have just refuted the existence of such a general principle.

## REFUTING A PERMANENT GENERAL PRINCIPLE

*Prasangika:* [131] We experience pleasure and so forth from such things as wearing woollen cloth. In this way they are shown to be the cause of pleasure. If they (the cause) were lacking then it would follow that pleasure and so forth (the result) could not occur. At such a time when no pleasure is present a balanced state of the three feelings in the general principle also could not exist. In which case the general principle would have previously existed with a balanced state of the three qualities as its nature and then it would have subsequently changed into an unbalanced state. In this case it would be seen to change and hence your assertion that it is permanent would be adversely affected.

[132] Furthermore, it is incorrect to state that the general principle is permanent because then its nature of pleasure, for example, would also have to be permanent and this is something that has never been cognized by a valid cognition. If pleasure is permanent why is it not apprehended at the times when pain is being experienced? If you say that at

those times the gross state of pleasure becomes subtle, then are you not saying that it changes? In which case how can you maintain that it is permanent?

*Samkhya:* It is simply a case of rejecting the gross state and becoming subtle.

*Prasangika:* [133] But this clearly shows that pleasure must be impermanent because it has the ability to change in this way. In the same way you should assert that all things are impermanent because they too have the nature of arising or coming into existence and then perishing. [134ab] Is gross pleasure the same nature as pleasure itself, or different? If it is of a different nature, then upon its ceasing the experience of pleasure should nevertheless remain. And if it is of the same nature, then when gross pleasure ceases pleasure would also have to cease, in which case it could no longer be considered permanent. If feelings were subject to change, the general principle would also have to be subject to change, and thus could not be permanent.

## REFUTING AN EFFECT EXISTING AT THE SAME TIME AS ITS CAUSE

The Samkhyas assert that everything that is produced exists at the time of its cause. For them all effects are produced from causes that are identical in nature. For example, a sprout (effect) is produced from a seed (cause) and exists already at the time of the seed. The two are one in nature. They do not say, however, that the sprout exists in its manifest state at the time of its cause; it exists in a non-manifest condition. When the sprout changes from a non-manifest to a manifest state they say that it has thus been produced from the seed. The same is true for all conditioned phenomena.

*Prasangika:* [134cd] You assert that the manifest phenomenon does not exist at the time of its cause and thus the product does not exist at the time of its cause. [135ab] You also claim that nothing is born anew, but in reality you would have to assert that things are born anew. A manifest sprout does not exist at the time of its cause; it is produced at a later time. Surely anything that does not exist at the time of its cause and then comes into existence later is a perfect example of a newly born phenomenon. [135cd] If you believe that a sprout can exist at the time of the seed, do you also believe that excrement exists at the same time as its cause, food? This must be so; thus to eat food must be the same as eating excrement. [136ab] Furthermore, instead of purchasing woven cotton you should spend your money only on its cause, the cotton seeds, and proceed to wear them.

*Samkhya:* [136c] Even though in reality food and excrement are of the same nature, owing to confusion the people of the world do not behold excrement in their food and thereby do not eat it.

*Prasangika:* [136d] But what about your Teacher the Rishi Kapila? He, being omniscient, must know that excrement exists in food, so would you say that he eats excrement? [137ab] Furthermore, you teach this view of yours to the people of the world, so why is it that they do not come to understand and see that the effect already exists in its cause?

*Samkhya:* [137c] The perceptions of worldly people are not valid cognizers, therefore they are unable to see the effect at the time of the cause.

*Prasangika:* [137d] In that case it would follow that a worldly person's visual perception of manifest phenomena would also not be valid and therefore untrue. In fact, such a perception is correct and unmistaken with regard to its object.

Those who would like to investigate these points in further detail should consult the commentaries of Chandrakirti and Buddhapalita to Nagarjuna's *Fundamental Wisdom of the Middle Way* (Skt. *Prajnanamamulamadhyamakakarika*), and the book *Ocean of Nectar*, a commentary to Chandrakirti's commentary *Guide to the Middle Way*.

## REFUTING THE CLAIM THAT THE MADHYAMIKA SCHOOL IS AT FAULT

*Other Schools:* [138] According to you, since a valid cognizer is not truly existent, it must be false. Therefore any object established by it likewise must be false. In this case the emptiness you talk of must in fact be false because the valid mind that realizes it is false. In which case it does not make much sense to meditate on emptiness.

*Prasangika:* [139] Although the valid cognizer that realizes emptiness and emptiness itself are both non-truly existent and thus falsely existent, to realize what we mean by 'non-true existence' depends upon correctly identifying the true existence that is to be negated. Without identifying the object to be negated (true existence) there can be no apprehension by a valid mind of its being non-existent, that is, of its emptiness. Similarly, there is no truly existent negation; thus the absence of true existence (emptiness) is also established as non-truly existent. So when we say that all phenomena are non-truly existent and are falsely existent we are not saying that they are utterly untrue and false but rather that they are empty of a falsely imagined true existence that we have mistakenly attributed to them. [140] For example, we cannot consider the death of the son of a childless woman until we have identified the son himself. Similarly, without recognizing what we mean by true existence it is impossible to realize the emptiness of true existence. Through understanding the meaning of true existence in the correct way we will realize that there is no contradiction in saying that a false subject can realize a falsely existent object.

When a mother dreams that her son has died she apprehends the non-existence of her son. Such an apprehension has the effect of eliminating the conception of her son's existence. Although both conceptions (of the son's dying and of his being alive) are in fact false because of their occurring in a dream, nevertheless the former has the ability to overcome the latter. In a similar way, although both the mind realizing emptiness and the conception that grasps at true existence are false, that is, non-truly existent, the former is still able to overcome the latter. In the same way there is no contradiction in saying that the falsely existent realization of emptiness understands the falsely existent emptiness.

It is important to recognize the distinction between phenomena being false and being falsely existent. All phenomena are falsely existent because they are devoid of true existence. Even the ultimate truth of emptiness is empty of true existence and thus is said to be falsely existent. However, only conventional truths are said to be false phenomena. Here we should understand false as meaning that the phenomenon's mode of appearance and the phenomenon's mode of existence are not the same. A conventional phenomenon is false because although it appears as truly existent this is in fact a false mode of appearance. An ultimate truth, that is, an emptiness, is not a false phenomenon because when it appears to a direct perceiver its mode of appearance corresponds to its mode of existence.

## A SUMMARY OF THE REFUTATION OF PRODUCTION FROM NO CAUSE

[141ab] Through the above reasonings we have established that production does not occur without a cause, and that neither the god Ishvara nor the general principle is the creator of the world and the sentient beings that inhabit it. However, if they are not created in these ways how, we may wonder, are they created?

All conditioned phenomena depend for their production upon the collection of a substantial cause and circumstantial conditions. For example, a crop has as its substantial cause a seed. This is the substantial cause because it is what actually transforms into the crop itself. The circumstantial conditions for the crop are heat, water, fertilizer, earth and so forth. These are only circumstantial causes since they merely help the substantial cause, the seed, to grow into the crop. Without the circumstantial conditions the seed will be unable to produce its fruit. In the same way all internal and external conditioned phenomena are produced in dependence upon these two causes.

The production of the world and the sentient beings within it can thus be understood to be the result of a beginningless series of such causes and conditions. What are the substantial cause and the circumstantial conditions for the entrance of a child's consciousness into the womb of its mother? The substantial cause is the continuum of consciousness that has come from a previous existence, and the circumstantial conditions are the actions committed by that being in his or her past lives. If we accept that all conditioned phenomena have to be produced from these two causes it will be easy for us to accept the fact of rebirth.

Some people believe that past lives exist but that future lives do not. However, surely this present life is the future life in relation to a former life? In which case what is there to prevent this present life from having a future life in relation to it as well? If you say that a past life has a future life, it is illogical to deny the possibility of this life also having a future life.

## REFUTING PRODUCTION FROM BOTH SELF AND OTHER

[141cd] The resulting sprout does not exist in the seed, water, earth or fertilizer, either individually or collectively. However, to maintain that the effect is produced from a cause that is of one nature with itself is to accept the view of production from self. This is the view of the Samkhya school that we have already refuted above.

Furthermore, the sprout is not a product of any cause that is inherently other than itself. If it were, it and such causes would be unrelated and thus it would make no sense to say that a cause and effect relationship existed between them. If a result could arise from an unrelated cause it would absurdly follow that darkness could arise from fire. Those who accept the view that effects are produced from causes that are inherently other than themselves are said to have the view of production from other. All Buddhist schools, except the Prasangika, are said to subscribe to this view because they correctly accept production from causes but incorrectly believe cause and effect to be inherently existent.

Having refuted the possibility of these two modes of production (production from self and production from other) the Prasangikas are able to arrive at the conclusion that all conditioned phenomena are not produced by self or other.

Thus it is clear that they cannot be produced from both self and other together.

In a syllogistic form the reasoning of vajra fragments can be presented in the following way: the person and the aggregates (the subject) are not inherently, or truly, produced (the factor to be established) because they are not produced from self, from other, from both self and other, or without a cause (the reason). This four-part reason acts as the logical proof whereby inherent production is refuted. For further clarification of these reasonings we should refer to the extensive works of Nagarjuna and Chandrakirti concerning the Madhyamika philosophy, and the book *Ocean of Nectar*.

## THE REASONING OF DEPENDENT RELATIONSHIP

A dependent-related phenomenon is one that is established in dependence upon its parts. This is a mode of existence that is true of everything that exists. However, this is only their general mode of dependent relationship; in addition there are both grosser and subtler levels of dependent relationship. The gross form is existing in dependence upon causes and conditions. This mode of dependent relationship applies only to conditioned, impermanent phenomena. It is said to be 'gross' because it is something that is relatively easy to understand. The subtle form of dependent relationship is existence in dependence upon imputation by a conceptual mind. This mode of existence belongs to all phenomena but is very subtle and difficult to understand. Nevertheless it is something that we should make every effort to try to comprehend.

[142-3] Even though a magician's magically created woman is not a real woman, she nevertheless appears as

such both to the magician and to the spectators of his show. Similarly, all phenomena have no true existence, but because of the confusion and ignorance of sentient beings they appear as if they did. It is in this way that we say that everything is like a dream, an illusion or a mirror's reflection. The magician's illusory horses and elephants are in fact manifested by him, and in the same way all things such as visual forms are manifested by their own particular causes and conditions. Both the magician's illusions and things such as visual forms are non-truly existent; if they were it would follow that when they were produced they would have come from elsewhere and when they perish they will have to depart elsewhere. However, upon analysis it will be discovered that when something is produced it does not come from anywhere else and when it perishes it does not go to any other place.

[144] We can all see by direct perception that a sprout is produced from a seed and that without a seed it is impossible for there to be a sprout. The sprout is solely a product of its causes and conditions and has no true, independent existence of its own. Thus we say that it is like a reflection in a mirror; it appears merely through the force of other conditions. In brief, all things are produced from their individual causes and conditions and are merely imputed upon the collection of their parts. Therefore they have no true or inherent existence.

The reasoning of dependent relationship that we have introduced above is known in the Madhyamika scriptures as 'the king of reasons'. In the same way that a minister is subordinate to his king, all other reasons that establish emptiness are subordinate to the reasoning of dependent relationship. A more detailed explanation of dependent relationship can be found in the books *The New Heart of Wisdom* and *Ocean of Nectar*.

# THE REASONING THAT REFUTES INHERENT PRODUCTION OF EXISTENTS AND NON-EXISTENTS

This has three parts:

1 Refuting inherently existent production through this reasoning
2 Thereby refuting truly existent cessation
3 Thus establishing the equality of samsara and nirvana from the point of view of lacking true existence

## REFUTING INHERENTLY EXISTENT PRODUCTION THROUGH THIS REASONING

*Prasangika:* [145] What need is there for an inherently or truly existent thing to be caused? There is no need because something that exists inherently does not have to be produced. And, if the result is non-existent, what need is there for a cause to produce it? It is something that is incapable of being produced by a cause. However, it is true that all results are non-existent at the time of their cause and thus it is not this fact that is being refuted here. We are refuting the production of something utterly non-existent. Likewise, in refuting the production of an existent thing we are only refuting the assertion of inherently existent results. It is these assertions that are logically untenable. Moreover, non-inherently existent causes and effects do exist and we regard these as being like illusions and reflections in a mirror.

We will now proceed to establish that a non-thing is unsuitable to act as a cause. The category of non-things comprises permanent phenomena such as unproduced space, and non-existents such as the son of a childless woman. Excluded are functioning things, namely impermanent phenomena that are able to produce effects and that are therefore also known as 'effective phenomena'.

*Non-Buddhists:* Since an existent thing already exists, there is no need for it to be produced. This is true. But why can't we say that a non-existent comes into being as an existent?

This question arises from the following doubt. The Buddhist schools maintain that an effect or fruit (for example, a sprout) does not exist at the time of its cause (a seed). The non-Buddhists then infer that, if this is so there must be a way for a non-existent to become an existent thing. Why? Because first the sprout was non-existent (at the time of the seed) and later it became existent (at the time of the effect, the sprout itself).

Before presenting Shantideva's tightly-reasoned refutation of this assertion – that a non-existent comes into being as an existent – it might be helpful to look at other examples of the non-Buddhist line of reasoning. They say that just as a yellow book need not become yellow because it is already yellow, so a thing need not produce another thing. Therefore what is a thing produced from? In the same way that a person who is a monk did not become a monk after already being a monk, but rather did so from having originally been a non-monk (that is, a lay person), a thing comes into existence as a thing from what had been a non-thing.

This reasoning is subtle but faulty, as Shantideva will reveal, and derives from an inability to understand how an earlier moment of a continuum (a cause) changes and transforms into a later moment of the same continuum (an effect or result). Without such an understanding non-Buddhists assert that an existent thing must come into existence from a non-existent, that is, that a non-thing must transform somehow into a thing.

*Prasangika:* [146] Even with a hundred million causes a non-thing will never transform into a thing. There is no condition whatsoever that is able to make a non-thing into a thing. No one is able to work with non-things.

If a non-thing were to become a thing, it would have to do so either (1) while retaining its condition of being a non-thing or (2) after having discarded that condition. Both of these are impossible. In the first case, how could something retaining the condition of a non-thing ever be a thing? This is impossible because the condition of effectiveness – the state of a thing – and the condition of ineffectiveness – the state of a non-thing – are mutually exclusive. The second case is also impossible; there is no intermediate state of being into which a non-thing could first transform and then afterwards become a thing.

[147] Furthermore, if the condition of being a non-thing is not discarded, at the time of it not being a thing, it cannot exist as a thing. If this is so, when would it ever become a thing? Also, were it to become a thing upon having discarded the condition of being a non-thing, without first having become a thing it would not have been able to become separate from being a non-thing. [148] And without being separate from being a non-thing, it is impossible for the state of a thing to arise. In the same way that a non-thing cannot become a thing, a thing cannot become a non-thing when it ceases to exist. If it existed half as a thing and half as a non-thing it would absurdly follow that one phenomenon would have two mutually exclusive natures.

These reasons refute that any non-existent or non-thing can produce results. We are therefore led implicitly to the refutation of inherent production. The syllogism can be stated as follows: a sprout (the subject) is not inherently produced (the factor to be established) because neither an existent nor a non-existent is inherently produced (the reason), as in the case of the son of a childless woman (the example). Without either an existent or a non-existent sprout being inherently produced, we can be sure that the subject – the sprout – is not inherently produced at all. As was stated above, there is no need for either an inherently existent thing or a non-existent thing to be produced.

## THEREBY REFUTING TRULY EXISTENT CESSATION

[149] Just as production has been established as non-truly existent, likewise cessation can be established as non-truly existent. In this way all things can be seen to lack true existence. All living beings are never truly born nor do they ever truly cease. From beginningless time they have been empty of inherent existence and in this way are said to be in a 'state of natural nirvana'.

## THUS ESTABLISHING THE EQUALITY OF SAMSARA AND NIRVANA FROM THE POINT OF VIEW OF LACKING TRUE EXISTENCE

[150] Upon application of the logical reasons that have been explained we will come to understand that all sentient beings have no true existence and are like a dream. If we analyze sentient beings in search of an ultimate identity, we will find nothing at all. It will be like looking for the substance of a

plantain tree. If we are not satisfied that things exist merely as conceptual imputations and try to find a real solid essence, however much we may search not even one such atom will be found. The same is true of all phenomena. Therefore the state of nirvana that is beyond sorrow and the sorrowful state of samsara are the same in that they both completely lack true existence. In this respect they are identical and there is not the slightest bit of difference between the two.

## ENCOURAGING THE PRACTITIONER TO STRIVE TO DEVELOP THIS WISDOM

This has four parts:

1 Showing the meaning of sublime, precious emptiness
2 The need to strive to realize emptiness
3 Explaining great compassion by showing the faults of samsara
4 Showing the conceived object of great compassion

### SHOWING THE MEANING OF SUBLIME, PRECIOUS EMPTINESS

[151] If we analyze whether or not all things exist from their own nature we will not find even one object to which we can be attached. Therefore what is gained from an object of attachment? What pleasure arises from gaining the object and what displeasure from not gaining it? Through contemplating that the objects of attachment are not truly existent we will be able to abandon the first and second of the eight worldly concerns: being pleased when receiving

resources and respect and being displeased when not receiving resources and respect. Since sentient beings are not truly existent, from whom are praise and blame received? Through contemplating that both praise and blame are non-truly existent we are able to abandon the third and fourth of the eight worldly concerns: being pleased when receiving praise and being displeased when receiving blame.

[152] There is not one truly existent atom; there is no truly existent benefit or truly existent harm. Therefore, what is the point of being happy when benefited or unhappy when harmed? Contemplate that both happiness and unhappiness are non-truly existent and abandon the fifth and sixth of the eight worldly concerns: being pleased when experiencing pleasure and being displeased when experiencing harm. The seeker of a good reputation and the reputation itself are not truly existent, so why be happy when a good reputation is received or unhappy when a bad reputation is received? Consider this and contemplate that good and bad reputations are non-truly existent, and abandon the last two of the eight worldly concerns: being pleased when enjoying a good reputation and being displeased when receiving a bad reputation.

This explanation shows the method for abandoning the eight worldly concerns by meditating on emptiness. This method is extremely powerful and effective. By analysis we find there is no truly existent subject, so who craves for what object of attachment? [153] By examining living beings in this universe to see whether or not they exist from their own nature, we can never find any such sentient being at all. Therefore, all living beings in this universe are non-truly existent. If we investigate in this way, who lives in this world and who is it who will die? What will happen in a future life? What has already happened in a past life? Who are the pleasing, helpful relatives and who are the handsome and beautiful friends? All are non-truly existent.

## THE NEED TO STRIVE TO REALIZE EMPTINESS

As Shantideva says:

[154ab] O you who are just like me: as I, the composer of this text, have advised you before, please strive to realize that all phenomena are empty, like space. This is the sharpest sword to cut the root of samsara and is the main path to the attainment of enlightenment.

## EXPLAINING GREAT COMPASSION BY SHOWING THE FAULTS OF SAMSARA

This has five parts:

1 Contemplating the faults of this life
2 Contemplating the faults of future lives
3 Contemplating that even in fortunate realms it is difficult to find the time to practise Dharma
4 Contemplating the rarity and great meaning of finding this precious human life
5 Since we and others are afflicted by the sufferings of samsara, it is appropriate to feel sorrow

## CONTEMPLATING THE FAULTS OF THIS LIFE

[154cd-155] All human beings wish for happiness in this life but most of our time is spent under the power of suffering. For the sake of experiencing some pleasure or happiness we fight enemies and please our relatives and friends. Because our wishes are not fulfilled we experience great distress, dissatisfaction and problems. In an attempt to satisfy our desires we undergo great hardships and encounter many difficulties. Whenever we are harmed or our wishes are obstructed we return the harm, engage in quarrels and disputes and hurt each other with weapons, and because of all this we experience much physical pain. To fulfil the wishes of this life we also commit many non-virtues through our speech and mind. This precious fully-endowed life, obtained so rarely, is wasted without meaning; we spend all our time in the pursuit of this life's slight happiness, exposing ourself to needless hardship.

## CONTEMPLATING THE FAULTS OF FUTURE LIVES

[156] In future lives we may be able to meet a Spiritual Guide once or twice and because of that take a higher rebirth for a short time. But the joy of a god or a human is but briefly experienced before death comes and we fall into the extremely unbearable suffering of the lower realms for many aeons. [157] In samsara there are many pitfalls that lead to suffering. Since beginningless time until now we have not had the opportunity to be free from samsara.

Why have we not found release? The noble path that leads from the swamp of samsara is the realization of emptiness, but until now we have not found this path. Therefore, we are bound to samsara by the strong iron chain of self-grasping and we continue to wander, experiencing incessant suffering. Until we realize sublime emptiness we will remain in samsara and suffer always, tied by the bonds of this self-grasping. [158ab] In samsara it is extremely difficult and rare to find the path of emptiness, but unless we do we will experience an ocean of unbearable suffering that is beyond analogy. Knowing this, strive continuously to understand the correct view of emptiness.

## CONTEMPLATING THAT EVEN IN FORTUNATE REALMS IT IS DIFFICULT TO FIND THE TIME TO PRACTISE DHARMA

[158cd] Even though we may be born in the higher realms, as long as we remain in samsara we will have little ability to practise virtue. The life of freedom and endowment is extremely short, yet still we make plans for a long stay. [159] In order to secure a long life free from sickness we take medicine. To avoid hunger, thirst and cold, we apply great effort and encounter many problems to obtain food, drink and clothing. [160] Being faced with many external and internal obstacles, being harmed by others and coming under the influence of misleading friends, this life passes rapidly without meaning or the time to practise Dharma.

It is extremely difficult to investigate and develop the wisdom realizing emptiness that cuts the root of samsara. Therefore, knowing thoroughly the vicious state of samsara, realize how fortunate we are that today we have found a precious, fully-endowed human life, together with the rare opportunity to practise Dharma and to discriminate between virtue and non-virtue. We have met with the complete and flawless teachings of Buddha Shakyamuni, which lead to the state of full enlightenment. Such a rare occasion should not be wasted. We should strive to obtain the perfect state of Buddhahood!

## CONTEMPLATING THE RARITY AND GREAT MEANING OF FINDING THIS PRECIOUS HUMAN LIFE

[161] Since beginningless time we have never been separate from self-grasping, not even for a moment. We thus have strong familiarity with anger, attachment and all manner of distractions, and little power to oppose them. Many hindrances and obstacles prevent us from attaining enlightenment. Rarely have we had the opportunity to practise Dharma, and when we have, the demonic Devaputra Mara, employing many methods, has hindered us in our practice and led us into the vast wasteland of the lower realms. Thus many conditions and circumstances prevent us from finding release from samsara while very few lead us to that release.

Even though we are born human, we encounter many mistaken paths and misleading teachers. Because of this it is difficult to develop strong conviction and faith in the perfect path and Spiritual Guide. We remain filled with many doubts regarding karma and emptiness and thus it is extremely difficult to cross over this ocean of samsaric suffering. [162] At this time we have found a fully qualified Spiritual Guide who teaches the perfect, flawless path leading to enlightenment. If we do not strive to attain liberation or enlightenment, in the future it will be extremely difficult to find such conducive circumstances again.

A Buddha rarely appears in this world and it is very difficult to meet a qualified Mahayana Spiritual Guide. Therefore, it is extremely difficult to cross the river of delusion. Until we attain liberation or enlightenment our mind remains polluted by the stains of delusions. It is our great misfortune that we go from misery to misery unceasingly.

Considering well the faults of samsara and cultivating the appropriate disillusionment and renunciation, we should meditate daily on bodhichitta and emptiness and strive to attain enlightenment.

## SINCE WE AND OTHERS ARE AFFLICTED BY THE SUFFERINGS OF SAMSARA, IT IS APPROPRIATE TO FEEL SORROW

[163] Within samsara, despite oppression and affliction by unwanted suffering, certain states are thought to be happiness and our suffering is not recognized as suffering. Looking with great compassion on those who because of ignorance are unable to recognize such suffering, we should think, 'How wonderful it would be if their ignorance was dispelled and they were rescued from drowning in the ocean of suffering!' It is therefore appropriate to feel deep sorrow for mother sentient beings who are sinking in the swamp of samsara.

We should strive continuously to develop great compassion and think how ignorant beings bring torment upon themselves. [164] For example, some ascetics carry out their ablutions in freezing water and repeatedly burn themselves with fire. They experience great suffering but they do not recognize that they suffer at all. Indeed, they maintain that their practices lead to liberation! [165] In the same way, people experience the sufferings of birth, sickness, ageing, death, not fulfilling their wishes and meeting with undesirable circumstances, but they fail to recognize these as suffering. Instead, they cling to worldly activities as being real happiness, and without fearing samsara in general and the unbearable sufferings of the three lower realms in particular they think that they are as happy and free as Arhats and remain oblivious of future misery. Yet they do not have the slightest chance of avoiding such suffering; they will quickly experience the sufferings of ageing, sickness and death. When the Lord of Death finally arrives and kills his victims the inexpressible sufferings of death arise, and after death they will experience unbearable suffering in one of the lower realms for many aeons.

## SHOWING THE CONCEIVED OBJECT OF GREAT COMPASSION

[166] We first recollect that all sentient beings are suffering unbearable pains, similar to being tormented with flames of fire. Then from the clouds of our merit we send down rains of happiness that extinguish these fires of suffering. Thinking 'How wonderful it would be to alleviate the suffering of all sentient beings; I will act to relieve all others of their suffering,' we meditate on this continuously. When this thought arises spontaneously it is great compassion.

[167] In addition we should accumulate a collection of wisdom arising from the realization that all phenomena are empty of true existence, and a collection of merit arising from infinite good deeds such as giving and patience.

Because of self-grasping, sentient beings are wretched and sad. Therefore, in order to pacify their sufferings we should think, 'How wonderful it would be if all sentient beings were free from the sufferings of samsara! May I teach them about emptiness!' Thinking like this, we should meditate with great compassion.

Wishing to attain enlightenment for the sole purpose of benefiting all sentient beings – with the spontaneous thought to release them from their suffering and lead them to the ultimate state of happiness – is bodhichitta. The methods for developing bodhichitta have been explained extensively in the previous chapters, together with the ceremony for taking the Bodhisattva vows. In fact, Shantideva has explained all the essential stages of the Mahayana path. The correct view of reality has been presented in this, his ninth chapter, the development of meditative concentration in his eighth chapter, and the appropriate conduct of a Bodhisattva in the earlier chapters. With a proper union of view, meditation and action we can attain the desired state of full enlightenment very rapidly. Therefore, we should take all these teachings as sound and reliable words of advice and put them into practice for the benefit of all.

This concludes 'Wisdom', the ninth chapter of the text *Meaningful to Behold*, a commentary to Shantideva's *Guide to the Bodhisattva's Way of Life*.

# Dedication

## DEDICATION AND THE PRACTICE OF GIVING FOR THE BENEFIT OF ALL BEINGS

This section, the final chapter of Shantideva's *Guide*, has three parts:

1. An explanation of the brief dedication
2. An explanation of the extensive dedication
3. Remembering kindness and prostrating

## AN EXPLANATION OF THE BRIEF DEDICATION

In his tenth chapter Shantideva dedicates all the roots of virtue he has accumulated from his composition of this text for the benefit of himself and all other beings:

[1] Through the merit of composing this text, which contains the flawless meaning of Buddha's teaching of the stages of the Bodhisattva's path to enlightenment, may all sentient beings develop bodhichitta and engage in the six perfections and all the other Bodhisattva practices.

In general it is very important to dedicate the fruits of whatever Dharma practice we engage in. In the Kadampa text *Training the Mind in Seven Points* it says that for a Dharma

*Venerable Geshe Kelsang Gyatso Rinpoche*

action to be complete it must begin and end in a specific manner. At the start of every action it is extremely important to generate a pure motivation, and at the completion of that action it is important to dedicate all the accumulated merit. Our initial motivation determines whether our practice is pure or not. For instance, if we practise Dharma solely for the sake of the pleasures of this life – to gain a good reputation and so forth – our practice will be impure. If our motivation is to gain rebirth as a human or god, this is a Dharma practice but its aspiration is of a person of initial scope. Higher than this is the motivation of practising so that we can release ourself from suffering and attain liberation; this is the aspiration of a person of intermediate scope. Finally, if we practise Dharma with the aspiration to attain the highest enlightenment for the sake of all sentient beings, this motivation is an aspiration of a person of great scope. Thus we can see that the scope of our practice depends mainly on our motivation for performing that action. That is why it is extremely important to generate a pure motivation before we begin any Dharma practice whatsoever.

Generating the proper motivation is the correct way of beginning an action and dedicating merit is the proper way of ending it. If a single drop of water falls into the ocean it will remain for as long as the ocean remains. In a similar fashion, if we dedicate the merit gained from our practices for the attainment of enlightenment, that merit will remain undiminished until enlightenment is actually reached. As explained in the sixth chapter, virtue that has been dedicated can never be destroyed by anger; on the contrary, it will increase abundantly.

Dedication is defined as the mental factor intention that directs our accumulated virtue and acts as a cause of the results we desire. In this respect dedication is like the reins on the horse of virtue. Wherever a horse is led is determined by its reins, and whatever results are wished for are determined by our dedication of virtue. For all these reasons it is extremely important to dedicate our merit after every Dharma practice, no matter how insignificant.

## AN EXPLANATION OF THE EXTENSIVE DEDICATION

This has three parts:

1 Dedication for the sake of others
2 Dedication for the sake of ourself
3 Dedication for the flourishing of Buddhadharma, the source of all happiness

## DEDICATION FOR THE SAKE OF OTHERS

This has five parts:

1 Dedication to free others from their sickness
2 Dedication to remove the sufferings of the three lower realms
3 Dedication for all gods and humans
4 Universal dedication for all living beings
5 Dedication for all Bodhisattvas and Superior beings

## DEDICATION TO FREE OTHERS FROM THEIR SICKNESS

[2] By virtue of my merit may the beings who reside in all directions be released from their physical and mental torment and from all disease. May they find boundless oceans of joy and happiness.

## DEDICATION TO REMOVE THE SUFFERINGS OF THE THREE LOWER REALMS

[3] For as long as samsara exists may all beings experience without decline the temporary happiness and joy of the god and human realms. May they all eventually come to experience the everlasting joy of Buddhahood.

*Hell beings.* [4] May all embodied creatures throughout the universe who are experiencing the pains of hell find relief and come to enjoy the great bliss of Sukhavati Pure Land. [5] May the feeble ones suffering the blistering pain of the cold hells find warmth and pleasure. May those oppressed and burning within the hot hells be cooled by the boundless waters that issue forth from the great clouds of the Bodhisattvas' collections of merit and wisdom. [6] May the forest of razor-sharp leaves, situated near the hot hells, be transformed into a beautiful pleasure-grove. May the trees of splintered iron and sharp thorns grow into wishfulfilling trees.

[7] May all the regions of hell become joyful lands adorned with vast and fragrant lotus lakes that resound with the enchanting calls of geese, ducks and swans. [8] May the heaps of burning coals in the scorching hells become piles of various jewels. May the burning iron ground shine like a beautiful crystal floor. May those fearful crushing mountains, shaped like the heads of goats and rams, become palaces filled with Sugatas. [9] May the rains of lava, blazing stones and weapons from now on transform into a rain of flowers. May those who battle and kill one another with guns and swords in the reviving hells from now on engage in a playful exchange of flowers. [10] By the power of my virtue may those drowning in

the fierce torrents of acid, their flesh eaten away revealing bones as white as a water-lily, attain the bodies of glorious gods dwelling with beautiful goddesses in gently flowing streams.

When the hell beings find themselves suddenly released from suffering they will exclaim: [11] 'Why are the henchmen of the Lord of Death and the vultures and other terrifying birds so afraid? By whose power is joy brought to us now and the darkness of suffering dispelled?' Looking up they will behold in the midst of space the radiant form of Vajrapani. Through the force of the faith and joy that they will then experience may they all be freed from their past evil and abide with the glorious Holder of the Vajra.

[12] When they see the fires of hell extinguished by the rain of flowers and scented water, the hell beings will become full of joy and will wonder by whose hand this was brought about. At that time may all the inhabitants of hell behold Pemapani, Holder of the Lotus.

Then may the hell beings declare, [13] 'Dear friends, do not be afraid, but quickly gather here. There is no need to run away because above us is radiant youthful Manjughosha, with a topknot at his crown. Endowed with great compassion and the precious bodhichitta, he protects all living beings. Through his power all suffering is dispelled and all joy increases. [14] Behold him abiding in an enchanting palace resounding with the celestial songs of a thousand goddesses. While hundreds of gods bow down before him, their tiaras lowered towards his lotus feet, a vast rain of various flowers descends upon his head, his eyes moist with great compassion.'

May all the residents of hell cry out with joy at seeing Manjughosha. [15] By the roots of my virtue may all the inhabitants of hell, beholding the cool, sweet-scented rains falling from the joyful clouds created by Bodhisattvas such as Samantabhadra, Maitreya, Ksitigarbha, Akashagarbha and Sarvanivaranaviskambini, be truly happy.

*Animals.* [16ab] Through the power of my own and others' virtue may all animals be freed from the fears of being devoured by one another.

*Hungry spirits.* [16cd-17] May the beings in the northern continent enjoy the pleasures of food and clothing and other delights without difficulty. Like them, may the hungry spirits be satisfied with the food and drink that flows as a stream of milk from the hand of the noble Lord Avalokiteshvara. By bathing in this stream may they be constantly refreshed.

## DEDICATION FOR ALL GODS AND HUMANS

This dedication has two parts:

1 Dedication for relief from suffering
2 Dedication for the fulfilment of wishes

### DEDICATION FOR RELIEF FROM SUFFERING

[18] May those human beings who are blind and deaf become able to see forms and hear sounds. Just as it was with Mayadevi, the mother of Buddha, may all pregnant women give birth without any pain or difficulty. [19] May the naked find clothing, the hungry find food, and the thirsty find fresh water and other delicious drinks. [20] May those who are poor find wealth and possessions, those weak with sorrow and anxiety find joy, and may those exhausted from the loss of their wealth be refreshed, their minds made stable

and glorious. [21] May all who are sick be cured of their illness and may each and every disease be eradicated, never to arise again. [22] May those who are afraid of enemies be separated from their fear, and may all prisoners, captive without choice, be freed. May those who are powerless gain power and, without jealousy, may all beings have beneficial thoughts towards one another.

[23] May all travellers and merchants find happiness wherever they go. May they effortlessly accomplish whatever they wish for. [24] May those who travel by boats and ships upon the ocean obtain whatever they seek and then return safely to land to be reunited joyfully with their friends and relatives. [25] May those who are lost and distressed meet with fellow travellers. May they proceed without fear of thieves or wild beasts, and may their journeys be easy and without fatigue. [26] May those who wander in fearsome and dangerous places, children, the aged, the protectorless, as well as the bewildered and the insane, be safeguarded by kindly celestials.

## DEDICATION FOR THE FULFILMENT OF WISHES

This has two parts:

1. General dedication for all human beings
2. Specific dedication for the ordained

### GENERAL DEDICATION FOR ALL HUMAN BEINGS

[27] May all human beings be freed from the eight states of no freedom, and may they be endowed with faith, wisdom and compassion. May they have excellent food, follow pure

conduct and always be mindful of their past and future lives. [28] May all who are destitute find wealth as limitless as the treasury of space, and without any dispute or injury may they always abide in freedom. [29] May those who possess little splendour be endowed with great magnificence. May those whose bodies are weak and worn by the toils of asceticism find magnificent and noble forms. [30] May all the females throughout the universe who so desire be reborn in a male form. May the lowly of birth attain grandeur without ever displaying any pride.

[31] By the power of my merit may all sentient beings without exception abandon all evil and practise virtue at all times. [32] May they never be separated from bodhichitta, and may they always engage in the Bodhisattva practices of giving and other virtues. May they always be cared for by Spiritual Guides and Buddhas, and may they abandon all demonic activity. [33] May they be reborn in higher realms, and enjoy inconceivably long lives, and may they always live comfortably and happily without ever hearing the sound of the word 'death'.

[34] May all places become gardens of wishfulfilling trees, resounding with the sweet sounds of Dharma as it is proclaimed by the Buddhas and their Noble Sons and Daughters. [35] May the whole ground become completely pure, as level as the palm of the hand, free from rocks and thorns and as smooth as lapis lazuli. [36] May Bodhisattvas who possess clairvoyance, miracle powers and other excellent qualities increase in number for the sake of their circles of disciples. As with advanced Bodhisattvas [37] may all living beings continuously hear the sound of Dharma issuing forth from the singing of birds, from the rustling of trees and from space itself. [38] May all beings come to meet the

Buddhas and their Sons, and may the Spiritual Guides of the world be venerated with clouds of offerings.

[39] May the glorious gods send timely rains so that harvests may be plentiful. May kings rule in accordance with Dharma, and may the people of the world prosper. [40] May all medicines be effective in curing disease, and may the recitation of mantras fulfil all wishes. May spirits, cannibals, wild animals and the like possess the mind of great compassion. [41] May no one ever experience physical pain or the mental anguish of frustration or unhappiness. May no one ever be afraid or belittled.

## SPECIFIC DEDICATION FOR THE ORDAINED

[42] In all temples and monasteries may the practice of reciting scriptures and meditating on them flourish forever. May the members of the Sangha forever be harmonious and may their wishes to benefit others be fulfilled. [43] May monks who desire to keep their ordination purely and follow their practices stainlessly, find quiet and solitary places for these purposes. By abandoning all distractions, may they meditate with mental suppleness.

[44] May nuns be materially provided for without any difficulty, and during retreat may they be free of all harm from men. May the morality of all those who have taken ordination never decline but be perfected. [45] May all those who have broken their moral vows come to regret it deeply, and completely purify their downfalls by the power of confession. May they thereby attain fortunate rebirths and never let their morality decline again.

[46] May those who are learned in the three sets of the teachings be honoured and respected, and may they always

find sustenance and receive material support. May their minds be pure and peaceful, and may their fame be proclaimed in all directions. [47] May they never experience the sufferings of the lower realms or meet with hardships of body, speech and mind. May they have physical forms endowed with excellent qualities and superior to those of the gods. May they swiftly attain Buddhahood.

## UNIVERSAL DEDICATION FOR ALL LIVING BEINGS

[48] May all sentient beings again and again make offerings to the Buddhas. May they practise the Bodhisattva way of life and thereby find eternal joy in the inconceivable bliss of a fully enlightened being.

## DEDICATION FOR ALL BODHISATTVAS AND SUPERIOR BEINGS

[49] Through the virtue of composing this text may all Bodhisattvas fulfil the welfare of the world in the very manner they have intended. May all sentient beings receive whatever the protecting Buddhas have intended for them. [50] In the same manner, may all the Solitary Conquerors and Hearers who strive to find the happiness of nirvana attain it.

## DEDICATION FOR THE SAKE OF OURSELF

[51] Through the virtue of composing this text and through the kindness of Manjughosha, may I always remember my past and future lives and always receive ordination until I attain the level of the Joyous One. [52] May I be sustained by simple food, and may I abide in solitude throughout all

my lives and always find ideal conditions for achieving my goals.

[53] Whenever I wish to see something such as a scripture of Buddha or to compose even a single verse, may I be able to see without any obstruction Protector Manjughosha. [54] In order to fulfil the needs of all beings who extend without limit throughout the ten directions, may my way of life resemble that of Manjughosha.

[55] For as long as space exists and for as long as beings remain in samsara, may I live among them in order to dispel their misery. [56] Whatever are the sufferings of living beings may they ripen solely upon me, and by the power of the Bodhisattvas' virtue and aspirations may all beings experience happiness.

## DEDICATION FOR THE FLOURISHING OF BUDDHADHARMA, THE SOURCE OF ALL HAPPINESS

[57] Through the power of my own and others' virtue, may Buddhadharma – the sole medicine for all suffering and the foundation of all joy – be upheld and honoured, and may it remain for a very long time.

## REMEMBERING KINDNESS AND PROSTRATING

[58] I prostrate to Manjughosha through whose kindness I developed the precious bodhichitta and received the opportunity to practise the six perfections and develop the wisdom enabling me to compose this text on the flawless path that leads to the attainment of Buddhahood. I also prostrate to my other Spiritual Guides through whose kindness I received ordination and developed the three wisdoms of listening,

contemplating and meditating, and thereby increased all my virtuous qualities.

The tenth chapter has explained in detail Shantideva's dedication to others of his body and wealth, and specifically the roots of his virtue. Such a dedication is therefore a detailed exposition of the perfection of giving. Additional discussions of this perfection are to be found throughout the other chapters of this text.

This concludes 'Dedication', the tenth chapter of the text *Meaningful to Behold*, a commentary to Shantideva's *Guide to the Bodhisattva's Way of Life*.

# Conclusion

## THE MEANING OF THE CONCLUSION

This has two parts:

1 About the author
2 About the translators

### ABOUT THE AUTHOR

*Guide to the Bodhisattva's Way of Life* is the one text that has formed the main basis of listening, contemplating and meditating for all the previous Indian Yogis as well as for the wise and learned followers of all the Mahayana Buddhist traditions. It is invaluable for training the minds of all, whether they have superior or inferior intelligence, and whether they are ordained or lay, male or female. In this text the general Mahayana path – specifically renunciation, bodhichitta and the correct view of emptiness – is explained clearly, extensively and profoundly.

In brief, this text contains the complete and flawless path to highest enlightenment. The author of this *Guide* is the great Bodhisattva Shantideva. Under the care of Manjushri he abandoned his kingdom as if it were dust, seeing no meaning in it. Through following the Mahayana path in general and the path of the Highest Yoga Tantra in particular, Shantideva attained Buddhahood in one lifetime.

## ABOUT THE TRANSLATORS

*Guide to the Bodhisattva's Way of Life* was originally translated from Sanskrit into Tibetan by the Abbot Sarvajanadeva and the Tibetan translator Bende Peltseg from the Kashmiri edition of the text. Later this translation was revised by the Indian Abbot Dharmashribhadra and the Tibetan translator Rinchen Sangpo. A further translation was subsequently made, in accordance with the Magadha edition and related commentaries, by the Indian Abbot Shakyamati, again with the assistance of the Tibetan translator Rinchen Sangpo. Further excellent revisions were made by the Indian Abbot Sumatikirti and the Tibetan translator Gelong Loden Sherab from the Kashmiri edition of the text.

This book, *Meaningful to Behold*, is the teachings of Venerable Geshe Kelsang Gyatso Rinpoche. These teachings were recorded and transcribed, and then edited principally by him and some of his senior students.

# The Condensed Meaning of the Commentary

**The commentary to Guide to the Bodhisattva's Way of Life has three parts:**

1. The pre-eminent qualities of the author
2. An introduction to the text
3. The explanation of the actual text

The explanation of the actual text has four parts:

1. The meaning of the title
2. The homage of the translators
3. The explanation of the meaning of the text
4. The meaning of the conclusion

**The explanation of the meaning of the text has two parts:**

1. The preliminary explanation
2. The actual explanation of the stages of the path to enlightenment

The preliminary explanation has three parts:

1. The expression of worship
2. The promise of composition
3. The reason for composition

The actual explanation of the stages of the path to enlightenment has two parts:

1. The exhortation to grasp the significance of this precious human life
2. The method for making this precious human life meaningful

The method for making this precious human life meaningful has two parts:

1. Contemplating the benefits of bodhichitta
2. How to practise the six perfections once bodhichitta has been developed

Contemplating the benefits of bodhichitta has four parts:

1. An explanation of the benefits of bodhichitta
2. Recognizing bodhichitta
3. The reasons for the benefits of bodhichitta
4. Praise to the one who gives birth to bodhichitta

An explanation of the benefits of bodhichitta has ten parts:

1. The conquest of all great evils
2. The attainment of the most sublime happiness
3. Wish-fulfilment
4. Bodhichitta carries with it a special name and meaning
5. Transformation of the inferior into the supreme
6. The value of the precious bodhichitta, so difficult to find
7. The inexhaustible and increasing fruits of bodhichitta
8. The power of protection from great fear
9. The swift and easy destruction of great evil
10. Scriptural citations of the benefits of bodhichitta

Recognizing bodhichitta has three parts:

1. The divisions of bodhichitta
2. The benefits of the aspiring mind of bodhichitta
3. The benefits of the engaging mind of bodhichitta

**How to practise the six perfections once bodhichitta has been developed has two parts:**

1. Maintaining bodhichitta
2. How to practise the six perfections

Maintaining bodhichitta has two parts:

1. How to destroy obstacles and purify evil
2. How to accept and hold on to the actual bodhichitta

How to destroy obstacles and purify evil has two parts:

1. The preliminary limbs of practice
2. The confession of non-virtue

The preliminary limbs of practice has three parts:

1. Offering
2. Prostration
3. Going for refuge

Offering has two parts:

1. The necessity of making offerings, and recognizing the objects of offering
2. The actual offering

The actual offering has three parts:

1. Unowned offerings
2. Offering our own body
3. Mentally transformed offerings

Mentally transformed offerings has two parts:

1 Ordinary offerings
2 Sublime offerings

Going for refuge has five parts:

1 The causes of going for refuge
2 The objects of refuge
3 The measurement of going for refuge perfectly
4 The commitments of going for refuge
5 The benefits of going for refuge

The confession of non-virtue has four parts:

1 The power of regret
2 The power of reliance
3 The power of the opponent force
4 The power of promise

**How to accept and hold on to the actual bodhichitta has three parts:**

1 The preparatory practices for accumulating merit
2 Fully accepting bodhichitta
3 Concluding activities

The preparatory practices for accumulating merit has five parts:

1 Rejoicing in virtue
2 Requesting the Buddhas to turn the Wheel of Dharma
3 Beseeching the Buddhas not to pass away
4 Dedicating merit
5 Training the mind in giving

Dedicating merit has four parts:

1. General dedication
2. Dedication for the sick
3. Dedication to relieve hunger and thirst
4. Dedication to fulfil the wishes of sentient beings

Concluding activities has three parts:

1. Meditating on the happiness of fulfilling our own wishes
2. Meditating on the happiness of benefiting others and fulfilling their wishes
3. Exhorting others to meditate on happiness

Meditating on the happiness of benefiting others and fulfilling their wishes has three parts:

1. Relieving others of their suffering
2. Eliminating the two obstructions
3. Bestowing great benefit and happiness upon others

**How to practise the six perfections has four parts:**

1. Meditating on conscientiousness so that the bodhichitta practice and precepts do not degenerate
2. How to train in moral discipline by practising mindfulness and alertness
3. Explanation of the four remaining perfections: patience, effort, concentration and wisdom
4. Dedication and the practice of giving for the benefit of all beings

Meditating on conscientiousness so that the bodhichitta practice and precepts do not degenerate has three parts:

1 An introduction to conscientiousness
2 An extensive explanation of conscientiousness
3 Summary

An extensive explanation of conscientiousness has two parts:

1 Meditating on conscientiousness with respect to bodhichitta
2 Meditating on conscientiousness with respect to the precepts

Meditating on conscientiousness with respect to bodhichitta has two parts:

1 The reasons why it is unwise to abandon bodhichitta
2 The faults of abandoning bodhichitta

The faults of abandoning bodhichitta has three parts:

1 We are led to the three lower realms
2 The benefit to others will decrease
3 We are far removed from the Bodhisattva grounds

Meditating on conscientiousness with respect to the precepts has three parts:

1 Conscientiousness in abandoning non-virtue
2 Conscientiousness in meditating on virtue
3 Conscientiousness in abandoning delusions

CONDENSED MEANING OF THE COMMENTARY

Conscientiousness in meditating on virtue has six parts:

1 Striving to abandon the infinite evils collected in previous lives
2 Merely experiencing the sufferings of lower realms will not lead to release
3 Not applying effort to the practice of virtue now that we have attained a precious human life is self-deception
4 If we do not practise virtue now we will experience suffering in this life
5 If we do not practise virtue now we will experience the sufferings of lower realms in future lives
6 Following from the above, it is appropriate to strive to abandon non-virtue and practise virtue

Conscientiousness in abandoning delusions has three parts:

1 Contemplating the faults of delusions
2 The inappropriateness of grieving over the hardships to be endured while abandoning delusions
3 Contemplating the joy of being able to abandon delusions

Contemplating the faults of delusions has six parts:

1 Delusions give us no choice
2 Delusions bring infinite sufferings
3 Delusions harm us for a long time
4 Following delusions as if they were friends is unwise
5 Being patient with delusions is unwise
6 Developing encouragement to dispel delusions

Contemplating the joy of being able to abandon delusions has three parts:

1. Unlike ordinary enemies, delusions cannot return once they have been eradicated
2. As the cause of delusions is wrong views, with diligence they can be abandoned
3. For these reasons it is suitable to abandon delusions

**How to train in moral discipline by practising mindfulness and alertness has five parts:**

1. The method of guarding the practice is to guard the mind
2. The method of guarding the mind is to practise mindfulness and alertness
3. How to practise moral discipline by means of mindfulness and alertness
4. How to prevent our practice from degenerating
5. In conclusion, the necessity of following the meaning and not merely the words of the practice

The method of guarding the mind is to practise mindfulness and alertness has six parts:

1. A brief presentation of the two factors
2. Without mindfulness and alertness our virtue will have little power
3. Without mindfulness and alertness we will not develop pure wisdom
4. Without mindfulness and alertness we cannot practise pure moral discipline
5. Without mindfulness and alertness previously accumulated virtue will degenerate

6 Without mindfulness and alertness new virtue cannot be accumulated

How to practise moral discipline by means of mindfulness and alertness has three parts:

1 Practising the moral discipline of restraint
2 Practising the moral discipline of gathering virtue
3 Practising the moral discipline of benefiting sentient beings

Practising the moral discipline of gathering virtue has two parts:

1 Abandoning attachment to the body
2 Practising virtue with skilful means

Practising virtue with skilful means has three parts

1 Following pure conduct of the body
2 Following skilful conduct when associating with others
3 Following skilful conduct of body, speech and mind

## Explanation of the four remaining perfections: patience, effort, concentration and wisdom has four parts:

1 How to practise patience
2 How to practise effort
3 How to train in the concentration of tranquil abiding
4 How to develop the wisdom of superior seeing

How to practise patience has two parts :

1 The method of meditating on patience
2 The method of practising patience

The method of meditating on patience has two parts:

1 The faults of anger
2 The benefits of patience

The method of practising patience has five parts:

1 Preventing the cause of anger
2 Meditating on the patience of voluntarily enduring suffering
3 Meditating on the patience of definitely thinking about Dharma
4 Meditating on the patience of not retaliating
5 An extensive explanation of the benefits of patience

Meditating on the patience of definitely thinking about Dharma has four parts:

1 Because the angry person and the anger are both dependent upon causes, there is no choice
2 Refuting the assertion that the cause of anger is independent
3 The necessity of abandoning anger
4 Summary

Refuting the assertion that the cause of anger is independent has three parts:

1 Refuting the Samkhya school's assertion of an inherently existent general principle and self
2 Refuting the Vaisheshika school's assertion of an inherently existent self
3 Recognizing all beings as illusions, and thus the inappropriateness of generating anger towards them

Meditating on the patience of not retaliating has three parts:

1. Reflecting with attention on the methods for developing compassion
2. Overcoming the cause of anger
3. Contemplating our own faults when undesirable situations arise

**How to practise effort has four parts:**

1. An exhortation to practise effort
2. Recognizing effort
3. Overcoming the opponent to effort
4. Increasing the force of effort

Overcoming the opponent to effort has two parts:

1. Recognizing the opponent, laziness
2. How to overcome laziness

How to overcome laziness has three parts:

1. Overcoming the laziness of indolence
2. Overcoming the laziness of being attracted to what is meaningless or non-virtuous
3. Overcoming the laziness of discouragement

Overcoming the laziness of indolence has three parts:

1. Examining the cause of indolence
2. Contemplating the faults in this life of indolence
3. Contemplating the suffering in future lives caused by indolence

Increasing the force of effort has four parts:

1. Recognizing the four powers that increase the force of effort
2. An extensive explanation of the four powers
3. Practising earnestly with mindfulness and alertness
4. Using suppleness of body and mind to engage in virtuous conduct

An extensive explanation of the four powers has four parts:

1. The power of aspiration
2. The power of steadfastness
3. The power of joy
4. The power of rejection

**How to train in the concentration of tranquil abiding has four parts:**

1. Why we need to attain tranquil abiding
2. Exhortation to abandon the opponents to tranquil abiding
3. How to abandon the opponents to tranquil abiding
4. How to attain tranquil abiding

How to abandon the opponents to tranquil abiding has six parts:

1. Recognizing the causes of our attachment to worldly life
2. Recognizing the opponent to our attachment
3. How to generate the opponent to attachment
4. The faults of worldly associations
5. The benefits of living in solitude
6. How to abandon disturbing conceptions

## CONDENSED MEANING OF THE COMMENTARY

How to generate the opponent to attachment has two parts:

1. Abandoning attachment to sentient beings
2. Abandoning attachment to inanimate things

How to attain tranquil abiding has two parts:

1. A general explanation of the stages of tranquil abiding meditation
2. Explanation of the particular use to which tranquil abiding is to be put: meditating on equalizing and exchanging self with others

A general explanation of the stages of tranquil abiding meditation has four parts:

1. The six necessary conditions for attaining tranquil abiding
2. The nine mental abidings
3. The five obstacles to attaining tranquil abiding
4. The eight opponents to the five obstacles

Explanation of the particular use to which tranquil abiding is to be put: meditating on equalizing and exchanging self with others has two parts:

1. How to meditate on equalizing self and others
2. How to exchange self with others

How to meditate on equalizing self and others has five parts:

1. A brief explanation of the meditation
2. The meaning of equalizing self and others
3. The actual meditation on equalizing self and others
4. The benefits of meditating on equalizing self and others
5. How we are able to develop the mind in this meditation

How to exchange self with others has four parts:

1. A brief explanation of the exchange
2. The way to exchange self with others
3. Completing the exchange by means of reflection
4. Completing the exchange by means of action

The way to exchange self with others has four parts:

1. Gaining familiarity with cherishing others
2. Abandoning self-cherishing
3. Reflecting on the disadvantages of self-cherishing and the advantages of cherishing others
4. Summary

Completing the exchange by means of reflection has five parts:

1. A brief explanation
2. Meditation on jealousy towards a superior
3. Meditation on competitiveness towards an equal
4. Meditation on pride towards an inferior
5. The results of this meditation

**How to develop the wisdom of superior seeing has five parts:**

1. Showing why those who wish to attain liberation need to develop the wisdom realizing emptiness
2. The presentation of the two truths
3. Showing the reasons why those who seek only personal liberation need to develop the wisdom realizing emptiness
4. An extensive explanation of the reasons that establish emptiness
5. Encouraging the practitioner to strive to develop this wisdom

The presentation of the two truths has five parts:

1. The distinctions between the two truths
2. The definition of the two truths
3. The distinctions between the individuals who assert the two truths
4. The distinctions between their varying degrees of mental capacity
5. Refuting the argument that it is not necessary to realize emptiness in order to attain liberation

Refuting the argument that it is not necessary to realize emptiness in order to attain liberation has two parts:

1. A refutation of the proponents of things in general
2. A refutation of the Chittamatrins in particular

A refutation of the Chittamatrins in particular has four parts:

1. Refuting self-cognizers by scriptural authority
2. Refuting self-cognizers by reasoning
3. Refuting the Chittamatrins' proofs of the existence of self-cognizers
4. Refuting the assertion that all imputed existents must have as their basis something truly existent

Refuting the assertion that all imputed existents must have as their basis something truly existent has three parts:

1. The reason why a magician can have desire for the illusory woman he manifests
2. The reason why meditation on emptiness can abandon all delusions and their imprints
3. Showing that excellent results will come from abandoning grasping at true existence and its imprints

An extensive explanation of the reasons that establish emptiness has two parts:

1 An extensive explanation of the reasons that establish selflessness of persons
2 An extensive explanation of the reasons that establish selflessness of phenomena

An extensive explanation of the reasons that establish selflessness of persons has three parts:

1 Refuting the conceived object of the innate self-grasping of persons
2 Refuting the conceived object of the intellectually-formed self-grasping of persons
3 Refuting arguments against these refutations

Refuting the conceived object of the intellectually-formed self-grasping of persons has two parts:

1 Refuting the permanent self posited by the Samkhya school
2 Refuting the permanent self posited by the Vaisheshika and Naiyayika schools

An extensive explanation of the reasons that establish selflessness of phenomena has three parts:

1 Explaining selflessness of phenomena by means of the four close placements of mindfulness
2 Refuting arguments concerning the two truths
3 Explaining the reasoning that establishes selflessness

Explaining selflessness of phenomena by means of the four close placements of mindfulness has four parts:

1. Close placement of mindfulness of body
2. Close placement of mindfulness of feelings
3. Close placement of mindfulness of mind
4. Close placement of mindfulness of phenomena

Close placement of mindfulness of body has four parts:

1. Establishing the non-true existence of a body as possessor of its parts
2. Establishing the non-true existence of the parts of the body
3. Therefore it is inappropriate to be attached to this dream-like non-truly existent body
4. Through this, establishing the non-true existence of the person

Close placement of mindfulness of feelings has four parts:

1. Refuting the true existence of the nature of feeling
2. Refuting the true existence of the cause of feeling
3. Refuting the true existence of the object of feeling
4. Refuting the true existence of the subjective experiencer of feeling

Refuting the true existence of the nature of feeling has three parts:

1. Refuting the true existence of painful feelings
2. Refuting the true existence of pleasant feelings
3. Explaining the yoga of meditating on the non-true existence of feelings

Refuting the true existence of the cause of feeling has three parts:

　　1　Refuting a truly existent meeting between a sense power and an object
　　2　Refuting a truly existent meeting between an object and a consciousness
　　3　Thus establishing the non-true existence of the contact that arises from the meeting of an object, sense power and consciousness

Close placement of mindfulness of mind has two parts:

　　1　Establishing the non-true existence of mental consciousness
　　2　Establishing the non-true existence of the five sense consciousnesses

Explaining the reasoning that establishes selflessness has three parts:

　　1　The reasoning of vajra fragments
　　2　The reasoning of dependent relationship
　　3　The reasoning that refutes inherent production of existents and non-existents

The reasoning of vajra fragments has five parts:

　　1　Refuting production from no cause
　　2　Refuting production from a permanent cause that is other
　　3　Refuting production from a permanent general principle
　　4　A summary of the refutation of production from no cause
　　5　Refuting production from both self and other

Refuting production from a permanent cause that is other has three parts:

1. Refuting what is meant by the god Ishvara
2. Refuting that Ishvara is the cause of everything with the reason he is permanent
3. Refuting permanent partless particles as the cause of everything

Refuting production from a permanent general principle has four parts:

1. Refuting a general principle that is the cause of all manifestations
2. Refuting a permanent general principle
3. Refuting an effect existing at the same time as its cause
4. Refuting the claim that the Madhyamika school is at fault

The reasoning that refutes inherent production of existents and non-existents has three parts:

1. Refuting inherently existent production through this reasoning
2. Thereby refuting truly existent cessation
3. Thus establishing the equality of samsara and nirvana from the point of view of lacking true existence

Encouraging the practitioner to strive to develop this wisdom has four parts:

1. Showing the meaning of sublime, precious emptiness
2. The need to strive to realize emptiness

3 Explaining great compassion by showing the faults of samsara
4 Showing the conceived object of great compassion

Explaining great compassion by showing the faults of samsara has five parts:

1 Contemplating the faults of this life
2 Contemplating the faults of future lives
3 Contemplating that even in fortunate realms it is difficult to find the time to practise Dharma
4 Contemplating the rarity and great meaning of finding this precious human life
5 Since we and others are afflicted by the sufferings of samsara, it is appropriate to feel sorrow

**Dedication and the practice of giving for the benefit of all beings has three parts:**

1 An explanation of the brief dedication
2 An explanation of the extensive dedication
3 Remembering kindness and prostrating

An explanation of the extensive dedication has three parts:

1 Dedication for the sake of others
2 Dedication for the sake of ourself
3 Dedication for the flourishing of Buddhadharma, the source of all happiness

Dedication for the sake of others has five parts:

1 Dedication to free others from their sickness
2 Dedication to remove the sufferings of the three lower realms
3 Dedication for all gods and humans

4 Universal dedication for all living beings
5 Dedication for all Bodhisattvas and Superior beings

Dedication for all gods and humans has two parts:

1 Dedication for relief from suffering
2 Dedication for the fulfilment of wishes

Dedication for the fulfilment of wishes has two parts:

1 General dedication for all human beings
2 Specific dedication for the ordained

**The meaning of the conclusion has two parts:**

1 About the author
2 About the translators

*Appendix I:*
*Liberating Prayer*

# *Liberating Prayer*

## PRAISE TO BUDDHA SHAKYAMUNI

O Blessed One, Shakyamuni Buddha,
Precious treasury of compassion,
Bestower of supreme inner peace,

You, who love all beings without exception,
Are the source of happiness and goodness;
And you guide us to the liberating path.

Your body is a wishfulfilling jewel,
Your speech is supreme, purifying nectar,
And your mind is refuge for all living beings.

With folded hands I turn to you,
Supreme unchanging friend,
I request from the depths of my heart:

Please give me the light of your wisdom
To dispel the darkness of my mind
And to heal my mental continuum.

Please nourish me with your goodness,
That I in turn may nourish all beings
With an unceasing banquet of delight.

Through your compassionate intention,
Your blessings and virtuous deeds,
And my strong wish to rely upon you,

May all suffering quickly cease
And all happiness and joy be fulfilled;
And may holy Dharma flourish for evermore.

**Colophon:** This prayer was composed by Venerable Geshe Kelsang Gyatso Rinpoche and is recited at the beginning of teachings, meditations and prayers in Kadampa Buddhist Centres throughout the world.

# Glossary

*Absorption without discrimination*   A concentration of the fourth form realm that observes nothingness and that is attained by stopping gross feelings and gross discriminations. See *Ocean of Nectar*.

*Aggregates*   In general, all functioning things are aggregates because they are an aggregation of their parts. In particular, a person of the desire or form realm has five aggregates: the aggregates of form, feeling, discrimination, compositional factors and consciousness. A being of the formless realm lacks the aggregate of form but has the other four. A person's form aggregate is his or her body. The remaining four aggregates are aspects of his mind. See *The New Heart of Wisdom*.

*Amitabha*   The manifestation of the aggregate of discrimination of all Buddhas. He has a red-coloured body. See *The New Eight Steps to Happiness*.

*Atisha*   (AD 982-1054) A famous Indian Buddhist scholar and meditation master. He was Abbot of the great Buddhist monastery of Vikramashila at a time when Mahayana Buddhism was flourishing in India. He was later invited to Tibet where he re-introduced pure Buddhism. He is the author of the first Lamrim text, *Lamp for the Path*. His tradition later became known as the 'Kadampa Tradition'. See *Joyful Path of Good Fortune*.

*Avalokiteshvara*   The embodiment of the compassion of all the Buddhas. Sometimes he appears with one face and four arms, and sometimes with eleven faces and a thousand arms. At the time of Buddha Shakyamuni, he manifested as a Bodhisattva disciple. Called 'Chenrezig' in Tibetan. See *Living Meaningfully, Dying Joyfully* and *The Mirror of Dharma*.

***Awakened One*** An epithet for Buddha, referring to anyone who has awakened from the sleep of ignorance and is completely free from dream-like samsaric problems and suffering. The 'sleep of ignorance' is the sleep of self-grasping in which living beings always remain and from which they have never awakened.

***Blessing*** The transformation of our mind from a negative state to a positive state, from an unhappy state to a happy state, or from a state of weakness to a state of strength, through the inspiration of holy beings such as our Spiritual Guide, Buddhas and Bodhisattvas.

***Buddha's bodies*** A Buddha has four bodies – the Wisdom Truth Body, the Nature Body, the Enjoyment Body and the Emanation Body. The first is Buddha's omniscient mind. The second is the emptiness, or ultimate nature, of his or her mind. The third is his subtle Form Body. The fourth, of which each Buddha manifests a countless number, are gross Form Bodies that are visible to ordinary beings. The Wisdom Truth Body and the Nature Body are both included within the Truth Body, and the Enjoyment Body and the Emanation Body are both included within the Form Body. See *Joyful Path of Good Fortune* and *Ocean of Nectar*.

***Buddha Shakyamuni*** The fourth of one thousand founding Buddhas who are to appear in this world during this Fortunate Aeon. The first three were Krakuchchanda, Kanakamuni and Kashyapa. The fifth Buddha will be Maitreya. See *Modern Buddhism* and *Introduction to Buddhism*.

***Buddhist*** Anyone who from the depths of their heart goes for refuge to the Three Jewels – Buddha, Dharma and Sangha. See *Introduction to Buddhism*.

***Chandrakirti*** (circa 7th century AD) A great Indian Buddhist scholar and meditation master who composed, among many other books, the well-known *Guide to the Middle Way*, in which he clearly elucidates the view of the Madhyamika-Prasangika school according to Buddha's teachings given in the *Perfection of Wisdom Sutras*. See *Ocean of Nectar*.

***Chekhawa, Geshe*** (AD 1102-1176) A great Kadampa Bodhisattva who composed the text *Training the Mind in Seven*

*Points*, a commentary to Bodhisattva Langri Tangpa's *Eight Verses of Training the Mind*. He spread the study and practice of training the mind throughout Tibet. See *Universal Compassion*.

***Close retreat*** A retreat during which we strive to draw close to a particular Deity. This can be understood in two ways: drawing close in the sense of developing a special relationship with a friend, and drawing close in the sense of becoming more and more like the Deity. An action close retreat is a close retreat in which we collect a certain number of mantras and conclude with a fire puja. See *Heart Jewel, The New Guide to Dakini Land, Essence of Vajrayana* and *Tantric Grounds and Paths*.

***Collection of merit*** A virtuous action motivated by bodhichitta that is a main cause of attaining the Form Body of a Buddha. Examples are: making offerings and prostrations to holy beings with bodhichitta motivation, and the practice of the perfections of giving, moral discipline and patience.

***Collection of wisdom*** A virtuous mental action motivated by bodhichitta that is a main cause of attaining the Truth Body of a Buddha. Examples are: listening to, contemplating and meditating on emptiness with bodhichitta motivation.

***Commitments*** Promises and pledges taken when engaging in certain spiritual practices.

***Consciousness*** The six consciousnesses, or primary minds, are the eye consciousness, ear consciousness, nose consciousness, tongue consciousness, body consciousness and mental consciousness. See *How to Understand the Mind*.

***Contact*** A mental factor that functions to perceive its object as pleasant, unpleasant, or neutral. See *How to Understand the Mind*.

***Deity*** 'Yidam' in Tibetan. A Tantric enlightened being.

***Direct perceiver*** A cognizer that apprehends its manifest object. See *How to Understand the Mind*.

***Direct valid cognizer*** A non-deceptive cognizer that apprehends its manifest object. See *How to Understand the Mind*.

***Doubt*** A mental factor that wavers with respect to its object. See *How to Understand the Mind*.

*Eight worldly concerns* The objects of the eight worldly concerns are happiness and suffering, wealth and poverty, praise and criticism, and good reputation and bad reputation. These are called 'worldly concerns' because worldly people are constantly concerned with them, wanting some and trying to avoid others. See *Universal Compassion* and *Joyful Path of Good Fortune*.

*Emanation Body* 'Nirmanakaya' in Sanskrit. A gross form body of a Buddha that can be seen by ordinary beings. See also *Buddha's bodies*.

*Enjoyment Body* 'Sambhogakaya' in Sanskrit. A Buddha's subtle Form Body that can be perceived only by Mahayana Superiors. See also *Buddha's bodies*.

*Faith* A mental factor that functions principally to eliminate non-faith. Faith is a naturally virtuous mind that functions mainly to oppose the perception of faults in its observed object. There are three types of faith: believing faith, admiring faith and wishing faith. See *Modern Buddhism, How to Transform Your Life, Joyful Path of Good Fortune* and *How to Understand the Mind*.

*Feeling* A mental factor that functions to experience pleasant, unpleasant or neutral objects. See *How to Understand the Mind*.

*Foe Destroyer* 'Arhat' in Sanskrit. A practitioner who has abandoned all delusions and their seeds by training on the spiritual paths, and who will never again be reborn in samsara. In this context, the term 'Foe' refers to the delusions. See also *Hearer*.

*Four noble truths* True sufferings, true origins, true cessations and true paths. They are called 'noble' truths because they are supreme objects of meditation. Through meditation on these four objects, we can realize ultimate truth directly and thus become a noble, or Superior, being. Sometimes referred to as the 'four truths of Superiors'. According to the Madhyamika-Prasangika school, there are two types of four noble truths: gross and subtle. This is because there are two types of self-grasping of persons, gross self-grasping of persons – grasping at a self-supporting, substantially existent person, and subtle self-grasping of persons – grasping at an inherently existent person. See also *Sixteen characteristics of the four noble truths*. See *How to Solve Our Human Problems, Joyful Path of Good Fortune* and *Ocean of Nectar*.

*Four ways of gathering disciples*   The four ways of gathering disciples practised by Bodhisattvas are: (1) pleasing others by giving them material things or whatever they need; (2) teaching Dharma to lead others to liberation; (3) helping others in their Dharma practice by giving them encouragement; and (4) showing others a good example by always practising what we teach. See *Joyful Path of Good Fortune*.

*Functioning thing*   A phenomenon that is produced and disintegrates within a moment. Synonymous with impermanent phenomenon, thing and product.

*God*   'Deva' in Sanskrit. A being of the god realm, the highest of the six realms of samsara. There are many different types of god. Some are desire realm gods, while others are form or formless realm gods. See *Joyful Path of Good Fortune*.

*Ground/Spiritual ground*   A clear realization that acts as the foundation of many good qualities. A clear realization is a realization held by spontaneous renunciation or bodhichitta. The ten grounds are the realizations of Superior Bodhisattvas: Very Joyful, Stainless, Luminous, Radiant, Difficult to Overcome, Approaching, Gone Afar, Immovable, Good Intelligence and Cloud of Dharma. See *Ocean of Nectar* and *Tantric Grounds and Paths*.

*Guide to the Middle Way*   A classic Mahayana Buddhist text composed by the great Indian Buddhist Yogi and scholar Chandrakirti, which provides a comprehensive explanation of the Madhyamika-Prasangika view of emptiness as taught in the *Perfection of Wisdom Sutras*. For a translation and full commentary, see *Ocean of Nectar*.

*Happiness*   There are two types of happiness: mundane and supramundane. Mundane happiness is the limited happiness that can be found within samsara, such as the happiness of human beings and gods. Supramundane happiness is the pure happiness of liberation and enlightenment.

*Hearer*   One of two types of Hinayana practitioner. Both Hearers and Solitary Conquerors are Hinayanists, but they differ in their motivation, behaviour, merit and wisdom. In all these respects, Solitary Conquerors are superior to Hearers.

Hearers are of eight types according to the level of delusions they have abandoned: (1) approachers to the accomplishment of a Stream Enterer, (2) abiders in the accomplishment of a Stream Enterer, (3) approachers to the accomplishment of a Once Returner, (4) abiders in the accomplishment of a Once Returner, (5) approachers to the accomplishment of a Never Returner, (6) abiders in the accomplishment of a Never Returner, (7) approachers to the accomplishment of a Foe Destroyer, and (8) abiders in the accomplishment of a Foe Destroyer. A Stream Enterer is on the path of seeing and will never again be reborn in the three lower realms; a Once Returner will return to the desire realm only once more; and a Never Returner will never again return to the desire realm. See *Ocean of Nectar*.

**Highest Yoga Tantra** The supreme quick path to enlightenment. The teachings on Highest Yoga Tantra are Buddha's ultimate intention. See also *Tantra*. See *Mahamudra Tantra* and *Tantric Grounds and Paths*.

**Hinayana** Sanskrit term for 'Lesser Vehicle'. The Hinayana goal is to attain merely one's own liberation from suffering by completely abandoning delusions. See *Joyful Path of Good Fortune*.

**Hungry spirit** A being of the hungry spirit realm, the second lowest of the six realms of samsara. Also known as 'hungry ghost'. See *Joyful Path of Good Fortune*.

**Ignorance** A mental factor that is confused about the ultimate nature of phenomena. See *How to Understand the Mind*.

**Impermanent phenomenon** Phenomena are either permanent or impermanent. 'Impermanent' means 'momentary'; thus an impermanent phenomenon is a phenomenon that is produced and disintegrates within a moment. Synonyms of impermanent phenomenon are functioning thing, thing and product. There are two types of impermanence: gross and subtle. Gross impermanence is any impermanence that can be seen by an ordinary sense awareness – for example the ageing and death of a sentient being. Subtle impermanence is the momentary disintegration of a functioning thing. See *The New Heart of Wisdom*.

*Imprint* There are two types of imprint: imprints of actions and imprints of delusions. Every action we perform leaves an imprint on the mental consciousness, and these imprints are karmic potentialities to experience certain effects in the future. The imprints left by delusions remain even after the delusions themselves have been abandoned, rather as the smell of garlic lingers in a container after the garlic has been removed. Imprints of delusions are obstructions to omniscience, and are completely abandoned only by Buddhas.

*Imputation, mere* According to the highest school of Buddhist philosophy, the Madhyamika-Prasangika school, all phenomena are merely imputed by conception in dependence upon their basis of imputation. Therefore, they are mere imputations and do not exist from their own side in the least. See *Modern Buddhism*, *The New Heart of Wisdom* and *Ocean of Nectar*.

*Imputed object* An object imputed by the mind in dependence upon its basis of imputation. See *The New Heart of Wisdom* and *Ocean of Nectar*.

*Innate delusions* Delusions that are not the product of intellectual speculation, but that arise naturally. See *How to Understand the Mind*.

*Intellectually-formed delusions* Delusions that arise as a result of relying upon incorrect reasoning or mistaken tenets. See *How to Understand the Mind*.

*Intention* A mental factor that functions to move its primary mind to the object. It functions to engage the mind in virtuous, non-virtuous and neutral objects. All bodily and verbal actions are initiated by the mental factor intention. See *How to Understand the Mind*.

*Intermediate state* 'Bardo' in Tibetan. The state between death and rebirth. It begins the moment the consciousness leaves the body, and ceases the moment the consciousness enters the body of the next life. See *Clear Light of Bliss*, *Joyful Path of Good Fortune* and *Living Meaningfully, Dying Joyfully*.

*Je Tsongkhapa* (AD 1357-1419) An emanation of the Wisdom Buddha Manjushri, whose appearance in fourteenth-century

Tibet as a monk, and the holder of the lineage of pure view and pure deeds, was prophesied by Buddha. He spread a very pure Buddhadharma throughout Tibet, showing how to combine the practices of Sutra and Tantra, and how to practise pure Dharma during degenerate times. His tradition later became known as the 'Gelug', or 'Ganden Tradition'. See *Heart Jewel*, *Great Treasury of Merit* and *The Mirror of Dharma*.

***Kadampa*** A Tibetan term in which 'Ka' means 'word' and refers to all Buddha's teachings, 'dam' refers to Atisha's special Lamrim instructions known as the 'stages of the path to enlightenment', and 'pa' refers to a follower of Kadampa Buddhism who integrates all the teachings of Buddha that they know into their Lamrim practice. See also *Kadampa Buddhism*, *Kadampa Tradition* and *New Kadampa Tradition*. See *Modern Buddhism*.

***Kadampa Buddhism*** A Mahayana Buddhist school founded by the great Indian Buddhist Master Atisha (AD 982-1054). See also *Kadampa*, *Kadampa Tradition* and *New Kadampa Tradition*.

***Kadampa Tradition*** The pure tradition of Buddhism established by Atisha. Followers of this tradition up to the time of Je Tsongkhapa are known as 'Old Kadampas', and those after the time of Je Tsongkhapa are known as 'New Kadampas'. See also *Kadampa*, *Kadampa Buddhism* and *New Kadampa Tradition*.

***Karma*** Sanskrit term meaning 'action'. Through the force of intention, we perform actions with our body, speech and mind, and all of these actions produce effects. The effect of virtuous actions is happiness and the effect of negative actions is suffering. See *Joyful Path of Good Fortune* and *Modern Buddhism*.

***Liberation*** Complete freedom from samsara and its cause, the delusions. See *Joyful Path of Good Fortune*.

***Lord of Death*** Although the mara, or demon, of uncontrolled death is not a sentient being, it is personified as the Lord of Death, or 'Yama'. The Lord of Death is depicted in the diagram of the Wheel of Life clutching the wheel between his claws and teeth. See *Joyful Path of Good Fortune*.

***Love*** A mind wishing others to be happy. There are three types: affectionate love, cherishing love and wishing love. See *Joyful Path of Good Fortune* and *The New Eight Steps to Happiness*.

***Lower realms*** The hell realm, hungry spirit realm and animal realm. See also *Samsara*.

***Madhyamika*** A Sanskrit term, literally meaning 'Middle Way'. The higher of the two schools of Mahayana tenets. The Madhyamika view was taught by Buddha in the *Perfection of Wisdom Sutras* during the second turning of the Wheel of Dharma and was subsequently elucidated by Nagarjuna and his followers. There are two divisions of this school, Madhyamika-Svatantrika and Madhyamika-Prasangika, of which the latter is Buddha's final view. See *Ocean of Nectar*.

***Mahayana*** Sanskrit term for 'Great Vehicle', the spiritual path to great enlightenment. The Mahayana goal is to attain Buddhahood for the benefit of all sentient beings by completely abandoning delusions and their imprints. See *Joyful Path of Good Fortune*.

***Mala*** A rosary used to count recitations of prayers or mantras, usually with one hundred and eight beads. See *The New Guide to Dakini Land*.

***Mandala offering*** An offering of the entire universe visualized as a Pure Land, with all its inhabitants as pure beings. See *The New Guide to Dakini Land* and *Great Treasury of Merit*.

***Manjushri*** The embodiment of the wisdom of all the Buddhas. At the time of Buddha Shakyamuni he manifested as a Bodhisattva disciple. See *Great Treasury of Merit* and *Heart Jewel*.

***Mara*** Sanskrit term for 'demon', which refers to anything that obstructs the attainment of liberation or enlightenment. There are four principal types of mara: the mara of the delusions, the mara of contaminated aggregates, the mara of uncontrolled death and the Devaputra Maras. Of these, only the last are actual sentient beings. The principal Devaputra Mara is wrathful Ishvara, the highest of the desire realm gods, who inhabits Land of Controlling Emanations. A Buddha is called a 'Conqueror' because he or she has conquered all four types of mara. See *The New Heart of Wisdom*.

***Marpa*** (AD 1012-1096) Marpa Lotsawa, or Marpa the Translator, was a great lay Tantric Yogi and the Spiritual Guide of Milarepa. See *Joyful Path of Good Fortune*.

***Meditation*** Meditation is a mind that concentrates on a virtuous object, and is a mental action that is the main cause of mental peace. There are two types of meditation – analytical meditation and placement meditation. When we use our imagination, mindfulness and powers of reasoning to find our object of meditation, this is analytical meditation. When we find our object and hold it single-pointedly, this is placement meditation. There are different types of object. Some, such as impermanence or emptiness, are objects apprehended by the mind. Others, such as love, compassion and renunciation, are actual states of mind. We engage in analytical meditation until the specific object that we seek appears clearly to our mind or until the particular state of mind that we wish to generate arises. This object or state of mind is our object of placement meditation. See *The New Meditation Handbook*.

***Mental continuum*** The continuum of a person's mind that has no beginning and no end.

***Mental excitement*** A deluded mental factor that wanders to any object of attachment. See *How to Understand the Mind*.

***Mental factor*** A cognizer that principally apprehends a particular attribute of an object. There are fifty-one specific mental factors. Each moment of mind comprises a primary mind and various mental factors. See *How to Understand the Mind*.

***Mental sinking*** A mental factor that destroys the clarity of concentration and its firm hold upon the object. See *Joyful Path of Good Fortune*.

***Merit*** The good fortune created by virtuous actions. It is the potential power to increase our good qualities and produce happiness.

***Method practice*** Any spiritual path that functions to ripen our Buddha lineage. Training in renunciation, compassion and bodhichitta are examples of method practices.

***Milarepa*** (AD 1040-1123) A great Tibetan Buddhist meditator and disciple of Marpa, celebrated for his beautiful songs of realization.

***Mind*** That which is clarity and cognizes. Mind is clarity because it always lacks form and because it possesses the actual power to perceive objects. Mind cognizes because its function is to know or perceive objects. See *How to Understand the Mind*, *Mahamudra Tantra* and *Clear Light of Bliss*.

*Miserliness* A deluded mental factor that, motivated by desirous attachment, holds on to things tightly and does not want to part with them. See *How to Understand the Mind*.

*Mistaken awareness/mind* A mind that is mistaken with respect to its appearing object. Although all minds of ordinary beings are mistaken, they are not necessarily wrong. A wrong mind is a mind that is mistaken with respect to its engaged object. Thus our eye awareness perceiving this page is a mistaken mind because the page appears as inherently existent, but it is a correct mind because it correctly apprehends the page as a page. See *How to Understand the Mind*.

*Mount Meru* According to Buddhist cosmology, a divine mountain that stands at the centre of the universe.

*Nagarjuna* A great Indian Buddhist scholar and meditation master who revived the Mahayana in the first century AD by bringing to light the teachings on the *Perfection of Wisdom Sutras*. Nagarjuna's extraordinary life and works were prophesied by Buddha Shakyamuni. See *Ocean of Nectar*.

*Nalanda Monastery* A great seat of Buddhist learning and practice in ancient India.

*Naropa* (AD 1016-1100) An Indian Mahasiddha and a lineage Guru in the Highest Yoga Tantra practice of Vajrayogini. See *The New Guide to Dakini Land*.

*Nature Body* The ultimate nature of a Buddha's mind. Also known as 'Entity Body'. See also Truth Body. See *Joyful Path of Good Fortune*, *Tantric Grounds and Paths* and *Ocean of Nectar*.

*Never Returner* See *Hearer*.

*New Kadampa Tradition-International Kadampa Buddhist Union (NKT-IKBU)* The union of Kadampa Buddhist centres, an international association of study and meditation centres that follow the pure tradition of Mahayana Buddhism derived from the Buddhist meditators and scholars Atisha and Je Tsongkhapa, introduced into the West by the Buddhist Teacher Venerable Geshe Kelsang Gyatso. See also *Kadampa*.

***Nirvana*** Sanskrit term meaning 'state beyond sorrow'. Complete freedom from samsara and its cause, the delusions. See *Joyful Path of Good Fortune*.

***Non-virtue*** A phenomenon that functions as a main cause of suffering. It can refer to non-virtuous minds, non-virtuous actions, non-virtuous imprints or the ultimate non-virtue of samsara. See *How to Understand the Mind*.

***Non-virtuous actions*** Paths that lead to the lower realms. Non-virtuous actions are countless, but most of them are included within the ten: killing, stealing, sexual misconduct, lying, divisive speech, hurtful speech, idle chatter, covetousness, malice and holding wrong views. See *Joyful Path of Good Fortune*.

***Object of negation*** An object explicitly negated by a mind realizing a negative phenomenon. In meditation on emptiness, or lack of inherent existence, it refers to inherent existence. Also known as 'negated object'.

***Obstructions to liberation*** Obstructions that prevent the attainment of liberation. All delusions, such as ignorance, attachment and anger, together with their seeds, are obstructions to liberation. Also called 'delusion-obstructions'.

***Obstructions to omniscience*** The imprints of delusions, which prevent simultaneous and direct realization of all phenomena. Only Buddhas have overcome these obstructions.

***Once Returner*** See *Hearer*.

***Parinirvana*** Sanskrit term literally meaning 'passing away to a state-beyond-sorrow'. It refers to a Buddha's Emanation Body appearing to die and pass beyond this world.

***Perfection of Wisdom Sutras*** Sutras of the second Turning of the Wheel of Dharma in which Buddha revealed his final view of the ultimate nature of all phenomena – lack of inherent existence. See *The New Heart of Wisdom*.

***Permanent phenomenon*** Phenomena are either permanent or impermanent. A permanent phenomenon is a phenomenon that does not depend upon causes and that does not disintegrate moment by moment. It lacks the characteristics of production, abiding and disintegration.

***Person*** An I imputed in dependence upon any of the five aggregates. Person, being, self and I are synonyms. See *How to Understand the Mind*.

***Prasangika*** See *Madhyamika*.

***Preceptor*** A Spiritual Guide who give us vows or commitments to observe.

***Pride*** A deluded mental factor that, through considering and exaggerating one's own good qualities or possessions, feels arrogant. See *How to Understand the Mind*.

***Pure Land*** A pure environment in which there are no true sufferings. There are many Pure Lands. For example, Tushita is the Pure Land of Buddha Maitreya, Sukhavati is the Pure Land of Buddha Amitabha, and Dakini Land, or Keajra, is the Pure Land of Buddha Vajrayogini and Buddha Heruka. See *Living Meaningfully, Dying Joyfully*.

***Renunciation*** The wish to be released from samsara. See *Joyful Path of Good Fortune*.

***Retreat*** A period of time during which we impose various restrictions on our actions of body, speech, and mind so as to be able to concentrate more fully on a particular spiritual practice. See also *Close retreat*. See *The New Guide to Dakini Land* and *Heart Jewel*.

***Root Guru*** The principal Spiritual Guide from whom we have received the empowerments, instructions and oral transmissions of our main practice. See *Great Treasury of Merit, Joyful Path of Good Fortune* and *Heart Jewel*.

***Samsara*** There are six realms of samsara. Listed in ascending order according to the type of karma that causes rebirth in them, they are the realms of the hell beings, hungry spirits, animals, human beings, demi-gods and gods. The first three are lower realms or unhappy migrations, and the second three are higher realms or happy migrations. Although from the point of view of the karma that causes rebirth there, the god realm is the highest realm in samsara, the human realm is said to be the most fortunate realm because it provides the best conditions for attaining liberation and enlightenment. See *Joyful Path of Good Fortune* and *Modern Buddhism*.

***Sangha*** According to the Vinaya tradition, any community of four or more fully-ordained monks. In general, ordained or lay people who take Bodhisattva vows or Tantric vows can also be said to be Sangha.

***Seed-letter*** The sacred letter from which a Deity is generated. Each Deity has a particular seed-letter. For example, the seed-letter of Manjushri is DHI, of Tara is TAM, of Vajrayogini is BAM and of Heruka is HUM. To accomplish Tantric realizations, we need to recognize that Deities and their seed-letters are the same nature.

***Sense power*** An inner power located in the very centre of a sense organ that functions directly to produce a sense awareness. There are five sense powers, one for each type of sense awareness – the eye awareness and so forth. They are sometimes known as 'sense powers possessing form'. See *How to Understand the Mind*.

***Sentient being*** Any being who possesses a mind that is contaminated by delusions or their imprints. Both 'sentient being' and 'living being' are terms used to distinguish beings whose minds are contaminated by either of these two obstructions from Buddhas, whose minds are completely free from these obstructions.

***Seven limbs*** Special practices for purifying negativity and accumulating merit. They are prostration, offering, confession, rejoicing, beseeching the holy beings not to pass away, requesting the turning of the Wheel of Dharma and dedication. They are called 'limbs' because they provide support for the main body of our practice, which is the actual meditations on the paths of Sutra and Tantra. See *Joyful Path of Good Fortune* and *Great Treasury of Merit*.

***Shariputra*** One of Buddha Shakyamuni's principal disciples. He has the aspect of a Hinayana Foe Destroyer. See *The New Heart of Wisdom*.

*Sixteen characteristics of the four noble truths* Buddha taught that each of the four noble truths has four special characteristics. The four characteristics of true sufferings are: impermanent, suffering, empty and selfless. The four characteristics of true origins are: cause, origin, strong producer and condition. The four characteristics of true cessations are: cessation, peace, supreme attainment and definite abandoner. The four characteristics of true paths are: path, antidote, accomplisher and definite abandoning. See *Ocean of Nectar*.

*Solitary Conqueror* One of two types of Hinayana practitioner. Also known as 'Solitary Realizer'. Both Hearers and Solitary Conquerors are Hinayanists, but they differ in their motivation, behaviour, merit and wisdom. In all these respects, Solitary Conquerors are superior to Hearers. See *Ocean of Nectar*.

*Spiritual Guide* 'Guru' in Sanskrit, 'Lama' in Tibetan. A Teacher who guides us along the spiritual path. See *Joyful Path of Good Fortune* and *Great Treasury of Merit*.

*Stream Enterer* See *Hearer*.

*Substantial cause* Main cause.

*Sugata* Another Sanskrit term for a Buddha. It indicates that Buddhas have attained a state of immaculate and indestructible bliss.

*Sukhavati* Sanskrit term for 'Pure Land of Bliss' or 'Blissful Land' – the Pure Land of Buddha Amitabha.

*Superior being* 'Arya' in Sanskrit. A being who has a direct realization of emptiness. There are Hinayana Superiors and Mahayana Superiors.

*Superior seeing* A special wisdom that sees its object clearly, and that is maintained by tranquil abiding and the special suppleness that is induced by investigation. See *Joyful Path of Good Fortune*.

*Suppleness* There are two types of suppleness, mental and physical. Mental suppleness is a flexibility of mind induced by virtuous concentration. Physical suppleness is a light and flexible tactile object within our body that develops when meditation causes a pure wind to pervade the body.

***Sutra*** The teachings of Buddha that are open to everyone to practise without the need for empowerment. These include Buddha's teachings of the three turnings of the Wheel of Dharma.

***Svatantrika*** See *Madhyamika*.

***Tantra*** Synonymous with Secret Mantra. Tantric teachings are distinguished from Sutra teachings in that they reveal methods for training the mind by bringing the future result, or Buddhahood, into the present path. Tantric practitioners overcome ordinary appearances and conceptions by visualizing their body, environment, enjoyments and deeds as those of a Buddha. Tantra is the supreme path to full enlightenment. Tantric practices are to be done in private and only by those who have received a Tantric empowerment. See *Tantric Grounds and Paths* and *Mahamudra Tantra*.

***Tathagata*** The Sanskrit for 'A Being Gone Beyond', which is another term for Buddha.

***Ten directions*** The four cardinal directions, the four intermediate directions, and the directions above and below.

***Three higher trainings*** Training in moral discipline, concentration, and wisdom motivated by renunciation or bodhichitta.

***Three Jewels*** The three objects of refuge: Buddha Jewel, Dharma Jewel and Sangha Jewel. They are called 'Jewels' because they are both rare and precious. See *Joyful Path of Good Fortune*.

***True cessation*** The ultimate nature of a mind freed from any obstruction by means of a true path. See *Joyful Path of Good Fortune* and *The New Heart of Wisdom*.

***True origin*** An action or a delusion that is the main cause of a true suffering. See *Joyful Path of Good Fortune* and *The New Heart of Wisdom*.

***True path*** A spiritual path held by a wisdom directly realizing emptiness. See *Joyful Path of Good Fortune* and *The New Heart of Wisdom*.

***True suffering*** A contaminated object produced by delusions and karma. See *Joyful Path of Good Fortune* and *The New Heart of Wisdom*.

***Truth Body*** See *Buddha's bodies*.

***Ultimate nature*** All phenomena have two natures: a conventional nature and an ultimate nature. In the case of a table, for example, the table itself, its shape, colour and so forth are all the conventional nature of the table. The ultimate nature of the table is the table's lack of inherent existence. See *Modern Buddhism*, *The New Heart of Wisdom* and *Ocean of Nectar*.

***Vajra*** Generally the Sanskrit word 'vajra' means indestructible like a diamond and powerful like a thunderbolt. In the context of Secret Mantra it means the indivisibility of method and wisdom.

***Vajradhara Trijang Rinpoche*** (AD 1901-1981) A special Tibetan Lama of the twentieth century who was an emanation of Buddha Shakyamuni, Heruka, Atisha, Amitabha and Je Tsongkhapa. Also known as 'Kyabje Trijang Rinpoche', 'Trijang Dorjechang' and 'Losang Yeshe'.

***Vajrapani*** The embodiment of the power of all the Buddhas. He appears in a wrathful aspect displaying his power to overcome outer, inner and secret obstacles. At the time of Buddha Shakyamuni he manifested as a Bodhisattva disciple.

***Vajrayogini*** A female Highest Yoga Tantra Deity who is the embodiment of indivisible bliss and emptiness. She is the same nature as Heruka. See *The New Guide to Dakini Land*.

***Valid cognizer*** A cognizer that is non-deceptive with respect to its engaged object. There are two types: inferential valid cognizers and direct valid cognizers. See *The New Heart of Wisdom* and *How to Understand the Mind*.

***Virtue*** A phenomenon that functions as a main cause of happiness. It can refer to virtuous minds, virtuous actions, virtuous imprints or the ultimate virtue of nirvana. See *How to Understand the Mind*.

***Vow*** A virtuous determination to abandon particular faults that is generated in conjunction with a traditional ritual. The three sets of vows are the Pratimoksha vows of individual liberation, the Bodhisattva vows and the Secret Mantra or Tantric vows. See *The Bodhisattva Vow* and *Tantric Grounds and Paths*.

***Wheel of Dharma*** A collection of Buddha's teachings. Buddha gave his teachings in three main phases, which are known as 'the three turnings of the Wheel of Dharma'. During the first Wheel he taught the four noble truths, during the second he taught the *Perfection of Wisdom Sutras* and revealed the Madhyamika-Prasangika view, and during the third he taught the Chittamatra view. These teachings were given according to the inclinations and dispositions of his disciples. Buddha's final view is that of the second Wheel. Dharma is compared to the precious wheel, one of the possessions of a legendary chakravatin king. This wheel could transport the king across great distances in a very short time, and it is said that wherever the precious wheel travelled the king reigned. In a similar way, when Buddha revealed the path to enlightenment he was said to have 'turned the Wheel of Dharma' because, wherever these teachings are present, deluded minds are brought under control.

***Wrong awareness*** A cognizer that is mistaken with respect to its engaged, or apprehended, object. See *How to Understand the Mind*.

***Yogi/Yogini*** Sanskrit terms usually referring to a male or a female meditator who has attained the union of tranquil abiding and superior seeing.

# *Bibliography*

Venerable Geshe Kelsang Gyatso Rinpoche is a highly respected meditation master and scholar of the Mahayana Buddhist tradition founded by Je Tsongkhapa. Since arriving in the West in 1977, Venerable Geshe Kelsang has worked tirelessly to establish pure Buddhadharma throughout the world. Over this period he has given extensive teachings on the major scriptures of the Mahayana. These teachings provide a comprehensive presentation of the essential Sutra and Tantra practices of Mahayana Buddhism.

### Books

The following books by Venerable Geshe Kelsang Gyatso Rinpoche are all published by Tharpa Publications.

*The Bodhisattva Vow* A practical guide to helping others. (2nd. edn., 1995)

*Clear Light of Bliss* A Tantric meditation manual. (3rd. edn., 2014)

*Essence of Vajrayana* The Highest Yoga Tantra practice of Heruka body mandala. (2nd. edn., 2017)

*Great Treasury of Merit* How to rely upon a Spiritual Guide. (2nd. edn., 2015)

*Guide to the Bodhisattva's Way of Life* How to enjoy a life of great meaning and altruism. (A translation of Shantideva's famous verse masterpiece.) (2002)

*Heart Jewel* The essential practices of Kadampa Buddhism. (2nd. edn., 1997)

*How to Solve Our Human Problems* The four noble truths. (2005)

*How to Transform Your Life* A blissful journey. (3rd edn., 2016)

*How to Understand the Mind* The nature and power of the mind. (4th. edn., 2014)

*Introduction to Buddhism* An explanation of the Buddhist way of life. (2nd. edn., 2001)

*Joyful Path of Good Fortune* The path to the supreme happiness of enlightenment. (4th. edn., 2018)

*Living Meaningfully, Dying Joyfully* The profound practice of transference of consciousness. (1999)

*Mahamudra Tantra* The supreme Heart Jewel nectar. (2005)

*Meaningful to Behold* Becoming a friend of the world. (6th. edn., 2016)

*The Mirror of Dharma with Additions* How to find the real meaning of human life (2nd. edn., 2019)

*Modern Buddhism* The path of compassion and wisdom. (2nd. edn., 2013)

*The New Eight Steps to Happiness* The Buddhist way of loving kindness. (3rd. edn., 2016)

*The New Guide to Dakini Land* The Highest Yoga Tantra practice of Buddha Vajrayogini. (3rd. edn., 2012)

*The New Heart of Wisdom* Profound teachings from Buddha's heart (An explanation of the *Heart Sutra*). (5th. edn., 2012)

*The New Meditation Handbook* Meditations to make our life happy and meaningful. (5th. edn., 2013)

*Ocean of Nectar* The true nature of all things. (2nd. edn., 2017)

*The Oral Instruction of Mahamudra* The very essence of Buddha's teachings of Sutra and Tantra. (2nd. edn., 2016)

*Tantric Grounds and Paths* How to enter, progress on, and complete the Vajrayana path. (2nd edn., 2016)

*Universal Compassion* Inspiring solutions for difficult times. (4th. edn., 2002)

## Sadhanas and Other Booklets

Venerable Geshe Kelsang Gyatso Rinpoche has also supervised the translation of a collection of essential sadhanas, or ritual prayers for spiritual attainments, available in booklet or audio formats.

*Avalokiteshvara Sadhana* Prayers and requests to the Buddha of Compassion.

*The Blissful Path* The condensed self-generation sadhana of Vajrayogini.

*The Bodhisattva's Confession of Moral Downfalls* The purification practice of the *Mahayana Sutra of the Three Superior Heaps*.

*Condensed Long Life Practice of Buddha Amitayus*.

*Dakini Yoga* The middling self-generation sadhana of Vajrayogini.

*Drop of Essential Nectar* A special fasting and purification practice in conjunction with Eleven-faced Avalokiteshvara.

*Essence of Good Fortune* Prayers for the six preparatory practices for meditation on the stages of the path to enlightenment.

*Essence of Vajrayana* Heruka body mandala self-generation sadhana according to the system of Mahasiddha Ghantapa.

*Feast of Great Bliss* Vajrayogini self-initiation sadhana.

*Great Liberation of the Father* Preliminary prayers for Mahamudra meditation in conjunction with Heruka practice.

*Great Liberation of the Mother* Preliminary prayers for Mahamudra meditation in conjunction with Vajrayogini practice.

*The Great Mother* A method to overcome hindrances and obstacles by reciting the *Essence of Wisdom Sutra* (the *Heart Sutra*).

*A Handbook for the Daily Practice of Bodhisattva and Tantric Vows*.

*Heart Jewel* The Guru yoga of Je Tsongkhapa combined with the condensed sadhana of his Dharma Protector.

*Heartfelt Prayers* Funeral service for cremations and burials.

*The Hundreds of Deities of the Joyful Land According to Highest Yoga Tantra* The Guru Yoga of Je Tsongkhapa as a Preliminary Practice for Mahamudra.

*The Kadampa Way of Life* The essential practice of Kadam Lamrim.

*Keajra Heaven* The essential commentary to the practice of *The Uncommon Yoga of Inconceivability*.

*Lay Pratimoksha Vow Ceremony*.

*Liberating Prayer* Praise to Buddha Shakyamuni.

*Liberation from Sorrow* Praises and requests to the Twenty-one Taras.

*Mahayana Refuge Ceremony and Bodhisattva Vow Ceremony*.

*Medicine Buddha Prayer* A method for benefiting others.

*Medicine Buddha Sadhana* A method for accomplishing the attainments of Medicine Buddha.

*Meditation and Recitation of Solitary Vajrasattva*.

*Melodious Drum Victorious in all Directions* The extensive fulfilling and restoring ritual of the Dharma Protector, the great king Dorje Shugden, in conjunction with Mahakala, Kalarupa, Kalindewi and other Dharma Protectors.

*The New Essence of Vajrayana* Heruka body mandala self-generation practice, an instruction of the Ganden Oral Lineage.

*Offering to the Spiritual Guide* (*Lama Chopa*) A special way of relying upon a Spiritual Guide.

*Path of Compassion for the Deceased* Powa sadhana for the benefit of the deceased.

*Pathway to the Pure Land* Training in powa – the transference of consciousness.

*Powa Ceremony* Transference of consciousness for the deceased.

*Prayers for Meditation* Brief preparatory prayers for meditation.

*Prayers for World Peace*.

*A Pure Life* The practice of taking and keeping the eight Mahayana precepts.

*Quick Path to Great Bliss* The extensive self-generation sadhana of Vajrayogini.

*Request to the Holy Spiritual Guide Venerable Geshe Kelsang Gyatso from his Faithful Disciples*.

*The Root Tantra of Heruka and Vajrayogini* Chapters One & Fifty-one of the *Condensed Heruka Root Tantra*.

*The Root Text: Eight Verses of Training the Mind*.

*Treasury of Wisdom* The sadhana of Venerable Manjushri.

*The Uncommon Yoga of Inconceivability* The special instruction of how to reach the Pure Land of Keajra with this human body.

*Union of No More Learning* Heruka body mandala self-initiation sadhana.

*The Vows and Commitments of Kadampa Buddhism*.

*Wishfulfilling Jewel* The Guru yoga of Je Tsongkhapa combined with the sadhana of his Dharma Protector.

*The Yoga of Buddha Amitayus* A special method for increasing lifespan, wisdom and merit.

*The Yoga of Buddha Heruka* The essential self-generation sadhana of Heruka body mandala & Condensed six-session yoga.

*The Yoga of Buddha Maitreya* Self-generation sadhana.

*The Yoga of Buddha Vajrapani* Self-generation sadhana.

*The Yoga of Enlightened Mother Arya Tara* Self-generation sadhana.

*The Yoga of Great Mother Prajnaparamita* Self-generation sadhana.

*The Yoga of Thousand-armed Avalokiteshvara* Self-generation sadhana.

*The Yoga of White Tara, Buddha of Long Life.*

To order any of our publications, or to request a catalogue, please visit www.tharpa.com or contact your nearest Tharpa office listed on pages 577-578.

NKT-IKBU

# *Study Programmes of Kadampa Buddhism*

Kadampa Buddhism is a Mahayana Buddhist school founded by the great Indian Buddhist Master Atisha (AD 982-1054). His followers are known as 'Kadampas'. 'Ka' means 'word' and refers to Buddha's teachings, and 'dam' refers to Atisha's special Lamrim instructions known as 'the stages of the path to enlightenment'. By integrating their knowledge of all Buddha's teachings into their practice of Lamrim, and by integrating this into their everyday lives, Kadampa Buddhists are encouraged to use Buddha's teachings as practical methods for transforming daily activities into the path to enlightenment. The great Kadampa Teachers are famous not only for being great scholars but also for being spiritual practitioners of immense purity and sincerity.

The lineage of these teachings, both their oral transmission and blessings, was then passed from Teacher to disciple, spreading throughout much of Asia, and now to many countries throughout the world. Buddha's teachings, which are known as 'Dharma', are likened to a wheel that moves from country to country in accordance with changing conditions and people's karmic inclinations. The external forms of presenting Buddhism may change as it meets with different cultures and societies, but its essential authenticity is ensured through the continuation of an unbroken lineage of realized practitioners.

Kadampa Buddhism was first introduced to the modern world in 1977 by the renowned Buddhist Master, Venerable Geshe Kelsang Gyatso Rinpoche. Since that time, he has worked tirelessly to spread Kadampa Buddhism throughout the world by giving extensive teachings, writing many profound texts on Kadampa Buddhism, and founding the New Kadampa Tradition – International Kadampa Buddhist Union (NKT-IKBU), which now has over 1200 Kadampa Buddhist Centres and groups worldwide. Each Centre offers study programmes on Buddhist psychology, philosophy and meditation instruction, as well as retreats for all levels of practitioner. The emphasis is on integrating Buddha's teachings into daily life to solve our human problems and to spread lasting peace and happiness throughout the world.

The Kadampa Buddhism of the NKT-IKBU is an entirely independent Buddhist tradition and has no political affiliations. It is an association of Buddhist Centres and practitioners that derive their inspiration and guidance from the example of the ancient Kadampa Buddhist Masters and their teachings, as presented by Venerable Geshe Kelsang.

There are three reasons why we need to study and practise the teachings of Buddha: to develop our wisdom, to cultivate a good heart, and to maintain a peaceful state of mind. If we do not strive to develop our wisdom, we will always remain ignorant of ultimate truth – the true nature of reality. Although we wish for happiness, our ignorance leads us to engage in non-virtuous actions, which are the main cause of all our suffering. If we do not cultivate a good heart, our selfish motivation destroys harmony and good relationships with others. We have no peace, and no chance to gain pure happiness. Without inner peace, outer peace is impossible. If we do not maintain a peaceful state of mind, we are not happy even if we have ideal conditions. On the other hand, when our mind is peaceful, we are happy, even if our external conditions are unpleasant. Therefore, the development of these qualities is of utmost importance for our daily happiness.

Venerable Geshe Kelsang, or 'Geshe-la' as he is affectionately called by his students, has designed three special spiritual programmes for the systematic study and practice of Kadampa Buddhism that are especially suited to the modern world – the General Programme (GP), the Foundation Programme (FP), and the Teacher Training Programme (TTP).

## GENERAL PROGRAMME

The General Programme provides a basic introduction to Buddhist view, meditation and practice that is suitable for beginners. It also includes advanced teachings and practice from both Sutra and Tantra.

## FOUNDATION PROGRAMME

The Foundation Programme provides an opportunity to deepen our understanding and experience of Buddhism through a systematic study of six texts:

1 *Joyful Path of Good Fortune* – a commentary to Atisha's Lamrim instructions, the stages of the path to enlightenment.
2 *Universal Compassion* – a commentary to Bodhisattva Chekhawa's *Training the Mind in Seven Points*.
3 *The New Eight Steps to Happiness* – a commentary to Bodhisattva Langri Tangpa's *Eight Verses of Training the Mind*.
4 *The New Heart of Wisdom* – a commentary to the *Heart Sutra*.
5 *Meaningful to Behold* – a commentary to Bodhisattva Shantideva's *Guide to the Bodhisattva's Way of Life*.
6 *How to Understand the Mind* – a detailed explanation of the mind, based on the works of the Buddhist scholars Dharmakirti and Dignaga.

The benefits of studying and practising these texts are as follows:

(1) *Joyful Path of Good Fortune* – we gain the ability to put all Buddha's teachings of both Sutra and Tantra into practice. We can easily make progress on, and complete, the stages of

the path to the supreme happiness of enlightenment. From a practical point of view, Lamrim is the main body of Buddha's teachings, and the other teachings are like its limbs.

(2) and (3) *Universal Compassion* and *The New Eight Steps to Happiness* – we gain the ability to integrate Buddha's teachings into our daily life and solve all our human problems.

(4) *The New Heart of Wisdom* – we gain a realization of the ultimate nature of reality. By gaining this realization, we can eliminate the ignorance of self-grasping, which is the root of all our suffering.

(5) *Meaningful to Behold* – we transform our daily activities into the Bodhisattva's way of life, thereby making every moment of our human life meaningful.

(6) *How to Understand the Mind* – we understand the relationship between our mind and its external objects. If we understand that objects depend upon the subjective mind, we can change the way objects appear to us by changing our own mind. Gradually, we will gain the ability to control our mind and in this way solve all our problems.

## TEACHER TRAINING PROGRAMME

The Teacher Training Programme is designed for people who wish to train as authentic Dharma Teachers. In addition to completing the study of fourteen texts of Sutra and Tantra, which include the six texts mentioned above, the student is required to observe certain commitments with regard to behaviour and way of life, and to complete a number of meditation retreats.

A Special Teacher Training Programme is also held at Manjushri Kadampa Meditation Centre, Ulverston, England, and can be studied either by attending the classes at the centre or by correspondence. This special meditation and study programme consists of twelve courses based on the books of Venerable Geshe Kelsang Gyatso Rinpoche: *How to Understand the Mind; Modern Buddhism; The New Heart of Wisdom; Tantric*

*Grounds and Paths*; Shantideva's *Guide to the Bodhisattva's Way of Life* and its commentary, *Meaningful to Behold; Ocean of Nectar; The New Guide to Dakini Land; The Oral Instructions of Mahamudra; The New Eight Steps to Happiness; The Mirror of Dharma; Essence of Vajrayana*; and *Joyful Path of Good Fortune*.

All Kadampa Buddhist Centres are open to the public. Every year we celebrate Festivals in many countries throughout the world, including two in England, where people gather from around the world to receive special teachings and empowerments and to enjoy a spiritual holiday. Please feel free to visit us at any time!

For further information about NKT–IKBU study programmes or to find your nearest centre visit www.kadampa.org, or please contact:

NKT-IKBU Central Office
Conishead Priory, Ulverston,
Cumbria LA12 9QQ, UK
Tel: +44 (0) 01229-588533
Email: info@kadampa.org
Website: www.kadampa.org

*or*

US NKT-IKBU Office
KMC New York
47 Sweeney Road
Glen Spey, NY 12737, USA
Tel: +1 845-856-9000
*or* 877-523-2672 (toll-free)
Fax: +1 845-856-2110
Email: info@kadampanewyork.org
Website: www.kadampanewyork.org

# *Tharpa Offices Worldwide*

Tharpa books are currently published in English (UK and US), Chinese, French, German, Italian, Japanese, Portuguese and Spanish. Most languages are available from any Tharpa office listed below.

**Tharpa UK**
Conishead Priory,
ULVERSTON,
Cumbria,
LA12 9QQ, UK
Tel: +44 (0)1229-588599
Web: tharpa.com/uk
Email: info.uk@tharpa.com

**Tharpa US**
47 Sweeney Road,
GLEN SPEY,
NY 12737, USA
Tel: +1 845-856-5102
Toll-free: 888-741-3475
Fax: +1 845-856-2110
Web: tharpa.com/us
Email: info.us@tharpa.com

**Tharpa Asia**
1st Floor Causeway Tower,
16-22 Causeway Road,
Causeway Bay,
HONG KONG
Tel: +(852) 2507 2237
Web: tharpa.com/hk-en
Email: info.asia@tharpa.com

**Tharpa Australia**
25 McCarthy Road,
MONBULK, VIC 3793, AU
Tel: +61 (0)3 9756 7203
Web: tharpa.com/au
Email: info.au@tharpa.com

**Tharpa Brasil**
Rua Artur de Azevedo 1360
Pinheiros, 05404-003
SÃO PAULO, SP, BR
Tel: +55 (11) 3476-2328
Web: tharpa.com.br
Email: info.br@tharpa.com

**Tharpa Canada (English)**
631 Crawford St.,
TORONTO, ON, M6G 3K1, CA
Tel: (+1) 416-762-8710
Toll-free: 866-523-2672
Fax: (+1) 416-762-2267
Web: tharpa.com/ca
Email: info.ca@tharpa.com

**Tharpa Canada (Français)**
835 Laurier est Montréal H2J
  1G2, CA
Tel: (+1) 514-521-1313
Web: tharpa.com/ca-fr
Email: info.ca-fr@tharpa.com

**Tharpa Deutschland (Germany)**
Chausseestraße 108,
10115 BERLIN, DE
Tel: +49 (030) 430 55 666
Web: tharpa.com/de
Email: info.de@tharpa.com

**Tharpa España (Spain)**
Calle La Fábrica 8, 28221,
Majadahonda, MADRID, ES
Tel: +34 911 124 914
Web: tharpa.com/es
Email: info.es@tharpa.com

**Tharpa France**
Château de Segrais
72220 SAINT-MARS-D'OUTILLÉ, FR
Tél/Fax : +33 (0)2 43 87 71 02
Web: tharpa.com/fr
Email: info.fr@tharpa.com

**Tharpa Japan**
KMC TOKYO, JP
Web: kadampa.jp
Email: info@kadampa.jp

**Tharpa México**
Enrique Rébsamen Nº 406
Col. Narvate Poniente,
CUIDAD DE MÉXICO,
CDMX, C.P. 03020, MX
Tel: +52 (55) 56 39 61 80;
+52 (55) 56 39 61 86
Web: tharpa.com/mx
Email: info.mx@tharpa.com

**Tharpa New Zealand**
2 Stokes Road, Mount Eden,
AUCKLAND 1024, NZ
Tel: +64 (0)9 631 5400
DD Mobile: +64 21 583351
Web: tharpa.com/nz
Email: info.nz@tharpa.com

**Tharpa Portugal**
Rua Moinho do Gato, 5,
Várzea de Sintra,
SINTRA, 2710-661, PT
Tel: +351 219231064
Web: tharpa.pt
Email: info.pt@tharpa.com

**Tharpa Schweiz (Switzerland)**
Mirabellenstrasse 1
CH-8048 ZÜRICH, CH
Tel: +41 44 401 02 20
Fax: +41 44 461 36 88
Web: tharpa.com/ch
Email: info.ch@tharpa.com

**Tharpa South Africa**
26 Menston Road, Dawncliffe,
Westville, 3629, KZN,
REP. OF SOUTH AFRICA
Tel: +27 (0)31 266 0096
Web: tharpa.com/za
Email: info.za@tharpa.com

**Tharpa Sverige (Sweden)**
Bastugatan 41, 1 tr ned
118 25 STOCKHOLM, SE
Tel: +46 72 251 4090
Email: info.se@tharpa.com

# *Index*

*The letter 'g' indicates an entry in the glossary*

## A

Abhidharma Pitaka 10
absorption without
 discrimination 435, g
accumulating merit
 preparatory practices for
 112–131
accumulation of merit. *See*
 collection of merit
accumulation of wisdom. *See*
 collection of merit
actions. *See also* karma
actions and their effects/
 cause and effect 36, 84, 89,
 95, 158, 170, 252, 253, 258,
 299, 448–449, 489. *See also*
 karma
 factors for completion
 211–214
aggregates 405, 408–409,
 440–441, 451, g
Akashagarbha 99, 511
*Akashagarbha Sutra* 231
alertness 185–227, 291,
 308–311, 355–356
 guarding 185–227
Amitabha 299, g
Ananda 102

anger 56, 104, 112, 173, 176,
 192, 248–249, 254–266, 507
 faults 235–239
 necessity to abandon 252
 no independent cause
 249–251
animals 17, 27, 92, 255, 511
Arhat 102, 103, 114, 417, 434,
 435. *See also* Foe Destroyer
Aryadeva 410
Asanga 30, 47
Ashoka 65
aspiration 221, 354
 power of 295–299
Atisha 24, 30, 83, 221, 225,
 261, 342, 374, 410, g
attachment 104, 112, 171–172,
 176, 265–266, 269–271, 290,
 305, 457, 496
 opponents to 317–321
 to others' bodies 330–338
 to worldly life 317–318
Avalokiteshvara 62, 66, 69,
 99, 373, 511, g
Awakened One 44, 53

## B

basis of imputation *See*
 imputation, basis of

baskets, the three. *See* sets, the three
Bende Peltseg 520
Ben Gungyel 181–182, 309
Bodh Gaya 75
bodhichitta 5–8, 45, 133–142, 235, 504.
  aspiring 30, 45–48
  bases for generating 75
  benefits of 20–29, 46, 47–52
  engaging 30, 45–48, 135
  faults of abandoning 152–157
  how to develop 30–43
  prevent degenerating 145–181
Bodhisattva 3, 23, 45, 51, 56, 127, 132, 235, 429. *See also* Superior Bodhisattva
  grounds 119, 156
  paths 118–119
  praise of 52–57
*Bodhisattvacharyavatara*. See *Guide to the Bodhisattva's Way of Life*
Bodhisattva vows 7, 45, 134–136, 155, 157
  maintaining 157–182
body
  abandoning attachment to 216–218
  close placement of mindfulness 453–456
  impurity of 24–25, 331–336, 412–414
Buddha 9, 11–13, 18, 22, 23, 25, 62, 79, 97, 98, 115, 119, 139, 143, 274–275, 278, 293
  beseeching not to pass away 111–112, 120–121
  blessings of 21, 123
  bodies of 120–121, g
  four characteristics of 45, 80
  lack of conceptual mind 429–430
  offerings to 61–70
  requesting to turn the Wheel of Dharma 111–112, 119–120
Buddhadharma. *See* Dharma
Buddhahood 5, 9, 14, 45, 79, 83, 129, 267, 398, 452. *See also* enlightenment
Buddha Jewel 80, 82
Buddhapalita 410, 486
Buddha Shakyamuni 23, 30, 38, 47, 49, 56, 73, 75, 96, 127, 148, 158, 175, 188, 229, 273, 275, 282, 437, 500, g
Buddhist 83, g
Buddhist cosmology 63–64

# C

cause 484–485, 489, 491–493. *See also* actions and their effects
  circumstantial 107–108, 478, 488
  substantial 107–109, 478, 488
chakravatin king 278
Chandragomin 43
Chandra, King 188–189
Chandrakirti 43, 374, 410, 486, 490, g
Charavaka 474

Chekhawa, Geshe 374, g
cherishing others 360, 362, 364, 367, 369, 370–371, 372–375
  advantages of 377–380
Chittamatra 402, 407, 408, 436, 472–473
  refutation of 417–428
clairvoyance 29, 71, 137, 225, 513
close placement of mindfulness 453–468
  of feelings 458–465
  of phenomena 469–470
  of the body 453–456
  of the mind 466–468
close retreat 344, g
*Cloud of Jewels Sutra* 189
collection of merit 291, 429, g
collection of wisdom 291, 429, g
commitments 76, 81, 134
compassion 25, 34, 51–50, 55, 83–82, 124, 132, 247, 254–256, 264, 450–451, 451. *See also* great compassion
competitiveness 385–386
concentration 8, 80, 193, 198, 313–387. *See also* tranquil abiding
confession of non-virtue 84–107, 111
confusion 244, 435
conscientiousness 145–181, 395
consciousness 463–465
  continuity of 36–39
  mental 194, 467
  non-true existence of 467–468
  sense 467–468
consciousness-basis-of-all 409
contact 461, 464–465, g
conventional truth 398, 399–401, 413, 470
covetousness 147, 214–215, 375
craving 435, 464
'crazy virtue' 307
cushion, meditation 344–345
cyclic existence. *See* samsara

# D

death 85–87, 93–96, 104–105, 139, 159–161, 167, 168, 263, 287–288, 327–329, 502.
dedication 8, 26, 112, 121–125, 505–515
definite goodness 116
Deity 1, 138, 142, g.
deluded view 175–176
delusion-obstructions 79
delusions 13, 78, 90, 104, 114, 155, 176, 194, 202, 246, 252, 255, 259, 268, 309, 437
  abandoning 170–182, 427–428
  faults of 170–178
  imprints of 80, 119, 120
  innate 80, 439–440, g
  intellectually-formed 80, 439–440, g
  six root 171–176
dependence 248–249, 473, 490
dependent arising 249

dependent relationship 14, 490–491
Devaputra Mara 501
Dharma 11–13, 16, 36, 55, 57, 62, 75, 79, 91, 98, 139, 141, 147, 160, 210, 264, 272, 505–506
  definition 165–166
  rarity of practising 501
Dharma Jewel 81, 82
Dharmakaya 428, 430. *See* Truth Body
Dharmashribhadra 520
Dharmodgata 127–130
direct perceiver 412, 472, 475, g
direct valid cognizer 400, g
discouragement 284, 290–293
distractions 271, 313–319, 347
disturbing conceptions 316–317
  how to abandon 330–338, 346–347
divisive speech 90, 147, 213, 266, 375
doubt 174–175, g
dream 409
Drugpa Kunleg 282
dualistic appearance 400–401

# E

effect(s) 484–485, 489, 493
  the three 92–93
effort 8, 129, 193, 281–309, 354
  increasing the force of 295–310
  overcoming opponents to 284–293
  types 284–285
eight worldly concerns 497–498, g
elements
  the four 476
Emanation Body 121, g
emptiness 65, 102, 114, 118, 119, 122, 127, 130–131, 173, 183, 193, 293, 399, 401, 427–428, 430, 434–435, 487
  importance of realizing 496–503
  of feelings 458–465
  of persons 404–409, 439–452
  of phenomena 453–492
  of the body 453–456
  of the mind 466–468
  reasons establishing 438–490
endowments, the ten 17–18, 165
Enjoyment Body 121, g
enlightenment 5, 7, 19, 21, 29, 78, 116, 117, 118, 141, 277, 281, 282, 291–292, 295, 315, 503, 507
equalizing self and others 31, 359–370
  benefits of 368–369
  meaning of 360–361
  meditation on 361–367
equanimity 31–34
evil 6, 27. *See also* non-virtue
exchanging self with others 5, 30, 276, 291, 371–392
  completing by action

388–394
  completing by reflection 381–387
existents, production of 492–495
expression of worship 11–13
external objects 417–418, 424
extreme of attachment 437–438
extreme of fear 437–438

## F

faith 54, 56, 72, 78, 140, 223, 264, 273, 274, 354, 430, g
false 486–488
falsely existent 464, 486–487
familiarity 245–246, 294, 371, 372, 427
faults 257, 259
feeling 458–465, g
  close placement of mindfulness of 458–465
field
  of benefit 222
  of excellence 222
  of suffering 222
five sense objects 305
*Flower Garland Sutra* 300
Foe Destroyer 114, g. *See also* Arhat
four close placements of mindfulness 453–468
four noble truths 65, 175, 431, g
  sixteen characteristics of 434–435
  true cessation 81
  true path 81
four opponent powers 6, 84–106, 163
four ways of gathering disciples 157, g
freedoms, the eight 17–18, 165
fully endowed human life 15–19. *See also* precious human life
functioning thing 493, g
future lives 36, 489, 499, 513

## G

general principle 250, 446–447, 479–485, 488
giving 7, 16, 26, 108, 116, 126–133, 191, 221–222, 226–227, 272, 273, 294, 397, 505–515
goals, the three 19–20
god 17, 117, 499, g
goddesses 69
god realm 49, 193
*Gone to Lanka Sutra* 420
great compassion 42–43, 49, 52, 78, 97, 127, 205, 227, 367, 387, 437, 498–502, 514
ground/spiritual ground g. *See* Bodhisattva grounds
guarding the mind 185–227, 268, 309
*Guide to the Bodhisattva's Way of Life* vii, 1, 3, 9, 10, 519, 520
*Guide to the Middle Way* 374, 486, g
guilt 88–89

Gungtang Jampelyang 115
Gungtang Rinpoche 160
Guru 54, 67. *See also* Spiritual Guide

# H

happiness 22, 25, 51, 107, 109, 113, 115, 136, 477, g
hatred 78
Hearer 47, 294, 515, g
hell/hell being 17, 27, 49, 56, 89, 96, 96–97, 99, 104, 153, 163, 173, 259, 266, 288, 300, 509–511
higher rebirth 499
Highest Yoga Tantra 519, g
Hinayana 48, 228, 341, 402, 431, 433, 436, g
homage 10–11, 11–13, 23
human beings 18, 19, 27–28, 117, 512
hungry spirits 17, 27, 511, g
hurtful speech 147, 213, 375

# I

I 175, 362–364, 403–409, 440–443
idle chatter 147, 214, 375
ignorance 44, 80, 85–84, 85, 90, 95, 104, 114, 159, 174–175, 502, g
illusion(s) 252, 411–416
immediate retribution, five actions of 18
impermanence 286, 327, 413
impermanent phenomenon g
imprint(s) 39, 49, 71, 89, 114, 294, 301, 322, g
imputation 365–366, 401, 471, 490
  basis of 409, 425, 451–452, 455, 469–470
  mere g
imputed existents 425–430
imputed object g
indolence 284–288
inherent existence/inherently existent 241, 250–251, 366, 399–401, 417, 442–443, 460, 492–495
intention 21, 23, 48–50, 51, 100, 202, 211, 354, 437, 507, g
intermediate state 433, g
Ishvara 475–478, 488

# J

Jampa Rinpoche 74
Jangkya 407
jealousy 78, 113–114, 220, 266–268, 383–385, 387
Je Tsongkhapa 47, 66, 74, 400, 407, 410, g
joy, power of 296, 304–306

# K

Kachen Yeshe Gyaltsen 54, 326–327
Kadampa 374–373, 505, g
Kadampa Buddhism 571–572, g
Kailash, Mount 75
karma 49, 164, 176, 191, 259, 264–265, 501, g
  collective 91
  non-virtuous 92

Kashyapa 434
Khedrupje 407
killing 92, 147, 212, 374
Ksitigarbha 99, 511
Kushinagar 76

# L

Lam Chung 100–102
*Lamp for the Path* 342
laziness 282–295, 352
  types 285–293
legless man, story of 20
*Liberating Prayer* 545–546
liberation 19, 78, 102, 114,
  117, 141, 173, 305, 398, 404,
  406, 417, 425, 430, 501,
  507, g. *See also* nirvana
Loden Sherab 520
Lord of Death 85–87, 160,
  166–167, 287, 289, 300, 310,
  503, g
love 34, 132, 274, 275, 450, g
  affectionate 41, 42
  wishing 43
lower realms 27, 77, 83,
  87–86, 95, 116, 152–153,
  162–163, 164–165, 166, 169,
  269, 271, 303, 305, 499,
  508–509, g
Lumbini 76
lying 147, 204–205, 213, 375

# M

Madhyamika 400–403, 409,
  412, 486, 490, g
magician's illusions 411–416,
  426, 491
Mahayana 31–30, 54, 55, 75,
  99, 114, 122, 137, 154–156,
  165, 519, g
  paths 45, 48, 80, 397
  scripture 431–433
  Teacher 120
Maitreya 27, 30, 74, 99, 511
Maitribala 56
mala 366, g
malice 147, 214, 375
mandala offering 64, g
manifestations of Superior
  beings 70–71
Manjughosha 10, 62, 69, 70,
  510, 516
Manjushri 2–3, 30, 99, 519, g
mara g. *See* Devaputra Mara
Marpa 67, 71, 73, 346, g
Mayadevi 511
meditation 156, 309, 344–358, g
  analytical 39, 142–143, 177,
    299
  breathing 347
  placement 39, 142–143, 299
meditation cushion 344–345
meditation posture 345–346
mental continuum 38, g
mental excitement 197–198,
  352, 355–357, g
mental factors 194, 196–199, g
mental sinking 197–198, 353,
  355–357, g
merit 6, 26, 29, 47, 49, 65, 72,
  73, 75, 83, 91, 111, 133, 235,
  272, 274, 429, 430, 513, g
method 397–398, g
Milarepa 57, 67, 70–71, 156,
  195, 283, 325, g
mind 36–38, 210, 238, g
  close placement of

mindfulness of the 466–468
creator of all 189–190
mindfulness 187, 196–227, 275, 291, 308–311, 355, g
close placement of 453–468
mind of enlightenment. *See* bodhichitta
miracle powers 29, 71, 137, 513. *See* clairvoyance and miracle powers
miserliness 67, 90, 111, 152, 191, 222
mistaken awareness 414, g
Mondrol Chodak 167–168
monks 148, 172, 195, 226, 514
moral discipline 8, 16, 116, 147, 185–227, 375, 397
how to practise 201–227
of benefiting sentient beings 224–230
of gathering virtue 215–222
of restraint 202–215
mother
recognizing all living beings are our 32, 35–39
remembering the kindness of 40
repaying kindness of 41
motivation 78, 202, 290, 346, 507
Mount Meru 64, g

# N

Nagarjuna 410, 486, 490, g
Naiyayika 447, 476–477
Nalanda 2–3
Naropa 73, g

Nature Body 121, g
Never Returner 103, g
New Kadampa Tradition 572, g
nine mental abidings 348–353
nirvana 5, 65, 436, 515, g
natural state of 417, 467, 472, 495
non-application 353, 358
non-existents, production of 492–495
non-things, production of 492–494
non-virtue 6, 21, 93, 500, g
abandoning 157–162
purifying 29, 61–105
non-virtuous actions 27, 89, 100, 203, 299, 300, 375, 458, g
heaviness of 92
the ten 117, 211–215
non-virtuous minds 177–178
nuns 172, 195, 226, 514

# O

object of negation 403–406, 440, g
obstructions 5, 44, 55, 68, 79, 438
eliminating the two 141
to liberation 79, 81, g
to omniscience 79, 81, 114, 119, 397, g
*Ocean of Nectar* 400, 486, 490, 491
offering 61–70, 111, 430
omniscient mind 38, 121, 200
Once Returner 103, g
opponent force, power of 100–105

opponent powers, the four 6, 84–106
  opponent force 100–105
  promise 106–109
  regret 84–97
  reliance 98–99
ordination 172
other-powered phenomena 439

# P

Padmasambhava 155
parinirvana 120, g
partless particles 461–462, 479
past lives 32, 36–39, 488, 513
path of accumulation 80, 118
path of meditation 80, 118
Path of No More Learning 80, 119
path of preparation 80, 118
path of seeing 80, 118
patience 8, 192–193, 233–275
  benefits of 239, 277–279
  meditating on 233–238
  of definitely thinking about Dharma 247–254
  of not retaliating 254–277
  of voluntarily enduring suffering 243–247
Pemapani 510
*Perfection of Wisdom Sutra* 127, 431, 433–434, g
perfections, the six. *See* six perfections

permanent/permanence 251–252, 444–445, 448, 477, 483, 492
permanent phenomenon g
personal liberation 19, 47, 65, 116, 405, 431
person(s) g. *See* I, self
  non-true existence of 457
Padampa Sangye 70–71
phenomena
  close placement of mindfulness of 469–470
  selflessness of 442, 453–492
plantain tree, analogy of 25, 450, 496
pleasure 482, 483, 496
powers, the four 295–306
  aspiration 295–299
  joy 295, 304–306
  rejection 295, 306–307
  steadfastness 295, 300–302
praise 220, 266–267, 270–271
Prasangika 400, 402, 409, 410, 411, 417, 419, 425, 428, 430, 436, 444, 471, 489
Prasenajit, King 115, 116
prayer(s) 16, 28, 70, 116, 118, 121, 124–126, 127
Preceptor 13, 46, 72, 134, 200, g
precepts 47, 157
  of aspiring bodhichitta 46
precious human life 15–19, 105, 160, 165, 169, 205, 209, 227, 270, 279, 289, 297, 311, 498, 501

cause of 15–16
preliminary limbs of practice 61–81
pride 111, 173, 220, 247, 303, 386–387, g
production 474–490
  from a general principle 479–488
  from no cause 474, 488–489
  from other 475–478
  from self and other 489–490
  of existents and non-existents 492–494
  of non-things 492–494
promise, power of 106–109
proponents of things 402, 410–416
prostration 11, 72–75, 111, 516–517
Purchog Jampa Rinpoche 54
Pure Land 300, 509, g. *See also* Dakini Land
purification 6, 61–105, 230, 231

# R

*Ratnachudapariprrcha Sutra* 420
Ratna Pemachandra 367
rebirth 24, 36–38, 89
  higher 116, 141
refuge 11–13, 76–83, 230
regret 100, 168, 268
  power of 84–97
rejection, power of 306–307
rejoicing 111, 113–118, 136, 266
relationship of the text 14
reliance, power of 98–99

renunciation 50, 117, 153, 172, 244, 247, 271, 293, 502, 519, g
retreat 2, 74, 122, 210, 304, 343–344, 359, 514, g
Rinchen Sangpo 520
Rishi Kapila 479, 485
root Guru 24, g. *See also* Guru; Spiritual Guide

# S

Sadaprarudita 127–131
Samantabhadra 69, 70, 99, 511
Samkhya 250, 444–447, 479–486, 489
samsara 13, 19, 47, 55, 67, 93, 117, 140, 156, 172, 176, 243, 271, 417, 434–435, 454, 465, 481, g
  equality with nirvana 495
  faults of 498–502
  four characteristics of 159
  sufferings of 21, 25, 50, 78, 164, 176, 502–503
Sangha 11–13, 62, 79, 514, g
Sangha Jewel 81, 82
Sarnath 57, 76
Sarvajanadeva 520
Sarvanivaranaviskambini 99, 511
Sautrantika 402, 408
scopes, the three 165–166, 166, 507
scripture(s) 14, 431–432, 516
seed-letter 347, g
self 250, 361–364, 403–409, 444–452, 476, 479–482

self-cherishing 50, 67, 112, 188, 205, 364, 369, 370, 371–393
  abandoning 375–376
  disadvantages of 377–380
self-cognizer 420–423, 472
self-grasping 114, 172, 174, 183, 240, 293, 297, 403–404, 440, 452–453, 454, 499, 503
  innate 118, 440–443
  intellectually-formed 118, 443–448
self-importance 303
selflessness of persons 404–408, 439–452
  gross and subtle 405
selflessness of phenomena 441, 453–492
self-supporting, substantially existent self 405–407, 435
sense power 461, 464, g
sentient being(s) 22, 221, 274, 276–277, 450–453, 488, 495, 503, 515, g
  kindness of 278
Serlingpa 24, 30
sets, the three 10, 18, 433, 514
sevenfold cause and effect 5, 31, 133
seven limbs 111–112, 134, g
sexual misconduct 147, 212, 374
Shakyamati 520
Shantideva 1–4, 31, 43, 45, 153, 400–401, 402, 428, 493, 519
Shariputra 152, g
sickness 508, 512

six perfections 7, 45, 134, 135, 145, 150, 157, 191–194, 398, 411, 505, 516
sixteen characteristics of the four noble truths 434–435, g
skilful means 55, 218–222, 436
sleep 229
snake 442–443, 450
Solitary Conqueror 47, 515, g
solitude 320–321, 324–329
Spiritual Guide 46, 71, 85, 120, 133, 134, 175, 231, 264, 310, 352, 358, 454, 499, 501–502, 513, g
*Stalks in Array Sutra* 27, 73, 231
steadfastness, power of 295, 300–302
stealing 147, 212, 374
Stream Enterer 103, g
substantial cause g
suffering 95, 108, 247, 259
  cause of 88, 95, 107, 176–177, 253, 259–260, 371, 477
  enduring our own 242, 243–247
  of others 42
  relieving others' 44, 51, 52, 139–140, 180–181
Sugata 11, 22, 134, g
Sukhavati 299, 509, g
Sumatikirti 520
Superior being 70, g
Superior Bodhisattva 70, 76, 80, 81, 85, 98, 118–119, 121, 294, 437
superior intention 43, 45

superior seeing 80, 118, 173, 397–495, g
suppleness 355, g
Supushpachandra 367
*Sutra Interpreting the Intention* 434
*Sutra of the Three Superior Heaps* 230
*Sutra on Skilful Means* 224
Sutra Pitaka 10
*Sutra Requested by Subahu* 48
Sutra(s) 57, 326, 341, 399, 431, 434, g
Svatantrika 402, 409, g
syllogism 490, 495

## T

Tantra 57, 138–139, g
Tathagata 62, g
ten directions 85, 181, 516, g
tenets 402, 410, 431
  four schools 402–409, 436–437
*The Bodhisattva Vow* 47, 231
*The New Heart of Wisdom* 491
three higher trainings 117, 433, g
  concentration 10, 117
  moral discipline 10, 117
  wisdom 10, 117
Three Jewels 11–13, 57, 65, 73, 77, 79–83, 98, 140, 222, 264, 274, g
Togme Sangpo 370
*Training the Mind in Seven Points* 374, 505
tranquil abiding 143, 156, 173, 193, 313–387
  benefits 313–315
  eight opponents to the five obstacles 354–357
  five obstacles to attaining 352–354
  how to abandon the opponents 316–337
  how to attain 340–357
  nine mental abidings 348–353
  particular use of 359–392
  six conditions for attaining 342–347
translators 10, 520
true cessation g
true origin g
true path g
true suffering g
true existence/truly existent 400, 418, 424–427, 431, 434, 473, 482, 487, 495
Truth Body 13, 121, g
turtle analogy 162
two truths 398, 399–427, 470–473
  definition of 400–401
  different presentations of 401–409
  distinctions between 399
  union of 398

## U

ultimate nature 102, 470, g
ultimate truth 398, 399–401, 470, 487
union of abandonment. *See also* ordinary union
union of the two truths 398

# INDEX

*Universal Compassion* 374
universe 63–64
unnecessary application 354–355
ushnisha 74–73

## V

Vaibhashika 402, 408, 411, 431, 433
Vaisheshika 251, 447, 476–477, 479
vajra g
vajra body 121
Vajradhara Trijang Rinpoche vii–viii, g
*Vajradotsa Sutra* 300
vajra fragments 474–490
Vajrapani 99, 510, g
Vajrayogini 1, g
valid cognizer 400, 419, 451, 486, g
 direct 400, g
view 436, 439
Vinaya 10
virtue/virtuous actions 6, 18, 21–22, 52–53, 71, 107, 109, 162, 165–169, 203, 235–236, 260, 268, 299–300, 310, 375–376, 500–501, g
 meditation on 163–170
 practice of 218–222
 rejoicing in 113–118

virtuous object 315
visualization 64, 142, 198, 347–348
vow(s) 83, 148, 514, g

## W

Wheel of Dharma 57, 65, 76, 119, 158, 413, 429, 433, 436, g
wisdom 1, 8, 15, 55, 183, 197, 397–495
 encouragement to develop 496–503
 perfection of 7, 130–131, 193
 realizing emptiness 183, 193, 199, 294, 439
wisdoms, the three 198
wishes
 fulfilling others' 139–141
 fulfilling our own 136–138
wishfulfilling jewel 25
worldly associations, faults of 322–323
worldly life 290, 317–321
wrong awareness 398, 404, 442, g
wrong views 90–91, 112, 147, 174, 183, 214, 375

## Y

Yogi 401–402, 414, g

# *Further Reading*

If you have enjoyed reading this book and would like to find out more about Buddhist thought and practice, here are some other books by Geshe Kelsang Gyatso that you might like to read, or listen to. They are all available from Tharpa Publications.

## GUIDE TO THE BODHISATTVA'S WAY OF LIFE
### How to Enjoy a Life of Great Meaning and Altruism

This famous and universally loved poem for daily living has inspired generations of Buddhists and non-Buddhists since it was first composed in the eighth century by the great Indian Bodhisattva Shantideva.

This new translation, made under the guidance of Venerable Geshe Kelsang Gyatso, conveys the great lucidity and poetic beauty of the original, while preserving its full impact and spiritual insight.

The poem invokes special positive states of mind, moves us from suffering and conflict to happiness and peace, and gradually introduces us to the entire Mahayana Buddhist path to enlightenment. It is a perfect companion to *Meaningful to Behold*.

Also available as an audiobook and eBook.

## HOW TO TRANSFORM YOUR LIFE
**A Blissful Journey**

A practical manual for daily life that shows how we can develop and maintain inner peace, how we can reduce and stop our experience of problems, and how we can bring about about positive changes in our lives that will enable us to experience deep and lasting happiness. This is a significantly revised edition of one of Venerable Geshe Kelsang's most popular and accessible books. Also available as an audiobook.

For a free eBook of *How to Transform Your Life* please visit www.howtotyl.com.

## HOW TO UNDERSTAND THE MIND
**The Nature and Power of the Mind**

This book offers us deep insight into our mind, and shows how an understanding of its nature and functions can be used practically in everyday experience to improve our lives.

The first part is a practical guide that shows us how to recognize and abandon states of mind that harm us, and to replace them with peaceful and beneficial ones. The second part describes different types of mind in detail, revealing the depth and profundity of the Buddhist understanding of the mind. It concludes with a detailed explanation of the meditations that lead to a lasting state of joy, independent of external conditions. Also available as an audiobook and eBook.

## JOYFUL PATH OF GOOD FORTUNE
**The Path to the Supreme Happiness of Enlightenment**

We all have the potential for self-transformation, and a limitless capacity for the growth of good qualities, but to fulfil this potential we need to know what to do at every stage of our spiritual journey. With this book, Venerable Geshe Kelsang Gyatso offers us step-by-step guidance on the meditation practices that will lead us to lasting inner peace and happiness. With extraordinary clarity, he presents all Buddha's teachings in the order in which they are to be practised, enriching his explanation with stories and illuminating analogies. Also available as an audiobook and eBook.

'This book is invaluable.' *World Religions in Education*

## THE MIRROR OF DHARMA WITH ADDITIONS
### How to Find the Real Meaning of Human Life

This book gives practical advice on how we can solve our daily problems of uncontrolled desire, anger and ignorance, and how to make our human life meaningful. The author explains as practical instructions the complete path to enlightenment, based on his deep experience gained from a lifetime spent in meditation. Also available as an eBook.

## THE NEW HEART OF WISDOM
### Profound Teachings from Buddha's Heart

This completely new presentation offers truly liberating insights and advice for the contemporary reader. It reveals the profound meaning of the very heart of Buddha's teachings – the *Perfection of Wisdom Sutras*. The author shows how all our problems and suffering come from our ignorance of the ultimate nature of things and how we abandon this ignorance and come to enjoy pure, lasting happiness through a special wisdom associated with compassion for all living beings. Also available as an eBook.

'....both excellent and comprehensive.' *North American Board for East West Dialogue*

'An excellent book... for the serious student of Buddhism a better book would be hard to come across.' *The Middle Way*

## MODERN BUDDHISM
### The Path of Compassion and Wisdom

By developing and maintaining compassion and wisdom in daily life, we can transform our lives, improve our relationships with others and look behind appearances to see the way things actually exist. In this way we can solve all our daily problems and accomplish the real meaning of our human life. With compassion and wisdom, like the two wings of a bird, we can quickly reach the enlightened world of a Buddha. Also available as an audiobook.

For a free eBook or PDF of Modern Buddhism please visit www.emodernbuddhism.com

## THE ORAL INSTRUCTIONS OF MAHAMUDRA
### The Very Essence of Buddha's Teachings of Sutra and Tantra

This book reveals the uncommon practice of Tantric Mahamudra of the Ganden Oral Lineage, which the author received directly from his Spiritual Guide. It explains clearly and concisely the entire spiritual path from the initial preliminary practices to the final completion stages of Highest Yoga Tantra that enable us to attain full enlightenment in this life. Also available as an audiobook and eBook.

## THE NEW EIGHT STEPS TO HAPPINESS
### The Buddhist Way of Loving Kindness

This inspiring book explains how to transform all life's difficulties into valuable spiritual insights, by meditating on one of Buddhism's best-loved teachings, *Eight Verses of Training the Mind*, by the great Tibetan Bodhisattva Geshe Langri Tangpa. This ancient wisdom is now available for those seeking lasting happiness and greater meaning in their lives. Also available as an eBook.

'... induces calmness and compassion into one's being.' *The New Humanity Journal*.

## OCEAN OF NECTAR
### The True Nature of All Things

*Ocean of Nectar* is the first complete explanation in English of Chandrakirti's *Guide to the Middle Way*, a classic Mahayana scripture, which to this day is regarded as the principal presentation of Buddha's profound view of emptiness, the ultimate nature of reality. Also available as an eBook.

## THE BODHISATTVA VOW
### A Practical Guide to Helping Others

How to engage in the essential practices of Mahayana Buddhism by taking and keeping the Bodhisattva vows – practical guidelines for compassionate living – including a purification practice based on the *Sutra of the Three Superior Heaps*. With this handbook as our companion, we can enter the Bodhisattva's way of life and progress with confidence along the path to full enlightenment. Also available as an audiobook and eBook.

## UNIVERSAL COMPASSION
### Inspiring Solutions for Difficult Times

The heart of Buddha's teachings is unconditional love and compassion. This inspiring explanation of the popular Buddhist poem, *Training the Mind in Seven Points*, reveals powerful and far-reaching methods for us to develop these altruistic states. Ancient meditative techniques that have been tried and tested for centuries are brought alive and made relevant to our everyday experiences. Also available as an audiobook and eBook.

'It could be read with profit by anyone whose religion demands the exercise of compassion.' *Faith and Freedom*.

To order any of our publications, or to request a catalogue, please visit www.tharpa.com or contact your nearest Tharpa office listed on pages 577-578.

# *Finding Your Nearest Kadampa Meditation Centre*

To deepen your understanding of this book, and other books published by Tharpa Publications, and its application to everyday life you can receive support and inspiration from qualified Teachers and practitioners.

Tharpa Publications is part of the wider spiritual community of the New Kadampa Tradition. This tradition has a growing number of centres and branches in over 40 countries around the world. Each centre offers special study programmes in modern Buddhism and meditation, taught by qualified Teachers. For more details, see *Study Programmes of Kadampa Buddhism* (see pages 571-575).

These programmes are based on the study of books by Venerable Geshe Kelsang Gyatso Rinpoche and are designed to fit comfortably with a modern way of life.

**To find your local Kadampa centre**
**visit:** tharpa.com/centres